Abstracts of the Land Records of GRANVILLE COUNTY North Carolina

Dockets H-M, O, N

1765–1793

Abstracted by
Bonnie Zae Hargett Gwynn

Transcribed [and Annotated] by
Trudie Davis-Long

Heritage Books
2024

HERITAGE BOOKS
AN IMPRINT OF HERITAGE BOOKS, INC.

Books, CDs, and more—Worldwide

For our listing of thousands of titles see our website
at
www.HeritageBooks.com

Published 2024 by
HERITAGE BOOKS, INC.
Publishing Division
5810 Ruatan Street
Berwyn Heights, MD 20740

Abstracted by Bonnie Zae Hargett Gwynn

Heritage Books by the author:
1889 List of Taxpayers of Frederick County, Maryland
Abstracts of the Land Records of Granville County, North Carolina: Dockets H-M, O, N, 1765–1793
Abstracts of the Land Records of Granville County, North Carolina: Dockets P, Q, R, S, T, 1793–1810
Abstracts of the Land Records of Granville County, North Carolina, Dockets V, W, X, Y, Z, 1, 2, 1810–1826
Abstracts of the Wills and Estate Records of Granville County, North Carolina, 1833–1846 by Zae Hargett Gwynn
Abstracts of the Wills and Estate Records of Granville County, North Carolina, 1846–1863 by Zae Hargett Gwynn
Abstracts of the Wills and Estate Records of Granville County, North Carolina, 1863–1902 by Zae Hargett Gwynn
Frederick County, Maryland Estate Docket Index Book, Volume 1: A to G, 1815–ca 1950
Frederick County, Maryland Estate Docket Index Book, Volume 2: H to R, 1815–ca 1950
Frederick County, Maryland Estate Docket Index Book, Volume 3: S to Z, 1815–ca 1950
Frederick County, Maryland Estate Docket Index Book, Volume 4: Combined Compiled Index, 1815–ca 1950

International Standard Book Number
Paperbound: 978-0-7884-2865-4

Table of Contents

Introduction

This publication continues the series of land record abstracts originally begun by [Bonnie] Zae Hargett Gwynn for Granville Co., NC.

In the 1990s there was a book published by the abstracter on some of the early Deeds but the series was not continued. And the book that was put in print did not include the full data of the manuscript as it currently exists.[1]

The proofing process involved scanning and Optical Character Recognition (OCR) processing of the Gwynn manuscripts. The result was compared to the manuscript by this compiler. Items of questionable interpretation were checked against the courthouse records.

It is important to note there were handwritten notes on the original Gwynn manuscript. This information is included. Obvious spelling errors were corrected and some punctuation was changed, however all names are spelled as listed in the manuscript.

The original pagination from the abstract is included for anyone who wants to check individual pages against Ms. Gwynn's work. However since the annotations include the Liber Folio designation for the items listed, it would probably be more practical to reference the microfilm[2] or originals at the Granville County Courthouse in Oxford, NC or the NC State Archives in Raleigh.

During my research, I realized that Ms. Gwynn left out details from the original records important to contemporary researchers. Most significantly, Ms. Gwynn left out the given names of the slaves that were listed in the docket books.

[Annotations] are in brackets.

Surnames are listed in **Bold**. Tracts of land, those given a particular name are shown in *Italics*. Notes that couldn't be included are shown as footnotes.

Images are included of court clerk handwriting that need to be included for understanding the transcription.
In some cases, where a significant change needed to be made, the information from the court ledger books is included and the wording used by Gwynn is included in a footnote.

As researchers, it is important to be able to find places, occupations, tract names and other data items when looking for family information, so all of these topics and others are included in the index. The only phrase not included in the index is 'Granville' because it would appear on every page.

Gwynn was haphazard about showing possessives in names. As a general rule, all possessive names are universally written this way. In the same way, periods were added to the end of sentences and abbreviations. Periods are not used in the index.

I am also including the information about Zae Gwynn, as she preferred to be called, at the end of the index.

This work is a guide only to records that are available. The originals should be consulted for verification and to authenticate information.

Trudie Davis-Long
2024

---

[1] Abstracts of the early deeds of Granville County, North Carolina, 1746-1765. Authors: Zae Hargett Gwynn, Joseph W. Watson Print Book, English, 1993

[2] https://www.familysearch.org/search/catalog/360398?availability=Family%20History%20Library

North Carolina Department of Cultural Resources
June 25, 2002

Dear Ms. Montague,

It was good to hear from you that Zae Hargett Gwynn's notebooks of Granville County record abstracts have been useful to you. I wish the donor of them, Mrs. Mary Jeffreys Rogers, were still alive so that I could pass on to her your remarks about them.

Mrs. Rogers and Mrs. Gwynn had been great friends, and after the death of Mrs. Gwynn, Mr. Gwynn gave to Mrs. Rogers all the notebooks of unpublished abstracts of records of North Carolina counties that Mrs. Gwynn had made during her life. Mrs. Gwynn, herself, as you will remember, published her abstracts of Jones County and Onslow County records--but nothing more.

In the early 1970s Mrs. Rogers lent the notebooks of Gwynn abstracts to Joseph W. Watson of Rocky Mount so that he could publish such of them as he chose. You will recall that he issued, six volumes based on the Granville County abstracts: deeds, 1746-1765; wills and estates in two volumes, 1746-1833; court minutes, 1746-1820; guardian accounts, 1810-1856; and "kinfolks" based on land records, 1765-1826. Mr. Watson's opinion was that little market existed for published data later than about 1820.

Fearing that the notebooks would be put out as trash following the death of Mrs. Rogers, I suggested to her that the Thornton Library would be a good home for the three Granville County notebooks if the Library were willing to give them a home. She accepted the suggestion, and it was at that time that I talked with Joanna McDaniel about them. It is probable that Mrs. McDaniel was no longer officially connected with the library when we talked, but she thought the Library would like to have them, and she was willing to pick them up in Raleigh and take them to Oxford if I would collect them from Mrs. Rogers at Louisburg and bring them to the Archives for her. I brought the notebooks to Raleigh, put with them the name and address of Mrs. Rogers (425 Sledge Road, Louisburg, NC 27549), and held them until they were collected for Thornton Library by Mrs. McDaniel on March 7, 2000. I don't know whether the gift was ever acknowledged to Mrs. Rogers, or not, but she was glad to know that they had gone on to the Library as a permanent gift from her. Mrs. Rogers died on December 5, 2000.

If the Library decides to publish such of the abstracts as were not published by Mr. Watson, I assume that Zae Hargett Gwynn will be given credit on the title page as the abstracter in the same way that Mr. Watson gave her credit.

George Stevenson
Private Manuscripts Archivist
North Carolina State Archives

163

1- May 7, 1765- John **Raigan** to Samuel **Benton** for 35 pds. 50 acres on Reedy Branch on **Benton**'s line.
Wts: Reuben **Searcy**, Tho. **Sanders (Landers)**.

2- May 4, 1765- Jane **Braswell**, widow, to Samuel **Benton** for 16 pds. 80 acres at **Benton**'s corner, **Person**'s line.
Wts: Charles **Bruce**, Thos **Sanders (Landers)**.

3- Apr. 15, 1765- Jeremiah **Reaves** to Miles **Wells** for 60 pds. 270 acres on Fishing creek along **Taylor**'s line, **Frazer**'s line, Robert **Duke**'s line.
Wts: Lark **Johnston**, Thomas **Morris**.

4- May 8, 1765- Andrew **Hampton** to John **Hampton** for 125 pds. Land on south side of Indian Field creek in **McCulloch**'s line.
Wts: none.

4, 5- May 9, 1765- Michael **Wilson** to James **Young** for 66 pds. 14 shls. 663 acres which was granted to Moses **Linsey** Feb. 6, 1762 on **Hatcher**'s Run on both sides of Tar river, on **Benton**'s line.
Wts: Robert **Reed**, John **Morris**.

5, 6- Feb. 13, 1765- Dennis **Sullivant** to Thomas **Chestar** of Johnston Co., N.C. for 26 pds. 200 acres on branch of News [Neuse] river called Ledge of Rocks granted by Henry **McCulloch** Aug. 8, 1763-
Wts: Edward and Gillum **Harris**.

7, 8- May 7, 1765- John **Hawkins** and wife Mary of Bute Co., N.C. to Terisha **Turner** of Bedford Co., VA. for 70 pds. 700 acres in Granville Co. on both sides of **Rogers** branch and on Little Nut Bush creek, **Templey**'s line.
Wts: George **Lamkin**, Philemon **Hawkins**.

8, 9- Mar. 2, 1765- Robert **Mitchel** and wife Tanner to Sherwood **Sims**, Sr. for 50 pds. 330 acres on both sides of Reedy Branch.
Wts: Reuben **Searcy**, Sherwood **Sims**.

9- July 25, 1763- Henry **McCulloch** to John **West** for 10 pds. 100 acres on Ledge of Rocks creek.
Wts: Richd **Clements**, James **Boyd**.

9, 10- Aug. 13, 1763- Henry **McCulloch** to John **West** for 10 pds. 200 acres on Dennis **Sullivant**'s line being part of *tract No. 12* at John **West**'s.
Wts: Robert **Rainey**, Samuel **Boyd**.

10 thru 13- Aug. 6, 1765- Henry **Hawson** by Power of Attorney of Wilkshire, Great Brittain and Henry Eustice **McCulloch** of Halifax Co., N.C.- Henry **McCullock** granted 100,000 acres by King of England in 1745 and on Jan. 20, 1757, conveyed to Henry **Hawson** 12,500 acres known as *tract No. 12* and by mistake Henry **McCulloch** deeded on Aug. 10, 1763, to Henry Eustice **McCulloch**, his only son, 1,240 acres on forks of Beaverdam creek in Granville Co., N.C. and now Henry Eustice **McCulloch**, since he has settled this land, wished to purchase the tract. . . so for 86 pds. said **Hawson** deeds to Henry Eustice **McCulloch** the entire *tract No. 12*- signed by Jno. **Campbell**, agent.
Wts: Alex **Ford**, Ambrose [**Knox**].

13, 14- Mar. 1, 1765- Philip **Pryor**, Esq., sheriff, to Robert **Jones** of Northampton Co., N.C. attny at law -
The land of James **Wilson** and Robert **Cade**, Jr. for debt- and 559 acres belonging to Robert **Cade** was sold to highest bidder, on Poplar swamp on Horse creek and a parcel of Indian corn on the said land, there being no other property of James **Wilson** or Robert **Cade**, Jr. found- Robert **Jones** was highest bidder-
Wts: Richard **Henderson**, C. **Bruce**.

15, 16- Apr. 1, 1765- Grant to James **Bridges** for 370 acres on both sides of Aaron's creek along **Harris**'s line at rate of 3 shls sterling per year paid to Lord Granville for each 100 acres.

164

16, 17- Oct. 6, 1764- John **Hayes** and wife Susanna to Leonard **Linsey** for 100 pds. 226 acres on Crooked Run at

Linsey's corner.
Wts: Reuben **Searcy**.

17, 18- Oct. 6, 1764- Richard **Searcy** to John **Hayes** for 50 pds. 190 acres on Crooked Run.
Wts: Reuben **Searcy**.

18, 19- Aug. 6, 1765- Jonathan **Parker** to Groves **Howard** for 9 pds. 120 acres on Haw branch at **Howard**'s line.
Wts: James **Davenport**, Tho. **Landers (Sanders)**.

19, 20- Oct. 6, 1764- Humphry **Marshall** and wife Mary of Halifax Co., N.C. to John **Champion**, Jr. for 35 pds. 300 acres on both sides of Middle creek which was granted to Alexander **McCulloch**, Esq. Oct. 14, 1759 by special agent Francis **Corbin**, and he conveyed to Humphry **Marshall** Mar. 16, 1762.
Wts: John and Osborn **Pope**.

20, 21- May 9, 1764- Gillam **Harris** to Joseph **Lemon** of Halifax Co., N.C. for 20 pds. 232 acres in Granville Co. on both sides of Newlite creek being part of tract granted to **Harris** Jan. 1, 1762 for 700 acres.
Wts: Osborn **Pope**, David **Harris**.

22- Aug. 14, 1764- Edward **Bond** and Judith **Bond** to John **Davis** for 30 pounds, 208 acres on N side of Grassy creek in King's line.
Wts: Thos. **Person**, William **Hicks**.

23- Sept. 8, 1762 Edward **Brown**, Sr. to Dennis **Bradley** for 20 pds. 130 acres on S side of Red Bud creek at Horsepen branch being part of tract patented by George **Nicholson**.
Wts: Ann **Bradley**, Anne **Brown**.

23, 24- Aug. 9, 1765- Robert **Boyd** to John **Boyd**, his son, for 50 pds. 200 acres on branch of Tar river at John **Landess**'s line on N. side of Tar river at **Patten**'s line, **Ross**'s line, which was granted to Jane **Reeks** July 1743-
Wts: Will **Moore**, Carter **Hudspeth**.

24, 25- May 8, 1764- Nimrod **Ellis** to John **Rae** for 20 pds. 100 acres on N. side of Grassy branch at Thomas **Winningham**'s line.
Wts: Joseph **Garrison** and Hugh **Montgomery**, Presley **Harrison**.

25, 26- Aug. 9, 1765- Robert **Boyd** to Thomas **Boyd**, his son, for 50 pds. 300 acres on S side of Tar river.
Wts: William **Moore**, Israel **Eastwood**.

26, 27- May 8, 1765- Michael **Wilson** to John **Morris** for 20 pds. 200 acres on both sides of Reedy creek at **Wilson**'s other line.
Wts: Samuel **Benton**, Charles **Bruce**.

27, 28- May 14, 1765- Warham **Glen** of Orange Co., N.C. to James **Dyar** of Granville Co. for 70 pds. 200 acres on both sides of Reedy creek in Robert **Callior**'s line being tract bought by James **Alston**, deceased, late of Orange Co., N.C. of H. E. **McCulloch** and willed to Warham **Glen**.
Wts: Charles **Bruce**, Solo. **Alston**, W. **Moore**.

28, 29- Aug. 7, 1765- William **Gowin** to his son Joseph **Gowin** for gift, 350 acres in **Gowin**'s line.
Wts: Stephen **Jett**, James **Davenport**.

29, 30- Apr. 5, 1765- Benjamin **Cooke** to Daniel **Dennis** for 60 pds. 70 acres on both sides of **Haral**'s creek, on **Bullock**'s line, **Hester**'s line.
Wts: Mich **Bullock**, Zebedee **Dennis**.

30, 31- Aug. 6, 1765- John **Stovall**, Sr. to Bartholomew **Stovall** for 12 pds. 210 acres on both sides of Jonathan's creek
Wts: Chas. **Bruce**.

31, 32- Apr. 8, 1765- Benjamin **Cook** to James **Hester** for 60 pds. 340 acres on S. side of **Harris** creek at line made

by **Cook** and **Hester**, **Hicks**' line, near **Anderson**'s path.
Wts: Chas. **Cook**, Howel **Lewis**, Henry **Parkman**.

32, 33- Dec. 1, 1764- Isaac **Arnold** to his daughter Sarah **Arnold** for 30 pds. 100 acres on E side of Fishing creek at Thomas **Morris**'s corner.
Wts: Ann and Thomas **Hopkins**.

165

33, 34- Aug. 6, 1765- John **Stovall**, Sr. to John **Stovall**, Jr. for 12 pds. 210 acres on both sides of Jonathan's creek.
Wts: Ch. **Bruce**.

34, 35- Feb. 21, 1765- Luke **Carrol** and wife Anne to James **Coffield** of Halifax Co., N.C. for 30 pds. 215 acres on Spring branch being part of tract granted Feb. 6, 1762 to **Carrol** at **Cowell**'s line.
Wts: Robert **Harris**, John **Carrol**.

36, 37- Aug. 7, 1765- Jonathan **Parker**, carpenter, to Edward **Moore** for 50 pds. 200 acres in **Taylor**'s line along the original line and along the old line on **Bennett**'s creek.
Wts: Wm. **Williams**, Joel **Chandler**.

37, 38- Apr. 7, 1765- Daniel **Nowlin** planter, to Benjamin **Hardy** of Johnston Co., N.C. for 25 pds. 180 acres on Neuse river on Horse creek.
Wts: Joseph **McGehee**, Brittian **Fuller**.

38, 39- Nov. 3, 1764- David **Clanton** from Ephriam **Clanton** for 100 pds. 320 acres on N. side of Flat creek near old court house road-
Wts: Chrismas and Fanny **Ray**, Amea [**Flugausnion**, Richard R. **Clanton**, Jr.]

39, 40- Apr. 1, 1764- Briten **Fuller** to Solomon **Fuller**, Jr. for 40 pds. 388 acres on Jos. **Fuller**'s corner, Peter **Vincent**'s corner, which was granted to Philemon **Bradford** for 570 acres Nov. 13, 1756 and conveyed to James **Vincent** Oct. 15, 1761 and by him to Brittain **Fuller**.
Wts: James **Fuller**, Booth **Peary**.

41- Dec. 1, 1764- Henry **Jones** to John **Brown** of Halifax Co., N.C. for 50 pds. 335 acres at Luke **Rawl**'s line, at Phil **Pryor**'s corner, **Benton**'s line, **Braswell**'s corner, **Reaves**' line, John **Lewis**' line.
Wts: Patrick **Callehan**, Elizabeth **Callehan**.

42, 43- Aug. 3, 1765- Jonathan **Night** to James **Reed** for 15 pds. 160 acres on Spewmarrow creek in Benjamin **Hendrick**'s line, Peter **Oliver**'s line and Mocoal **Kounts** line (?).
Wts: M. **Hunt**, Richd **Harris**, William **Knight**.

43, 44- May 18, 1765- William **Bullock** to John **Gilliam** for 200 pds. 530 acres on Flat branch at **Hargrove**'s corner, William **Potter**'s line, near Little Nut Bush creek.
Wts: Zach **Bullock**, Peter **Gilliam**.

44, 45- Aug. 5, 1765- William **Allin** to John **Layton** for 25 pds. 100 acres on lower side of Grassycreek on **Smith**'s and **Cragg** lines.
Wts. M. **Hunt**.

45, 46- Mar. 15, 1765- John **Hyndman** of London, by attny Robert **Jones**, Jr. to John **Gillam** of Lunenburg Co., VA. for 45 pds. 320 acres on W side of Great Nut Bush branch which was patented by John **Glover** Nov. 21, 1754 at Nathaniel **Norwood**'s line, on Crooked Run now called Flat creek.
Wts: none.

46, 47- Apr. 10, 1765- Andrew **Hampton** to Samuel **Sneed** for 50 pds. 300 acres on **Person**'s line, Ephraim's **Hampton**'s line, **Landis**'s line, **Phis**' line.
Wts: Samuel **Benton**.

47, 48- Apr. 6, 1765- Benjamin **Cook** to Lewis **Pettiford** for 16 pds. 50 acres on Harrels creek at John **Knot**'s line. Wts: James **Hester**, Christopher **Hunt**.

48, 49, 50- Aug. 6, 1765- John **Stovall**, Sr. to his son William **Stovall** land containing 286 acres on N. side of Jonathan's creek in sd. John **Stovall**'s and **Clayton**'s lines.
Wts: None.

50, 51- Aug. 3, 1765- John **Knight** of Lunenburg Co., VA. to Jonathan **Knight** of Granville Co., N.C. for 60 pds. 300 acres in Granville Co. on lower side of Grassy creek.
Wts: William and Peter, and John **Knight**, Jr.

51, 52- Mar. 1, 1764- Luke **Carroll** to Thomas **Harris** for 8 pds. 100 acres in Robert **Harris**'s corner.
Wts: David and Robert **Harris**.

166

52, 53- Apr. 17, 1765- Benjamin **Cook** to Charles **Cook** for 30 pds. 200 acres on both sides of **Harrel**'s creek on James **Hester**'s corner, near George **Anderson**'s path, at John Knot's and **Bullock**'s and **Morris**'s lines.
Wts: Thomas **Tait**, Howel **Lewis**, Henry **Parkman**.

53 thru 55- Mar. 4, 1765- Joseph **McDaniel** to John **Earl**, late of Lunenburg Co., VA. for 50 pds. 200 acres in Joseph **McDaniel**'s first corner in **Chaver**'s line.
Wts: William **Spears**, Danl **Hunter**, Philip **Brown**.

55 thru 57- Aug. 3, 1765- Drury **Smith** of Mecklinburg Co., VA. to John **Haley** of Drysdale Parish, Caroline Co., VA. for 42 pds. 301 acres on S side of Aaron's creek in Granville Co., N.C. at **Yancey**'s and **Smith**'s lines, formerly belonging to Zachariah **Smith**, deceased.
Wts: Spencer **Pescud**, Thos. **Haley**.

58, 59- Aug. 1, 1765- Jonathan **Knight** to Richard **Harris** for 10 pds. 50 acres at **Hockinging** line and **Hunt**'s line.
Wts: James **Reed**, William **Knight**, M. **Hunt**.

59, 60- June 11, 1763- Joseph **Mase** to Brittan **Fuller** for 7 pds. 225 acres on [sic] granted to James **Sandland** on **Wells**' and **Wade**'s lines, who sold it to **Mase**.
Wts: Jones **Fuller**, Solomon **Fuller**.

60, 61- Feb. 16, 1765- Edward **Ballinger** and wife Mary of Johnston Co., N.C. to John **Pullen** of Granville Co. for 65 pds. 376 acres, being part of land granted to Nathan **McGehee** in 1762 on Tar river below Fort creek.
Wts: William **Young**, Richard **Cureton**.

63- Nov. 19, 1764- James **Bass** to Benjamin **Bass** for 5 pds. 50 acres in Northampton Co., N.C. at Thomas **Bryant**'s patent on S side of Maples springs-
Wts: Edward **Bass**, Reuben **Bass**.

63, 64- Apr. 5, 1764- Augustine **Bate** to Henry **Jones** for 20 pds. 334 acres at **Jones**'s corner, **Pryor**'s, **Benton**'s, **Braswell**'s lines, **Reavis**' and **Hicks**', **Lewis**'s lines.
Wts: Samuel **Benton**, Stephen **Jett**.

64 thru 66- Sept. 1, 1764- James **Madewell** to John **Pope** for 12 pds. 100 acres on N. side of Fort creek on James **Young**'s line granted to Peter **Vinson** Nov. 28, 1760 for 639 acres and by deed for 150 acres Nov. 8, 1762 and from **Vinson** to James **Madewell**.
Wts: George **Levister**- 50 acres has been sold to John **Hatcher** whereon he formerly lived-

67, 68- Mar. 24, 1765- Daniel **Blackman** to Joseph **McDaniel** for 40 pds. 200 acres on both sides of Tabbs creek at **Blackman**'s lower corner on **Dickerson**'s line.
Wts: Henry **Fuller**, William **Roberts**, Daniel **Hunter**.

68, 69- Aug. 7, 1765- Philemon **Hawkins** and wife Dille of Beaut Co., N.C. to Richard **Harris** for 50 pds. 332 acres on both sides of Grassy creek at Benjamin **Hendrick**'s line to **Fegines**' line, **Smith**'s line.
Wts: William **Byars**, William **Graves**.

70- July 4, 1763- Henry **McCulloch** to William **Rose** for 27 pds. 300 acres on Nap of Reeds creek being part of *No. 12*, on **Kemp** creek.
Wts: Robt. **Rainey**.

70, 71- July 4, 1763- Henry **McCulloch** to Thomas **Rose** for 24 pds. 404 acres being part of *tract 12*, at John **Walker**'s corner, Joseph **Walker**'s.
Wts: Edmund **Fanning**, Robert **Rainey**.

71, thru 74- May 30 1766- James **Forsyth**, **Forsyth** and **Watson** and Robert **Mackie**, merchants, all of N.C.- In order to pay to creditors of **Forsythe**, **Watkins** and Co. that is James **Dunlop**, **Tabb** and **Hunter**, David **Forsythe**, James **Murdock** and Co., and James **Robeson** merchants- mortgages lots, land, houses in town of Campbeleton and all other lands belonging to **Forsythe** and **Watson** being in Cumberland and Granville Co., N.C., all stock, household furniture, debts due from sundry persons amounting to 2,604 pds. 9 shls.- mortgage to run four years-
Wts: Thos **Smith**, John **Cuming**, John **Waldrop**.

167

74 thru 76- July 6, 1765- John **Ross** to Edward **Stabler** of Petersburg, VA., merchant, for 103 pds. 8 shls., 11 pence, 320 acres including the plantation whereon John **Ross** now lives and another tract of 332 acres on both sides of Nicholas creek- mortgage.
Wts: Tom **Spencer**, John **Williams**, Jr.

76, thru 73- Dec. 6, 1762 James **Willingham** to John **Boddie** for 100 pds. 200 acres on both sides of Cedar creek on John **Pope**'s and Richard **Bridges**' line, being part of tract granted to **Bridges** Mar. 11, 1760 for 600 acres and sold to **Willingham** Nov. 13, 1760-
Wts: William **Winston**, John **Pope**, Alex **Collbeath**.

79, 80- May 3, 1766- John **Ross** to William **Rose** for 37 pds. 200 acres on Neus river.
Wts: Saml **Benton**, Jesse **Benton**.

80, 81- May 7, 1765- John **Brown** of Halifax Co., N.C. to Samuel **Benton** for 5 pds. 110 acres on Fishing creek at John **Luise**'s line, **Pryor**'s line, **Benton**'s and **Baswell**'s lines, **Hicks**' corner.
Wts: Hannah **Yancey**.

81, thru 82- July 23, 1766- Francis **Hutchins** to William **Hamileton** of Nansemond Co., VA. for 16 pds. 200 acres on **Hatcher**'s Run at **Weldon**'s line.
Wts: Chas **Bruce**, Wm. **Stone**.

83, 84- Aug. 5, 1766- William **Taylor**, Esq. to James **Young** of Halifax Co., N.C., merchant, for 125 pds. 400 acres on E side of Fishing creek in Sherwood **Harris**'s line, **Anderson**'s line, **Bradford**'s old line.
Wts: Robert **Reid**, Jos **Taylor**.

84, 85- Mar. 6, 1765- Ghiles **Hudspeth** to Michael **Wilson** for 7 pds. 80 acres on both sides of Fishing creek at **Hudspeth**'s line.
Wts: Ralph **Hudspeth**, John **Tudor**.

85, 86- Oct. 20, 1765- James **Knot** gave to his son James **Knott**, Jr. 310 acres on Grassy creek whereon he now lives at **Robertson**'s line, **Black**'s line being part of tract whereon he lives.
Wts: James **Roberts**, David **Knott**.

86, 87- Oct. 31, 1765- William **Gillam**, Sr. to William **Gillam**, Jr. for 100 pds. 320 acres on W side of **Anderson**'s swamp at **Glover**'s road reserving to himself and to his wife Agnes, for their lifetime then to his son William, Jr.
Wts: Isham **Harris**, Jessey **Gillam**.

87 thru 89- Feb. 15, 1765- William **Reardon** of Fairfax Co., VA. to Reuben **Searcey** for 85 pds. 258 acres on Great Nut Bush creek on **Anderson**'s swamp at Reuben **Searcey**'s corner, on Samuel **Henderson**'s line.
Wts: William **Reardon**, Jr.

89, 90- Oct. 7, 1765- William **Yancey** and wife Sophia to John **Walker** for 30 pds. 260 acres on Little Island creek.
Wts: Reuben **Searcy**, James **Forsyth**.

90, 91- May 17, 1765- Samuel **Smith** to Samuel **Walker** for 30 pds. 300 acres on S side of Tabbs creek at **Smith**'s corner.
Wts: Chas **Bruce**, Thomas **Sanders** (**Landers**).

91, 92- May 17, 1765- Samuel **Smith** to Samuel **Walker** for 81 pds. 200 acres on Tabbs creek at **Peace**'s corner.
Wts: Charles **Bruce**.

92, 93- Aug. 15, 1765- Ezekiel **Hampton** to Ephraim **Hampton** for 16 pds. 50 acres on **Harris**'s line at William **Jones** corner, whereon I now live along **Person**'s corner, and also 26 hogs-
Wts: Robert **Harris**.

94 thru 96- Aug. 6, 1766- Robert **Harris**, executor of Sherwood **Harris** deceased, to James **Young** and Co. of Halifax Co., N.C. for 120 pds.- land on Fishing creek at **Young**'s, formerly **Bradford**'s old line, to **Hamilton**'s line to the Forked road in Harrisburg and along Contentee old road to **Benton**'s corner, and at **Holtsclaus**' line, **Wilson**'s and **Hudspeth**'s lines **Hamilton**'s formerly **Farguson**'s line, John **White** and **Arnold**'s lines, **Hamilton**'s, formerly **Vaughn**'s line.
Wts: Charles **Bruce**.

168

96, 97- Aug. 5, 1766- John **Mitchel**, Jr. to Elisabeth **Kennon** of Virginia for 150 pds. 350 acres whereon John **Mitchel** now lives on both sides of Island creek.
Wts: Edmund **Taylor**, Saml **Hopkins**.

97 thru 99- Sept. 14, 1765- Thomas **Persons**, Esq., to Phillip **Pryor** for 20 pds. 250 acres at John **Hill**'s corner being part of grant to **Person** Jan. 1, 1763.
Wts: Phil **Pryor**, Waters **Dunn**.

99- May 9, 1754- Grant to John **Rainwater** for 480 acres on both sides of Sandy creek.

100- Apr. 11, 1763- Grant to Henry **Fuller** for 700 acres on **Bullock**'s line, and on Tar river.

100, 101- Nov, 13, 1756- Grant to Philemon **Bradford** for 470 acres on Joseph **Fuller**'s corner on both sides of Little creek on lines of Arthur **Fuller** and Peter **Vincent**.

101 thru 103- July 1, 1762 Grant to John **Pope** for 468 acres on both sides of Cedar creek on **Hawkins**' line, **Hewlin**'s line.

103, 104- May 8, 1765- Solomon **Fuller**, Jr. to John **Pope** for 100 pds. 388 acres on Cedar creek at Joseph **Fuller**'s corner, Peter **Vincent**'s line being land whereon Brittan **Fuller** formerly lived.
Wts: Osborn **Pope**, Wm. **Nailing**.

104, 105- Nov. 6, 1764- John **Vaughn** to Michael **Wilson** for 40 pds. 70 acres on W side of Fishing creek on Isaac **Arnold**'s and Sherwood **Harris**'s lines.
Wts: Larkin **Johnson**, John **Hamilton**.

105 thru 107- Dec. 5, 1764- James **Cook** and wife Lucy to Edmund **Taylor** of Lunenburg Co., VA. for 88 pds. 150 acres whereon James **Cook** now lives on Island creek which he bought of Benjamin and Charles **Cook**.
Wts: John **Oliver**, Veazey **Husband**, Howel **Lewis**, Henry **Parkmon**.

107 thru 109- Nov. 15, 1762- Samuel **Ware** to William **Gray** for 20 pds. 100 acres on S side of Tar river on both sides of Middle creek on **Ballinger**'s line, and his mill path at **Shapard's** line, granted to **Ware** July 27, 1761-
Wts: John **Neville**, John **Pope**.

109, 110- Mar. 14, 1765- David **Clanton** to Benja **Ragland** for 150 pds. 640 acres on both sides of Flat creek including 40 acres more lying on **Clanton**'s line and which land was bought of Ephraim **Clanton**.
Wts: Nath **Harris**, Evan and William **Ragland**.

110 thru 112- Aug 6, 1756- [sic] Francis **Howard**, Sr. and wife Anne to John Williams **Graves** for 120 pds. 350 acres on both sides of West creek.
Wts: Richd **Harris**, William **Graves**.

112, thru 114- Mar. 25, 1765- James **Reaces** to Robert **Hicks** for 11 pds. 100 acres on **Hicks** line at Thomas **Person**'s corner on lines of Benjamin **Bass**, Lawrence **Pettiford** and Robert **Hicks**, on creek where old mill stands-
Wts: Abagail **Hicks**, Lucretia **Hicks**.

114, 115- July 28, 1766 Henry **Howard** and wife Priscilla of Mecling [sic] Co, VA. to John **Owen** of Granville Co., N.C. for 150 pds. 380 acres on both sides of Grassy creek whereon John **Owen** now lives on line between John **Owen** and Daneil[sic] **Grant**.
Wts: Danl **Grant**, Richardson **Owen**.

116 thru 118- Aug. 18, 1765- William **Young** to John **Pullion** for 25 pds. 111 acres on N. side of Fort creek on **Moxley**'s branch.
Wts: Thos **Banks**, Joseph **Wade**.

118, 119- Oct. 23, 1765- Samuel **Henderson** to Joseph **Waldrop** for 40 pds. 220 acres on both sides of Beaverdam swamp being part of grant to **Henderson** July 27, 1760 on **Arnold**'s line.
Wts: Daniel **Williams**, Luke **Waldrop**.

120, 121- Aug. 10, 1766- Malechy **Reeves** to Robert **Hicks** for 17 pds. 10 shls. 100 acres on **Hicks**'s own line.
Wts: Abagail and Lucretia **Hicks**.

121, 122, 123, 124- Aug. 5, 1766- James **Young** and wife Mary to Joseph **Wade** for 25 pds. 111 acres on both sides of Fort creek being part of

169
tract granted to **Young** at James **Young**'s and John **Pullen**'s lines and at a line between **Young** and **Moxley**'s land.
Wts: Joseph **Hill**, John **Pullen**.

124 thru 125- Oct. 30, 1765- John **Gomer** of Mecklinburg Co., VA. to Nathaniel **Robinson** for 35 pds. 100 acres in Granville Co., N.C. on N. side of Nut Bush creek on **Dodson**'s branch, at Charles **Dotson**'s and **Hargrove**'s line.
Wts: John **Hargrove**, George **Duncan**, Jerem **Ward**.

125 thru 127- Sept 10, 1765- William **Arnold** to William **Potter** of Dinwiddie Co., VA. for 100 pds. 300 acres which was granted to James **Mitchel** Apr, 27, 1754 on both sides of Beaverdam creek.
Wts: John **Potter**, Thos **Ferrar**, Thos **Moore**.

127, 128- Aug. 2, 1766- Richard **Briggs** and wife Mary to Egbert **Haywood** of Halifax Co., N.C. for 14 pds. 80 acres being part of land, whereon **Briggs** formerly lives, conveyed to Maj. Phillip **Pryor** on S side of Hico road at Thomas **Person**'s line, Chesley **Daniel** and sold to **Briggs**.
Wts: Chesley **Daniel**, David **Knott**, Joseph **Miller**.

128, 129- July 8, 1766- Henry **Howard** and wife Priscilla of Mecklenburg Co., VA. to Daniel **Grant** for 150 pds. 380 acres on both sides of Grassy creek whereon **Grant** now lives on N. side of Bear branch at John **Owen**'s line at John **Potter**'s mill pond.
Wts: Richardson **Owen**, Thomas **Brooks**, Spencer **Pescud**.

129, 130- Apr. 11, 1765- Benjamin **Cook** to James **Criswell** for 125 pds. 566 acres on both sides of Lick branch on **Parker**'s line.
Wts: John **Foushee**, Howel and Isabella **Lewis**.

131, 132- Mar. 14, 1764- Daniel **Blackman** to Joseph **Rogers** for 60 pds. 266 acres on both sides of Tabbs creek on **Blackman**'s line.
Wts: Claborn **Harris**, Joseph **Daniel**.

132, 1333- Apr. 28, 1766- William **Briant** of Brunswick Co., Virginia to John **Herndon** of Bute Co., N.C. for 130 pds. 215 acres on both sides of Ruin Creek at George **Woodlief**'s corner and at **Herndon**'s corner which was granted to **Briant** by deed from Daniel **Hunter** Feb. 10, 1763- .
Wts: John and Sarah **Herndon**.

134, 135- May 29, 1765- Isham **Parham** to John **Smith** for 62 pds. 10 shls. 650 acres on W. side of Tabbs creek in **Chaver**'s line granted to George **Moore**- Dec. 1, 1760.
Wts: Wm. **Moore**, John **Herndon**, Daniel **Hunter**.

135, 136- Jan. 29, 1765- Grimes **Halcom** to Richard **Hargrove**'s for 45 pds. 100 acres on **Hargrove**'s line.
Wts: Edmund **Taylor**, Josiah **Mitchel**.

136, 137- Sept. 2, 1765- Augustine **Davis** to Thomas **Lanier** for 10 pds. 14 shls. 6 pence, 600 acres at **Davenport's** corner.
Wts: Robert **Lanier**, Nat **Harris**, Elizabeth **Davis**.

137 thru 139- Aug. 9, 1766- Larkin **Johnston** to James **Young** and Co. of Halifax Co., N.C. for 32 pds. 11 pence, 65 acres on both sides of Jonathan's creek.
Wts: Charles **Bruce**.

139, 140- Oct. 30, 1765- Richard **Briggs** to Phillip **Pryor** for 25 pds. 200 acres on Canway's branch at **Person**'s line, **Hill**'s line.
Wts: Tabitha and Haden **Pryor**.

140 thru 142- May 12, 1765- Richard **Currington** and wife Martha to John **Dickerson** for 100 pds. 450 acres on both sides of Long creek at **Fuller's**, **Smith**'s lines.
Wts: John **Finch**, Thos. **Dickerson**.

142, 143- May 11, 1762 Arthur **Jordan** to Thomas **Reeks** for 50 pds. 200 acres on W side of **Anderson**'s swamp on **Jordan**'s line.
Wts: Reuben **Searcy**, Richd **Henderson**.

143 thru 145- May 27, 1765- Peter **Vinson** and Judey **Vinson** to James **Sandland** of Bute Co., N.C. for 25 pds. 180 acres on both sides of Tabbs creek, west part of tract granted to **Vinson**- Nov. 28, 1760.
Wts: John **Champion**, Jr., Sander (Lander) **Vincent**.
This name, spelled both **Vinson** and **Vincent**-

170

145, 146- May 10, 1765- Charles **Williams** to David **Gunter** for 5 shls. sterling, 100 acres being part of tract granted to William **Williams**.
Wts: Francis **Fowler**.

146, 147- Jan. 2, 1765- John **Searcy** to Len Henley **Bullock** for 112 pds. 316 acres on Nut Bush creek on **Bullock**'s line, **Henderson**'s line, John **Sims** and John **Wade**'s line.
Wts: John **Williamson**, Thos. **Ray**.

147 thru 149- Oct. 18, 1765- Solomon **Fuller**, Sr. to Jones **Fuller** for 50 pds. 170 acres on both sides of North Fork of Newlight creek and on N. side of Tar river, granted to William **Hall** May 7, 1757.

Wts: Jeremiah **Baley**, Solomon **Fuller**, Barnaby **Fuller**.

149, 150- Dec. 17, 1764 [sic]- Augustine **Davis** to William **Holley** for 81 pd. 246 acres on both sides of **Michael**'s creek on Edward **Henderson**'s line.
Wts: Nat **Harris**, Solomon **Davis**, Joseph Pomphrett **Davis**.

150 thru 152- Oct. 31, 1765- Phillip **Pryor**, Esq., sheriff of Granville Co., N.C. to John **Williams**, Jr., attny at law - - In Salisbury, N.C. the court ordered Mar. 2, 1765, that property of Elisha **Brooks** was to be sold at public auction to cover his debts due and suit brought by John **Alloway**- Land containing 430 acres was sold to John **Williams**, Jr., located on Flat creek in Granville Co., N.C.

153 thru 155- Aug. 5, 1766- Phillip **Pryor**, sheriff, to James **Young** of Halifax Co., N.C.-
Property of William **Moxley** sold at public vendue at suit brought by James **Young** and Co. for debt due them- 200 acres on both sides of Fort creek sold, James **Young** was highest bidder-

155, 156 Oct. 31, 1765- Philip **Pryor** to John **Goodloe**-
Property of Christopher **Hunt** sold by court order at suit brought by William **Hamilton** and Co. in Town of Halifax, N.C.- and land on Fishing creek at Henry **Day**'s line in Granville Co., N.C. sold to John **Goodloe**.
Wts: Sml **Benton**.

157 thru 159- Oct. 31, 1765- Philip **Pryor**, Esq., sheriff of Granville Co. ordered to sell property of Henry **Jones**, by order of court at suit for debt against him- 150 acres on branch of Fishing creek at **Mead**'s, Joseph **Bass**'s, John **Lewis**'s, Robert **Hicks**'s lines- bought by John **Goodloe** as highest bidder.

160- Aug. 6, 1766- Philip **Pryor**, sheriff, sold property of Robert **Duke**, William **Jordan** and Thomas **Newby**- suit brought by David **Mitchel**- sold 492 acres belonging to Thomas **Newby** in Granville Co., at **Hudspeth**'s line on both sides of Fishing creek.

162 thru 164- Aug. 5, 1766- Sheriff Philip **Pryor** sold property of Ephraim **McLemore** at suit brought by James **Young** for debt. 250 acres sold to Robert **Harris** as highest bidder.

164 thru 167- Aug. 5, 1766- Sheriff Philip **Pryor** sold at public vendue property of James **Coffield** at suit of Luke **Carrol** 215 acres at line of Luke **Carrol**'s land in Granville Co., N.C. sold to Robert **Harris**.

167- thru 169- Aug. 9, 1766- Sheriff **Pryor** sold at public auction the property of Haul **Hudson** at suit of William **Hamilton** and Co. 200 acres on Nathaniel **Henderson**'s line in Granville Co. sold to William **Hamilton** as highest bidder.

169- thru 172- Aug. 6, 1766- Sheriff **Pryor** sold at public auction the property of Isaac **Arnold** to William **Hamilton**, he being highest bidder.

172- thru 174- Aug. 5, 1766- Sheriff **Pryor** sold at public auction the property of Philip **Chavers** by order of court by Clerk Samuel **Benton**, at suit brought by **Hamilton** and Co.- 700 acres at lines of **Hawkims** and **Person**'s lands sold to William **Hamilton** and Co, as highest bidder.

174, 175- Mar. 16, 1761 Grant from Lord Granville to John **Pope** in Granville Co. on both sides of Capes branch, **Magehee**'s line, **Fuller**'s line containing 582 acres.
Wts: Joseph **Montfort**, Wm. **Clanton**.

175, 176- Aug. 4, 1766- John **Williams**, Sr. to Nathaniel **Williams** for 10 pds. 400 acres on both sides of River creek granted to **Williams** (John).

171
to John **Williams**- Nov. 7, 1760.
Wts: Samuel **Henderson**, Jr., John **Williams**, Jr.

177- 178- Nov. 17, 1764- Henry **Howard** of Lunenburg Co., VA. to David **Wilkerson** of Granville Co., N.C. for 10

pds. 10 acres on S side of Bearskin creek in Henry **Howard**'s line in Granville Co., N.C.
Wts: Phil **Pryor**, Spencer **Pescud**.

178, 179- Mar. 5, 1765- Sherwood **Harris** to Michael **Wilson** for 50 pds. 340 acres on Hatcher's Run at Isaac **Arnold**'s alias **Harris**'s corner.
Wts: Wm. **Ogelvie**, James **Moore** (**Oglevie** also a spelling of this name.)

180, 181- Oct. 4, 1764- Josiah **Roberts** of Bute Co., N.C. to John **Warmouth** of Granville Co. for 12 pds. 65 acres on branches of Grassy creek at **Dobbin**'s corner, Thomas **Person**'s line.
Wts: James **Downey**, Daniel **Standard**, Mary **Downey**.

181, 182- Aug. 5, 1766- Nathaniel **Williams** to John **Williams**, Sr. and wife Mary for 10 pds. 300 acres in Granville Co., N.C. on S side of Ruin creek which was conveyed to Nathaniel **Williams** by John **Williams**, Sr. John **Williams**, Sr. and wife Mary to have land for their lifetimes.
Wts: Samuel **Henderson**, John **Williams**, Jr.

182, 183- Aug. 6, 1766- John **Bearden** to Richard **Head** for 15 pds. 100 acres on Lovet **Gates**' line, **Feagins**'s line.
Wts: Benj **Beardon**, John **Beardon**, Jr.

183, 184- May 18, 1765- John **Busbee** to Mathew **Caviness** for 11 pds. the land whereon **Caviness** now lives on head of **Mitchel**'s creek at Jeremiah **Ward**, **Busbee**'s, Richard **Hargrove**, Luke **Waldrop**'s line.
Wts: Benjamin **Mitchel**, Abraham **Mitchel**, Thomas **Caviness**, Josiah **Mitchel**, William **Caviness**.

184 thru 186- Sept. 30, 1765- Peter **Calder** to John **Pope** for 20 pds. 200 acres on S side of Flat River path, about 6 yards from path being part of tract granted to John **Pope**- May 16, 1761 for 582 acres and conveyed to **Calder**- Dec. 31, 1762.
Wts: Wm. **Nailing**, Shemuel **Kearne**, James **Winningham**, Henry **Pott**.

186, 187- Aug. 8, 1765- John **Gillam** to William **Bullock** for 350 pds. 844 acres on Great Nut Bush creek at **Glover**'s line on Flat creek on **Norwood**'s, Joseph **Glover**'s, David **Mitchel**'s lines.
Wts: Zac **Bullock**, Peter **Gillam**, Richard **Henderson**, Samuel **Benton**.

187 thru 189- Dec. 23, 1765- Samuel **Weaver** to William **Mitchel** for 200 pds. 70 acres on Long Creek at Solomon **Fuller**'s line.
Wts: John **Spears**, Henry **Fuller**, John **Bowie**.

189, 190- Oct. 30, 1765- Richard **Bradford** to Thomas **Bradford** for 50 pds. 472 on both sides of Low Ground creek on **Wilkerson**'s line.
Wts: George **Hudspeth**, William **Wilkerson**, John **Tisdale**.

190 thru 192- Sept. 3, 1766- James **Reid** and wife Margaret to Samuel **Smith** for 48 pds. 100 acres on Buffalo creek, at William **Graves**' line.
Wts: William **Graves**, Benja **Kendrick**, Richard **Norris**.

192, 193- Sept. 1, 1766- Benjamin **Ragland** to Richard **Clanton** for 5 pds. 320 acres on both sides of Flat creek on **Ragland**'s north line being half the tract that did belong to Ephraim **Clanton**.
Wts: Thos. **Critcher**, Banjamin **Clarke**.

193, 194- May 11, 1765- West **Harris** and wife Mary of Bute Co. to Isham **Harris** for 100 pds. 640 acres at Joseph **Kimball**'s, Jr., corner.
Wts: Arthur **Jordan**, Tanner **Jordan**.

194, 195- Nov. 4, 1766- Joseph **Bishop** and wife Thaena to Joseph **Linsey** for 100 pds. 237 acres on **Anderson**'s swamp and a tract of 100 acres on John **Daniel**'s' and **Williams**' lines.
Wts: Reuben **Searcy**.

196, 197- Nov. 4, 1766- Joseph **Linsey** and wife Rachel to Joseph **Bishop** for 100 pds. 240 acres at George

Jordan's corner on **Worley**'s branch.
Wts: Reuben **Searcy**.

197, 198- May 29, 1766- Bartholomew **Kimball** to Joseph **Kimball** for 80 pds. 460 acres on **Anderson**'s swamp at James **Daniel**'s' corner, Daniel **Williams**'s line.
Wts: John **Reagin**, Robert **Robinson**, Geo. **Lamkin**, Miles **Williams**.

172

198 thru 200- May 16, 1766- Arthur **Jordan** to Joseph **Smith** for 12 pds. 70 acres on **Anderson**'s swamp, at Thomas **Parish**'s line, George **Reid**'s line.
Wts: Maryman **Thorne**, Thomas **Parrish**, Robert **Hight**.

200, 201- Aug. 20, 1765- Ezekiel **Hampton** and wife Jenny to William **Jones** for 40 pds. 130 acres on Spring branch, N. side of Indian Field creek on **Jones**'s line.
Wts: George **Thompson**, John **Hampton**.

201 thru 203- Feb. 4, 1765- Luke **Landers** to Micajah **Crenshaw** for 45 pds. 329 acres on both sides of Grassy creek in John **Willingham**'s corner at Francis **Howard**'s line whereon **Crenshaw** now lives.
Wts: James **Walker**, James **Mathews**, Gign **Crenshaw**.

203, 204- Oct. 16, 1766- Thomas **Aspen** and wife Hannah to Thomas **Critcher** for 120 pds. 135 acres on both sides of Crooked creek and on Nut Bush creek.
Wts: Benjamin **Ragland**, Benjamin **Smith**.

204, 205- Aug. 30, 1766- Leonard **Sims** to his mother, Sarah **Sims** 200 acres, whereon she now lives, as a gift to her for her lifetime. Land on Reedy and Mitchell's branch including the dwelling house.
Wts: William, Nathan and Dorcas **Sims**.

206, 207- Nov. 3, 1766- Bryan **Fuller** to Samuel **Fuller** for 100 pds. 340 acres on Tabbs creek.
Wts: Henry **Fuller**, William **Roberts**.

207, 208. . .1766- Thomas **Lanier** to John **Williams** for 5 pds. 5 acres whereon he lives at said **Lanier**'s line.
Wts: None.

208, 209- June 26, 1766- Thomas **Parish** to Joseph **Smith** for 5 pds. 30 acres on **Anderson**'s swamp at Maryman **Thorne**'s line.
Wts: Arthur **Jordan**, Robt. **Hightower**.

210, 211- June 19, 1766- Ephraim **Hampton** to William **Jones** for 30 pds. 70 acres whereon **Jones** lives on N. side of Indian Field creek, at **Harris**'s line, Thomas **Person**'s line.
Wts: Robert **Harris**, Wm. **Ogilvie**.

211, 212- June 5, 1766- John **Hogins** to Isum **Cordill** for 36 pds. 150 acres on both sides Ready branch at John **Hogans**' own line, **Benton**'s line.
Wts: John **Hamilton**, Edwd. **Moore**.

212, 213- Oct. 17, 1766- Vincent **Bodine** and wife Phebee to George **Tillman** of Brunswick Co., Va. for 60 pds. 280 acres on both sides of Mirey creek at Len **Linsey**'s line, John **Hase**'s line.
Wts: John **Craft**, Thomas **Craft**.

214, 215- Oct. 29, 1766- West **Harris** and wife Mary to Joseph **Wood** for 150 pds. 300 acres on head of Island creek.
Wts: Richard **Figures**, Mical **Harris**, Turner **Harris**.

215, 216- Nov. 6, 1766- Thomas **Craft** and wife Elizabeth to David **Mitchel** for 130 pds. 200 acres on S side of Flat creek, adjoining Reuben **Moss**, Thomas **Aspen** and said **Mitchell**'s lines.
Wts: Reuben **Searcy**.

217, 218- Nov. 6, 1766- David **Mitchel** to Samuel **Walker** for 30 pds. 492 acres on both sides of Fishing creek in **Hudspeth**'s line.
Wts: Stephen **Jett**.

218, 219- Jan. 16, 1765- Harris **Gillam** and wife Elizabeth to Bartholomew **Kimball** for 32 pds. 75 acres on **Anderson**'s swamp at William **Gillam**'s line.
Wts: William **Gillam**, Len. Henley **Bullock**.

218, 219- Aug. 30, 1766- William **Sims** of Mecklenburg Co., N.C. to Leonard **Sims** of Granville Co for 150 pds. 189 acres in Granville Co on W side of Great Nut Bush creek on lines of Nathaniel **Bullock**, John **Hargrove**'s, William **Potter** and Luke **Waldrup**, Leonard **Sims** line.
Wts: Nathan, Dorcas, Sally **Sims**.

220, 221- Aug. 4, 1766- Vinson **Bodine** to John **VanLandingham** for 10 pds. 150 acres on S side of Ruin creek on Vinson **Bodine**'s and John **Hase**'s lines.
Wts: Samuel **Denton**, John **Bird**.

221, 222- Nov. 5, 1766- James **Hester** to Zachariah **Hester** for 50 pds. 150 acres on line of William **Cocke**, Absalom **Davis**, James **Butler**, Jos. **Minter** at fork of Island creek.
Wts: Reuben **Searcy**.

173

222, 223- Nov. 3, 1766- John **Rust** and wife Sarah to Thomas **Critcher** for 20 shls. 2 acres on E side of Nut Bush creek [in the parish of Granville.]
Wts: Benja **Ragland**, Nathaniel **Rochester**.

224, 225- Apr. 20, 1765- Samuel **Weaver** to Joshua **Hays** for 30 pds. 500 acres on both sides of Tabbs creek in **Dickerson**'s line.
Wts: Claborn and Judith **Harris**.

225 thru 227- Feb. 4, 1766- Gideon **Crenshaw** and wife Sarah to James **Williamson** for 20 pds. 200 acres being land whereon **Williamson** lives.
Wts: John **Williams**, Littleberry **Smith**, Luke **Landers**.

227, 228- July 10, 1762 Thomas **Jones** and wife Frances to John **Denbey** for 50 pds. 340 acres on E side of Cypress swamp on **Hobbs**' line which was granted to **Jones** for 680 acres Feb. 6, 1762.
Wts: Thomas **Jones**, William and James **Hobbs**.

228 thru 231- Feb. 5, 1767- James **Yancey**, sheriff of Granville Co. to Haden **Pryor**- property of William **Gowin**, ordered sold to pay debt to William **Whorton** who brought suit against said **Pryor**, land was sold, 300 acres on Charles **Harris**'s line.
Wts: Samuel **Walker**, Jos. **Farguson**.

231, 232- Feb. 2, 1767- William **Hamilton** and Co. of Nansemond Co., Va. merchants, to Nathaniel **Benton** for 20 pds. 100 acres in Granville Co. on James **Reaves** line.
Wts: Thomas **Mutter**, Charles **Bruce**.

233, 234- Jan. 31, 1767- William **Hamilton** and Co., of Nansemond Co., Va. to Thomas **Springfield** for 10 pds. 70 acres on W side of Fishing creek at dividing line between Isham **Arnold** and Sherwood **Harris**.
Wts: Samuel **Benton**, Saml **Clay**.

234, 235- Nov. 11, 1766- Jean **Braswell** to William **Hamilton** and Co. merchants, for 20 pds. 100 acres on James **Reaves**' corner.
Wts: Stephen **Jett**, Elizabeth **Gaultney**.

235 thru 237- Nov. 3, 1766- William **Chavers** to Daniel **Hunter** for 137 pds. 335 acres which was granted to

Chavers Mar. 22, 1752 on Tabbs creek by William **Kinchen**, Jr.
Wts: William **Spears**, Charles **Moore**, Alexander **Snelling**.

237, 238- Feb 6, 1767- Thomas **Lowe** and wife Mary to Charles Rust **Eaton** of Halifax Co., N.C. for 250 pds. Land on Tabbs creek known as the *courthouse tract* which was given to Mary **Lowe** by Will of William **Eaton**, her deceased husband.
Wts: Robert **Hightower**, William and Thomas **Eaton**.

239, 240- Jan. 15. 1767- James **Smith** and wife Elizabeth to William **Allen** son of Samuel **Allen** for 70 pds. 200 acres on William **Stovall**'s line, at **Beardon**'s line, **Hutchins**' line, John **Morgan**'s line.
Wts: Danl **Grant**, Benja **Beardon**, Richard **Harris**.

240, 241- Jan. 20, 1767- James **Smith** and wife Elizabeth to William **Allen**, Sr. for 45 pds. 200 acres at William **Allen**'s old line and Wm. **Roads** corner. at **Hutchins** and William **Harris**'s line.
Wts: Richard **Harris**, John **Wade**.

242, 243- Sept. 3, 1766- Richard **Harris** and wife Priscilla to Samuel **Smith** for 200 pds. 316 acres in William **Knight**'s line, on Buffalo creek-
Wts: William **Graves**, Banja **Kendrick**, James **Reed**.

243, 244, 245- Jan. 31, 1767- James **Reed** and wife Margaret to Samuel **Smith** for 10 pds. 45 acres on Samuel **Smith**'s corner, William **Graves**' line and on west side of Buffalo creek.
Wts: Richard and Priscilla **Harris**, Margaret **Reed**.

245 thru 247- Nov. 16, 1766- James **Cash** and wife Marget to Joseph **Miller** for 24 pds. 200 acres at **Hill**'s line, Philip **Taylor**'s line, George **King**'s line, which was taken up by Jonathan **Parker** and sold to **Cash**.
Wts: Joseph **Ballson**, Nahom **Landers**, William **Hicmon**.

247, 248, 249- Feb. 3, 1767- David **Gunter** to Israel **Eastwood** for 5 shls. 100 acres deeded to William **Williams** on S side of Tar river.
Wts: James **Langston**, Solomon **Langston**.

174

249, 250- Feb. 2, 1767- William **Allen** and wife Mary to William **Crag** for 40 pds. 304 acres in Edward **Bond's** line on William **Cragg**'s line.
Wts: Rich **Harris**, Ben **Bearden**.

250, 252- Nov. 3, 1766- James **Chandler** of Mecklenburg Co., Va. from Edmund **Bearden** of Mecklenburg Co., Va for 25 pds. 150 acres in Granville Co., N.C. on Henry **Feagin**'s line.
Wts: Benjamin, John, Jr., and John **Bearden** (**Beardon**).

252 thru 254- Dec. 18, 1766- George **Levister** to Pumphrey **Edwards** for 16 pds. 100 acres on S side of Tar river at **Ballinger**'s line.
Wts: John **Pullen**, Samuel **Walker**.

254 thru 256- Oct. 1, 1765- Abraham **Moore** to Thomas **Harris** for 30 pds. 265 acres on **Thompson**'s line, **McCulloch**'s corner, **Williams**' line.
Wts: John **Hampton**, Charles **Williams**.

256 thru 258- Oct. 21, 1766- Ephraim **Hampton** to Thomas **Veazey** for 30 pds. 202 acres being the land conveyed by Robert **Harris** to Ephraim **Hampton** on Alexander **Jones**'s line-
Leminder, wife of Ephraim **Hampton** relinquishes dower right.
Wts: James **Veazey**, James **Veazey**, Jr., Thomas **Littlejohn**.

258, 259- Jan. 20, 1767- John **Bybe** and wife Jean to Drury **Kimball** for 20 pds. 50 acres on Thomas **Parrish**'s and George **Rhodes**'s line on **Anderson** Swamp.

Wts: Thomas **Parrish**, William **McMerritt**.

259, 260- Jan. 26, 1767- George **Roads** and wife Juda to Drury **Kimball** for 10 pds. 50 acres on **Anderson**'s swamp.
Wts: Wm. **McMerritt**, Susanna **Roads**.

260 thru 262- Feb. 5, 1767- Thomas **Bradford** to William **Parham** for 75 pds. 150 acres on W side of Fishing creek being the west part of tract granted to Jonathan **White** Oct. 23, 1754.
Wts: Stephen **Jett**, Michael **Wilson**.

262 thru 264- Junly [sic] 28, 1766- Abraham **Landess** to Joseph **Landess** for [20] pds. sterling of England, 202 acres which was deeded to Abraham **Landes** Aug. 30, 1764 by John **Ross** on John **Ross**'s line, at Trading path.
Wts: Robert **Harris**, David **Harris**.

264 thru 266- Oct. 8, 1766- Gibea (Gibby) **Chavers** to Giles **Hudspeth** for 60 pds. 300 acres on N. side of Tar river on **Snelling**'s line where John **Shepard** now lives being part of tract purchased by Gibby **Chavers** from John **Metisock** (**McKissock**?).
Wts: Isham **Parham**, John **Parham**.

266, 267- Nov. 20, 1766- Richard **Harris** to his son John **Harris**, a gift of 144 acres on Jonathan **White**'s line.
Wts: Daniel **Standland**, John **Kittrell**.

267 thru 268- Nov. 8, 1765- William **Dobbins** to William **Frazer** for 30 pds. 140 acres on branch of Grassy creek.
Wts: Jeremiah, James and Elizabeth **Walker**.

268 thru 270- Feb. 4, 1767- John **Oliver** and wife Fanny to Robert **Lewis**, Jr. for 200 pds. 320 acres on N. side of Island creek, **Hawkins**' line adjoining Robert **Lewis**, Jr.
Wts: Thomas **Butler**, William **Cocke**, Charles **Kennon**.

270, 271- Oct. 19, 1765- Reuben **Searcy** to William **Cooper** for 50 pds. 155 acres on Nut Bush creek at Robert **Hutchins**' line.
Wts: James **Forsythe**, John **Walker**.

271 thru 273- Aug. 19, 1766- Robert **Searcy** to Samuel **Henderson** for 5 pds. 30 acres on **Anderson**'s swamp whereon **Henderson** lives.
Wts: Richard **Henderson**, John **Litterill**.

273, 274- Aug. 26, 1766- William **Bullock** and Reuben **Searcy** to Gulielmus **Smith** for 88 pds. 12 shls. 6 pence. 277 acres on **Anderson**'s swamp on Mill pond.
Wts: John **Williams**, Jr., William **Williams**.

274, 275- Dec. 1, 1766- John **Haly** (**Haley**) of Caroline Co, Va to Richard **Duty** for 20 pds. 301 acres on W side of **Aaron's** creek on **Yancey**'s Line.
Wts: Micajah **Crenshaw**, George **Brasfield**.

175

276 Sept. 3, 1762- Henry **McCulloch** to George **Byar** for 15 pds. 5 shls 2 pence, part of *tract No. 12*, 271 acres at George **Miller**'s corner.
[no witnesses listed.]

277 thru 279- Feb. 13, 1757- James **Boyd** and wife Mary to Henry Eustice **McCulloch** for 350 pds. 640 acres being tract purchased of James **Kelly** Dec. 1, 1755 and **Kelly** bought of Henry **McCulloch** Dec. 7, 1754 near the Trading Path in Granville Co.
Wts: Ann and William **Johnston**.

279, 280- Mar. 25, 1766- Andrew **Hampton** of Georgia, to George **Boyer** of Granville Co., N.C. for 60 pds. 200

acres in Granville Co., N.C. granted to **Hampton**- July 11 17. . .
Wts: Frederick **Peck**, Ezekiel **Hampton**.

280, 281- July 27, 1761- Grant to Sherwood **Harris** for 685 acres on both sides of Fishing creek at **Hudspeth**'s line.

281 thru 283- May 17, 1767- David **Wicker** to James **Currin** for 25 pds. 200 acres whereon **Wicker** now lives which was granted to him July 24, 1761.
Wts: Edmund **Fanning** (wife Sukey **Wicker** also signs deed.).

283, 284- May 7, 1767- Howel **Lewis** and wife Isabell to John **Johnston** for 60 pds. 369 acres on both sides of lower fork of Grassy creek at James **Pettigrew** [corrected from **Pettigres**] line, Drury **Smith**'s line.
Wts: John **Bell**, James **Pettegrew**.

285, 286- Mar. 28, 1767- Thomas **Person** to Thomas **Owen** for 40 pds. 327 acres along **Collin**'s line and **Howard**'s line.
Wts: John **Owen**, Francis **Howard**.

286, 287- Apr. 10, 1767- Thomas **Lanier** to Robert **Lanier** for 15 pds. 600 acres on both sides of Lick Branch at **Davenport**'s corner, **Davis**'s line.
Wts: William **Byers**.

287, 298- Apr. 13, 1767- John **Brooks** to **Young**, **Miller** and Co. for 75 pds. 150 acres along Ester **Shockley**'s line, on N. side of Jonathan's crk. and N. side of the Mountain Fork of said creek, at **Williams** line, and Jeremiah **Clayton**'s lines.
Wts: Stephen **Jett**, Thomas **Mutter**.

289, 290- Aug. 11, 1766- Robert **Searcy** to Joshua **Moss** for 5 pds. 40 acres on branches of **Anderson**'s fork in Leonard Henley **Bullock**'s line, John **Daniel**'s' line.
Wts: Daniel and Joseph **Williams**.

290, 291- Aug. 5, 1766- Samuel **Henderson** to Joshua **Moss** for 30 pds. 333 acres on branches of Great Nut Bush creek at Nimrod **Williams**' line.
Wts: Richard **Henderson**, John **Litterell**, Jr.

291 thru 293- Feb. 6, 1767- Thomas **Parish** to William **Hamilton** and Co. of Nansemond Co., Va. for 10 pds. 50 acres on **Anderson**'s swamp on West **Harris**'s line and Thomas **Parish**'s line.
Wts: Wm. **Reeves**, John **Hampton**.

292 thru 295- Feb. 4, 1767- John **Herndon** late of Bute Co., N.C. now of Granville to William **Briant** of Brunswick Co., Va. for 37 pds. 215 acres on Tabbs and Ruin creeks at **Woodlief**'s lower corner, **Henderson**'s line which was granted by **Bryant** to **Herndon**- Apr. 28, 1766-
Wts: Samuel **Kittrell**, Danl **Hunter**.

295, 296- May 4, 1767- John **Bearding** and wife Lettice to Guy **Smith** of Mecklenburg Co., Va. for 100 pds. 300 acres on Lovet **Gates** line, Richard **Head**'s line and line of land of orphans of Henry **Fagin** and of James **Chandler**.
Wts: Mary **Smith**, Baxter **Davis**, Samuel **Smith**.

296 thru 298- [no date] James **Reade** and Margaret his wife to Samuel **Smith** for 12 pds. 60 acres at **Smith**'s line, on Richard **Harris**'s line, Benjamin **Kendrick**, William **Graves**' line.
Wts: Ben **Bearden**, Richd **Harris**, William **Knight**, Baxter **Davis**.

298 thru 300- June 10, 1764- Joseph **Kimball**, Jr. to Philemon **Hawkins** for 30 pds. 10 shls, 6 pence- 530 acres at **Kimball**'s corner.
Wts: Geo. **Martin**.

300, 301- May 2, 1767- John Michael **Redwine** to William **Ogelvie** for 35 pds. 445 acres being tract sold by **Ogelvie** to **Redwine** on **McCulloch**'s line and on **Ogelvie**'s line.

Wts: Richard and Thomas **Harris**.

176

301 thru 303- Jan. 20, 1767- James **Smith** and wife Elizabeth to William **Head** for 20 pds. 160 acres on William **Allens** line.
Wts: Richard **Harris**, John **Wade**.

303, 304- Mar. 4, 1767- James **Hester** and wife Frances to James **Butler** of Brunswick Co., Va. for 20 pds. 100 acres on **Howlett** creek at Zachariah **Hester**'s line.
Wts: Thomas **Butler**, John **Terrell**, George **Pitlock**.

304 thru 306- May 5, 1767- Phillemon **Bradford**, Sr. to Timoth[sic] **Reach** for 30 pds. 360 acres on Beaverdam creek.
Wts: Gillam **Harris**, John **Bridges**.

306 and 3099- May 5, 1767- James **Yancey** to Jesse **Saunders** for 50 pds. (this name also spelled **Sanders** or is it **Landers**?) 150 acres above Jesse **Sanders** house on Jonathan Creek at Ester **Shockley**'s line.
Wts: Haden **Pryor**, Jesse **Benton**.

307, 308- May 2, 1767- George **Boyer** to William **Patterson** for 60 pds. 200 acres which was granted **Hampton** and conveyed to **Boyer**.
Wts: R. **Harris**.

310, 311- May 5, 1767- Richard **Duty** to Isaac **Winfrey** for a tract of land on **Smith**'s line on a creek at **Yancey**'s line for 577 acres granted to Drury **Smith**- Nov. 7, 1760.
Wts: Dan. **Hunter**, Wm. **Ring**.

311 thru 313- Mar. 14, 1767- Richard **Harris** to Philemon **Bradford** for (Margaret wife of Richard **Harris**) 10 pds. 265 acres on Beaver Pond Creek.
Wts: Jonathan **Kittrell**, Thomas **Mutter**, Margaret **Harris**.

314, 315- Mar. 23, 1767- Ephraim **Hampton** to Robert **Harris** for 150 pds. 400 acres being same land given by Andrew **Hampton** on S side of Tar river and on Mill creek.
Wts: Richard **Foster**, Nicholas **Medlock**, Jr.

315, 316- May 20, 1765- Joseph **Walker** to Andrew **Hampton** for 50 pds. 200 acres granted to **Walker** by **McCulloch**- July 8, 1763- on John **Walker**'s lines.
Wts: John **Ross**, Denis **Sulivin**.

316 thru 318- Dec. 6, 1767- John **Hunt** to William **Vickary** for 63 pds. 200 acres on both sides of **Michaels** creek being part of grant to John **Bird**- Nov. 27, 1760 from Lord Granville (Wife Sarah relinquishes dower right).
Wts: None.

318,- July 16, 1767- John **Trevillian** of Rowan Co., N.C. to Capt James **Mitchel** for 7 pds. 76 acres on **Mitchell**'s line, James **Trevillians**' and **Bullock**'s line.
Wts: Richard **Henderson**, Richd **Trevillian**.

319, 320- Aug. 4, 1767- Thomas **Lanier** to Joseph **Winston** for 700 pds. 200 acres at John **Searcy**'s line on **Glover**'s and on John **Mitchell**'s lines.
Wts: Reuben **Searcey**, Robert **Lanier**.

320 thru 322- Mar. 15, 1767- John **Hawkins** of Bute Co., N.C. to James **Boyd** for 48 pds. 200 acres on W side of Cattail branch.
Wts: Len Henley **Bullock**, Reuben **Searcy**.

322, 323- Feb. 2, 1767- Henry **Melton** to William **Crag** for 70 pds. 234 acres on both sides of **Howlet**'s creek on **Harris**'s line, **Ester**'s line, **Cook**'s line being a half of tract whereon **Melton** now lives granted to him June 25, 1761 by

Granville and also land Benjamin **Whicker**, Jr. lived on.
Wts: Veazey **Husband**, Thomas **Whicker**, Banjamin **Wickee**[sic].

323, 324- Jan. 18, 1767- Andrew **Hampton** to Ezekiel **Hampton** for 50 pds. 200 acres granted to **Hampton** by Henry **McCulloch**- Jan. 18, 1767- at William **Jones**'s line.
Wts: Moses **Bonner**, John **Hampton**, Corls. **Keith**.

324, 325- Jan. 28, 1767- John **Pope** to Thomas **Brummitt** for 15 pds. 25 acres on Fort creek near Ridge path at John **Pullin**'s corner being remainder tract sold by James **Maidwell** to John **Pope**.
Wts: John **Pullin**, Shemuel **Kearne**.

325 thru 326- Aug. 5, 1767- Nathan **Sims** to Leonard **Sims** for 60 pds. 645 acres on Nut Bush creek.
Wts: John **Wms**., Nathaniel **Bullock**.

177

326, 327- May 1, 1760 Leonard **Linsey** and wife Sarah to Thomas **Craft** for 105 pds. 421 acres on both sides of Crooked Run on **Linsey**'s line.
Wts: Reuben **Searcy**, Richard **Searcy**, John **Craft**.

328- May 1, 1767- Leonard **Linsey** and wife Sarah to George **Tilman** of Brunswick Co., Va for 60 pds. 200 acres at **Linsey**'s corner.
Wts: Reuben, Richard **Searcy**, John **Craft**.

329- 330- Nov. 7, 1766- William **Hamilton** and Co. of Nansemond Co., Va. to John **Hogan** for 50 pds. 200 acres on **Hatcher**'s Run at **Wilson**'s corner.
Wts: Reuben **Searcy**, Edwd **Moore**.

330, 331- July 22, 1767- Nathan **Sims** to Richard **Clanton** for 6 pds. 40 acres on Old courthouse road on north side of Flat creek, at Richard **Clanton**'s line.
Wts: Gillam **Norwood**, John **Mayes**.

331 thru 333- Aug. 3, 1767- John **Pope** to John **Pullin** for 9 pds. 5 shls. 65 acres on S side of Tar river being part of tract granted to **Pope** by deed from James **Maidwell** on Simons **Secret**'s line, **Pullim**'s [sic] line.
Wts: William **Henley**, Osborn **Pope** (Also spelled **Hendley**.)

333, 334- June 17, 1767- James **Trevilion** to James **Mitchell** for 8 pds. 15 shls. 37 acres at James **Mitchell**'s and James **Trevillion**'s line, **Bullock**'s.
Wts: William **Taylor**, Mich. **Satterwhite**.

334, 335- June 22 1767- Richard **Bradford** to Jeremiah **Reach** for 20 pds. 240 acres on both sides of Beaverdam creek.
Wts: John **Bridges**, Timothy **Reach**, Philemon **Bradford**, Jr.

335 thru 337- July 7, 1767- James **Pettegrew**, Sr. to Howel **Lewis**, Joseph **Linsey**, Robert **Lewis**, Chesley **Daniel** and John **Oliver**, trustees for the Presbyterian Congregation on waters of Grassy creek- in order to promote the worship of God, granted to trustees one acre on Grassy creek to be used as a place of worship.
Wts: Ben **Wade**, Samuel **Smith**, Grorge **Brasfield**.

337, 338- Apr. 1, 1760 Absalom **Wells** of Bute Co., N.C. to Benjamin **Ward** of Bute Co. for 25 pds. 247 acres on S side of Court house Prong of Sand [sic] creek in Granville Co. including land whereon Thomas **Ballard** lived former.
Wts: John **Pernell**, Richard **Ward**, M. **Wells**.

338, 339- July 5, 1767- Acquiler **Snelin** to Alexander **Snelin** for 10 shls 100 acres where Acquiller **Snelin** now lives on John **Smith**'s line, and on Long Creek-
Wts: Jos. **Peace**, James **Blackley**.

339, thru 341- Aug. 4, 1767- John **Howell** to Jeremiah **Frazier** for 45 pds. 150 acres where Thomas **Howel** now lives at lands of Jeremiah **Frazer** and Martin **Wheelor**, Jonathan **Parker** and Thomas **Howell**.
Wts: John **Verner**, Xtopher **Hunt**, Thos. **Howel**.

341, 342- Aug. 3, 1767- John **Willingham**, Sr. to James **Downey** for 37 pds. 520 acres on Thos. **Willingham**'s line, on Grassy creek.
Wts: Luke **Landers**, Thos. **Willingham**, James **Williamson**.

342, 343- Feb. 9, 1767- John **Reaves** to John **Harris** of Rowan Co., N.C. for 100 pds. 200 acres on both sides of Fishing creek.
Wts: Wm. **Moore**, Ro. **Harris**.

344, 345- Aug. 3, 1767- James **Downey** to John **Willingham** for 50 pds. 229 acres on **Gill**'s line.
Wts: James **Williamson**, Luke **Landers**, Abram **Crenshaw**.

345 thru 347- May 10, 1767- John **Roberts** of Mecklenburg Co., Va. to Daniel **Grant** for 50 pds. 310 acres on Jonathan creek on Bare branch of Grassy creek in William **Gill**'s line, John **Owen**'s line.
Wts: Hezekiah and Susannah **Tabor** and William **Tabor**.

347 thru 348- May 5, 1760- Capt. Henry **Howard** of Mecklenburg Co., Va to Daniel **Grant** for 30 pds. 57 acres on both sides of Grassy creek and Bearskin creek known as **Potter**'s Mill on Capt. **Willingham**'s line.
Wts: James **Yancey**, Haden **Pryor**.

348 thru 350- Aug. 3, 1767- James **Downey** to Thomas **Willingham** for 50 pds. 228 acres on **Gill**'s, **Royster**'s lines.
Wts: None.

178

350, 351- Oct. 1, 1766- Joseph John **Alston** of Halifax Co., N.C. to Philip **Alston**, Jr. for 50 pds. 350 acres which was granted to J. J. **Alston** Apr. 10, 1745 on both sides of Tar river.
Wts: Montfort **Elbeck**.

351 thru 353- Oct. 1, 1766- Joseph John **Alston** of Halifax Co., N.C. to Philip **Alston**, Jr. for 50 pds. 680 acres granted to J. J. **Alston** Apr. 20 1745 on both sides of Tar river at Robert **Donevant**'s line.
Wts: Montofrt [sic] **Eelbeck**.

353 thru 354- July 2, 1765- J. J. **Alston** of Halifax Co., N.C. to Philip **Alston**, Jr. for 50 pds. 300 acres granted to J. J. **Alston** Feb. 22, 1739 on NE side of the river at mouth of creek.
Wts: Montfort **Eelbeck**.

354 thru 356- July 8, 1765- J. J. **Alston** of Halifax Co., N.C. to Philip **Alston**, Jr. for 50 pds. 130 acres formerly granted to J. J. **Alston**- Sept. 25 1742, about a quarter mile above **Donevant**'s plantation on the river.
Wts: Montfort **Eelbeck**.

356- Receipt from James and Mary **Boyd** to Henry Eustace **McCulloch** for 350 pds.- Nov. court 1767.

357 thru 359- Feb. 28, 1767- Henry **Fuller** to William **Phillips** for 25 pds. 175 acres on N. side of Tar river.
Wts: Danl **Hunter**, Henry **Fuller**, Robert **Phillips**.

359 thru 361- Oct. 7, 17 Joseph **Gowin** to Isaac **Winfree** for 100 pds. 350 acres on William **Gowin**'s line.
Wts: John **Cunningham**, John **Winfree**.

361, 362- May 7, 1767- Howell **Lewis** and wife Isobell to James **Petegrew** for 60 pds. 369 acres on both sides of Lower fork of Grassy creek at John **Johnson**'s and Robert **Downey**'s lines.
Wts: John **Bell**, Jr., John **Johnson**.

363, 364- Sept. 7, 1767- Isaac **Winfree** to Richardson **Owen** for 75 pds. 577 acres on both sides of **Andrews** Branch.

Wts: Thos. **Owen**, Dan **Grant**, John **Winfree**.

364, 365- Aug. 15, 1767- William **Meadows** of Orange Co., N.C. to Lodwick **Redwine** of Granville Co., N.C. for 50 pds. on branches of **Shelton**'s creek east of Michael **Pealer**'s line in **Slaughter**'s line- 233 acres.
Wts: Thomas **Person**.

366, 367- Aug. 8, 1767- John **Herndon** to Pomffrett **Herndon** his son, a gift of 216 acres on both sides of Tabbs and River Creek at Daniel **Hunter**'s line, **Bryant**'s corner.
Wts: Humphrey **Herndon**, Priscilla **Langford**.

368, 369- Aug. 28, 1767- Joseph **Lefavour**, taylor [sic], to James **Young**, merchant, for 10 pds. 10 shls one acre on both sides of Sharman's road in **Hamilton**'s line.
Wts: Stephen **Jett**, Robert **Goodloe**, Jr.

369 thru 371- Aug. 21, 1767- Benjamin **Goodman** to Joseph **Williams** for 200 pds. 20 acres being the land devised to Benjamin **Goodman** in Will of Daniel **Williams**. deceased, on Little Nut Bush creek at Joseph **Williams** corner-
Wts: Bromfield **Ridley**, Thomas **Henderson**.

371 thru 373- Sept. 4, 1766- John **West** to Samuel **Denton** for 10 pds. 135 acres on Little Nut Bush creek at John **Craft**'s line.
Wts: John **Craft**, Samuel **Morse**.

373, 374- Sept. 30, 1767- Benjamin **Ragland** to Evan **Ragland** for 50 pds. 320 acres on N. side of Flat creek.
Wts: William **Potter**, Thomas **Lanier**.

375, 376- Dec. 26, 1767- James **Daniel** to John **Rust** for 25 pds. one acre on S side of N. fork of **Anderson**'s swamp at Joseph **Kimball**'s land whereon his mill stands which is land Bartholomew **Kimball** is to erect a mill on.
Wts: John **Williams**, Gulielmus **Smith**.

376, 377- Jan. 15, 1768- John **Trevillian** of Mecklenburg Co., N.C. to James **Mitchell** of Granville Co. for 5 pds. 4 shls. 50 acres on **Taylor**'s road, at head of **Mathews** branch.
Wts: Richd **Henderson**, Zach **Bullock**.

179

377, 378- Sept. 7, 1767- William **Stone** to Evan **Ragland** for 1 pds. 12 shillings, 4 acres on bank of Flat creek to Lick branch on **Ragland**'s line.
Wts: Cutbird **Hudson**, Benjamin **Ragland**.

379, 380- May 30, 1767- Moses **Street** of Mecklinburg Co., Va. to Jeremia[h] **Ward** for 50 pds. on S fork of **Taylor**'s Mill creek containing 205 acres being between the land of Edmund **Taylor**, John **Hargrove**, Mathias **Cavernis** and Robert **Gillam** and the county line.
Wts: Edmund **Taylor**, Thos. **Leach**, Charles **Kennon**.

380, 381- Dec. 28, 1767- Joseph **Kimball** to John **Rust** for 130 pds. 5 shl. 360 acres on **Anderson**'s swamp including the Mill at James **Daniel** corner, and Daniel **Williams**' line.
Wts: Miles **Williams**, Gulielmus **Smith**.

382, 383- Aug. 15, 1767- John Rodwell **Buzzard** to James **Hopper** for 5 shl 200 acres on S side of Tar river.
Wts: Jno. **Stone**, Jacob **Williams**, Isral **Eastwood**.

383 thru 385- Sept. 11, 1767- John **Green** late of Bute Co., N.C. to James **Caudle** of Granville Co. for 50 pds. 200 acres being part of 400 acres granted to Isaac **Ricks** July 25, 1743 on S side of Tar river.
Wts: John **Fowler**, William **Fowler**.

385, 386- Nov. 7, 1767- John **Bowdown** to John **Robinson** for 60 pds. 350 acres on **Lowe**'s line.
Wts: Miles **Williams**.

387, 388- Nov. 2, 1767- Ralph **Hudspeth** to Robert **Ellison** for 100 pds. 220 acres on E side of Fishing creek.
Wts: Jno. **Benton**, Wm. **Reeves**.

388, 389- Aug. 20, 1766- John **Hays** to Bartlet **Searcy** for 15 pds. 197 acres on Crooked Run.
Wts: Reuben **Searcy**, John **Searcy**, Sr.

390, 391- Aug. 11, 1763- Joseph **Davenport** to Nathaniel **Harris** for 30 pds. 300 acres on **Williams**' line which was granted to him July 24, 1761.
Wts: Edwd. **Stabler**, Christopher **Morgan**, John **Williams**, Jr.

391 thru 393- Feb. 3, 1768- Nathaniel **Harris** to Michael **Satterwhite** for 100 pds. 272 acres on **Harris**'s line, Michael **Murry**'s line, **Davenport**'s corner on **Michaels** creek.
Wts: Reuben **Searcy**, Joseph **Williams**.

393, 394- Nov. 3, 1767- James **Currin** to John **Sears** for 30 pds. 200 acres on Fishing creek part of land purchased by David **Wicker** whereon he now lives.
Wts: none (James **Currin**'s wife (not named) relinquishes dower right.

395, 396- Jan. 24, 1768- William **Crag** to Benjamin **Whicker**, son of Thomas **Whicker** for 80 pds. 320 acres on a branch of Fishing creek adjoining **Harris**, **Bullock** and **Sneed**'s lands which land was deeded by Banja **Wade** and granted July 24, 1761 by Lord Granville.
Wts: Thomas **Wicker**, David **Wicker**.

396 thru 398- Jan. 25, 1768- George **Rhodes** to Ansil **Parrish** for 55 pd s. 200 acres on **Anderson**'s swamp along Thos. **Parrish**'s line to Drury **Kimball**'s.
Wts: Joseph **Smith**, Thos. **Parrish**, John **Harris**.
Judah, wife of George **Rhodes** also signed the deed.)

398 thru 400- Feb. 1, 176[7]- John **Williams** to Charles **Williams** for 20 pds. part of 640 acres granted to John **Williams** Nov. 27, 1760 on a branch of Nut Bush creek called Ruin Creek.
Wts: John **Williams**, Jr., John **Keeling**.

400 thru 402- Oct. 17, 1767- John **Wade** to John **Young** of Essex Co., VA. for 100 pds. the land known as *Pincens* containing 200 acres on Jonathan's creek in Granville Co., N.C. (Mary **Wade**, wife of John, also signs deed).
Wts: Samuel **Smith**, David **Allen**, Tom **Yancey**.

402 thru 404- Oct. 17, 1767- John **Wade** to John **Young** of Essex Co., Virginia, for 250 pds. (also Mary, wife of John **Wade** is selling land here.) 479 acres on both sides of Grassy creek to Jonathan's creek at **Stovall**'s line, on Drury **Allen**'s line.
Wts: Tom **Yancey**, David **Allen**, Samuel **Smith**.

180

404 thru 406- Mar. 9, 1767- William **Bowdon** and wife Elizabeth to Travis **Bowdon**. for 20 pds. 140 acres at **Brack**'s corner on both sides of Great Nut Bush creek, along **Lowe**'s line.
Wts: John **Bowdon**.

406 thru 408,- Sept. 30, 1767- Philemon **Bradford** to Lawrence **Peteford** for 20 pds. 300 acres on Beaver Dam creek at **Bradford**'s own corner to **Parnel**'s line in **MoColer**'s [sic] line.
Wts: Gillum **Harris**, Philemon **Bradford**, Jr.

408 thru 409- Mar. 16, 1761 Grant from Granville to John **Baynes** of Granville Co. for 376 acres at James **Yancey**'s corner, Jeremiah **Clayton**'s

410- 411- Mar. 1, 1764- Henry Eustace **McCulloch** to William **Burford** for 32 pds. 200 acres on both sides of Ledge of Rocks creek.
Wts: Jas. **Campbell**, H. **McCulloch**.

412- May 2, 1768- John **Busbee** to George **White** and John **White**, sons of George **White**, Sr. of Mecklinburg Co., Virginia for 45 pds. 231 acres in Granville Co., N.C. on S fork of **Mitchel**'s creek along land John **Busbee** formerly held and between the lands of John **Hargrove**, Mathew **Caviness**, Jeremiah **Ward** and George **White** and the county line.
Wts: John **Bullock**, Ruth **Elickson**.

413, 414- Apr. 27, 1768- Roger **Badget** to Elizabeth **Drawhorn** for 200 pds. 300 acres which was granted to him- Nov. 22, 1760 and now in possession of Elizabeth **Drawhorn**.
Wts: Edward **Moore**, Thomas **Bagget**.

414, 415- Feb. 10, 1768- Edmund **Taylor** of Mecklenburg Co., VA. to William **Townes** of same place for 57 pds. land adjoining that of Jonathan **Parker**.
Wts: Thomas **Glass**, Ann **Brown**, Charles **Kennon**.

415- Apr. 10, 1768- Jeremiah **Anderson** to William **Hester** for 34 pds. 200 acres at Robert **Hicks** line, George **Anderson**'s line, Edward **Basse**s line.
Wts: John **Trevillion**, James **Currin**, John **Wicker**, John **Fullilove**, Benjm **Wicker**.

416- Nov. 17, 1767- Joseph **King** of St. George Parish, Georgia to Ephraim **Hampton** of Granville Co., N.C. for 12 pds. 202 acres on Nap of Reeds creek.
Wts: Andr **Hampton**, Sherwood **Harris**.

417- Apr. 26, 1768- Memucan **Hunt** to John **Gordon** and Co. of Mecklenburg Co., N.C. for 275 pds. 300 acres on Grassy creek.
Wts: Jonath **Knight**, Benjamin **Glaze**.

418- May 4, 1768- Thomas **Howell** gave to his son William, 140 acres being part of 200 acre tract on S side of Fishing creek.
Wts: James **Kanaday**, Philip **Lak**.

418, 419- Jan. 14, 1768- Richard **Clanton** and his wife Susannah to Leonard **Linsey** for 25 pds. 300 acres on courthouse road, s side of Flat creek along **Tynes** line, **Wilson**'s line. **Ragland**'s and **Clanton**'s lines.
Wts: Reuben **Searcy**, Nathl **Norwood**.

420- Aug. 7, 1766- Robert **Black** to John **Knott** for 40 pds. 240 acres in Granville Co., N.C.
Wts: James **Knott**, Thomas **Forsythe**, James **Howell**, David **Knott**.

421- May 2, 1768- Nathaniel **Bullock** of Bute Co., N.C. to Thomas **Leach** of Granville Co. for 100 pds. 130 acres at Len **Sims** line, on Great Nut Bush creek at **Hargrove**'s corner being land whereon Richard **Bullock**, deceased lately lived, he now deceased, and willed land to Nathaniel **Bullock**.
Wts: Lennard **Sims**, Natl. **Sims**.

422- Aug. 27, 1767- Abraham **Cook** of Rowan Co., N.C. to Edmund **Taylor** of Mecklenburg Co., for 20 pds. 162 acres on Thomas **Lanier** line, Benjamin **Johnson**'s line.
Wts: Wm. **Potter**, David **Mitchel**.

423- Feb. 6, 1768- Thomas **Willingham** to Robert **Beasley** of Lunenburg Co., VA. for 55 pds. 866 acres on both sides of Grassy creek at **Howard**'s and **Grant**'s lines, **Downey**'s line, John **Willingham**'s line.
Wts: Daniel **Malone**, James **Downey**, Luke **Landers**.

424- Feb. 6, 1768- Thomas **Willingham** to John **Willingham** for 5 shls. 200 acres on both sides of Grassy creek at the land whereon John now lives.
Wts: James **Downey**, Daniel **Malone**.

181

425- Oct. 7, 1768- James **Yancey** to Jesse **Landers** (**Sanders**?)**Sanders** sued for debt owed him by Esther **Shockley** and 200 acres sold to highest bidder who became Jesse Snders.- **Yancey** is sheriff.

Wts: Daniel **Malone**, George **Brasfield**.

427- Aug. 4, 1768- Daniel **Mitchel** of Mecklenburg Co., Va to Robert **Crawle[y]** of same place for 200 pds. 450 acres on each side of Island creek in the county line- signed by Mary **Mitchel** also, she the wife of Daniel.
Wts: Stephen **Jett**.

428, 429- July 6, 1768- Jeremiah **Reach** of Johnston Co., N.C. to Timothy **Reach** of Granville Co., N.C. for 20 pds. 240 acres on Beaverdam creek.
Wts: Peter **Vincent**, James **Willenham**, James **Betty**.

429, 430- Aug. 3, 1768- Richard **Harris** and wife Priscilla to Joseph **Glover** for 80 pds. 670 acres on E side of Little Island creek on **Goss**es branch in John **Taylor**'s line.
Wts: William **Byars**, Richd **Hargroves**.

430, 431- Aug. 2, 1768- Richard **Harris** to James **Reed** for 10 pds. 40 acres at James **Reed**'s corner to the school house glade on **Hunt**'s line.
Wts: William **Groves**, Benjamin **Kendrick**.

431, 432- Mar. 7. 1768- Ephraim **Hampton** to William **Jones** for 30 pds. 202 acres.
Wts: David **Harris**, Ro. **Harris**.

433, 434- Aug. 3, 1768- John Williams **Graves** and wife Mary to John **Oliver** for 130 pds. 210 acres on Island creek where John **Oliver** now lives on **Hawkins**, **Holley**'s lines at Benja **Cook**'s line.
Wts: Thomas **Person**, Philip **Yancey**.

434, 435- Aug. 2, 1768- Micajah **Crenshaw** to Charles **Spaulding** for 65 pds. 220 acres on both sides of Grassy creek at **Graves**' line whereon **Spaulding** now dwells.
Wts: John Williams **Graves**, Mary **Graves**.

435, 436- Mar. 14, 1768- James **McGehee**, Jr. and wife Ann to James **Kelley** for 25 pds. 100 acres on W side of Middle creek being part of grant to John **Pope** Mar. 16, 1761 for 582 acres.
Wts: Wm. **Nailing**, John **Champion**, Jr.

436, 437- July 26, 1768- John **Wade** to Drury **Allen** for 20 pds. 30 acres W of Jonathan's creek at **Allen**s own line.
Wts: John **Gordan**, Memucan **Hunt**.

437, 438- July 21, 1768- Robert **Harris**, Esq. to Malachi **Dickinson** for 125 pds. 635 acres (excepting the 65 acres given to Sherwood **Harris**) as per grant to Robert **Harris** by Granville Mar. 1, 1762 at Sherwood **Harris**'s corner to Tar river.
Wts: Robert **Harris**, Jr., David **Harris**.

439- Jan. 9, 1768- John **Van Landingham** to Joseph **Fletcher** for 16 pds. 50 acres on both sides of Crooked Run at John **Craft**'s line, **Wiggins**' line.
Wts: Philip **Gathings**, William **Aplewhite**, Drury **Kimball**.

440- May 20, 1768- Alexander **Gray** from Orange Co., N.C. to Thomas **Person** of Granville Co. for 100 pds. land in Granville and Orange counties on both sides of Nap of Reeds creek containing 700 acres.
Wts: William **Bennett**, Jeremiah **Johnson**.

441- Aug. 3, 1768- Thomas **Person** and Joanna, his wife, to Jesse **Harper** for 150 pds. 504 acres on both sides of Little Island creek in two tracts opposite to each other, one tract formerly the property of Nathl **Harris** at Thos **Barnet**'s line, Robt. **Mitchell**'s line containing 504 acres and the other tract formerly the property of John **Reynolds** containing 296 acres on Little Island creek at Thos **Barnett**'s line.
Wts: Stephen **Jett**, Len Henley **Bullock**.

443- Oct. 10, 1767- Robert **Mitchel** to James **Walace** for 20 pds. 140 acres at Sherwood **Sims**'s line on both sides of Ready Branch.

Wts: Thomas **Mitchel**, James **Waldrop**.

444- Mar. 30, 1768- John **Williams**, Jr. to John **Potter** for 275 pds. 330 acres on Little Island creek being land **Williams** bought at sheriffs sale of property of Josiah **Mitchel**, late of this county.
Wts: Wm. **Potter**, Richard **Henderson**.

182

445- Aug. 3, 1768- William **Dodson** gave to his brother- in- law Nathaniel **Robinson**, land on N. side of Nut Bush creek adjoining the plantation whereon **Robinson** now lives at **Hargrove**'s line.
Wts: Stephen **Jett**.

446- Aug. 3, 1768- William **Dodson** gave to his brother Charles **Dodson** 200 acres on N. side of Nut Bush creek at John **Hargrove**'s line, but since my brother Francis **Dodson** is living on part of the land he is to remain thereon for life.
Wts: Stephen **Jett**.

446, 447- Aug. 3, 1768- Drury **Allen** to John **Young** for 10 pds. 30 acres on Grassy creek near **Young**'s mill.
Wts: Stephen **Jett**.

448- Nov. 27, 1767- Thomas **Ray** of Georgia to David **Mitchel** of Granville Co., N.C. for 100 pds. 100 acres on Nut Bush creek at Long Branch on the Main road along **Williams**'s line to Buffalo branch.
Wts: John **Potter**, John **Satterwhite**.

449- Aug. 3, 1768- Nathaniel **Norwood** and wife Mary to Joseph **Williams** for 300 pds. 400 acres on Great Nut Bush creek on **Bullock**'s and **Mitchel**'s lines.
Wts: Joseph **Williams**, Jr., Jonathan **Kittrell**.

450, 451- July 20, 1767- William **White**, Jr. and wife Molley of Mecklinburg Co., Va to Thomas **Rudd** of Granville Co., N.C. for 40 pds. 296 acres on Grassy creek in Granville Co. at **Graves** corner.
Wts: John Williams **Graves**, Abraham **Crenshaw**, Isaac **White**.

451, 452- July 2, 1768- William **Cragg** to William **Amis** of Essex Co., Va.- for 37 pds. 10 shls. 100 acres in Granville Co., N.C. on B**ond**'s line.
Wts: Richard **Bush**, Mary **Smith**, Samuel **Smith**.

453- July 11, 1768- John **Potter** of Mecklenburg Co., Va to Vinckler **Jones** of same county and State for 275 pds. 230 acres on Little Island creek in Granville Co., N.C. which was purchased by John **Potter** from John **Williams**, Jr.
Wts: William **Taylor**, Thomas **Person**.

454 thru 456- Aug. 3, 1768- James **Yancey** to Edmund **Taylor**, William **Kennon** and Charles **Kennon**- since in 1765 the property of James **Forsythe**, John **Watson**, Robert **Mackie** ordered sold to highest bidder for debt- Sheriff of Granville sold 125 acres on Island creek at John **Williams** line, James **Mitchel**s line and **Taylor** was highest bidder- Land now deeded to **Taylor** and **Kennon**.

456, 457- Sept. 1, 1762 Grant to William **Cragg** for 400 acres on Cool Spring branch on **Williamson**'s corner.

457 thru 460- Mar. 1, 1762 Grant from Lord Granville to William **Chavis** for 686 acres on **Spivey**'s line, in Granville Co., NC.

461- Aug. 24, 1767- James **Mitchel**, Jr. and wife Frances to Benjamin **Harrison** for 20 pds. 50 acres on Island creek to mouth of Reedy branch to **Ragland**'s line.
Wts: Joseph **Davenport**, William **Arnall**.

462- Apr. 2, 1768- Prettyman **Berry** of Orange Co., N.C. to Michael **Wilson** of Granville Co. for 70 pds. 100 acres on E side of Fishing creek at **Morris**'s line.
Wts: George **Alston**, Robert **Thorn**.

463, 464- July 16, 1768- James **Pettigrew** and wife Mary to James **Johnston** of Cumberland Co., Va. for 220 pds. 369 acres on both sides of the Lower fork of Grassy creek along John **Johnston**'s new line to Robert **Downey**'s line.
Wts: Chesley **Daniel**, John **Witherspoon**, Ebenezar **Pettegrew**.

464, 465- Feb. 3, 1768- Joseph **Landess** to John Rodwell **Buzzard** for 20 pds. 202 acres which was sold to Abraham **Landess** by Thomas **Ross** Aug. 30, 1764 at John **Ross**'s line on the Trading Path.
Wts: Joseph **Landess** (can't read other two.)

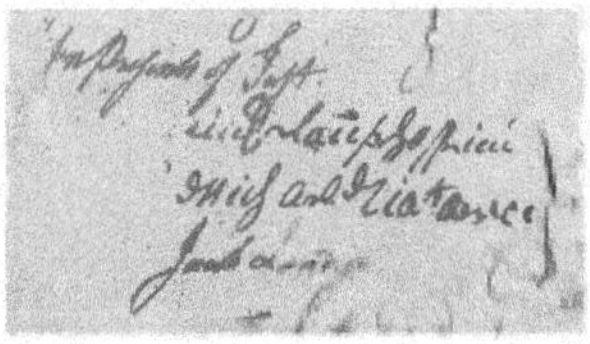

465, 466- Sept. 10, 1768- William **Ferris** to Elizabeth **Kennon** of Goochland Co., Va. for 20 pds. 240 acres at **Ferris**, and **Kennon**'s lines.
Wts: Robert **Lanier**, Charles **Kennon**.

183

466, 467- July 26, 1768- Michael **Satterwhite** and wife Amey, to Nathaniel **Norwood** for 250 pds. 290 acres on Little Island creek at mouth of **Goss**'s creek.
Wts: Joseph **Williams**, Robert **Mitchel**, Joseph **Glover**, Evan **Ragland**.

468, 469- May 28, 1768- Evan **Ragland** and wife Amey to William **Potter** for 400 pds. 560 acres on Little Island creek at Joseph **Glover**'s line to Reedy Branch.
Wts: David **Mitchel**, Charles **Kennon**, John **Satterwhite**.

460, 461- Nov. 1, 1768- Malecky **Reaves** to Mourning **Hunt** for 50 pds. 100 acres on Fishing creek.
Wts: John **Tatom**, Ab. **Tatom**.

470, 471- Nov. 1, 1768- John **Harris** to John **Tatom** for 100 pds. 200 acres on both sides of Fishing creek.
Wts: Agra **Tatom**, John **Compton**, Jonathan **Kittrell**.

471, 472- May 7, 1768- Robert **Mitchel** and wife Tanner to Len Henley **Bullock** for 360 pds. 430 acres at Bartlet **Searcy**'s line, Elisha **Sims**'s line, William **Cooper**'s line on Great Nut Bush which land Robert **Mitchel** purchased on Edward **Moore** and sold part of to John **Sims** and 85 acres granted from Granville July 24, 1761.
Wts: Robert **Lanier**, John **Bullock**.

572, 573 [sic] - Sept. 10, 1768- Benjamin **Fuller** to Samuel **Fuller** for 100 pds. 270 acres on Tabbs creek called Littleton **Spivey**'s branch to Henry **Fuller**'s branch along Henry **Jones**'s line.
Wts: Henry **Fuller**, John **Person**.

573, 574 [sic]- Oct. 20, 1768- Larrine **Pettiford** to Reuben **Bass** for 4 pds. 10 shls. 50 acres near **McCulloch**'s line.
Wts: Benjamin **Bass**, Lewis **Anderson**.

575, 576 [sic]- Feb. 1, 1769 (9) John **Wilson** to Ezekiah **Massey** for 2 pds. 10 shillings, 75 acres on Tar river at **Massey**'s own line to William **Smith**'s line granted to William **Smith** by Granville Oct. 7, 1752.
Wts: Wm. **Massey**, Joseph **Wright**, John **Boyton**.

476, 477- May 1, 1768- Littleton **Spivey**, executor, Ann **Spivey** and Henry **Fuller** to Benjamin **Fuller** for 20 pds. 75 acres on Henry **Fuller**'s branch on Tabbs creek and along Littleton **Spivey**'s branch.
Wts: William **Roberts**, Mourning **Roberts**, Molley **Spivey**.
signed Ann **Spivey** and Henry **Fuller**.

478, 479- Sept. 10, 1765- Philip **Pryor**, Esq. to Thomas **Person**- property of Gowing **Black (Gowin)** containing 350 acres on **Morris**'s creek in county for debt he owes- sold at public vendue.

479, 480- Sept. 10, 1765- Sheriff Philip **Pryor** sold at public sale, property of Thomas **Phillips** as ordered by court, sold to Thomas **Persons** as highest bidder 25 acres including Thomas **Phillips** plantation on both sides of Cattail branch of Grassy creek in Granville Co.

481, 482- Feb. 2, 1768- William **Gray** to Moses **Jewel** alias **Gowin** for 15 pds. 100 acres on S side of Tarr river both sides of Middle creek at **Shappard**'s and **Balinger**'s lines being part of 420 acres granted to Samuel **Ware** July 27, 1761 by Lord Granville.
Wts: Crafford **Pope**, John **Pope**.

482, 483- Nov. 13, 1769 Sherwood **Harris** to William **Hamilton** and Co. merchants, for 15 pds. 30 acres on Tar river at Nicholas's creek.
Wts: William **Beaver**, William **Humphries**, Aaron **Read**, Stephen **Jett**.

483, 484- Dec. 1, 1768- Phillip **Alston**, Jr. to Solomon **Alston**, Jr., of Bute Co., N.C. for 750 pds. four tracts of land in Granville Co. containing in the whole 1,467 acres on both sides of Tar river including the plain known as *Great Low Grounds*, one tract of 300 acres, one of . . 37 acres one of 680 acres, one of 350 acres at **Donivant**'s land.
Wts: Stephen **Jett**, Robert **Reed** (?)

486- Jan. 14, 1769 John **Hampton** to Edward **Wilburn** of Fauquier Co., Va. for 140 pds. 200 acres on S side of Indian Field creek.
Wts: Robert **Harris**, William **Little**, David **Harris**.

487- Aug. 4, 1768- James **Yancey** Esq. sheriff, to Richard **Henderson**- land of James **Gowin** as per order of court at suit brought by James **Trevillion**

184
sold 429 acres on **Wharton**'s branch and waters of Grassy creek at **Cunningham**'s line, **Melone**'s line.

488, 489- Nov. 6 1767- John **Bricket** to Len Henley **Bullock** for 125 pds. 925 acres on Island creek called Great Branch and Lick branch which was granted by Lord Granville to **Bricket** for 420 acres Apr. 26, 1753 and one for 400 acres- Apr. 27, 1754 in Granville Co., N.C.
Wts: B. **Ward**, Richard **Ward**, Zachariah **Bullock**.

490- Dec. 8, 1767- James **Hester** to Lewis **Collins** for 15 pds. 2 shls the land conveyed from Banjamin **Cook** to James **Hester** on **Harrel**'s creek containing 330 acres being same whereon James **Hester** now lives.
Wts: Bromfield **Ridley**, Richard **Henderson**.

491, 492- Feb. 10, 1768- George **Boyer** to John **Hampton** for 20 pds. 200 acres which was sold to **Boyer** by John **Campbell** one of agents for Chauncey **Townsend** July 11, 1763 near the Trading Path at John **Pope**s line-
Wts: Robert **Harris**, Sr. and, Jr.

492, 493- Aug. 6, 1768- Daniel **Hunter** to John **Lowrey** of Bartie Co, N. C for 125 pds. land on Long creek a branch of Tabbs creek which land was deeded to **Hunter** by William **Chavers** Nov. 3, 1766 containing 335 acres.
Wts: Jonathan **Kittrell**, William **Spars**, Henry **Roades**.

494, 495- Nov. 8, 1768- Joseph **Davenport** to Charles **Kennon** for 375 pds. 611 acres on Little Island creek.
Wts: Robert **Lanier**, William **Potter**.

495, 496- Nov. 29, 1768- Joseph **Davenport** to John **Walker** for 15 pds. 34 acres on **Lanier**'s line, **Walker**'s line on the branch.
Wts: William **Potter**.

496, 497- Jan. 8, 1769 Jeremiah **Lewis** to Philip **Lewis** for 10 pds. 160 acres on both sides of **Shelton**'s creek at Thomas **Person**'s line, **Redwine**'s.
Wts: Saml **Benton**.

497, 498- May 20, I768. Thomas **Person** to John **Bowling** for 80 pds. 577 acres on Nap of Reeds creek.
Wts: Jeremiah **Lewis**, William **Bennett**.

498, 499- Dec. 29, 1768- John **West** of Georgia to Francis **West** of Orange Co., N.C. for 25 pds. 200 acres on both sides of Ledge of Rocks creek at Dennis **Sullivan**'s, John **West**'s line.
Wts: Richard **Clements**, Peyton **Clements**, William **Burford**.

500- Jan. 18, 1769 Philemon **Hawkins** of Bute Co., N.C. to John **Hawkins** of same place for 50 pds. 680 acres at **Blackman**'s corner, **Parrish**'s line on **Kittrell**'s line.
Wts: Reuben **Searcy**, Stephen **Jett**.

501- Nov. 10, 1767- John **Blackley** to Charles **Moore** for 30 pds. 100 acres on both sides of Long creek a branch of Tabbs creek at **Dickerson**'s lower line which was deeded to **Blackley** by Richard **Curreton** May 29, 1764.
Wts: Dan **Huntor**, William **Roberts**.

502, 503- Oct. 12, 1768- William **Williams**, Whitmell **Hill** executors of will of John **Hill**, deceased, to Robert **Dickins** for 120 pds. 675 acres on **Hicks** road which was sold to John **Hill**, May 9, 1757 by Robert **Harris**.
Wts: Haden **Pryor**, Benj **Person**, William **Moore**.

504, 505- Mar. 17, 1769 Thomas **Wicker** to Robert **Lewis** for 150 pds. 221 pds.[sic] on S side of Island creek.
Wts: William **Burch**, Howel **Lewis**, John **Harris**.

505, 506- Apr. 14, 1769 Zachariah **Denney** of Orange Co., N.C. to John **Harris** of Granville for 18 pds. 100 acres at **Harris**'s line and is part of land granted to John **Harris**.
Wts: Robert **Sandford**, Seth **Pool**.

506, 507- . . . 1769- Peter **Pettepool** and wife Elizabeth to Robert **Sandford** for 60 pds. 100 acres on Upper side of Aaron's creek.
Wts: Armbross **Jones**, James **Yancey**, John **Pettepool**.

507, 508- Sept. 19, 1768- Thomas **Bradford** to George **Hudspeth** (**Hudsparth**) for 16 pds. land where **Hudspeth** now lives being part of larger tract granted to John **Plant** at road leading from **Wilkerson**'s to **Bradford**'s containing 200 acres.
Wts: Geo **Thompson**, Richard **Bradford**, Solomon **Fuller**.

185

509, 510- Jan. 21, 1769- John **Kittrell** of Hartford county, N.C. to Moses **Kittrell** of same place for 5 shls., land in Granville bought by John **Kittrell** of Samuel **Benton** Mar. 11, 1760 on Rocky branch which is 382 acres which is a grant to Samuel **Benton** from Lord Granville.
Wts: Jonathan **Kittrell**, Samuel **Kittrell**, Henry **Goodman**.

510, 511- Apr. 17, 1769- Richard **Fowler**, Sr. to Richard **Fowler**, Jr. for 20 pds. 150 acres on Tar river being part of the grant to Richard **Fowler** at **Davenport**'s line.
Wts: William **Oakley**, James **Wilson**.

511, 512- Jan. 12, 1769- Robert **Harris** to Ephraim **Hampton** for 150 pds. 400 acres on S side of Tar river at **Griggs**' and **Boyd**'s corners.
Wts: Mary **Ogilivie**, Sarah **Harris**, Robert **Harris**, Jr.

512, 513- Mar. 9, 1767- Joel **Chandler** and wife Jean to Thomas **Mutter**, merchant, for 10 shillings, 10 acres on N. side of Jonathan's creek at **Chandler**'s line.
Wts: Joshua **Moss**, Larkn [sic] **Johnston**.

513, 514- Nov. 4, 1766- James **Roberts** to John **Warmouth** for 25 pds. 165 acres on Grassy creek on **Person**'s line.
Wts: William **Freeman**, Thomas **Person**.

514, 515- Feb. 6, 1769- Luke **Waldrop**e to James **Waldrop**e for 32 pds. 621/2 acres on Little Nut Bush creek at James **Mitchell**'s line.
Wts: Reuben **Searcy**, William **Farrar**, Jr.

515, 516- Nov. 8, 1768- Lewis **Pettyford** to James **Yancey** for 14 pds. 80 acres on **Harrill**'s creek at John **Wicker**'s line, **Anderson**'s corner being the land Lewis **Pettyford** bought of Abraham **Cook** including the plantation whereon he lately lives.
Wts: Wm. **Green**, Philip **Yancey**.

516, 517- Apr. 15, 1769- William **Person** of Bute Co., N.C. to Thomas **Person** of Granville Co. for 100 pds. 600 acres on both sides of **Shelton** creek or West fork of Tar river and also land on both sides of Fox creek containing 532 acres.
Wts: Benjamin **Person**, John **Moseley**.

518, 519- Feb. 1, 1769- Phillemon **Hawkins** of Bute Co, N.C. to Phillemon **Hawkins**, Jr. of Granville Co., N.C. for love of his son, two tracts of land on **Anderson**'s swamp containing 1170 acres in Granville Co., N.C. at Arther **Jordan**'s line, Daniel **Williams**' corner which was granted to Joseph **Kimball**, Jr. by Lord Granville Mar 11, 1760 and sold to **Hawkins** Aug. 23, 1763, and the 2nd tract of 530 acres on both sides of Reedy branch of **Anderson**'s swamp at **Bartholomew**'s **Kimball**'s line which was bought of Jos **Kimball** and was granted to him Apr. 11, 1763.
Wts: Len H. **Bullock**, John **Hawkins**, Jr.

519, 520- July 19, 1769- John **Dickerson** to John **Finch** for 30 pds. 200 acres between Tabbs creek and Long Creek at **Dickerson**'s line, being part of tract granted by William **Creech** to **Dickerson**.
Wts: Dan **Hunter**, Wm. **Green**.

521, 522 Mar 20, 1769- Jesse **Sanders** (**Landers**) and wife Annas to George **Alston**, merchant. for 62 pds. 10 shls. land on John **Newton**'s corner on Mountain fork of Jonathan's creek- 200 acres.
Wts: Thomas **Mutter**, James **Yancey**.

523, 524- Oct. 28, 1768- John **Brown** of Craven Co., South Carolina to William **Daniel** of Halifax Co., N.C. for 10 pds. 234 acres in Granville Co., N.C. on Henry **Jones**'s former line in John **Lewis**'s branch, Robert **Hicks** line, Samuel **Benton**'s line, Philip **Pryor**'s line along Augustine **Bates** line.
Wts: Phil **Kearney**, Stephen [**Jett**].

524, 525- Oct. 24, 1766- James **Young** of Halifax Co., N.C., merchant, to John **Hightower** of Lunenburg Co., Va. for 24 pds. 17 shls., 3 pence land on Jonathan creek at William **Gill**'s line containing 321 acres.
Wts: John **White**, James **Hepburn**.

525, 526- Jan. 15, 1768- Abraham **Cook** and wife Amy, late of Granville Co., N.C. to Alexander **Douglas** for 35 pds. 369 acres on branches of Little Island creek on Patrick's branch at Thomas **Barnet**'s line between William and John **Wallace**'s lines in division of tract intended for **Wallace** and

186
Benjamin **Harrison** running to line of Col. Edmund **Taylor** and contains 369 acres.
Wts: Richard **Henderson**.

527, 528- Mar. 15, 1769- Robert **Hicks** to Robert **Bell** of Bute Co., N.C. for 5 shls. 277 acres on **Reaves**'s line on Tabbs creek in Granville Co.
Wts: William **Gibson**.

528, 529 . . .1769- George **Anderson** to Benjamin **Whicker** for 70 pds. 169 acres being part of tract on both sides of Great Branch granted to **Anderson** by Lord **Carteret** 1769.
Wts: William **Kendrick**, Gideon **Crews**, William **Hester**.

530, 531- July 18, 1769- Elisha **Sims** to Leonard **Sims** for 35 pds. 143 acres on Reedy Branch near Ridge of Rocks, where **Vandyke**'s line crosses.
Wts: Jesse **Landers** (**Sanders**), Joseph **Taylor**.

531, 532- Mar. 14, 1769- Philemon **Bradford** to Lewis **Anderson** for 20 pds. 265 acres on Beaverdam creek.
Wts: Thos **Bradford**, Mary **Bradford**.

533- July 19, 1769- John **Hightower** of Lunenburg Co., Va. to William **Puryear** of Granville Co., N.C. for 250 pds. 321 acres on William **Gill**'s corner.
Wts: None.

534- Mar. 10, 1769- William **Chavers** to Joseph **McDaniel**, for 25 pds. 360 acres on E side of Long Creek a branch of Tabbs creek at **Chavers** corner.
Wts: Claborn **Harris**, David **Hunter**.

536- Jan. 1, 1769- Joseph **Bishop** and wife Thana to Samuel **Huckaby** of Bute Co, N.C. for 100 pds. 240 acres on Waleys branch at George **Jordan**'s corner at mouth of David **Parrish**'s branch, **Forgoson**'s line.
Wts: Thos **Bell**, Francis **Mabry**.

537, 538- Jan. 20, 1769- William **Hamilton** and Co. of Halifax Co., N.C. to John **Hampton** of Granville for 50 pds. 340 acres late the property of Sherwood **Harris**, Jr. at Isaack **Arnold**'s alias **Harris**'s line.
Wts: Samuel **Benton**, N. **McCulloch**.

539,- July 19, 1769- Thornton **Yancey** to Aron **Pinson** for 20 pds. 50 acres on N. side of Jonathan's creek at William **Stoval**'s line.
Wts: Thos **Stovall**, Henry **Graves**.

541- 542- Jan. 14, 1768- Abraham **Cook** and wife Amy late of Granville Co., N.C. to Benjamin **Harrison** for 115 pds. 450 acres on Little Island creek at line of Isabel **Wallace**'s land (widow), at James **Mitchel**, Jr.'s, Col. Edmund **Taylor**'s, **Harrison**'s to Spring branch (Schoolhouse branch) and on land of John **Walker** with the acres set aside for a mill, by said **Cook**.
Wts: Richard **Henderson**.

542, 543- May 21, 1768- Henning **Temble (~~Temple~~)** of Halifax Co., N.C. to James **Dunlop** of Nansimond Co., Va. for 1079 pds. a tract of land in Halifax. formerly Edgecombe, N.C. containing 820 acres from Sheriff Abraham **Jones** May 4, 1758 recorded in Edgecombe Co/ and a tract of 200 acres in Halifax Co. bought of William **Webb** Feb. 26, 1760 and a tract of 384 acres in Halifax Co. granted July 7, 1760, and 480 acres in Granville Co. granted Oct. 30, 1751 and a tract of 640 acres granted Dec. 3, 1753 in Granville Co.
Wts: Thomas **Fisher**, Alexa **Roxburgh**, Henning **Webb**.

End of Book- - - H - - -

187

Granville Go., N.C. - Record of Deeds
Book I (eye) - 1769- 1772
L. **Gilliam**, Register

1 Feb. 20, 1765- George **Moore** to Richard **Clopton** for 7 pds. 150 acres on both sides of Long Branch at **Chavers** line, Edward **Harris**'s line and along the Ridge Path.
Wts: Jonathan **Davis**, Charles **Moore**, Samuel **Smith**, Jr.

1, 2- Dec. 2, 1768- Joseph **Davenport** and wife Jemima to Moses **Overton** for 50 pds. 360 acres on both sides of Island Creek.
Wts: Reuben **Searcy**, John **Satterwhite**.

2, 3- Oct. 22, 1768- Thomas **Brumet** from John **Hatcher** for 12 pds. 75 acres on Fork creek at John **Pullin**'s corner.
Wts: Phillemon **Bradford**, John **Brumit**.

3, 4- Oct. 29, 1768- Samuel **Fuller**, executor and Deborah **Lawrence**, excrx. of will of William **Lawrence**, deceased, to Daniel **Hunter** for 7 pds. 160 acres between Tabb and Long Creek branch of Long Creek at **Fuller**'s corner in **Lawrence**'s line, of which 95 acres was brought of Samuel **Kittrell**.
Wts: Henry and Mary **Fuller**.

4, 5- Oct. 17, 1769- Henry **Graves** to David **Lewis**, Jr. of Albermarle Co., Va. for 70 pds. 300 acres on Tar River in lines of Benjamin **Hubard**, David **Gunter**, Rice Dollis **Buzzard**'s [treated as all one name in index] line, **Stovall**'s and William **Rose**'s line.
Wts: None.

5, 6- Oct. 18, 1769- Thomas **Bradford** to Richard **Bradford** for 50 pds. 272 acres on both sides of Low Ground creek, at **Wilkerson**'s line.

6, 7- Oct. 31, 1768- William **Paschall** of Bute Co., N.C. to his son Elisha **Paschall** of Granville Co., N.C. a deed of gift of 825 acres on Bartlet **Searcy**'s line, James **Paschall's** line, Samuel **Paschall's** line.
Wts: Jemima and John **Paschall**.

7, 8- Aug. 23, 1768- Charles **Williams** and wife Susannah to Henry **Graves** for 70 pds. 200 acres on Rice Dollas **Buzzard**'s line, 300 acres, 200 in my name and 100 left me by my father in his will on Tar river joining Benjamin **Hubbard** and David **Gunter**, **Stovall**'s line.
Wts: Thomas **Little**, Samuel **Crawford**, Feebe **Rann**, David **Lewis**.

8, 9- May 15, 1769- Capt. Jno. **Hawkins** of Bute Co., N.C. to, George **Wilson** for 10 pds. 50 acres on Little **Callier**k in **Adamson**'s line and **Hawkins** old line.
Wts: Fennell **Marks**, Thomas **Wilson**.

9 thru 11- Aug. 10, 1769- Benjamin **Ward** to Elias **Guest** for 18 pds. 53 acres which **Guest** purchased of William **Eaton** to whom it was granted May 10, 1753 and now occupied by **Guest** on E side of Tabbs creek on Saml **Kittrell**'s and Joseph **Rogers** line.
Wts: Jonathan and John **Kittrell**.

11, 12- July 6, 1768- John Winckler, silversmith, to George **Byer** for 45 pds. 200 acres which was deeded by Chauncey **Townsend** to Andrew **Hampton** who sold to **Byer** and he sold to William **Patterson**.
Wts: Frederick **Beck**.

13- Oct. 27, 1768- Joseph **Kimball**, and Bartholomew **Kimball** to Miles **Williams** for 5 pds. one acres [sic] of land on E side of Indian creek.
Wts: Robert **Robinson**, William **Gillam**, Bartho **Kimball**.

14, 15- July 20, 1768- James **Caudle** late of Granville Co., N.C. to Peter **Nowland** for 30 pds. 100 acres, being part of 400 acres granted to Isaac **Ricks** July 25, 1743 on S side of Tar river on **Ricks** line at James and at Isom **Caudle**'s lines.

Wts: Isom **Caudle**, William **Willis**.

16, 17- Sept. 18, 1769- Malachi **Dickerson** to John **Harris** for 30 pds. 150 acres on N. side of Tar river at mouth of Cattail creek at Sherwood **Harris**'s line.
Wts: Sherwood **Harris**.

16 thru 18- Oct. 18 1769- John **Pope** to Thomas **Banks** for 100 pds. 380 acres being part of tract granted to Philemon **Bradford**, Sr. Nov. 1756 and deeded to William **Vincent** and by him to Brittan **Fuller** and by

188
him to Solomon **Fuller**, Jr. who sold to John **Pope**.
Wts: None.

18, 19- Jan. 19, 1770 William **Hamilton** and Co., merchants, to William **Wilson** for 115 pds. 160 acres on Fishing creek at Thomas **Bradford**'s line.
Wts: Stephen **Jett**, Robert **Reid**.

120, 121 [sic]- Oct. 18, 1769- Samuel **Boyd** and wife Darity to William **Jones** for 40 pds. 330 acres on both sides of Pictur branch on Trading Path at James **Boyd**'s corner.
Wts: Solomon **Alston**, Jr., James **Langston**.

21 thru 23- Jesse **Sanders (Landers)**- June 29, 1769- to John **Gordon** & Co for 14 pds. 11 shls. land on Jonathan's creek at Mountain Fork, at Larkin **Johnston**'s line, which land formerly belonged to Hester **Shockley**, and is land whereon Jesse **Landers** now lives- this is a mortgage- or trust deed.
Wts: Haden **Pryor**, William **Wilson**.

23, 24- Feb. 1, 1770- Reuben **Searcy** and, wife Susanna to Jacob **Mitchel** of Mecklenburg Co., Va. for 60 pds. 202 acres on both sides of Beaver Pond creek at Baxter **Davis**'s line.
Wts: Richard **Henderson**, Isaac **Mitchel**.

24 thru 26- Nov. 7, 1769- Samuel **Benton** to Robert **Reid** and Co., Merchants for 160 pds. 125 acres on Fishing creek at **Bradford**'s corner, **Benton**'s old line, **Hamilton**'s, formerly Michael **Wilson**'s corner, **Holt**'s line and along lines of **Young** and Co., and Capt **Sherwood**'s old line, to uppermost Race Path near St. George Chapel.
Wts: Solomon **Alston**, Jr., Alexander **Munn**, Thomas **Satterwhite**.

26, 27- Oct. 17, 1768- Evan **Ragland** to William **Hanks** of Dinwiddie Co., Va. for 112 pds. 150 acres on N. side of Nut Bush creek at John **Weaver**'s old line.
Wts: Thomas **Craft**, Buckner **Robinson**.

28, 29- Dec. 8, 1769- William **Moore**, Jr. to John **Cobb**, Jr. for 250 pds. 318 acres on both sides of Island creek on **Hawkins** line.
Wts: Howel and Mary **Lewis**, Thos. **Cobb**.
Sary [sic], wife of William **Moore**, Jr. relinquishes her dower right.

29 thru 32- Jan. 16, 1700- Sheriff Len Henley **Bullock** to Philip **Yancey**- sale of property of William **Mitchel** for debt due William **Searcy** which land was 70 acres- sold to highest bidder- Philip **Yancey** was highest.
Wts: None.

32, 33- Dec. 29, 1766- John **Keys** of Orange Co., N.C. to Moses **Bonner** for 80 pds. 247 acres being part of land bought of Joseph **Walker** on Nap of Reeds creek.
Wts: Ezekiel **Hampton**, James **Dyar**, William **Jones**.

33 thru 35- Aug. 29, 1769- Phillemon **Bradford**, Sr. to William **Parnel** for 25 pds. 350 acres being a half tract granted Aug. 1, 1762 to said **Bradford** on Beaverdam creek on **Reach**'s line, **McCowlow**'s line.
Wts: Timothy **Reach**, Gillam **Harris**.

35 thru 37- Aug. 1, 1769- Leonard Henley **Bullock**, sheriff- to Samuel **Walker**- Property of John **Glover**, Jr., sold at

public auction for debts due and 212 acres sold to Samuel **Walker** as highest bidder.
Wts: Richard **Henderson**, Bromfield **Ridley**.

37- Aug. 29, 1760- Grant from Granville to William **Myrick** for 596 acres on both sides of Reedy creek on branches of Nut Bush creek on **Anderson**'s swamp at **Kimball**'s corner, **Jordan**'s line.

38, 39- Feb. 17, 1769- Isum **Caudle** to James **Willis** for 36 pds. 150 acres on John **Hogan**'s line, **Smith**'s and **Benton**'s corners.
Wts: James **Caudle**, Littleton **Moss**.

39, 40- Nov. 14, 1768- John **Speed** of Mecklenburg Co., Va. to William **Potter** for 25 pds. 100 acres on William **Potter**'s line and at Joseph **Winston**'s corner.
Wts: Reuben **Searcy**, Joseph **Glover**.

40, 41- Dec. 26, 1769- John **Boyd** to Jacob **Landers** (**Sanders**) for 100 pds. land on Cattail branch containing 200 acres which was granted Oct. 23, 1754 to **Landers**.
Wts: Joseph **Landress**, Peter **Noland**.

189

42, 43- Dec. 9, 1769- Benjamin **Harrison** and wife Elan to Joseph **Williams** for 100 pds. 292 acres on Island creek at Samuel **Wheelor**'s line, at William **Potter**'s corner of Reedy branch.
Wts: Richard **Henderson**.

43, 44- Dec. 11, 1769- Charles **Cook** of Lunenburg Co., Va. to George **Bruce** for 40 pds. 200 acres on both sides of **Harrel**'s creek on George **Anderson**'s path on Mirey branch at John **Knott**'s and **Bullock**'s line, **Hester**'s line.
Wts: William **Taylor**, John **Hunt**.

44, 45- Jan. 10, 1769- Samuel **Fuller** to Joseph **Parks** for 50 pds. 340 acres on Tabbs creek.
Wts: Henry **Fuller**, John **Duggar**.

45, 46- May 30, 1769- Leonard **Linsey** to Richard **Searcy** for 60 pds. 215 acres on John **Fleming**'s line on **Anderson**'s swamp.
Wts: Reuben **Searcy**, John **Rearden**,

47- Jan. 15, 1770- William **Potter** to John **Mitchel** for 135 pds. 225 acres on Beaver Pond creek.
Wts: Reuben **Searcy**, David **Mitchell**.

48, 49- Jan. 14, 1770- Thomas **Tate** and wife Elizabeth to John **Oliver** for 155 pds. 150 acres on both sides of Island creek which Benjamin **Cook** took up and 154 acres taken up by Benjamin **Cook**- in all 304 acres on Henry **Parkman**, West **Harris**, William **Moore**, the orphans of John **Oliver**, and on John **Lewis**'s lines.
Wts: Timothy **Cooper**, Sally **Cock**.

49 thru 51- Oct. 6, 1768- William **Potter** to John **Whitloe** for 50 pds. 190 acres on both sides of Flat creek on Miles **Williams**' line.
Wts: Thos **Satterwhite**, Charles **Kennon**.

51, 52- Oct. 30, 1765- John **Clarke** to John **Hightower** of Amelia Co., Va. for 25 pds. 170 acres on Jonathan creek which part of tract that **Hightower** bought of John **Ramund** on **Gill**'s line containing 170 acres.
Wts: James and Bartlet **Yancey**.

52, 53- Mar. 54, 1770- Joseph **Peace**, Sr. to John **Peace**, for 50 pds. 420 acres on both sides of Tabbs creek at **Hunt**'s, **Bryant**'s, Capt. **Dickerson**'s whereon Joseph **Peace** now lives which was bought of Darwin **Eelwick**.
Wts: Joseph **Hill**, David **Thomas**, Joseph **Peace**, Jr.

53, 54- Mar. 5, 1770- Joseph **Peace**, Sr. to John **Peace** for 30 pds. 581 acres on Tar river at **Bank**'s line, formerly **Nelson**'s line-
Wts: Joseph **Hill**, Joseph **Peace**, Jr., David **Thomas**.

54 thru 56- March. 28, 1770- Nathan **Childs** and wife Elizabeth to Nathaniel **Patterson** for 110 pds. 475 acres on both sides of King Lick branch at **Graggs** (Wm.) line, being part of tract granted, June 3 1762 to William **Yancey**.
Wts: George **Brasfield**, Betty **Knott**.

56, 57- Oct. 314. 1769- Malachi **Dickerson** to Abraham **Cook** for 100 pds. 485 acres being part of tract granted to Robert **Harris**, esq. Mar 1, 1762 on Cattail creek and Tarriver in **Lowe**'s line, John **Harris**'s line.
Wts: John **Harris**, Wm. **Jennings**.

57 thru 59- Apr. 17, 1770 Michael **Wilson** to John **Stainback**, for 25 pds. 100 acres on Thomas **Morris**'s corner on Fishing Creek.
Wts: None.

59 thru 61- Feb. 3, 1770 John **Hatcher** to John **Lunsford** for 21 pds. 75 acres on Joel **Moody**'s line and on Fort Creek being part of land granted to Peter **Vinson**.
Wts: James **Lunsford**.

61, 62- Feb. 2, 1770 Peyton **Clements** to Phillip **Burford** of Bute Co, N.C. for 2 pds. 20 acres on Thomas **Farril**'s path to David **Daniels** and, Phillip **Burford**'s lines.
Wts: Wm. **Burford**, Jesse **Christian**, Peyton **Meddison**.

62, 63- July 14, 1770 **eak** and wife Lucy to John Comer **Peak** for 100 pds. 225 acres on both sides of Nap of Reeds creek., in Tyree **Harris**'s line.
Wts: Robert **Reid**, William **Bradford**.

190

64, 65- July 19, 1770- Len Henley **Bullock** to Reuben **Piles** for 133 pds. 520 acres on both sides of the county road at John **Bullock**'s and Robert **Gilham**'s lines, James **Trevillion**'s line, Phillemon **Hawkins'** line- the 2nd tract adjoining the tract above and in both tracts 920 acres.
Wts: Michael **Satterwhite**.

65 thru 67- July 19, 1770- Leonard Henley **Bullock**, sheriff, to William **Wilson** for certain amount- the land of Isaac **Arnold** for debts due Thomas **Bradford** and 100 acres sold to William **Wilson** as highest bidder, on **Morris**'s line.

67, 68- Feb. 7, 1770- Elisha **Smallwood** of Orange Co., N.C. to James **Dyer** of same place for 32 pds. 4 shls. 304 acres on Nap of Reeds creek on S side of Trading path in Joseph **Walker**'s line which Elisha **Smallwood** bought of Henry Eustace **McCulloch** and willed to Elisha **Smallwood**.
Wts: Michael **Dent**, Thomas **Moore**.

69, 70- July 18, 1770- Thomas **Lowe** to Solomon **Alston**, Jr. for 10 pds. 190 acres on both sides of Tar river on said **Alston**'s line.
Wts: none.

70, 71- July 18, 1770- Thomas **Lowe** to Solomon **Alston**, Jr. for 50 pds. 2 tracts containing 1359 acres on both sides of Tar river on Low Ground at Dunaway's corner, on **Adcock**'s creek, one containing 671 acres and the 2nd tract 681 acres-
Wts: none.

72, 73- Nov. 23, 1769- Abraham **Cook** to James **Washburn** for 15 pds. 175 acres on **Glover**'s line, **Harris**'s and **Satterwhite**'s and **Cook**'s lines and on west side of Stony Ridge.
Wts: Howel **Moore**, James and Robert **Mitchel**.

73, 74- Jan. 1, 1762- Grant to Gillum **Harris** for 700 acres on both sides of Newlight creek at **Fuller**'s line.

74, 75776- July 18, 1770- William **Oglevie**, wife Mary to Richard Donaldson **Cooke** both of Granville Co., N.C. for 10 pds. and a bay gelding called Whistler, 200 acres known by name of "*Hard Bargain*".
Wts: none.

76, 77- Apr. 17, 1770- James **Kittrell** and wife Catherine to William **Hornsby**, school master, for 31 pds. 5 shls. 130 acres at Daniel **Hunter**'s corner, Samuel **Kittrell**'s line, Benjamin **Ward**'s and Henry **Fuller**'s line.
Wts: Richard **Searcy**.

78, 79- Mar. 19, 1770- Robert **Harris**, Esq., to William **Oglebey** for 10 pds. 53 acres on **Hampton** creek at Thomas **Harris**'s corner.
Wts: Wm. **Little**, Mary **Harris**.

79, 80- Oct: 8, 1768- Benjamin **Hubbard** of Orange Co., N.C. to Israel **Eastwood** for 65 pds. 200 acres on S side of Tar river on Charles **Williams**'s line.
Wts: Samuel and Jesse **Benton**.

80, 81- Nov. 4, 1769- Robert **Mitchel** to Robert **Wallace** for 15 pds. 135 acres at Francis **Keeling** and Sherwood **Sims**'s line, James **Wallaces**'s line.
Wts: Thomas **Mitchel**, Samuel **Henderson**.

82, 83- Sept. 27, 1769- Thomas **Parrish** to Joseph **Smith** for 20 pds. 55 acres on **Anderson**'s swamp at Merryman **Thorne**'s line.
Wts: Ansel and Elijah **Parrish**.

83, 84- Mar. 30, 1770- Thomas **Harris** to William **Oglebey** for 5 pds. 43 acres on both sides of **Hampton** Creek at William **Oglebey**'s line and on **Hampton**'s line.
Wts: David **Harris**.

84, 85- Apr. 21, 1770- Richard **Henderson** to Joseph **Williams** for 50 pds. land on W. side of Great Nut Bush creek being all land **Henderson** bought of Reuben Searcy.
Wts: Zach **Bullock**, Jos. **Williams**, Jr.

85 thru 87- July 7, 1770- Robert **Harris** to his son David **Harris** a gift of 360 acres being land granted to John Michael **Redwine** July 28, 1761.
Wts: Samuel and Thomas **Harris**.

87, 88- Aug. 4, 1768- Bartlet **Searcy** to Richard **Henderson** for 15 pds. 200 acres on **Paschal**'s line.
Wts: John **Henderson**.

191

88, 89- Apr. 13, 1770- Priscilla **Dennis**, relict of Daniel **Dennis**, and Abner **Dennis**, heir at law of Daniel **Dennis**, to George **Bruce** for 50 pds. 75 acres on **Harrells** creek at **Bullock**'s line, on **Heaters**' corner.
Wts: Ro. **Lewi[s]** David **Knott**, Daniel **Frazier**.

89 thru 91- Feb. 17, 1770- Robert **Harris** executor, of Sherwood **Harris**, deceased, to William **Parham** for 37 pds. 310 acres on both sides of Tabbs creek being part of tract known as the *Jonathan **White** Tract* at Absalom **Hicks** and Samuel **Hicks**, Sr.'s lines, Sherwood **Harris**, Jr.'s line.
Wts: Robert **Reid**, Cutbird **Hudson**.

91, 92- Feb. 7, 1770- William **Gill**, Sr. of Mecklenburg Co., Va. to William **Puryear** for 40 pds. 150 acres in Granville Co.
Wts: Thornton and Joseph **Yancey**.

93, 94- May 3, 1770- James **Young** late merchant of Halifax to James **Pucket** of Amelia Co., Va. for 33 pds. 200 acres on both sides of Fort creek.
Wts: Joseph **Wade**, George **Thompson**.

94, 95- Dec. 23, 1769- Rowland **Jordan** and wife Lucretia to Samuel **Jetor** for 70 pds. 200 acres at Samuel **Jeter**'s line, George **Jordan**'s and Samuel **Huckabie**'s and David **Parrish**'s line.
Wts: Evan **Ragland**, David **Parrish**, Samuel **Sneed**.

95 thru 97. May16, 1770- Ellot **Bohannon** of Botetourt Co., Va. to Woodson **Daniel** of Johnson Co., N.C. for 45 pds. 200 acres on N. side of Neuse river on Beaverdam creek.
Wts: William **Daniel**, Husselor **Burton**, Corl **Keith**.

97 thru 99- Jan. 23, 1770- Willie **Woods** to Robert **Dickens** for 120 pds. 300 acres being the land conveyed by Roger **Badget** to Elizabeth **Drawhorn** Apr. 7, 1768.
Wts: Roger **Badget**, Abraham **Womack**, Merryman **Barns.**
Elizabeth, wife of Willie **Woods** relinquished rightand witnessed by Peter **Brinkley**, Robert **Pryor**, Dempsey **Ruby**.

100, 101- May 5, 1770- John **Hawkins**, Sr. of Bute Co., N. C. to Robert **Callier** for 30 pds. 100 acres on Deep creek at **Addiman**'s line which **Hawkins** bought of Thomas **Addiman** and 50 acres granted to **Hawkins** Dec. 1 1760 on W side of Deep creek being part of 400 acres which **Hawkins** sold to Fountleroy **Wye** and he to Robert **Callier** and supposing land to be in Bute Co., since found that part is in Granville Co., N.C.
Wts: William **Moore**, Edward **Avery**.

102 thru 103 Dec. 4, 1769- Robert **Gillam** to Edmund **Taylor** of Mecklenburg Co, Va. for 150 pds. 1220 acres on both sides of Gillum branch on County line on **Bullock**'s line and at **Brickell**'s corner, at **Glover** and **Kennon**'s and **Crawley**'s corners.
Wts: John **Doswell**, Nat **Robinson**, Joseph **Taylor**.

103, 104, 105- July 19, 1770- Benjamin **Harrison** to Samuel **Wheelor** for 60 pds. 205 acres near **Walker**'s ford, at Edmund **Taylor**'s line crossing Little Island creek at the land of John **Walker** taking in one acre on W side of creek reserved for a mill.
Wts: Willis **Roberts**, Vincent **Harrison**.

105, 106- Feb. 9, 1770- Nathaniel **Harris** to Thomas **Person** for 30 pds. 293 acres on branches of **Michael**'s and Flat creeks including the fork of the roads, being the upper part of a larger tract, near Hico road at **Mitchell**'s and **Satterwhite**'s corners.
Wts: Solomon **Howard**, James **Benton**.

106, 107- Jan. 15, 1770- John **Mitchel** land wife Martha to Joseph **Williams** for 75 pds. 134 acres at Joseph **Williams**' line.
Wts: Richd **Henderson**, R. **Harrison**.

108- 109- Apr. 1, 1770- Joseph **Williams** to Richard **Henderson** for 50 pds. land on East side of Great Nut Bush. creek being all land bought of Nathaniel **Norwood** by Joseph **Williams**.
Wts: Reuben **Searcy**, Zach **Bullock**, Jos. **Williams**, Jr.

109, 110- Mar. 18, 1769- Reuben **Searcy** and wife Susanna to Baxter **Davis** of Mecklenburg Co., Va. for 60 pds. 202 acres at Baxter **Davis**'s line on Beaverdam Run at the county line.
Wts: Robert **Mitchel**, Wm. **Howard**.

192

110, 111- Apr. 1, 1770- John **Weatherspoon** and wife Martha to Peter **Oliver** for 150 pds. 262 acres on each side of Grassy creek commonly known as **Howard**'s Creek at lines of Drury **Smith**, Frances **King** and at John, David and Solomon **Howard**'s lines, George **Brasfield**'s being part of tract granted to Joab **Mitchel** Mar. 11, 1760.
Wts: George **Brasfield**, James **Johnston**, Francis **King**.

112, 113- July 18, 1770- Samuel **Walker** to Benja **Ragland** for 80 pds. 212 acres being part of a larger tract on both sides of Hico road and branches of Island creek at **Clanton**'s line, **Mitchel**'s and **Davenport**'s.
Wts: Reuben **Searcy**.

114, 115- Dec. 5, 1769- John **Searcy**, Jr. to Len Henley **Bullock** for 15 pds. 100 acres on **Anderson**'s swamp.
Wts: Will **Potter**, Reuben **Searcy**.

115, 116- July 15, 1769- Edward **Veazey** to his son Elijah **Veazey** the land he bought of Henry **McCulloch**, Esq. of Turnham Green, Great Britian, Middlesex Co.,- Jan. 12, 2nd year of reign of George 3rd. at George **Laws** line in Edward

Veazey's line- 200 acres.
Wts: Wm. **Burford**, Peyton **Clements**.

116, 117- Sept. 6, 1769- Allen **Jones** and Willie **Jones** to Robert **Goodloe** for 192pds. 10 shls. the land which Robert **Jones**, Jr. bought at auction at execution of **Gilchrist** and **Telfair** against **Wilson** and **Cade** being the land and manor plantation of **Cade** in Johnston and Granville Counties containing 550 acres on NE side of Horse creek.
Wts: Jo. **Long**, Thos **Short**.

118, 119- John **Alston** of City of Glasgow, North Britian, merchant, Robert **Carmichaell** of Broomley, late of Virginia, merchant and James **Young** of Neatherfield, late of Carolina, merchant, appoint Andrew **Miller**, William **Littlejohn** and George **Alston** of Carolina, merchants,- attorneys, to sell our property in North America, both that owned by **Carmichaell** and Co, which we owned as partners and that which we own individually- Oct. 25, 1770.
Wts: John **Wilson**, Andrew Murdock.
Colin **Dunlop**, Lord Provost attests to transaction above, he of Glasgow.

120, 121 John **Alston**, James **Morton** and Alexander **Grindley** of City of Glasgow, North Britain, merchants appoint Andrew **Miller**, William **Littlejohn** and George **Alston** as attorneys, they of N.C. to sell all belonging to us in Carolina as the firm of **Young**, **Miller** and Co or John **Alston** and Co. of Glasgow, Britain and also as individuals.
Wts: John **Wilson**, Andrew **Murdock** Oct. 29, 1770.
Registered in Chowan, Halifax and Granville Counties, N.C.

122, 123 Andrew **Miller** and William **Littlejohn** of North Carolina, merchants, appoint George **Alston** attorney, to sell our property in N.C.
Wts: Alexander **McHarg**, Henry L. **Martin**.

123, 124- June 7, 1771- James **Young**, John **Alston**, Robert **Carmichael** merchants, of Great Britain formerly in partnership of firm James **Young** and Co. to Thomas **Blount** of Edenton, N.C., merchant, for 20 pds. one acres in Granville Co., N.C., on both sides of road from Harrisburg to the courthouse in **Hamilton**'s line and also land on Fishing creek on **Young**'s, formerly **Bradford**'s line and **Hamilton**'s and **Young**'s, formerly **Mason**'s line, to the fork of road in Harrisburg and along Corbin Town old road at land formerly **Benton**'s, **Halsclaw**'s line, **Wilson**'s land to **Hedgepeth**'s, formerly **Ferguson**'s line at John **White**'s, **Arnold**'s line and land formerly **Vaughn**'s line in Granville Co., N.C.
Wts: Alexander **McHarg**, Henry L. **Martin**.

[no page 125 listed]

126, 127 June 7, 1771- James **Young**, merchant, In, Glasgow, Great Britain to Thomas **Blount** of Edenton, N.C. for 500 pds. one and a half acres conveyed to him by James **Mason** July 16, 1764 and also 50 acres sold by Isaac **Arnold** to him Sept. 8, 1764 and 50 acres conveyed to him by Joseph **Bass**, Feb. 26 1765 and 663 acres sold by Michael **Wilson** to him May 9, 1765 in Granville Co., N.C.
Wts: Alexander **McHarg**, Henry L. **Martin**.

193

129 thru 131- May 7, 1771- George **Alston** of Granville Co., N.C. to Thomas **Blount** of Edenton, N. CC. merchant, for 10 pds. 350 acres in Granville Co. on both sides of **Hatcher**'s Run.
Wts: Alexander **McHarg**, Henry L. **Martin**.

131 thru 134- May 8, 1771- Thomas **Blount** of Edenton, N.C., merchant, to John **Alston**, James **Young**, James **Morton** and Alexander **Grindley**, merchant in Glasgow, Great Britain and Andrew **Miller**, William **Littlejohn** and George **Alston** of N.C. for 530 pds. four tracts of land in Granville Co., N.C.- same land as described in above deeds to **Blount**.
Wts: Alexander **McHarg**, Henry L. **Martin**.

134, 135- Oct. 17, 1770- William **Potter** to William **Kennon** for 150 pds. 275 acres on Little Nut Bush creek at **Waldrop**'s line being part of a larger tract granted to James **Trevillion** by Granville Oct. 25, 1754.
Wts: Isaac **Edwards** C. C. registered in Book I 134, 135

135, 136- Aug. 19, 1769- Joseph **Davenport** and wife Jemima to Solomon **Walker** for 35 pds. 200 acres on Lick

branch along **Kennon**'s line, **Cleytons**.
Wts: W. **Potter**, John **Walker**, John **Satterwhite**.

137- Oct. 15, 1770- George **Bruce** to Nathan **Chiles** (**Childs**) for 250 pds. 302 acres on W side of Island creek at **Mintor**'s corner.
Wts: Thomas **Person**, John **Tuder**.

138, 139- Dec. 18, 1769- Thomas **Person** to Pleasant **Hart** for 35 pds. 250 acres on S side of **Aaron**'s creek at **Harrison**'s line, **Duty**'s corner.
Wts: Wm. **Webb**, David **Allin**.

139, 140- Oct. 15, 1770- Thornton **Yancey** and wife Elizabeth to John **Chandlor** for 50 pds. 50 acres on S side of Jonathan's creek at the former dividing line between Larkin **Johnston** and William **Clayton**.
Wts: John **Shearman**.

141- Nov. 11, 1769- Robert **Gillam** to William **Kennon** for 140 pds. 530 acres on N. side of Flat branch at **Hargrove**'s corner, Robert **Mitchel**'s line near Little Nut Bush creek, near **Dodson**'s branch.
Wts: Charles **Kennon**, Joseph **Williams**, John **Walker**.

142, 143- Oct. 17, 1770- Thomas **Craft** to Elijah **Hanks** for 50 pds. 200 acres on both sides of Crooked Run.
Wts: Wm. **Hanks**, Benja **Ragland**.

143, 145- Sept. 28, 1767- Robt. **Mills** Sr. to Joseph **Cooper** for 37 pds. 10 shls., 150 acres on S side of Tar river at **Addison**'s and **Pullin**'s lines being part of tract granted to Robert **Mills** Sr. Dec. 2, 1760 by Granville.
Wts: Jesse **Nevill**, Pump **Edwards**.
Wife (unnamed) relinquishes dower right.

145, 146- Oct. 7, 1770- John **Waldrop**, brick layer, to John **Fullilove** for 150 pds. 200 acres on Tabbs creek along Christopher **Harris**'s line to Richard **Harris**'s line.
Wts: none.
Taba, wife of **Waldrop**, relinquishes dower right.

146, 147- Feb. 15, 1769- James **Caudle** to Isom **Caudle** for 50 pds. 100 acres on S side of Tar river along **Jones**'s line.
Wts: James **Willis**, Littleton **Mapp**.

148, 149- May 8, 1770- Eliza **Kennon** of Goochland, Co., VA. to Edmund **Taylor** of Mecklenburg Co., Va. for 140 pds. 593 acres in Granville Co., N. C.- 354 acres bought of John **Mitchel** and 254 bought of Wm. **Farris**- Elizabeth **Kennon**.
Wts: Eliza **Kennon**, Richard **Marrion**, Robt. **Lewis**.

149- Apr. 21, 1769- Frances **Dodson** relict of Charles **Dodson**, deceased, to Charles **Dodson** for 20 pds. all land where on I lived and which was my husbands Charles **Dodson**'s, on Nut Bush creek in Granville Co., N.C.
Wts: John **Williams**, John Williams **Daniel**, James **Daniel**.

150, 151- Jan. . . 1771- George **Byars** to John **Ross** for 65 pds. 200 acres as per deed for land from Chauncey **Townsend** to Andrew **Hampton** and from him to George **Boyers** (Mary, wife of George **Byers** gives over dower.
Wts: Jesse **Benton**, Haden **Pryor**.

151, 152, [153]- Oct. 2, 1770- George **Byars** (**Boyers**) and wife Mary to Thomas **Yates** of Orange Co., N.C. for 137 pds., 10 shls. two tracts of land

184 [Gwynn's page # out of sequence]
on N. side of Ledge of Rocks creek one tract bought of George **Miller** Sept. 19, 1770 and other from Henry **McCulloh** Sept. 3, 1759 both on George **Miller**'s line containing 271 acres and the 2nd 200 acres-
Wts: John **Ross**, James **Bullock**, Richard D. **Cooke**.

154, 155- Oct. 16, 1770- Charles **Kennon** of Granville Co., N.C. to John **Kennon** of Goochland Co., Va for 340 pds., 611 acres on W side of Little Island creek near Tynes line, on **Mitchel**'s line.
Wts: William **Kennon**, John **Bullock**, Jr.

155 thru 157- Jan. 16, 1771- Robert **Harris**, sheriff of Granville Co sold to William **Burford**, land of Philip **Pryor** who was indebted 454 pds. 14 shls. 9 pence as suit brought by Governor **Tryon** against him . . sold for 220 pds. land on Hico road at Thomas **Person**'s line, **Dickens**' line one a grant from Granville Apr. 30, 1753, one from Richard **Briggs** July 15, 1762, 3rd from **Briggs** Oct. 30, 1765, 4th from Thomas **Person** Sept. 14,1765 and in all 950 acres.
Wts: Haden **Pryor**, Samuel **Harris**.

157, 158, 159- Jan. 15, 1771- John **Lowry** and wife Charity to Daniel **Hunter** for 125 pds. 335 acres on W side of Long Creek a branch of Tabbs creek which was sold to **Lowery** by **Hunter** Aug. 6, 1768.
Wts: Samuel **Kittrell**, Pomfrett **Herndon**, George **Bristow**.

159, 160- Sept. 12, 1770- James **Young**, late of Halifax Co., N. C., merchant, to Jonathan **White** of Granville Co., planter for 625 pds. land on W side of Fishing creek at **Anderson**'s and **Bradford**'s line.
Wts: Henry L. **Martin**, Archd **Heggie**.

162, 163- Jan. 11, 1770- John **Willingham** of Mecklenburg Co., Va to William **Willingham** of Granville Co., N.C. for 5 shls. 229 acres in Granville Co., N. C.
Wts: Thomas **Willingham**, John **Willingham**, Jarral **Willingham**.

163, 164- Nov. 26, 1770- Henry **Fuller** to Valentine **White** for 7pds. 130 acres at **Fuller**'s line, **Jones**'s line, Samuel **Fuller**'s corner, to Ridge Path-
Wts: Wm. **Hornsby**, Dan **Hunter**.

165- Aug. 2, 1770- Robert **Reed** to John **Blalock** for 100 pds. 158 acres on Fishing creek.
Wts: William **Wilson**, Lemuel **Goodwin**.

166, 167, July 10, 1770- James **McGehee**, Sr. to George **Levenston** for 12 pds. 10 shls. 100 acres at Benjamin **McGehee**'s spring branch on Talors creek-
Wts: James **Relly**, John **Brummit** (also spelled **Mcgehe**).

167, 168- Dec. 24, 1770- John **Harris** and wife Rachel to John **Waldrop** for 100 pds. 140 acres on Jonathan **White**'s line in Granville Co.
Wts: John **Fullilove**, Hennerita **Fullilove**.

169-170- Oct. 23, 1770- Jonathan **White** to John **Tatom** for 375 pds. 500 acres at the old mill, along the creek to John **Harris**'s line, along Jonathan **White**'s line crossing Nut Bush road to Lewis **Anderson**'s path, at Nicholas **Medlock**'s line.
Wts: Archd **Heggie**, Geo. **Alston**, Stephen **Jett**.

170, 171- May 21, 1771- George **White** of Mecklenburg Co., Va. to Fennel **Marks** of Granville Co., N. C, for 22 pds. 10 shls. 115 acres on **Taylor**'s Mill creek at John **White**'s line, at Richard **Johnston**'s, John **Hargrove**'s which is ½ of the land bought of John **Buzby**.
Wts: Howell **Moss**, Richd **Hargrove**.

171, 172- Mar. 17, 1770. William **Stone** to Thomas **Recks** for 60 pds. 313 acres on **Ragland**'s line, **Gillam**'s line on Lick creek.
Wts: Samuel **Morse**, Reuben **Morse**, Phillis **Morse**.

173, 174- Apr. 12, 1771- Stephen **Merritt** to Thomas **Philpot** for 60 pds. 404 acres on N. side of Tar river at **Langston**'s. line. **Washington**'s line.
Wts: James **Langston**, John **Williams**.

174, 175- [176 handwritten in]- Aug. 30, 1770. Thomas **Critcher** to Stephen **Williams** and Peter **Russil** for 83 pds. 4 shls.- mortgages 143 acres on N. side of Tar river to secure debt, land whereon Stephen **Williams** and his mother Elizabeth **Williams** now live, also stock, wagon, man's hat.
Wts: Robert **Dickins**, Israel **Eastwood**.

185

177, 178- Oct. 8, 1770- William **Townes** of Mecklenburg Co., Va to Edmund **Taylor** of same place for 57 pds. 200 acres at Jonathan **Parker**'s land.
Wts: Joseph **Taylor**, James **MacMurray**.

178, 179- May 20, 1771- Roger **Baget** to his son John **Baget** for 10 pds. 100 acres adjoining the former land given him by sd John **Baget**, by his father Roger **Baget** at his line at a branch called the Cornfield Branch.
Wts: Thos. **Oakley**, Frederick **Hutchins**.

179, 180- Sept. 10, 1770- Thomas **Lowe** and wife Salley gave to John **Malden** (**Maulden**) 129 acres being part of 529 acres granted by Earl Granville to Thomas **Lowe** Nov. 28, 1760 on both sides of Tabbs creek on **Loyd**'s corner.
Wts: William **Gowin**, Edward **Loyd**.

181, 182- Oct. 4, 1770- Samuel **Henderson** of Granville Co., N.C. and Nimrod **Williams** of Bute Co., N.C. to Nathan **Sims** of Granville Co. for 100 pds. 136 acres on **Anderson**'s swamp at **Linsey**'s corner, Robert **Williams** spring branch.
Wts: Reuben **Searcy**, William **Todd**.

183- Jan. 15, 1770- Nathaniel **Harris** to James **Mitchel** Senr. for 26 pds. 300 acres on Micals creek at Michael **Satterwhite**'s line on Hico rd.
Wts: Abraham **Mitchel**, Susanna **Mitchel**.

184, 185- Apr. 23, 1771- James **Byars** of Louisa Co., Va. to Rowland **Terry** of Granville Co., N.C. for 75 pds. 200 acres in Granville Co., N.C.
Wts: Joseph **Taylor**, Wm. **Byars**, James **Henderson**.

185, 186- Oct. 30, 1770- Edmund **Taylor** of Mecklenburg Co., Va. to Edward **Page** of Granville Co., N.C. for 35 pds. 350 acres in **Hargrove**'s line, at **Robinson**'s corner at county line- 100 acres is land whereon Thomas **Brown** the elder lives with his wife Mary and they are to remain thereon for their lifetime and then to Edward **Page**.
Wts: Joseph **Taylor**, Lewis **Taylor**.

187- May 22, 1771- Haden **Pryor** to Charles **Harris** for 166 pds. 300 acres on Charles **Harris**'s line.

188,189- May 22, 1771- Thomas **Craft** to Thomas **Person** for 60 pds. 525 acres on S side of **Anderson** Swamp along **McMillion**'s line and **Fleming**'s line.-
Wts: Samuel **Morse**, Reuben **Morse**.
Elizabeth, wife of Thomas **Craft**, relinquishes her dower right.

189, 190, 191- Dec. 3, 1770- James **Reade** and wife Margaret to Humphrey **David** of Essex Co., Va. for 45 pds. 2 shls. 6 pence, 100 acres in Granville Co., N.C. on Plum Tree Run, in **Harris**'s line, **Jordan**'s line.
Wts: Samuel **Smith**, Jonathan **Knight**, Banja **Kendrick**.

191, 192- Feb. 16, 1771- Richard **Head** and wife Sarah to Gideon **Scurry** for 55 pds. 100 acres on Lovet **Gates** line in **Feagin**'s line.

Wts: Henry **Graves**, Eli **Scurry**.

193, 194- Aug. 16, 1770- John **Hightower** of Lunenburg Co., Va to William **Puryear** of Granville Co., N.C. for 100 pds. 170 acres on fork of Jonathan's creek being part of tract **Hightower** bought of John **Raymond** on **Gill**'s line.
Wts: Stith **Hardaway**, Thomas **Leverett**, William **Gill**, Jr., Benja **Smith**.

195, 196- Jan. 3, 1771- John **Adcock** to Lonard **Adcock** for 40 pds. 50 acres at Indian Field creek to mouth of Spring branch to Henry **McCulloch** line
Wts: Chas **Partee**, Bolin **Adcock**, John **Adcock**.

196, 197- May 21, 1771- Mathew **Caviness** to Richard **Johnston** for 30 pds. 120 acres that **Caviness** bought of John **Buzbee** on head of **Mitchel**'s creek at lands of Jeremiah **Ward**, John **Hargrove** and Luke Waldrop.
Wts: Edmund and Lewis **Taylor**, Richard **Hargrove**, Fennil **Marks**.

197, 198- Apr. 1, 1771- Richard **Roberts** to James **Walker** for 120 pds. 190 acres being part of land whereon **Roberts** lives on Grassy creek at James **Walker**'s line.
Wts: Peter **Dunkin**, Elles **Dunkin**.

199, 200- May 7, 1771- Philip **Burford** of Bute Co., N.C. to George **Wilson** of Granville Co., N.C. for 17 pds. 76 acres in Granville Co. bought of George **Lampkin** at lands of Ann **Wood**, Saml **Paschall**, Jno. **Paschall**, and Capt. Jno. **Hawkins**-
Wts: Henry **Wilson**, Mildred **Burford**, Fennel **Marks**.

186

200 thru 202- May 18, 1771- John **Pope** and wife Elizabeth to Winfield **Wright**, Sr. for 332 pds. 16 shls. land on both sides of Cedar creek at Peter **Vinson**'s corner on Deep Branch, near James **Kelley**'s line on **McGehe**'s line at **Bradford**'s line, containing 800 acres being land whereon Arthur **Fuller** formerly lived, part of same conveyed to John **Pope** Dec. 10, 1760 and the other part being part of larger tract granted to John **Pope** May 10, 1761.
Wts: Benja **Wright**, Joseph **Wade**.

202 thru 204- Sept. 10, 1765- Philip **Pryor** Esq., sheriff, to Thomas **Person**- land of James **Briggs** sold at suit brought by Philip **Taylor**- 285 acres in Granville Co. at **Hill**'s line, **Haywood**'s line, on head of **Bennet**'s creek and is land conveyed by Richard **Briggs** to James **Briggs**-
Wts: Waters **Dunn**, Haden **Pryor**.

204, thru 206- Mar. 19, 1770- George **Hudspeth** to John **Blaylock** for 62 pds. 10 shls. land on waters of Low Ground Creek whereon George **Hudspeth** formerly lived which was granted to John **Plant** at path from **Bradford**'s to **Wilkerson**'s containing 200 acres.
Wts: Jonathan **White**, William **Parham**.

207, 208- Dec. 11, 1769- Thomas **Harris** to Robert **Allison** Jr. for 36 pds. 265 acres in **Thomson**'s line, at **McCulloch**'s line, along **Williamson**'s line.
Wts: Geo. **Alston**, Absalom **Tatom**.
Sarah, wife of Thomas **Harris** relinquishes her dower right.

208 thru 210- May 24, 1769, George **Keith** to William **Johnston** of Orange Co., N.C. (**Keith** of Granville) for 32 pds. 3 shls. land on Beaverdam creek in Granville Co., N.C. at Andrew **Hampton**'s line containing 200 acres.
Wts: This is a mortgage-

211, 212- May 3, 1771- Robert **Harris**, Esq. executor of will of Sherwood **Harris**, deceased, to George **Alston** for 53 pds. 8 shls., a half penny 350 acres being the land conveyed to Sherwood **Harris** May 8, 1762 on both sides of **Hatcher**'s Run.
Wts: Edwd **Moore**, Memucan **Hunt**.

213- Solomon **Alston** of Granville Co., N.C. owes Robert **Lewis** of Goochland Co., Va. 5000 pds. Apr. 23, 1771- and mortgages 2000 acres which he bought of Philip **Alston**, Jr. and Thomas **Lowe** and 640 acres which he bought of the

wife of Jacob **Catchings**-
Wts: Will and Charles **Kennon**.

214- Jan. 7, 1771- Sarah **Ball**, this day swore (she being of full age) that a negro woman was given to Ann **Hackney** who afterwards married Absalom **Davis** and after the marriage she heard the said William **Hackney** confirm the gift to her and her husband.
Wts: Stephen **Jett**.

215- Daniel **Ball** swears to negro woman being given to Ann **Hackney** by William **Hackney**. That Ann **Hackney** afterwards married Absalom **Davis** and he heard William **Hackney** confirm the gift to them- Jan. 17, 1771.

215, thru 218- July 22, 1772- Robert **Dickins**, Jr., from Daniel **Frazzer** for 55 pds. 9 shls., 3 pence- **Frazzure** indebted to **Dickins**- mortgages 2000 pds. tobacco, horses, cattle, furniture, corn to assure payment of debt.
Wts: James **Hunt**.

218- 219- Dec. 30, 1771- Joseph **Williams** and wife Sarah to John **Walker** for 110 pds. 292 acres on Island creek at Samuel **Whealor**'s line, William **Potter**'s line.
Wts: William **Bullock**.

220, 221- Sept. 14, 1771- John **Williams** and wife Mary to Joseph **Williams** for 400 pds. land on Great Nut Bush creek at mouth of John **Williams** Spring branch to the old race path's to head of Schoolhouse branch- 350 acres.
Wts: Jo. **Williams**, Jr.

222, 223- Oct. 28, 1771- Bartlet **Searcy** and wife, Lucy to Thomas **Wiggins** for 25 pds. 197 acres in Granville Co.
Wts: John **Williams**.

223, 224- Feb. 15, 1772- William **Gilliam** and wife Elizabeth to James **Daniel** for 5shls. one acre below **Daniel**'s mill at the pond.
Wts: Richd **Henderson**.

187

225, 226- July 7, 1770- Luke **Waldrop** and wife Christian to Daniel **Williams** for 162 pds. 187 ½ acres between Great Nut Bush and Little Nut Bush creeks in John **Bullock**'s and Leonard **Sims**'s line.

226, 227- July 7, 1770- John **Searcy**, Sr. to Daniel **Williams** for 60 pds. 262 acres on the branches of Nut Bush creek on John **Searcy**'s and Samuel **Henderson**'s lines- signed by John and Reuben **Searcy**.

228, 229- Aug. 7, 1771- Elisha **Paschal** to Thomas **Key** for 9 pds. 100 acres on Little Deep creek at Wm. **Paschal**'s line on E side of Jeffersons Ferry.
Wts: Len H. **Bullock**, Jos. **Williams**, Jr.

229, 230- Oct. 16, 1769- Bartholomew **Kembill** to William **Gillam**, Jr. for 18 pds., 15 shls. 30 acres on W side of **Anderson**'s swamp in William **Gilliam**'s line and along the line of William **Gilliam**, Jr.
Wts: Phil **Hawkins**, Jr., Drury **Kimball**.

231, 232- Dec. 13, 1770- Timothy **Drishell** of Lunenburg Co., Va from James **Washburn** for 25 pds. 175 acres at **Glover**'s line, **Harris**'s line at **Satterwhite**'s line along **Cook**'s line.
Wts: John **Smith**, Mich. **Satterwhite**.

[232, 233]- June 20, 1770- Isaac **Mitchell** and Mary his wife. to Edmund **Taylor** of Mecklinburg Co., Va. for 300 pds. 15 shls. 621 acres on both sides of Island creek being the land whereon **Mitchell** now lives.
Wts: Robert **Mchel**, Thomas **Mitchell**, James **Glover**, Drury **Smith**, Spencer **Pescud**.

234, 235- May 12, 1764- Reuben **Searcy** and wife Susanna to Richard **Henderson** for 420 pds. 600 acres on Great Nut Bush creek and **Anderson**'s swamp at Nathaniel **Norwood**'s lower corner at **Kimbal**s fork.
Wts: Samuel **Henderson**.

236, 237- May 5, 1771- Joseph **Waldrop** and wife, Hannah to John **Mitchell** for 45 pds. 220 acres at **Potter**'s line.
Wts: Joseph **Williams**, Jr., Abraham **Mitchell**.

237, 238- May 5, 1771- Richard **Johnson** to Joseph **Waldrop** for 100 pds. 100 acres on Lick branch.
Wts: Joseph **Williams**, Joseph **Williams**, Jr.

239, 240- Jan. 14 1771- John **Pullin** to John **Heffellin** for 30 pds. 176 acres on both sides of Fort creek at **Pucket**'s line.
Wts: Joel **Moody**, Thomas **Aderson**.

241, 242- Aug. 22, 1771- Joseph **Parrish** to Joseph **Rogers** for 7 pds. 20 acres on Ruin Creek in **Hawkins**' line, **Rogers**' line.
Wts: Thomas **Person**, David **Blalock**.
Wife (unnamed) relinquishes dower right.

242 thru 244 - Aug. 10, 1771 Richard **Roberts** to William **Wharton** for 30 pds. for his lifetime, and after his decease, to his daughter Lidia **Wharton** and her heirs, land on branches of Grassy creek being part of tract whereon **Wharton** now lives containing 300 acres.
Wts: James **Walker**, David **Howard**.

244, 245- Aug. 23, 1771- William **Burford** to Haden **Pryor** for 500 pds. 950 acres on Thomas **Parsons** line on Hico road to Robert **Dickens** line.

245, 246- Aug. 19, 1771- Jonathan **Knight** to Benjamin **Glaze** for 10 pds. 13 shls., 4 pence, 8 acres in the main fork of Grassy creek to the main creek, being part of land purchased of his brother Charles **Knight**.
Wts: Richard **Posey**.

247, 248- Feb. 5, 1770- George **Jourdan** and wife Elizabeth to Thomas **Ricks** for 125 pds., 200 acres on both sides of Flat creek at **Jordan**'s line.
Wts: Robert **Robinson**, Arpheus **Jordan**, Ansil **Parrish**.

248, 249- Aug. 20, 1771- Michal **Williamson** to Thomas **Williamson** for-[blank] pds., 247 acres which was granted to William **Gragg** May 13, 1756.
Wts: Jesse **Benton**- signed Michael **Williamson**.

250 thru 252- July 8, 1770- James **Yancey**, Sr., to James **Yancey**, Jr. for 100 pds. on both sides of Mountain Fork of Jonathans creek being part of land purchased by James **Yancey**, Sr. of Ruubert (Robert) **Jones**, attorney, as by deed Mar. 6, 1753 at Thornton **Yancey**'s line containing 320 acres.
Wts: Philip **Yancey**, Lewis **Yancey**.

188

252 thru 254- Sept. 24, 1773- Antony **Cozzart** (**Cozort**) to John **Cozart** for 50 pds. 150 acres in Granville Co.
Wts: George **Thompson**, Robert **Allison**, Sr. and, Jr.

254, 255- Aug. 21, 1771- Brissey **Parish** to Joseph **Parish** for 18 pds. 50 acres on N. side of Tabbs creek on Joseph **Rogers**' line to John **Hawkins** line. signs Brissie (also spelled Brise).

255, 256- Apr. 13, 1771- George **Miller** and wife Mary to Julius **King** for 34 pds. 120 acres adjoining land that Thomas **Bates** bought of George **Boyers** whereon George **Boyers** now lives being part of **Yates** land and all the tract patented for 320 acres.
Wts: Richd D. **Cooke**, Francis **Levinsone**, George **Boyers**, Mach **Rogers**.

[257, 258]- Sept. 19, 1770- George **Milner** to George **Boyers** (**Boyars**) for 30 pds. 200 acres on Ledge of Rocks creek at George **Buyarses** to George **Milner**'s line.
Wts: Richd D. **Cooke**, John **Ross**, James **McLemore**.

259, 260- Feb. 8, 1765- Robert **Cade**, Jr to Zachariah **Bullock**, for 20 pds. 200 acres in Bute and Granville Co., N.C.

in Joab **Mitchell**'s line, Thomas **Person**'s line on Horse creek at Danl **Nowlin**'s line, **Person**'s line, Britain **Fuller**'s line on waters of **Cade** creek to James **Winningham**'s line- 700 acres to John **Champion**'s line, also land in Bute Co at Isaac **Bledsoe**'s, Edward **Mobly**'s, **Benton**'s line 447 acres.
Wts: John **Pope**, Jeppthah **Terrell**.

260, 261- Aug. 3, 1765- - Julia **Nichols** of Bute Co., N.C. to Len Henley **Bullock** of Granville Co., N.C. for 100 pds. land in Granville Co., on Deep creek and Nut Bush creek on both sides of Hico road, containing 631 acres in **Bird**s line now **Williams**' line.
Wts: Philemon **Hawkins**, Thomas **Bell**, Will **Johnson**.

262, 263- Dec. 20, 1771- Thomas **Low** and wife Sarah to Thomas **Critcher** for 250 pds. land on both sides of Nut. Bush creek containing 1207 acres.
Wts: none.

264, 265- Feb. 19, 1771- George **Levister** to Charles **McGehee** for 6 pds. 5 shls. 50 acres on S side of Little Fork of Talers creek at **Levister**s Benj **McGehee** lines which was sold to **Levister** by James **McGehee**.
Wts: John **Nevill**, Elizabeth **Nevill**.

266, 267- June 6, 1771- William **Potter** and Edmond **Taylor**, to Howel **Moss** for 60 pds. 138 acres on **Davenport**'s line.
Wts: Samuel **Sneed**, Saml **Jeter**.

268, 269- Dec. 12, 1770. Absalom **Langston** to Samuel **Hambrick** for 125 pds. 450 acres on Cub creek of Tar river at **Washington**'s line.
Wts: James **Langston**, James **Wilson**, signed by Absalom and Christian **Langston**.

269, 270- Aug. 15, 1767- John Rodwell **Buzzard** to James **Hopper** for 5 shls 200 acres on S side of Tar river.
Wts: Jno. **Stone**, Jacob **Williams**, Israel **Eastwood**.
Elizabeth, wife of John Rodwell **Buzzard** relinquishes dower right.

271, 272- Aug. 20, 1771- John **Adcock**, Sr. to Lonard **Adcock** for 15 pds. 120 acres as per deed from Sarah **Danofins** to John **Adcock** at line that was between Sarah **Dunnafih** and John **Adcock** at Henry **McCulloch**'s line.
Wts: Chas. [&] Edm **Partee**.

273, 274- Mar. 13, 1770- Robert **Harris**, Esq. to Thomas **Harris** for 5 pds. 43 acres on Thomas **Harris**'s line, at Nicholas **Holstein**'s line, William **Oglebey**'s line.
Wts: Wm. **Oglevie**, Robert **Harris**, Jr.

274, 275- Nov. 1770 Edmond **Taylor** of Mecklenburg Co., Va. to William **Taylor** of Granville Co., N. C, for 20 pds. the tract of land Edmund **Taylor** bought of Abraham **Cook** on the main road between, Island and Nut Bush creek containing 162 acres at Thos. **Lanier**'s line, Benjamin **Johnson**'s line.
Wts: Joseph **Taylor**, Lewis **Taylor**.

276, 277- Apr. 3, 1771 Samuel **Morse** to David **Mitchel** for 5 pds. 30 acres on Buffaloe branch at land whereon Chrismas **Ray** did live at John **Williams**' line at Joseph **Glover**'s line.
Wts: Reuben **Morse**.

189

277 thru 279- Aug. 19, 1769- Robert **Mitchel** and wife Tanner to William **Todd** for 5 pds. 70 acres on Ready Creek at Leonard **Sims**'s line to James **Wallace**'s line and **Jefferson**'s Ferry road.
Wts: Haden **Pryor**, John **Mitchel**.

279, 280- Sept. 27, 1768- Reuben **Morse** and wife Martha to David **Mitchel** for 125 pds. 120 acres on W side of Great Nut Bush creek at **Critcher**'s to William **Bullock**'s line.
Wts: John **Satterwhite**, Samuel **Morse**, Jno. **Glover**.

281, 282- Nov. 27, 1770- James **Waldrop** and wife Mary to John **Bullock** 185 pds. 157 acres on Little Nut Bush

creek at Robert **Mitchel**'s former line on Little Nutbush creek.
Wts: none.

283, 284- June 16, 1769- James **Trevillion** of Rowan Co., N.C. to William **Taylor** of Granville Co., N.C. for 50 pds. 650 acres in Granville Co. on N. side of Great Island creek at **Henderson**'s corner at **Williams**'s line to James **Williams**'s line to **Doswell**'s line.
Wts: John **Trevillion**, Joab **Trevillion**, Richard **Trevillion**.

284, 285- Nov. 4, 1771- Luke **Waldrop** to Jos **Waldrop** for 20 pds. 100 acres whereon Sarah **Johnson** now lives being part of larger tract taken up by Luke **Waldrop** and sold to Jos. **Waldrop** son of Luke **Waldrop**.
Wts: Daniel **Williams**, Elisha **Sims**. (this is a mortgage)

286, 287- Jan. 12, 1771- William **Hamilton** and Co. of Halifax Co., N.C. merchants, to William **Alston** of Solomon, of the county of Granville, N.C. for 650 pds. land on both sides, of Tar river at **Harris**'s line, Sherwood **Harris**'s line on Nicholas creek containing 580 acres.
Wts: H **Hendric**, Stephen **Jett**, Jno. **McIndoe**. (signed John **Hamileton** for Wm)

287, 288- . . . 1771- William **Alston** and Charity his wife, to Reuben **Searcy** for 775 pds. 580 acres on both sides of Tar river at **Harris** line on Nicholas creek to Sherwood **Harris**'s line.

289, 290- Nov. 19, 1771- James **Dyer** to George **Wright** for 35 pds. 204 acres on Trading Path- Signed James and Anne **Dyer**.
Wts: Zepheniah **Waller**, George Lane **Moor**.

290, 291- May 10, 1771- James **Dyar** and Anne **Dyer** to George Lain **Moore** for 30 pds. 100 acres on Nap of Reeds creek (spelled here Napsareed.)
Wts: George **Wright**, Zepheniah and Nathaniel **Waller**.

292- Sept. 13, 1771- Robert **Dickens** to Charles **Kennon**. for 1000 pds. 675 ½ acres on Fox creek on Hico road which was sold by Robert **Harris** to John **Hill** June 9, 1757.
Wts: Jonathan **Parker**.

293, 294- Nov. 18, 1771- Jeremiah **Ward** to Mathew **Caviness** for 50 pds. 205 acres whereon Jer. **Ward** formerly lived at head of Col. Edmund **Taylor** Mill creek between the lands of Fennel **Marks**, Richd **Johnson**, Willm **Kennon** and the county line.
Wts: Fennl and William **Marks**, Abraham **Mitchell**.

294, 295- Nov. 18, 1771- John **Waldrop** and wife Tabe to Christopher **Harris** for 105 pds. 140 acres which was conveyed from Richard **Harris** to his son John **Harris** at Jonathan **White**'s line.

296, 297- Oct. 17, 1770- Phillip **Yancey** to William **Spier**, Sr. for 30 pds. 70 acres on Long Creek at Solomon **Fuller**'s line.
Wts: William **Roberts**, Samuel **Fuller**, Joseph **Rogers**.

297, 298- Aug. 14, 1770- Samuel **Whealer** to John **Winningham** for 80 pds. land on Little Island creek near **Walker**'s ford at Edmund **Taylor**'s line at John **Walker**'s line and reserving one acre for a mill- 205 acres.
Wts: C. **Hawkins**, W. **Potter**.

299, 300- Nov. 12, 1771- Luke **Waldro[p]** to Richard **Johnson** for 26 pds. 100 acres at Jos **Waldrop**'s line at Jeremiah **Ward**'s line, Jno. **Hargroves** being part of land taken up by Luke **Waldrop**, Sr.
Wts: Fennl **Marks**, Caleb **Caps**, Sally **Caps**. (this is a mortgage).

300, 301- Nov. 13, 1771- James **Jones** and wife Ann to Ambrose **Jones**, Sr. for 200 pds. all that land in Granville Co. willed to James **Jones** by Robert **Jones**, deceased, on Arons creek containing 640 acres.
Wts: Pleasant Ward, Jos **Chandler**, James **Yancey**.

302 thru 304- May 6, 1771- George **Alston** to Josiah **Farmer** for [blank] current money of VA, 200 acres on Mountain fork of Jonathan's creek at **Clayton**'s line, John **Newton**''s line.
Wts: Andrw **Miller**, Alexander **McHarg**, Christphr **Harris**.

304, 305- Apr. 15, 1771- Frances **Faulks** to Michael **Redwine** for 30 pds. 200 acres bought of Chauncy **Townsend** at tract whereon George **Boyers** lived in George **Miller**'s line on Ledge of Rocks creek.
Wts: Richard D. **Cooke**, George **Boyers**, James **McLemore**.

306, 307- Nov. 25, 1769- James **Trevillion** to Joseph **Taylor** for 10 pds. 10 shls. 40 acres on branches of Little Island creek in **Trevillion**'s line.
Wts: John and William **Taylor**, Henry **Williams**, Veazey **Husband**.

307, 308- Nov. 17, 1771- Isaac **Winfree** of Cumberland Co., Va. to Jacob **Winfree** of Granville Co., N.C. for 100 pds. 350 acres on Jonathan's creek at William **Gowin**'s former line.
Wts: Haden **Pryor**, M. **Hunt**.

309, 310- Sept. 16, 1771- John **Jackson** and wife Patience of Roan (Rowan) Co., N.C. to Joseph **Harp** of Orange Co., N.C. for 15 pds. 100 acres which is part of a larger tract formerly belonging to Robert **Prity**, Sr. who gave it to his granddaughter Patience **Pritty**, in Granville Co. N.C.
Wts: James [**Earp**](?), James **Maydwell**.

310, 311- July 10, 1769- Alexander **Gray** to Zachariah **Goss** for 30 pds. 200 acres on both sides of Nap of Reeds creek at Wm. **Bennett**'s line.
Wts: William **Bennett**, Robert **Sorrell**.

312, 313- Jan. 2, 1772- Thomas **Mutter** and Co. from John **Baynes** both of Granville Co. for 200 pds. a mortgage on 250 acres.
Wts: George **Reid**, Hugh **Garrett** ([**Galtt**]?)

314- Feb. 17, 1772- Len Henley **Bullock** for 20 pds. sold to John **Fleming** 100 acres on Anderson's swamp.
Wts: Lennord **Sime**, Howell **Tatum**.

315, 316, Oct. 14, 1771- Woodson **Daniel** to John **Hooker** for 45 pds. 200 acres being part of the 100,000 acres granted by the King to Henry **McCulloch** and is *No. 12 tract* on Beaverdam creek.
Wts: Alexander **Munn**, Adam **Potter**.

316, 317- Oct. 14, 1771- William **Jones** to Charles **Merryman** for 20 pds. 200 acres on N. side of Picture branch being part of land bought of Samuel **Boyd** by William **Jones**.
Wts: George **Wright**, James **Ham**, William **Merryman**.

317, 318- Jan. 21, 1772- John **Dickerson** to Justice **Parish** for 20 pds. 125 acres on S side of Tabbs creek at Maple Spring branch.
Wts: Jno. **Peace**, Jr., William **Dickerson**.

319, 320- Feb. 7, 1772- Henry **Howard**, and wife Prisilla of Mecklinburg Co., Va. to Charles **Edwards** of Granville Co., N.C. for 200 pds. 630 acres on S side of Bearskin creek and also 120 acres at **Roberts** corner, at **Willingham**'s line which lands were bought of Thomas **Hawkins** and David **Wilkerson**. . . and together are 750 acres.
Wts: James **Downey**, John and Abram **Potter**.

320, 321- Nov. 26, 1771- John **Dickerson** to Valentine **White** for 44 pds. 350 acres on N. side of Tabbs creek.
Wts: John **Peace**, Jr., Joseph **Rodgers**.

321, 322- Feb. 18, 1772- Zachariah **Goss** and wife Ann to James **Scarlett** of Orange Co., N.C. for 42 pds. part of 200 acres **Goss** bought of Ellexender **Gray** on Nap of Reeds creek whereon **Goss**, now lives being100 acres at James **Bennett**'s land.
Wts: William and Sarah **Bennett**.

323, 324- Jan. 25, 1772- Thomas **Person** to Abraham **Crenshaw** for 50 pds. 80 acres being part of larger tract granted to Thomas **Person** on **Malone**'s and **Crenshaw**'s lines.
Wts: James **Farquher**, Thomas **Bridges**.

324, 325- Feb. 17, 4772- Richard **Roberts** to Joseph **Roberts** for 30 pds. 296 acres on Grassy creek being tract of land whereon William **Wharton** and Joseph **Roberts** now live.
Wts: John **Howard**, Jr., Benjamin **Howard**.

191

325, 326- Nov. 30, 1771- Sarah **Alston**, widow of Solomon **Alston**, deceased being execrx. of his will to Robert **Lewis** of Goochland Co., Va. for 1200 pds. 2000 acres whereon he lived on both sides of Tar river which was willed to Robert **Lewis** by Solomon **Alston** in his last will, in fee simple.
Wts: M. **Hunt**, Betty **Ren**.

326, 327- June 10, 1769- Jeremiah **Baley**, Jr. to Richard **Baley** for 10 pds. 197 acres on Newlight creek in **Man**'s line, part of tract granted to Gillum **Harris** Dec. 1, 1760.
Wts: Joseph **Davis**, William **Balley**, Gillum **Harris**.

328, 329- Mar. 14, 1768- Solomon **Davis** and wife Elizabeth to Samiel **Tines** for 60 pds. 200 acres on **Mitchl**'s creek.
Wts: Mesenier **Davis**, Mich **Satterwhite**, Nat **Harris**.

329, 330- Jan 25 1772- Thomas **Person** to Patrick **O'Bryant** for 60 pds. 350 acres on both sides of Arons creek at **Hart**'s line, **Smith**'s line at **Duty**'s and Pleasant **Hart**'s line.
Wts: Thomas **Bridges**, James **Forquhar**.

331, 332- Feb, 7, 1772- Thomas **Person** to James C**hester** (**Chesher**) for 100 pds. 500 acres at Groves **Howard**'s and others on both sides of Reedy creek including the **Labinfields** at **Taylor**'s line.
Wts: John **Person**, Patience **Pryor**.

332, 333- Feb. 19, 1772- Christopher **Harris** to Daniel **Standard** for 5 pds. 18 ½ acres on Poplar creek.

333, 334- Nov. 24, 1770- Thomas **Person** to Joel **Pope** of Orange Co., N.C. for 20 pds. 200 acres on both sides of W fork of Aron's creek at **Pryor**'s corner-
Wts: Robert **Pryor**, Geo. **Martin**.

334, 335- Feb. 13, 1772- John **Dickerson** to Christian **Thomas** for 16 pds. 200 acres in Granville Co., N.C.
Wts: William **Ham**, Jno. **Peace**, Jr.

335, 336- Feb. 19, 1772- Pumphrey **Edwards** to Richard **Jones** for 25 pds. 100 acres on S side of Tar river at **Rust**'s line bought of Geo. **Levister**.
Wts: Richard **Hight**, Samuel **Walker**.

337, 338- Jan. 1, 1772- Jacob **Winfree** and wife Elizabeth to Thomas **Aplin** of Amelia Co., Va., for 150 pds. 350 acres in Granville Co, N.C. at William **Gawin**'s line.
Wts: John **Puryear**, Benja **Smith**, William **Puryear**.

338, 339- Nov. 21, 1771- John **Dickerson** to William **Dickerson** for 20 pds. 170 acres on Tar river.
Wts: Joseph **Cooper**, John **Piece**, Jr.

339, 340- Feb. 4, 1772- Gideon **Crenshaw** to Abraham **Crenshaw** for 10 shls. 140 acres on E side of Mountain creek being part of larger tract granted to Gideon **Crenshaw**.
Wts: Frances **Crenshaw**, Luke **Landers**.

340, 341- Feb. 8, 1772- Thomas **Bridges** to James **Bridges** for 300 pds. 600 acres on Grassy creek at Charles **Smith**'s line.
Wts: Thomas **Bradford**, Solomon **Fuller**.

342, 343- Feb. 18, 1772- James **Bridges** to Thomas **Bridges** for 300 pds. 475 acres granted to James **Bridges** Apr. 1, 1763 and Nov. 4, 1759 to Seth **Pettepool** and to James **Bridges** May 11, 1762 on both sides of **Aaron**'s creek at **Harris**'s line.
Wts: Solomon **Fuller**, Thos **Bradford**.

343, 344- Feb, 11, 1772- Valentine **White** to Judith **Highfield** for 11 pds. 10 shls. 130 acres at **Fuller**'s line, to her and her heirs-
Wts: Jonathan **Kittrell**, Samuel **Fuller**.

344, 345- July 20, 1771- Mellechiah **Reeves**, Sr. to Ann **Hopkins** for 5 pds. 100 acres on **Reeves** line.
Wts: Jesse **Benton**, John **Nelson**.

346- Dec. 10, 1771- James **Chandler** and wife Susannah to Thomas **Head** for 60 pds. 150 acres in Granville Co.
Wts: William **Head**, Richard **Head**, John **Head**.

347- Dec. 23, 1771- John **Taylor** of Caroline Co., VA. from Thomas **Doswell** for 1,050 pds. 2300 acres of which 958 acres was bought Nathaniel **Henderson** Feb. 11, 1761- 700 acres Mar. 1, 1762 as grant, 644 acres July 25, 1761 as a grant.
Wts: John **Penn**, Allen **Sears**, Lewis **Taylor**.

192

348, 349- Nov. 25, 1771- Joseph **Lamon** of Halifax Co., N.C. to John F. **Bridges** for 27 pds. 10 shls. 232 acres on both sides of Newlight creek.
Wts: John **Heffellin**, William **Hendly** (signed Joseph **Leamon**.

350, 351- Nov. 30, 1771- Joseph **Smith** to Ralph **Niel** for 45 pds. 55 acres on **Anderson**'s swamp, at Merryman **Thorne**'s line.
Wts: Len. H. **Bullock**, Ansel **Parish**, Wm. **Neal**, Sr. signed Joseph and Prudence **Smith**.

351, 352- Nov. 220 772- Mary **Dickens** wife of Robert **Dickins**, esq. relinquishes dower in and sold Sept. 30, 1772 on Fox creek to Charles **Kennon**-
Wts: Haden **Pryor**, Ro. **Lewis**.

352, 353- Dec. 9, 1772- Joseph **Harp** to William **Nailing** for 10 pds. 100 acres, which was left by Robert **Priddy**, deceased, to his granddaughter Patience **Priddy** by his will, on N. side of Middle creek and made over to Joseph **Harp**.
Wts: John **Shepard**, James **Kelley**.

354, 355- Apr. 29, 1772- Seth **More** (**Moore**- [written in the margin]) of Mecklenburg Co., VA. to John **Davis** of Granville Co., N.C. for 100 pds. 202 acres on NW side of Grassy creek at Daniel **Grant**'s Spring branch at Robert **Byley**'s, Wm. **Willingham**'s.
Wts: Thornton **Yancey**, Martin **Turman**.

355, 356- May 20, 1772- William **Sims** to Leonard **Sims** for 20 pds. 162 acres on E side of **Smith**'s creek.
Wts: Reuben **Searcy**.

356, 357- Jan. 28. 1767- James **Sandland** of Bute Co., N.C. to William **Champion** of Granville Co. for 20 pds. 180 acres on both sides of Fourt creek being west part of tract granted to **Sandland** from Peter **Vincent** May 27, 1765 signed by James and Elizabeth **Sandland**.
Wts: William **Wilkerson**, John **Lunsford**.

358, 359- Nov. 27, 1771- John **Bullock** to Henry **Lyne** of King and Queen Co., VA. (**Bullock** of Granville Co., N. C) for 550 pds. 1040 acres in Granville whereon John **Bullock** now lives at lines of the land of James **Mitchell**, Sr., Daniel **Williams**, William **Kennon**, John **Hargrove**. and Reubin **Piles**.
Wts: Joseph, William and Richard **Taylor**.

359, 360- Apr. 23, 1772- Isham **Malone** to Daniel **Malone** for 100pds. 100 acres on N, side of Mountain creek at Daniel **Malone**'s line, **Henderson** line.

Wts: Luke **Landers**, Nathan **Malone**, Thomas **Willingham**, James **Hunt**.

361, 362- Dec. 17, 1771- Robert **Beasley** of Lunenburg Co., VA. to Daniel **Grant** of Granville Co., N.C. for 10 shls. 2 acres adjoining the mill of Daniel **Grant** signed Robert **Beesley**.
Wts: Daniel and Nathl **Malone**, John **Ward**.

362, 363- Apr. 10, 1772- Henry **Fuller** to James **Fuller** for 5pds. 137 acres on both sides of Long creek at Samuel **Fuller**'s line.
Wts: Christian **Fuller**, John **Edwards**.

363, 364- May 18, 1772- William **Ogelvie** and wife Mary, Thomas **Harris** and wife Sarah to John **Searcy**, Sr. for 68 pds. 136 acres on both sides of **Hampton**'s creek at Nicolis **Holstein**'s upper corner at Ephraim **Hampton**'s.
Wts: William **Rardon**, Reuben **Searcy**.

364, 365 July 20, 1772- James **Buchannon**, Sr. to Woodford **Kelley** for 30 pds. 125 acres at John **Pascal**'s line, to mouth of Wolf Branch, to Isaiah **Pascal**'s line on Deep creek.
Wts: Thos **Henderson**, Ann **Williams**.

366, 367- July 2, 1772- William **Taylor** and wife Elizabeth to Nimrod **Williams** of Bute Co., N.C. for 106 pds. 6 shls. 8 pence at **Bullock**'s line and John **Bird**'s, George **Glover**'s lines- 420 acres.
Wts: R. **Harrison**, Wm. **Wallace**.

367, 368- May 21, 1772- Conaway **Garner** to Thomas **Person** for 25 pds. two tracts of land on both sides of Fishing creek at Geo. **Morris**'s former line in William **Reeves** line containing 70 acres [illegible handwritten note my copy] **Garner**'s and **Bandy**'s lines containing 15 acres.
Wts: Burgis **White**, Luke **Harp**.

369, 370- May 8, 1771- Francis **Williams** to Robert **Caller** of Bute Co., N.C. for 26 pds. 200 acres on Great Nut Bush creek.
Wts: Archelaus **Williams**, Saml **Hammond**.

193

370, 371- May 3, 1771- Robert **Williams** of Bute Co., N.C. to Francis **Williams** of Granville Co., N.C. for 50 pds. land on **Anderson**'s swamp at William **Taylor**'s line, in William **Browen**'s line to Simon **Williams** corner.
Wts: Archelous **Williams**, Simon **Beckham**- signed Robt. and Anne **Williams**.

371, 372- May 20, 1772- John **Pullin** and wife Ann of [blank] County to John **Rust** for 150 pds. 376 acres on Tar river at Nathan **Magehee**'s line.
Wts: Reuben **Searcy**- signed John and Anne **Pullen**.

373, 374- Apr. 23, 1772- Isham **Malone** to Nathaniel **Malone** for 50 pds. 232 acres on both sides of Mountain creek at Abraham **Crenshaw**'s line at Daniel **Malone's** line.
Wts: Luke **Landers**, Thomas **Willingham**, Daniel **Malone**.

374, 375- Feb. 18, 1772- Thomas **Willingham** to Isham **Malone** for 100 pds. 228 acres on **Gill**'s line-
Wts: Danl **Malone**, Charles **Spaulding**, Luke **Landers**.

376, 377- May 19, 1772- Leonard **Sims** executor of John **Sims**, deceased, to William **Sims** for 70 pds. 400 acres on both sides of **Smith**'s creek in John **Hargrove**'s line at William **Sims** line.
Wts: Reuben **Searcy**.

377, 378- Nov 29, 1771- Thomas **Banks** to John **Pope** for 200 pds. 388 acres in Bute and Granville Co., N.C. on Cedar creek that formerly Joseph **Fuller**'s and now Shemuel **Kearney**'s line and part of tract granted to Philemon **Bradford**, Sr. Nov. 13, 1756 and sold to William **Vincent** who sold to Britton **Fuller** and he sold to Solomon **Fuller**, Jr. and Solomon to Jno. **Pope** esq. and **Pope** esq. to Thos **Banks**.
Wts: John **Dickerson**, Wm. **Nailing**.

379, 380- May 18, 1772- Robert **Harris** to William **Ogilvie** for 20 pds. 173 acres at Nicolas **Holstein**'s line, along James **Bullock**'s line.
Wts: Reuben **Searcy**, Thos. **Harris**.

380, 381- Mar. 5, 1772- Joseph **Batson** to John **Knott** for 20 pds. mortgages all personal property.
Wts: Robert **Dickins**, Charles **Kennon**.

381, 382- May 20, 1772- James **Hopper** to William **Corder**, for 10 shls. 2op acres on S side of Tar river- signed James and Mary **Hopper**.

383, 384- Feb. 15, 1772- Thomas **Reeks** to Turner **Jourdan** for 100 pds. 200 acres on W side of **Anderson**'s swamp at Arthur **Jordan**'s line.
Wts: Gul **Smith**, Augtn **Davis**, Jr.

384, 385- Apr. 7, 1770- John **Neville** to William **Chavers** (**Chavis**) Sr. for 30 pds. 119 acres at **Cooper**'s corner, **Edwards** corner.
Wts: Samuel **Walker**.

385, 386- Aug. 20, 1771- Edward **Bond** and wife Sudey to William **Webb** of Essex Co., VA. for 125 pds. land whereon Edward **Bond** lives containing 225 acres on E side of Grassy creek at **Smith**'s, William **Amis** lines.
Wts: George **Bruce**, Samuel **Smith**, Joseph **Minter**.

387, 388- May 20, 1771- John **Rust** and wife Sarah to James **Daniel** for 135 pds. land on **Anderson**'s swamp below the mill, James **Daniel** corner and at Daniel **Williams** former line (amt. of acreage not given).
Wts: Reuben **Searcy**.

388, 389- Mar. 9, 1772- Jacob **Gray** and wife Jane of Mecklenburg Co., N.C. to Benjamin **Ragland** of Granville Co., N.C. for 20 pds. 250 acres on south side of Little Island creek above **Davenport**'s line.
Wts: James **Cook**, Bromfield **Ridley**.

390, 391- July 18, 1770- Len Henley **Bullock**, Esq., sheriff- to Benjamin **McCulloch** of Halifax Co., N.C.- Court ordered property of Andrew **Hampton** sold to highest bidder at suit brought by John **Thompson** and Co. for debt 225 acres in Granville Co. sold to **McCulloch**.
Wts: Jesse **Benton**, Thos **Henderson**.

392, 393- July 18, 1770- Len Henley **Bullock**, sheriff, to Benjamin **McCulloch** Land of Andrew **Hampton** sold to highest bidder and **McCulloch** bought it.

395, 396- Aug. 19, 1772- Richard **Bradford** to Robert **Allison**, Sr. for 73 pds. 6 shls, 8 pence 272 acres on Low Grounds in Granville Co. at **Wilkerson**'s line.
Wts: Jonathan **Kittrell**, Robt. **Bell**.

194

397, 398- Oct. 29, 1772- Susannah **Wilson**, widow of William **Wilson**, dec'd late of same county, taylor, to John **Alston**, James **Young**, James **Morton**, Alexander **Grindley**, Andrew **Miller**, William **Littlejohn**, George **Alston**. . . merchants and co.- for 11 pds., 2 shls, 3 pence land at Thomas **Bradford**'s line on E side of Fishing creek containing 160 acres and a tract at Isaac **Arnold**'s line 100 acres- in all 260 acres.
Wts: Robert **Bell**, Arch **Heggie**.

399, 400- May 20, 1772- Robert **Harris**, sheriff, to John **Alston**, James **Young**, James **Morton**, Alexander **Grindley**, Andrew **Miller**, William **Littlejohn** and George **Alston**, merchants by suit brought by William **Martin** against William **Wilson**- Court ordered Sheriff to sell property of William **Wilson**. Above persons became buyers.
Wts: Robert **Bell**, William **Crawford**.

402, 403- Apr. 14, 1770- John **Baynes** and wife Mary to Thomas **Mutter** for 100 pds. 112 acres on N. side of Jonathan's creek at Joel **Chandler**'s corner in **Whitehead**'s line.

Wts: Haden **Pryor**, Benjamin **Jones**.

403, 404- Mar. 16, 1770- Joel **Chandler** and wife Jean to Thomas **Mutter** for 100 pds. 55 acres on N. side of Jonathan's creek at **Mutter**'s line.
Wts: Thomas **Person**, Larkn **Johnston**.

405- 406- Mar. 20, 1770- Larkin **Johnston** to Thomas **Mutter** for 500 pds. land at his own line now Joel **Chandler**'s line, containing 618 acres granted to James **Yancey** Mar. 14, 1760 signed Larkin and Mary **Johnston**.
Wts: Haden **Pryor**, Thornton **Yancey**.

407, 408- Oct. 10, 1772. Nimrod **Williams** of Bute Co., N.C. io Joseph **Linsey** for 120 pds. 420 acres on **Anderson**'s swamp at **Bullock**'s old corner George **Glover**'s, now William **Green**'s line and **Williams** own line, John **Bird** line. signed Nimrod and wife Amey **Williams**.
Wts: Francis **Williams**, William **Green**, Robert **Caller**.

409, 410- Nov. 23, 1772- Young **Miller** and Co. to Burgess **White** for 47 pds., 15 shls., 7 pence, 140 acres where Burgess **White** now lives.
Wts: Robert **Bell**, Arch **Heggie** (this is a mortgage).

411, thru 413- Jan. 8, 1772- George **Alston** from John **Blalock**, wagoner, for 290 pds., 13 shls., 8 pence- land in Granville Co. near path from **Wilkerson**'s to **Bradford**'s containing 200 acres on W side of Fishing creek and also stock-mortgage-
Wts: Stephen **Jett**, Robt. **Bell**.

414, 415- Mar. 12, 1772- George **Alston** from Edward **Bullock**, wagoner, for 50 pds. 1 shl. 5 pence for which **Bullock** is indebted to **Alston**- mortgages a wagon, 6 horses, 2 guns and sundry household goods.
Wts: Archd **Heggie**, Robert **Bell**.

416, 417- Aug. 17, 1772- Richard **Searcy** to Bailey **Flemming** for 24 pds. 87 acres on **Anderson**'s swamp at John **Flemming**s line, James **Daniel**s line to the Great Spring Branch, **Person**'s line.
Len H. **Bullock**, Phil **Hawkins**- signed Richard **Searcy** and Mary **Searcy** her husband.

417, 420- Nov. 30, 1772- **Young**, **Miller** and Co. from John **Russel** for 288 pds., 17 shls., 9 pence for which **Russel** is indebted to **Young**, **Miller** Co mortgages land on both sides of North fork of Tarr river, containing 500 acres-
Wts: Robert **Bell**, Archd **Heggie**.

421, 422- Oct. 5, 1772- Israel **Eastwood** to Thomas **Person** for 5 pds. 130 acres on branches of N. fork of Tar river being part of land taken up by **Eastwood** at **Person**'s corner in **Russel**'s line, **Shearman**'s line.
Wts: Robert **Dickins**, Sally **Callier**.

422, 423- Oct. 26, 1771- John **Rust** and wife Sarah to Thomas **Person** for 125 pds. land purchased by John **Rust** of Len Henley **Bullock** on SE side of Great Nut Bush creek near **Mitchel**'s and **Bullock**'s lines, **Gillam**'s line on **Myrick**'s line, **Robertson**'s and **Williams**' line 550 acres.
Wts: John **Person**, Kitchin **Prim**.

195

424, 425- Oct. 1, 1771- Jesse **Nevil** of Orange Co., N.C. to Thomas **Person** for 100 pds. 302 acres near **Taylor**'s creek.
Wts: Will **Kennon**, Jonas **Parker**.

426, 427- Jan. 1, 1773- William **Wharton** and wife Jane, William **Chandler** and wife Lydia, to Thomas **Person** for 20 pds. 100 acres adjoining **Person**'s line in **Daniel**'s line along **Wharton**'s line.
Wts: George **Micklejohn**, Robert **Dickins**.

428, 429- Aug. 31, 1772- Francis **Davenport** to Thomas **Person** for 200 pds. 374 acres on both sides of West fork of Tar river on **Bumpas**'s line on N. side of River by **Person**'s and **Fowler**'s lines and **Person**'s line near a place called Lows Spring.

Wts: Robert **Kennan**, Isaac **Davenport**.

429, 430- Oct. 22, 1772- James **Trevillion** of Rowan Co., N.C. to William **Cooper** of Granville Co., N.C. for 133 pds. 390 acres on both sides of **Taylor**'s road, **Hawkins**' line, Joseph **Taylor**'s line at James **Mitchel**'s corner, formerly John **Bullock**'s line.
Wts: Veazey **Husband**, John **Trevillion**, Joab **Trevillion**.

431, 432- Sept. 14, 1772- Harris **Gillam** to James **Daniel** for 130 pds. 245 acres on W side of **Anderson**'s swamp at **Glover**'s road.
Wts: William **Gillam**, Ormond **Morgan**.
Elizabeth wife of Harris **Gillam** relinquishes her dower right in land.

432, 433- Nov. 17, 1772- Alexander **Gray** of Orange Co., N.C. from Robert **Sorrel** of Granville Co., N.C. for 80 pds. for which **Sorril** is indebted to **Gray**- mortgages 200 acres being part of a larger tract which **Sorril** bought of **Gray**.
Wts: Thomas **Person**, M. **Hunt**.
Susana **Sorrel** relinquishes her dower right in land- wife of Robert **Sorrel**.

END OF BOOK I (eye)

196

Granville Co., N.C. Record of Deeds
Book- K- 1772-1775
Reuben **Searcy**, C. C.- Jesse **Benton** Register

1- Aug. 19, 1772- James **Hunt** gave to his nephew John **Hunt**, 400 acres on both sides of Great Island creek known by the name of *The Poplar Ridge Tract* adjoining James **Hunt**'s land.
Wts: none-

2- Apr. 24, 1772- George **Fegins** of Mecklenburg Co., Va. to Henry **Graves** of Granville Co., N.C. for 152 pds. 10 shls, 416 acres on both sides of Lick branch at Richard **Harris**'s, Thos. **Head**'s lines, at Henry **Graves** old line.
Wts: Richard **Head**, John [**Speak**]

3, 4- Apr. 24. 1772- George **Fegins** of Mecklenburg Co., Va. to George **Norman** of Granville Co., N. C, for 37 pds. 10 shls., 117 acres at **Graves** old line. Also spelled **Fegan**.
Wts: John **Sleap**, Richard **Head**.

4, 5- Aug. 9, 1772- James **Hester**, Lewis **Collins** and William **Kennon** to George **Bruce** for 90 pds. 387 acres on **Harrald**'s creek, south side taken up by John **Knott** and sold to Benjamin **Cook** at George **Anderson**'s.
Wts: Robert **Reid**.

6- Aug. 19, 1772- John **Stovall**, Sr. gave to his son George **Stovall** 320 acres on Grassy creek.
Wts: Henry **Graves**, Geo. **Crenshaw**.

7, 8- May 11, 1772- William **Roberts** to John **Finch** for 25 pds. 200 acres in the fork of Long Creek on Lick branch.
Wts: John **Dickerson**, Henry **Finch**.

8, 9- Aug. 19, 1772- Stephen **Merritt** to Thomas **Philpot** for 50 pds., 404 acres on N. side of Tar river on **Langston**'s line, **Washington**'s line.
Wts: James **Langston**, Benjamin **Howard**.

10, 11- Jan. 3, 1771- William **Head** and wife Mary to John **Gordon** and Co. for 75 pds. 160 acres on William **Allen**'s line to William **Allin**'s, Sr. line, including dwelling, etc.
Wts: William **Williams**.

11, 12- July 31, 1772- Isham **Malone** to Isham **Malone**, Jr. for 100 pds. 68 acres on E side of Mountain creek at James **Walker**'s line, Thomas **Person**'s and Nathaniel **Malone**'s line being the land whereon Isham **Malone**, Jr., now lives.
Wts: Luke **Landers**, Thomas **Willingham**, Daniel **Malone**.

13, 14- Jan. 19, 1773- Fennel **Marks** to Alexander **Spears** and Co, of Glasgow for 45 pds. 115 acres on head branches of **Taylor**'s Mill creek on John **White**'s line, Richard **Johnston**'s line, John **Hargrove**'s line being half the tract George **White** had of John **Buzbey**.
Wts: David **Mitchel**, John **Lynch**, Jas. **McMurry**.

14, 15- Apr. 24, 1770- Alexander **Gray** of Orange Co., N.C. to Robert **Sorrel** of Granville Co. for 75 pds. 300 acres in Granville Co., N.C. on the Nappareed creek being part of larger tract granted to Thomas **Persons** and sold to **Gray**.
Wts: James **Scarlet**, Thomas **Manning**.

15 thru 17- July 25, 1772- Humphrey **Davis** from John **Gordon** for 200 pds. for which John **Gordan** is indebted, mortgages land and slaves to John **Gordon**.
Wts: James **M Callum**, Rich **Harris**.

17 thru 19- Feb. 17, 1773- John **Pope** to Thomas **Pope** for 200 pds. 388 acres in Bute and Granville Cos. N.C. on

Cedar and Little creek called by the name of Joes creek at Joseph **Fuller**'s, Shemuel **Kerney**'s lines which is part of larger tract granted to Philemin **Bradford**, Sr. Nov. 13 1756 and sold to William **Vincent** who conveyed it to Britain **Fuller** Jr. and he to John **Pope**, Esq. and **Pope** to Thomas **Banks** and he

197
back to John **Pope**, Esq. who conveyed it to Thomas **Pope**.
Wts: James **Blackwell**, John **Champion**, Jr.

20, 21- May 20, 1771- Robert **Sorell** to Thomas **Manning** for 50 pds. 100 acres at William **Bennett**'s corner on Nappareeds creek along Zachariah **Goss**'s line on both sides of **Dun**'s creek.
Wts: Thomas **Scarlett**, Alexander **Gray**.

21, 22- Mar. 30, 1772- Benjamin **Whicker** to Thomas **Crews** for 77 pds. 10 shls, at William **Hester**'s line, James **Currin**'s line- 150 acres.
Wts: John **Whicker**, William **Hester**.

23, 24- Aug. 22, 1771- Len Henley **Bullock** to Thomas **Crews** for 37 pds. 10 shls. 150 acres on **Ward's** corner, his old line, along **Knott**'s line.
Wts: John **Peace**, John **Whicker**.

24, 25- Feb. 17, 1773- David **Howard** to Benjamin **Howard** for 5 pds. 164 acres on both sides of Hay Meadow branch.
Wts: John **Howard**, Jr., Richard **Davis**.

25 thru 27- Dec. 20, 1771- Thomas **Person** to Mathew **Duty** for 105 pds. 400 acres on both sides of Grassy creek at Robert **Pryor**'s line, **Howard**'s line along **Bridges** and **Smith**'s lines.
Wts: Thomas **Bridges**, James **Bridges**.

27, 28- Feb. 15, 1771- William **Jones** and wife Elizabeth to Thomas Welmon **Culverhouse** for 20 pds. 130 acres being all that part of land bought of Samuel **Boyd** on S side of Picture branch.
Wts: James **Dyar**, George **Wright**.

28 thru 30- July 18, 1772- John **Hawkins** of Bute Co., N.C. to Robert **Caller** for 88 pds. 496 acres on Nut Bush at **Japtey**'s line on **Caller**'s line, **Bullock**'s line.
Wts: Powell **Potts**, John **Morrison**.

30 thru 32- Mar. 23, 1772- Benjamin **Hendrick** and wife Rachel to Samuel **Pittard** for 200 pds. 360 acres at Richd **Harris**'s line, **Graves**' corner.
Wts: Samuel **Pittard**, William **Hendrick**, William **Graves**, Richd **Harris**.

32, 33- Aug. 8, 1772- John **Shermon** to Thomas **Goss** for 5 shillings, 100 acres being part of tract taken up by John **Shermon** on both sides of Stony creek, the fork of Tar river at **Eastwood**'s line, Thos **Goss**'s old line.
Wts: George **Hunt**, Thomas **Goss**, Jr.

34, 35- Jan. 24, 1774- John **Ross** and wife, Mary to James **Bullock** for 120 pds. land on both sides of **Nicholas**es' creek at line formerly Earl Granville's containing 652 acres.
Wts: Thomas **Yates**, Jeremiah **Bullock**, Joshua **Bullock**.

35, 36- Nov. 9, 1771- Robert **Dickens** to Reuben **Piles** for 150 pds. 300 acres now in possession of **Piles**, granted by Granville Nov. 27, 1760.
Wts: Thos. **Stuckey**, Jonathan **Parker**.

37, 38- May 28, 1772- Haden **Pryor** and Micajah **Bullock** to Charles **Kennon** for 200 pds. part of three surveys two of which were taken up by Thomas **Person** and one by Richard **Briggs** together with one taken up by Philip **Pryor**, deceased, on Tar river and Grassy creek on S side of Hico road at **Daniel**'s cross path along **Briggs** original line, **Kennon**'s line and **Pryor**'s original line containing in all 925 acres.
Wts: Thomas **Person**, Tabitha **Pryor-** signed by Haden **Pryor**, Anne **Pryor**, and Micajah **Bullock**.

39, 40- Feb. 19, 1772- Gillam **Harris**, Sr. to Edward **Harris** for 10 pds. 100 acres on both sides of Newlight creek at John **Bridg**(es), line which is part of land granted to Gillam **Harris** and deeded to Edwd. **Harris**.
Wts: Gillum **Harris**, Jr., Nathan **Harris**.

40, 41, 42- May 16, 1772- Jiles (Giles) **Hudspeth** Sr: to William **Hudspeth** for 30 pds. 300 acres on N. side of **Hatcher**'s Run on **Hatcher**'s creek long **Wilson** and John **Hamilton**'s lines, Giles **Hudspeth**'s line.
Wts: John **Allison**.

42, 43- May 16, 1772- Giles **Hudspeth**, Sr. to Giles **Hudspeth**, Jr. for 30 pds. 300 acres on S side of Hatches creek at **Hudspeth**'s line.
Wts: John **Allison**.

198

43, 44- Sept. 2, 1772- Moses **Juel** to Luke **Harpe** for 40 pds. on S side of Middle creek at John **Rupe**'s line, Andrew **Shapherd**'s line
Wts: Joseph **Wade**, John **Rust**.

45, 46- Nov. 18, 1772- John **Boyd** and wife Mary to John **Oliver** for 135 pds. 200 acres at dividing line between **Landers** and **Boyd** on Tar river along **Person**'s line, **Rose**'s line.

46, 47, 48- Nov. 7, 1772- John **Peace** and wife Margaret to Thomas **Banks** for 66 pds. 13 shls., 4 pence, 581 acres, whereon Thomas **Banks** now lives, being part or a larger tract to Ebenezar **Wilson** Mar. 23, 1762 who deeded it to Joseph **Peace**, Sr. who conveyed it to me, John **Peace**, on S side of along **Banks**'s line
Wts: John **Pope**.

49, 50- Nov. 19, 1772- Len Henley **Bullock** to James **Foster** of Orange Co., N.C. for 100 pds. 640 acres surveyed for Robert **Eyre**, on both sides of the N. fork of Tar river on John **Sallis**'s line formerly.
Wts: S. **Hopkins**, Joseph **Taylor**.

50 thru 52- Feb. 15, 1772- George **Brack** to Frederick **Weaver** for 7 pds. 10 shls. 50 acres at the fork of Reedy Branch.
Wts: Sherwood **Parrish**, Thomas **Rolen** (**Rowland**).

52, 53- Nov. 14, 1770- Thomas **Critcher** and Ester (Easter) his wife to William **Williams** for 1000 pds. 700 acres on Nut Bush creek at David **Mitchel**'s line.

54, 55- May 25, 1772- Thomas **Howel**, Sr. to Thomas **Howel**, Jr. for 60 pds. 140 acres on S side of Fishing creek at John **Vernor**s corner to the Virginia State line.
Wts: John **Verner**, Jereme **Frazure**.

56, 57- Jan 21, 1773- Charles **Partee** to Abraham **Potter** for 200 pds. 400 acres at the widow **Dunnavan**'s former line to **Hampton**'s creek.
Wts: Reuben **Searcy**- (signed also by Barsheba, wife of Charles **Partee**).

57 thru 59- Mar. 10, 1771- Leonard **Linsey** to Bromfield **Ridley** for 130 pds. 300 acres on N and S side of Flat creek whereon **Linsey** now lives on the old courthouse road at Richard **Clanton**'s line, formerly, **Tiners**, **Wilson**'s lines at **Ragland**'s line.
Wts: John **Williams**, Saml **Sneed**.
Sarah **Linsey**, wife of Leonard, relinquishes her dower right.

59 thru 61- Jan. 13, 1770- Thomas **Burden** to Richard **Henderson** for 30 pds. 135 acres on both side of **Anderson**'s swamp at Thomas **Person**'s line of land he purchased of William **Glover** on E side of Nut Bush creek from **Bullock**'s Mill to the Granville old court house to Samuel **Henderson**'s old line-
Wts: John **Henderson**, Evan **Ragland**.

61, 62- Aug. 22, 1771- Robert **Lanier** to Richard **Clayton** for 20 pds. 310 acres on Lick Branch.
Wts: Charles **Kennon**, R. **Harrison**, Joseph **Williams**.

62 thru 65- Jan. 9, 1773- Young **Miller** to William **Hornsby** for 29 pds. 14 shls., 2 pence, 130 acres on which **Hornsby** lives conveyed from Samuel **Kittrell** to William **Hornsby**- this is a mortgage.
Wts: Robert **Bell**, James **Currin**.

65 thru 67- Dec. 1, 1772- Young **Miller** and Co. holds trust deed or mortgage on James **Currin** for money due of 471 pds. 11 shls. 6 pence, mortgage on 400 acres, negroes. **Currin** lives on the land adjoining David **Whicker** and Benjamin **Whicker**.
Wts: Robert **Bell**, Archd. **Heggie**.

68 thru 70- Mar. 23, 1774 John **Blalock** to George **Alston** for 133 pds. 6 shls., 8 pence, 158 acres on W side of Fishing creek.
Wts: Robert **Bell**, Archd **Heggie**, James **Duff**.

71- thru 73- Feb. 23, 1773- Moses **Bonner** to Young **Miller** and Co. for 136 pds. 7 shillings, 240 acres on both sides of Nappy Reed creek whereon he now lives which he purchased of John **Kees** Dec. 29, 1766- and also a gray horse- this is a mortgage.
Wts: Robert **Bell**, James **Carrington**, John **Kittrell**.

199

74- Mar. 23, 1773- John **Robinson** and wife Mary (also spelled **Roberson**) gave to their son Robert **Roberson** (**Robinson**) 560 acres on both sides of Indian Creek, whereon Robert Now lives-
Wts: James **Mitchell** Jr, Frances **Mitchell**.

75, 76- Dec. 7, 1773- Stephen **Merrit** to Thomas **Philpot** for 20 pds. 421 acres on N. side of Tar river at **Langston**'s line to **Goss**'s corner and on **Philpot**'s line.
Wts: James **Langston**, Jesse **Holder**.

76, 77- Mar. 9, 1773- Drury **Kimball** of Bute and wife Sarah to Sampson **Wiggins** for 100 pds. 200 acres on Indian creek.
Wts: John **Bell**, Joseph **Kimball**, Charles **McLemore**.

77, 78- Sept. 26, 1773- James **McGehee** to Nathaniel **McGehee** for 40 pds. 100 acres on Little fork of **Tyler**'s creek at Nathaniel **McGehee**'s line being part of land granted to James **McGehee** March 1761.
Wts: Moses **Jewell**, John **Shapherd**, John **McGehee**.

79- May 25, 1773. John **Dacrey** of Chatham Co., N. C. to Henry Eustace **McCulloh** of same place for 23 pds. 200 acres in Granville Co., N.C. on Middle fork of Beaverdam creek bought of Henry **McCulloh** Aug. 30, 1763.
Wts: Wm. **Johnston**, Adam **Dickson**.

80, 81- Dec. 29, 1768- John **West** of Georgia to Richard **Clements** of Orange Co., N.C. for 25 pds. 200 acres on both sides of Ledge of Rocks creek.
Wts: Wm. **Burford**, Peyton **Clements**, Lucy **Smith**.

81, 82- May 1, 1773- Richard **Clemants** of Wake Co., N.C., planter to Henry Eustace **McCulloh** for 23 pds. 200 acres on both sides of Ledge of Rocks being land granted or deeded from Henry **McCulloh** to John **West** in 1763 and bought by **Clements** from him.
Wts: Jas. **Watson**, Wm. **Johnston**.

83- Oct. 9, 1772- Samuel **Lynes** (**Tynes**?) to Richard **Wilkins** for 125 pds. 200 acres on both sides of **Michael**'s creek on a branch.
Wts: Wm. **Potter**.

84, 85- Dec. 23, 1772- Thomas **Mutter** and Co., merchants of Granville Co to John **Chandler** of same place for 45 pds. 5 shls. -11 pence, 100 -acres mortgages. Land was bought of Drury **Smith** and also a cow.
Wts: Ransom **Boswell**, William **Heggie**.

85, 86- Aug. 3, 17 John **Pope**, Esq. to Thomas **Mutter** for land of Larkin **Johnston** ordered sold by court at suit

brought by James **McCarver** containing 273 acres at George **Alston**'s line, Josiah **Farmer**'s and Thomas **Mutter**'s line of land bought of Larkin **Johnston**.
Wts: John **MacDonall**, Jonathan **Knight**.

88, 89- Oct. 7, 1772 Joseph **Williams** from Nathaniel **Robinson** for 142 pds. 6 shls. 3 pence- the land whereon Nathl **Robinson** lives at William **Dodson**, Richard **Hargrove** containing 125 acres- mortgage.
Wts: John **Hunt**, Jeremiah **Williamson**.

89- July 23, 1774- Joel **Pope** to McCall **Elliot** and Co of Glasgow, merchant, for 100 pds. a green handled penknife and 2 negroes.
Wts: James **McCallum**, Anderson **Smith**.

89, 90- Oct. 10, 1772- Richard **Johnston** to William **Traylor** for 60 Pds. 220 acres at Joseph **Waldrop**'s line, **Hargrove**'s, Fennel **Marks**, Mathew **Caviness**'s lines.
Wts: William and Fennel **Marks**.

90, 91- May 4, 1771- James **Buchannan** gave to his son Crawford **Bucannon** 100 acres on Deep creek at Elisha **Paschal**'s line along John **Chadwick**'s and James **Buchannon**'s line.
Wts: James **Buchannon**, Jr., Josiah **Paschal**.

91, 92- Aug. court 1772- (registered) **John Stovall** Sr. gave to his son Josiah **Stovall** 320 acres . . at Jonathan **Knight**'s line on Grassy creek.
Wts: Henry **Graves**, Gideon **Crenshaw**.

92, 93- Aug. 3, 1772- Alexander **Dougless** (**Doughless**, **Douglas**) to Joseph **Williams** for 100 pds. 400 acres on E side of Little Island creek at lines of John **Willingham**, Thomas **Barnet**, Jesse **Harper**, Timothy **Driscol**.

200
Benjamin **Johnston**, William **Taylor** whereon Alexander **Doughlas** now lives.
Wts: Richard **Harrison**, David **Mitchel**.

93, 94- July 16, 1772- William **Kennon** to William **Bullock** and Len Henley **Bullock**- William **Kennon** gave to his daughter, the only daughter, Betsey **Kennon**, by his last wife Betsey **Kennon**, six negroes that he had from his last wife, in trust with Len Henley **Bullock** and William **Bullock** for the benefit and only use of Betsey **Kennon** daughter of my last wife Betsey **Kennon**.
Wts: John **Bullock**, Catharine **Bullock**.

94, 95- July 28, 1772- John **Oliver** and wife Fanny to John **Gordon** for 300 pds. 514 acres at lines of land of Thomas **Cobb**'s, John **Cobb**'s, **Hawkins** orphans, Robt. **Lewis**, Henry **Beckman**, Richard **Wood**.
Wts: James **McCallum**, Howel **Lewis**.

96- Feb. 17, 1773- Robert **Wallace** to Bromfield **Ridley** for 33 pds. 135 acres at Francis **Keeling**'s line, Sherwood **Sims**'s line.
Wts: Jno. **Williams**.

97- 98- Feb. 15, 1773- Timothy **Rich** of Wake Co., N.C. to John **Husketh** of Mecklenburg Co., Virginia, for 146 pds., 6 shls. 8 pence 600 acres on both sides of Beaver Dam creek granted 1766.
Wts: Robert **Reid**- signed Timothy and Mary **Rich**, his wife.

98, 99- Jan. 23, 1771- Samuel **Henderson** and wife Mary Ann to James **Williams** for 110 pds. 400 acres at Isaac **Mitchell**'s corner along **Arnold**'s line, along **Williams**' line. signed Samuel and Maryann **Henderson**.
Wts: Thos **Henderson**, Thos **Satterwhite**.

99, 100- July. 25, 1771- Arthur **Jordan** to William **Neal** of Bute Co., N.C. for 20 pds. 18 acres on **Anderson**'s swamp at Joseph **Smith**'s line, **Hob**'s line to Reedy Branch.
Wts: William St. John, William **Neal**, Jr.

100, 101- Feb. 15, 1773- Anthony **Cozart** to Edmund **Partee** (Nancy, wife of Anthony **Cozart** also signs deed) for 30 pds. 100 acres at Henry Eustace **McCulloh**'s line where it crosses the creek bought of John **Adcock** by **Cozart** and along fork of Spring creek.
Wts: Peter **Cozart**, Charles **Partee**.

102- May 26, 1772- John **Finch** to Baxter **Ragsdale** of Lunenburg Co., VA. for 60 pds. 200 acres on Tabbs creek and Long Branch at **Dickerson** corner which was deeded to John **Finch** by John **Dickerson**.
Wts: John **Dickerson**, Richard **Hight**.

103, 104- Feb. 16, 1772- Zachariah **Goss** to James **Bennet** for 20 pds. 100 acres on both sides of Nap of Reeds creek being part of land bought by Alexander **Gray**.
Wts: James **Scarlet**, William **Bennitt**.

104, 105- Jan. 14, 1773- James **Chesher** to Charles **Kennon** for 221 pds. 500 acres on both sides of Reedy creek including the saline fields at **Howard**'s, **Taylor**'s lines.
Wts: John **Lewis**, Jr., James **Brown**.

105, 106- Feb. 17, 1773- John **Champion**, Jr. and wife Keziah to James **Blackwell** for 133 pds. 6 shls. 8 pence 300 acres on both sides of Middle creek a branch of Tar river granted to Alexander **McCulloch** by Francis **Corbin**, Esq. agent, Oct. 14, 1759 and sold to Humphrey **Marshal** Mar. 7, 1762 and from Humphrey **Marshall** and wife Mary to John **Champion**.
Wts: John **Pope**, Thomas **Pope**.

107- Nov. 19, 1774- Anne **Hopkins** to George **Alston** for 20 pds. 100 acres at Malachi **Reeves** line.
Wts: Jonathan **Kittrell**, Robert **Bell**, Archd **Heggie**.

108- Jan. 2, 1775- Malachi **Reeves** (**Reves**) to George **Alston** for 170 pds. 170 acres on Tabbs creek, at William **Hicks** line.
Wts: Jonathan **Reves**, Robert **Bell**, Archd **Heggie**.

109- Jan. 16, 1773- Benjamin **Ward** of Bute Co., N.C. to Kennon **Cooper** of Granville Co., planter 50 pds. 6 shls. 8 pence 247 acres on S. side of court house prong of Sandy creek including the plantation whereon Thomas **Ballard** formerly lived. (Tabitha, wife of Benjamin **Ward**, signs deed [handwritten]).
Wts: Joseph **Ward**, Thomas **Jarrott**, Jos **Mangum**.

201

110- Jan. 13, 1773- John **Johnston** to James **Downey** for 250 pds. 369 acres on N. side of Lower fork of Grassy creek on James **Patterson**'s and Drury **Smith**'s lines.
Wts James **Daniel**, David **Knott**.

111- Mar. 30, 1772- Thomas **Crews** to Benjamin **Wicker** for 37 pds. 10 shls 150 [or is it 50] acres on **Wade**'s and **Harris**'s lines.
Wts: John **Wicker**, William **Hester**.

112- Oct. 20, 1769- James **Terry** and wife Henritta to Joseph **Winston** for 100 pds. 200 acres on NW side of Little Nut Bush creek.
Wts: Reuben **Searcy**, Benja **Goodman**.

113, 114- Aug. 14, 1772- William **Chavers** to Daniel **Hunter** for 39 pds. 326 acres on Long creek a branch of Tabbs creek at William **Roberts**' line.
Wts: Thomas **Person**, Jonathan **Davis**.

114, 115- June 15, 1772- John **Neilson** to Reuben **Morse** for 100 pds. 215 acres being part of 315 acres granted to John **Glover** Nov. 12, 1755.
Wts: Samuel **Morse**, George **Bushop**.

115, 116- Oct. 20, 1772- Isaiah **Paschal** to William **Key** for 50 pds. 250 acres on Little Deep creek at Thomas

Addason's line, John **Chadwick**'s, James **Pashcal**'s lines.
Wts: Dennis **Paschal**, Leonard **Sims**, John **Paschal**, Bartlet **Searcy**, Thomas **Key**.

116- Oct. 7, 1772- Littleton **Mapp** to Solomon **Langston** for 20 pds. 50 acres whereon **Mapp** now lives at Stephen **Merritt**'s line on Cubb creek.
Wts: James, Joseph **Langston**, Samuel **Hamrick**.

117- Sept. 16, 1770- Moses **Span** to Solomon **Langston** for 40 pds. 130 acres whereon Span now lives at **Washington**'s line on Cubb Creek.
Wts: James **Langston**, Samuel **Hamrick**.

118- Oct. 30, 1772- John **Bridges** to David **Bridges** (John of Granville) David of Pitsilvania Co., VA. for 15 pds. 350 acres on branches of Newlight creek at Gilliam **Harris**'s line being half of land granted to John **Bridges** July 25,1761.
Wts: Richard **Bridges**, John **Rains**.

119- Dec. 15, 1772- Reuben **Searcy** to John **Searcy**, Sr. for 100 pds. 320 acres on both sides of Bolings creek.
Wts: Bartlet **Searcy**, Joseph **More**.

119, 120- Dec. 15, 1772- John **Searcy** to Reuben **Searcy** for 100 pds. 136 acres on **Hampton**'s creek at Nicholas **Holstein**'s line.
Wts: Joseph **More**, Bartlet **Searcy**.

120, 121- Apr. 12, 1773- Jacob **Landers** (**Sanders**), to Joseph **Landers** for 100 pds. 200 acres on W side of Cattle branch granted to Joseph **Landers** Oct. 23, 1754.
Wts: James **Langston**, Christopher **Harris**.

121, 122- Mar. 14, 1763- Joseph **Glover** and wife Phebee to David **Mitchel** for 100 pds. 35 acres on Josiah **Mitchel**'s line, James **Mitchel**, Jr.'s.
Wts: Thomas **Lanier**.

123- July 12, 1774- Joel **Pope** to John **Baird** and Co. for 57 pds. 19 shls. 3 pence 208 acres adjoining lands of Robert **Pryor**, Drury **Smith** and a negro and cattle- mortgaged.
Wts: William **Hart**, David **Watt**.

123, 124- Mar. 27, 1773. John **Hains** of Bute Co., N.C. to John **Dickerson** for 73 pds. 17 shls. 9 pence 140 acres on Buffaloe creek at **Overton**'s line, live stock and Furniture, tobacco, crop- mortgaged.
Wts: Jno. **Peace**, Jr., John **Smith**.

125, 126- Nov. 12, 1770- John **Mask**, Sr. and wife Katherine and John **Mask** Jr. and wife Drusilla, for 170 pds. (all of them of Anson Co., N.C.) to John **Dickerson** of N.C. 200 acres adjoining Samuel **Smith**'s land at Ezekiel **Fuller**'s line on Tabbs creek.
Wts: William **Mask** Jr., James **Blackwell**, Thomas **Banks** Jr., John **Peace**, Jr.

127, 128- May 28, 1773- James **Winningham** to John **Dickerson** for 200 pds. live stock, household goods-mortgage.
Wts: Jno. **Peace**, Jr.

202

128, 129- Oct. 29, 1772- Joseph **Parks** to John **Dickerson** for 130 pds. 250 acres on N. side of Tabbs creek.
Wts: Jno. **Peace**, Jr., Richard **Hight**.

129, 130- Nov. 231 1772- Samuel **Dispain** to John **Dickerson** for 100 pds. 180 acres on both sides of Horse creek.
Wts: John **McIver**, John **Peace**, Jr.

130, 131- Apr. 20, 1774- John **Lunsford** to John **Dickerson** for 10 pds. 75 acres on Fort creek at Simon **Secras**'s line.
Wts: John **Peace**, Jr., John **McIver**.

131, 132- May 2, 1774- Luke **Landers** to Thomas **Bond** for 4 pds. 20 acres on E side of Grassy creek at William **Mathews**'s line.
Wts: William **Puryear**, Caleb **Brasfield**.

132, 133, 134- Mar. 18, 1773- George **Alston** from John **Ross** for 40 pds. 17 shls. 3 pence mortgaged 200 acres at Trading road surveyed for John **Ross** Jan. 1771 registered Book 1 pages 150, 151-
Wts: Robert **Bell**, Thomas **Critcher**.

134, 135- Dec. 21, 1773- William **Wharton** and wife Jane, and William **Chandler** and wife Lidia to Joseph **Roberts** for 24 pds., 200 acres on **Person**'s corner at Joseph **Roberts**' line.
Wts: James **Walker**, Willis **Roberts**, Jesse **Jones**.

135, 136- Nov. 24, 1773- William **Gragg** to Thomas **Williamson** for 50 pds. 400 acres on E side of Cool Spring branch at **Mitchel**'s and **Williamson**'s lines which was granted to **Gragg** Sept. 1, 1762.
Wts: John **Hunt**, Jr., Willis **Roberts**.

137- Oct. 11, 1773- Isham **Malone** to James **Walker** for 100 pds. 125 acres whereon **Malone** lives at Mountain branch which divides it from Daniel **Malone**'s land and by Nathaniel **Malone**'s line, Thomas **Person**'s line, James **Walker**'s line.
Wts: William **Head**, Thomas **Head**, Robert **Malone**.

137, 138- Nov. 16, 1773- Burges **White** to Barnet **Tatom** for 146 pds. 13 shls. 4 pence 100 acres at the old mill on Tabbs creek at **Harris**'s line on Jonathan **White**'s old corner.
Wts: Robert **Bell**, Samuel **Goodwin**, Hugh **Currin**.

139, 140- Aug. 19, 1772- John **Stanback** to Ann **Hopkins** for 35 pds. 100 acres on E side of Fishing creek at Thomas **Morris**'s line.
Wts: John **Hampton**, Michael **Wilson**.

140, 141- Oct. 27, 1768- James **Winningham** to John **Dickerson** for 70 pds. 300 acres on both sides of Cedar creek being part of tract deeded to James **Winningham** Mar. 11, 1760 floe.
Wts: none (James and Luce **Winningham** sign deed.

141, 142- Nov. 10, 1773- John **Warmoth** to William **Cockrel** for 20 pds. 60 acres on branches of Grassy creek at **Frazure**'s, **Person**'s lines whereon William **Head** lives.
Wts: Howel **Sims**, William **Head**.

[142, 143]- Apr. 25, 1774- Nathaniel **Patterson** to his son William and daughter Jane **Patterson**-To Jane **Patterson** 26 pds. left her by her grandfather John **Orce** and delivered to me by her grandmother Jane **Orce** for her, my daughter, Jane **Patterson**. I, Nathaniel **Patterson** give to my children William and Jane **Patterson** all my personal estate of negroes, stock and all furniture except two beds deeded in trust to John **Gordan**.
Wts: Ann **Butler**, Mary **Whillock**, Wm. **Vickary**.

143, 144- Oct. 22, 1773- William **Huson** to Harris **Gilliam** for 25 pds. 100 acres on both sides of Fort creek being part of larger tract granted to **Huson** on **Gilliam**'s and **Rust**'s lines.
Wts: Wm. **Nailing**, James **Kelly**.

144- May 3, 1774- Richard **Henderson** to James **Walker** for 80 pds. 525 acres on branches of Grassy creek at James **Walker**'s, Robert **Beasley**'s and by land not yet taken up.
Wts: Thos. **Satterwhite**, Daniel **Malone**.

203

145- Mar. 15, 1774- Solomon **Fuller**, Sr. to Jones **Fuller** for 20 pds. 175 acres on middle fork of New Light creek.
Wts: John **Bridges**, Israel **Fuller**.

145, 146- Dec. 17, 1772- George Lane **Moore** to Roger **Phillips** for 50 pds. 100 acres on Nappareed creek.

Wts: George **Wright**, John **Curry**.

146, 147- Feb. 25, 1773- Anthony **Peelar** to Jacob **Slaughter** for 111 pds. 150 acres near **Meadows** on the old line. Wts: James **Langston**, Jacob **Landess**.

147, 148- May 3, 1774- William **Corder** to John **Corder** for 20 shillings 150 acres on S side of Tarr river. Wts: Ellis **Drewry**, Richard **Brinkley**.

148, 149- July 25, 1774- George **Alston**, attorney, for John **Alston**, James **Young**, James **Morton**, Alexander **Grindley** of Glasgow, Great Britain and William **Littlejohn** and Andrew **Millar** of Halifax Co., N.C.- to- James **Critcher** of Granville Co., N.C. for 1000 pds. 800 acres in Granville Co. on both sides of Fishing creek at line formerly Jonathan **White**'s at John **Blaylock**s line at line formerly **Benton**'s, **Ferguson**'s line.
Wts: Robert **Bell**, Archd **Heggie**.

150- 151- May 6, 1771- James **Young**, merchant, of Glasgow, Great Britain to Nathaniel **Snipes** of Granville Co., N.C. for 56 pds. 5 shls. 100 acres on S side of Fishing creek at mouth of Spring branch.
Wts: Andw **Miller**, Alexander **McHarg**.

151, 152- Sept. 28, 1772- Vincent **Bodine** and wife Phebe of Bute Co., N.C. to Samuel **Morse** of Granville Co., N. for 100 pds. 100 acres on both sides of Crooked creek.
Wts: David **Mitchel**, Joseph **Williams**.

152, 153- Sept. 28, 1772- Vincent **Bodine** and wife Phebe of Bute Co. to Samuel **Morse** for 100 pds. 100 acres on Nut Bush creek at Samuel **Denton**'s line.
Wts: David **Mitchel**, Joseph **Williams**.

153, 154- July 15 1773- Edward **Stabler** of Petersburg, VA. to James **Bullock** of Granville Co., N. C.- John **Ross** mortgages to Edward **Stabler** for 103 pds. 8 shld. 11 pence, certain land July 6, 1765, containing 650 acres to secure the debt to **Stabler**. James **Bullock** paid to **Stabler** for **John Ross**, 101 pds. 9 shls. 5 pence and **Stabler** deeded the 650 acres to James **Bullock**. . .
Wts: Jas. **Martin**, Joseph **Baxter**, Zebulon **Veazey**.

154, 155- Oct. 18, 1773- Joseph **Winston** to James **Mitchel** for 20 pds. 11 acres on Nut Bush creek and 10 and 3/4ths acres on Low Grounds of **Mathews** creek branch.
Wts: Thos **Satterwhite**, David **Mitchel**.

155, 156- Feb. 18, 1773- Israel **Eastwood** and wife Mary to Jeremiah **Mize** for 92 pds. 6. shls. 8 pence 277 acres on S side of Tar river at mouth of Reedy branch-
Wts: Reuben **Searcy**, Thos **Harris**.

156, 157- June 6, 1771- John **Alston**, Robert **Carmichael** and James **Young** merchants of Glasgow, Great Britain, co-partners in the Company of James **Young** and Co. to Ransom **Boswell** of Granville Co., N, C. the [sum of current Money of Virginia] for 65 acres in Granville Co. on S side of Jonathan's creek. [and registered in the county of Halifax]
Wts: Andrew **Miller**, Alexander **Macharg**.

158, 159- . . 1771- John **Alston**, James **Young**, James **Morton** and Alexander **Grindley**, merchants of Glasgow, G. B. co-partners in **Young**, **Miller** and Co- to Ransom **Boswell** of Granville Co., N. C. for . . pds. 150 acres on N side of Jonathan's creek, both sides of Mountain fork at **Williams** and Jeremiah **Clayton**'s line.
Wts: Henry L. **Martin**, Alexander **Macharg**.

160- Mar. 1, 1773- Jeremiah **Mize** to John **Mize** for 40 pds. 177 acres on S side of Tar river on a small branch.
Wts: John **Stone**, Samuel **Pitman**, James **Langston**.

204

160, 161- May 13, 1773- John **Searcy**, Sr. to William Hargraves **Searcy** and his wife Phebe for 50 pds. 160 acres on Tar river.
Wts: Wm. **Reardon**, Saml **Hopkins**, Jr., Richard **Taylor**.

161, 162- Dec. 10, 1772- Thomas **Head** and wife Elizabeth to William **Graves** for 50 pds. 150 acres at Henry **Graves** corner.
Wts: Richard **Head**, John **Spea[p]**, James **Hed**.

162, 163- May 4, 1773- Joseph **Kimball** and wife Sarah of Bute Co. to James **Harrison** of Surry Co., N.C. for 150 pds. 300 acres in **Roberson**'s line on East side of Indian Creek at **Eaton**'s line, Drury **Kimball**'s line-
Wts: Phil **Hawkins**, Jr., Drury **Kimball**.

164,- Apr. 23, 1773- John **Gordon** and wife Ann to James **Hunt** for 300 pds. 500 acres whereon John **Oliver** formerly lived at lines of Lewis **Parkman**, **Cobb** and others.
Wts: Wm. **Cocke**, Anderson **Smith**.

165, 166- Nov. 19, 1773- William **Mathews** to Thomas **Bond** for 40 pds. 140 acres on both sides of Grassy creek at Thomas **Person**'s line, Charles **Spaulding**'s line, Wm. **Mathew**, Thos **Bond**'s, **Daniel**'s line.
Wts: Luke **Landers**, John **Landers** (or **Sanders**?)

166, 167- July 30, 1774- John **Williams** to Samuel **Morse** for 5 pds. 15 acres on both sides of Flat creek where **Williams** and **Morse**'s lines cross.

167, 168- Nov. 24, 1773- William **Craig** to James **Hunt** for 265 pds. 1144 acres at **Amis's** line.
Wts: John **Hunt**, John **Hunt**, Jr.

168, 169- Apr. 17, 1772- Samuel **Kittrell** and wife Katherine to William **Floyd** for 25 pds. land at Samuel **Kittrell**'s line.
Wts: Richard **Rathel**, Wm. **Hornsbey**.

169, 170- Jan. 15, 1774- Thomas Welmon **Culverhouse** to Benjamin **Bonner** for 40 pds. 555 acres held by Michael **Wilson** by deed from Henry **McCulloh** July 11, 1763- on S side of Picter branch at James **Boyd**'s line, containing 130 acres deeded from William **Jones**, Sr.
Wts: James **Dyer**, John **Ross**, Wm. **Jones**.

170, 171- Nov. 4, 1768- Micajah **Crenshaw** to William **Mathews** for 20 pds. 140 acres on both sides of Grassy creek in James **Downey**'s line., being land whereon **Mathews** lives.
Wts: Luke **Landers**, Rachel **Landers**.

172, 173- Dec. 17, 1772- John **Penn,** of King and Queen Co., VA. from James **Hunt** and wife Sarah, John **Hunt** and wife Frances of Granville Co., N.C. for 1200 pds. 1602 acres, being all land owned by them in Granville Co., N.C. on both sides of Great Island creek at **Person**'s line, Rowland **Terry**'s line, Absalom **Davis**'s line, **Vickerey**'s line, Lewis **Collins** line, Joseph **Taylor**'s line, Sherwood **Harris**'s line, James Henderson's at John **Taylor**'s line.
Wts: M. **Hunt**, Jno. **Taylor**, Wm. **Taylor**, Saml **Hopkins**, Jr.

173, 174- Sept. 7, 1768- William **Jones** to Richard **Foster** for 24 pds. 150 acres which is part of tract granted to **Jones** Nov. 29, 1760 on Franks creek at **Jones**'s back line.
Wts: James **Caudle**, Peter **Nowland**.

174- Feb. 1774- James **McGehee** to Joseph **McGehee**, for 40 pds. 125 acres on N. side of **Tyler**'s creek to Winfield **Rights** line, Nathan **McGehee**'s.
Wts: Thomas **Pullen**, Benjamin **McGehee**.

175- June 5, 1773- John **Cozart** to James **Cozart** for 66 pds. 100 acre in **Thompson**'s line at Persimmon branch.
Wts: Peter and Anthony **Cozart**.

175, 176- Nov. 10, 1773- Jeremiah **Lewis** to Phillip **Lewis** for 100 pds. 320 acres on both sides of **Shelton**'s creek adjoining Thos. **Person**'s at Jacob **Slaughter**'s line.
Wts: Chas. **Kennon**, Thomas **Lewis**.

176, 177,- Oct. 25, 1774- Thomas **Rudd** of Mecklinburg Co., VA. to John William **Graves** for 50 pds. 296 acres on Rattle Snake creek and N. side of Grassy creek granted to Samuel **Rudd**.

Wts: Lar **Johnton**, Gideon **Crenshaw**, Isaac **White**, Daniel **Chandler**.

205

178- Nov. 3, 1774- James **Bridges** and wife Lidda to Thomas **Person** for 200 pds. 600 acres on both sides of Middle fork of Grassy creek at **Smith**'s corner, **Simmons**' line, **Dutie**'s line.
Wts: Thomas **Bridges**, Robert **Dickens**.

178, 179- Oct. 31, 1774- Benjamin **Whicker** to Joseph **Wood** of Northampton Co., N.C. for 150 pds. 319 acres on a branch of Fishing creek at **Harris**'s line and adjoining **Bullock**'s and **Sneed**'s lands granted July 24, 1761.
Wts: Benjamin **Thomas**, John Smith **Hunt**.
Charity **Whicker**, wife of Benjamin, relinquishes dower right.

180- Aug. 1, 1774- Thomas **Barnett** and wife Sarahcrosha, to Jesse **Barnett** [for 42 pds., 10 shls., VA money] 128 acres on W side of Little Island creek being part of Thomas **Barnett** land adjoining John **Walker**'s, Daniel **Clayton**'s lines to Hogpen branch.

181- July 9, 1774- Thomas **Leach** to John **Hargrove** for 100 pds. 130 acres on N. side of Nut Bush creek along **Sims**'s line and on **Hargrove**'s line being the land whereon Richard **Bullock** lived and willed to his son Nathaniel **Bullock** who sold it to Thomas **Leach**.
Wts: Richd **Wilkins**, Len H. **Bullock**.

182- Nov. 2, 1774- John **Hogan** to Nathaniel **Snipes** for fifty pounds 200 acres on **Hatcher**'s run and **Weldon**'s line.
Wts: Jesse **Benton**, Wm. **Wilson**.
Kezia, wife of John **Hogan** relinquishes her dower right.

183- Sept. 14, 1774- Robert **Allison** to Richard **Foster** for 35 pds. 150 acres being part of tract granted to William **Jones** Nov. 29, 1760 on Franks creek.
Wts: Paul **Nowland**, James **Hopper**.
Rachel, wife of Robert **Allison** relinquishes her dower right.

184- June 3, 1772- Charles **Kennon** to William **Kennon** for 300 pds. 925 acres on Tar river being part of three different tracts, two taken up by Thomas **Person** and one by Richard **Briggs** and including that taken up by Phillip **Pryor**, deceased, on S side of Hico road near **Daniel**'s's cross path at lines of land belonging to **Briggs**, **Kennon**, **Pryor** and **Daniel**'s.
Wts: Thomas **Person**.

185- May 6, 1774- Richard **Jones**, Sr. to Ephraim **Jones** for 30 pds. 100 acres on S side of Tar river on **Rust**'s line, Nevills and **Cooper**'s lines which land was bought of Pomphret **Edwards**.
Wts: Joseph **Hill**, John **Simmons**.

185, 186- Nov. 1, 1774- John **Whitlow** to Bromfield **Ridley** for 60 pds. 190 acres on N. and S sides of Flatt creek on Young **McLemore's** [old] line.
Wts: Joseph **Taylor**.
(Catherine, wife of **Whitlow** relinquishes her dower.

187- May 2, 1774- John **Hampton** to Robert **Wallace** for 60 pds. 200 acres near the Trading path at John **Ross**'s line.
Wts: Thos. **Harris**, Ephraim **Hampton**.

188- May 22, 1774- William **Jones** to **Dickens** and **Parker**, merchants of Orange Co., N.C. for 180 pds. 300 acres on S side of Indian Field creek on **Person**'s and **Harris**'s lines.
Wts: Geo. **Alston**, James **Langston**, John **Oliver**.

188, 189- July 1, 1769- John **Davis** to Drury **Smith** of Mecklinburg Co., VA. for 135 pds. 208 acres on NW side of Grassy creek at King's line.
Wts: Haden **Pryor**, Memucan **Hunt**.

189, 190- Feb. 3, 1773- John **Craft** to Reuben **Moss** for 100 pds. 135 acres and 241 acres- the 135 acres on S side of Nut Bush creek on Spring branch to the old trading path and the 241 acres at Vincent **Bodine**'s line.
Wts: Thos. **Satterwhite**, Len H. **Bullock**.
Elizabeth, wife of John **Craft** relinquishes dower right.

190, 191- Nov. 1, 1774- Howel **Lewis** to John **Lewis** (Mountain) of Halifax Co., VA. for 2000 pds. 2311 acres in Granville Co, on Grassy creek where Howell **Lewis** now lives and adjoining land of estate of Phillip **Taylor** deceased, **Person**'s tract known as *Mountain Tract*, and of John **Cobb**, **Hawkins** and James **Johnston** and the proprietor's land.
Wts: Robert **Lewis**, Esq., Charles **Kennon**.

206

192- Jan. 26, 1774- Samuel **Denton** and wife Elizabeth to William **Williams** for 100 pds. 135 acres on E side of Great Nut Bush creek at John **Craft**'s line.
Wts: John **Hunt**, Merryman **Barnes**.

193- Oct. 6, 1774- William **Fowler** to Thomas **Fowler** for 60 pds. 305 acres on branches of Tar river being part of land granted to Richard **Fowler**, Sr. **Davenport**'s line.
Wts: Littleton **Mapp**, John **Cragg**.

194- Feb. 23, 1774- William **Allen**, shoe leather, and Mary his wife to McCall **Elliott** and Co. for 47 pds. 200 acres being part of tract belong that belonged to James **Smith** at **Stovall**'s line, **Bearden**'s and Robt. **Hutchens**.
Wts: Robert **Thorn**, Henderson **Smith**, James **McCallum**.

195, 196- Apr. 24, 1773- William **Allen**, Jr. to John **Gordon** and Co.- mortgage stock and furniture.
Wts: Robert **Thorn**, John **Morgan**.

196- May 10, 1774- Peter **Nowland** to John **Oliver** for 50 pds. 62 1/4 acres on Tar river at Isham **Caudle**'s line.
Wts: Geo. **Alston**, Robert **Bell**, Reuben **Searcy**.

197- July 29, 1774- Isaiah **Phipps** to William **Jacob** for 50 pds. 100 acres on S side of Mill creek down the Mill race to the creek.
Wts: Saml **Harris**, Sherwood **Harris**.

197, 198- July 29, 1774- Isaiah **Phipps** to Robert **Russel** for 50 pds. 100 acres in Granville Co. on S side of creek.
Wts: Wm. **Reardon**, Joseph **Moore**.

198, 199- Aug. 3, 1774- Jesse **Benton** to Len Henley **Bullock** for 1500 pds. the land in Granville Co. whereon the court house now stands in the town of Oxford containing 1000 acres.
Wts: Richd **Benneham**, Alexander **Munn**, Duncan **Campbell**.

199, 200- July 29, 1774- William **Jacob** to Isaiah **Phipps** for 50 pds. 100 acres on N. side of Mill creek to the mill race and down the creek.
Wts: Sherwood **Harris**, Reuben **Searcy**, Saml **Harris**.

200, 201- Jan. 22, 1771- Benjamin **Hardy** of Johnston Co., N. C. esq, to Jesse **Benton** of Granville Co., N.C. for 1200 pds. 1000 acres in Granville Co, known by the name of Oxford whereon the county court house now stands.
Wts: James **Moore**, John **Dickerson**.

201, 202- Jan. 13, 1772- Robert **Williams** of Bute Co., N.C. to Simon **Williams** for 60 pds. 160 acres on N. side of **Anderson** Swamp being part of land granted to John **Bird** May 6, 1757 at William **Brown**'s line, Joseph **Linsies**, Robert **Williams**, Jr.'s line (signed by Robert and Anne **Williams**).
Wts: William **Darnall**, James **Baskett**.

202, 203- Dec. 1, 1772- Andrew **Ingrim** of Cumberland Co., N.C. to William **Nailing** of Granville Co., N.C. for 15 pds. 100 acres being part of a tract granted to Robert **Priddy**, deceased and left by Will to his granddaughter now wife of Andrew **Ingrim**.
Wts: James **Kelly**, John **Shepard**.

203- July 27, 1774- Valentine **White** to Zacharias **Higgs** for 50 pds. 350 acres on the north side of Tabbs creek including all the land on the north side of the creek.
Wts: Jno. **Peace**, Jr.

204- Jan. 21, 1771- Jesse **Benton** executor of Samuel **Benton**, deceased, to Benjamin **Hardy** of Johnston Co., N.C. for 1200 pds. 1000 acres.
Wts: James **Moore**, John **Dickerson**.

205- Jan. 17, 1771- John **West** and wife Mary of Bute Co., N.C. to James **Stark** of Granville Co., N. C, for 55 pd. 152 acres on Nut Bush creek on Great Branch along Thomas **Wiggins** line (signed John and Mary **West**).
Wts: Saml **Denton**, Miles **Williams**.

206- Aug. 14, 1774- Nathaniel **Snipes** to William **Douglass** for 50 pds. 100 acres on S side of Fishing creek at the mouth of Spring branch at the old line.
Wts: Jesse **Benton**, Daniel **Donnerly**.
Pleasant, wife of Nathaniel **Snipes** relinquishes her dower right.

207

207- Apr. 16, 1774- Peter **Vincent** to Abe **Mayfield** for 50 pds. 161 acres, on Fort creek at Simon **Sacras**'s line by the old original line at William **Champion**'s line by the original line.
Wts: Simon **Sacra**, William **Champion** (signed Peter and Judith **Vincent**.

208- Dec. 4, 1772. James **Pucket** and wife Martha to Harris **Gilliam** for 45 pds. 200 acres on both sides of Fort creek on the north side at a ridge. (Signed by James and Martha **Pucket**.
Wts: John **Rust**.

208, 209- Oct. 7, 1772- Samuel **Hambrick** of Orange Co., N.C. to Littleton **Mapp** of Granville Co. for 135 pds. 450 acres on Cubb creek of Tar river to the original line.
Wts: James **Langston**, Solomon and Joseph **Langston**.

209, 210- May 29, 1774- Benjamin **Wade** to McCall Elliot and Co. of Glasgow for 38 pds. mortgages a negro wench named Sucky about 13 yrs old.
Wts: Anderson **Smith**, James **McCallum**.

211- Apr. 3, 1773- Thomas **Manner** to James **Veazy** of Orange Co., N.C. for 35 pds. 101 acres on west side of Nap of Reed creek at James **Bennet**'s corner, William **Bennet**'s line.
Wts: James **Scarlet**, James **Bennet**.

212- Oct, 16, 1773- George **Tilman** to William **Bowdown** for 10 pds. 70 acres on Ruin creek and Crooked Run.
Wts: Turner **Jordan**, Travis **Bowdon** (Goodith, wife of George **Tilman** relinquishes her dower right in land.

213- Feb. 22, 1773- Ezekiel **Hampton** to Samuel **Adams** for 100 pds. 200 acres which was deeded to him by **Addonis** on Wm. **Jones**'s line.
Wts: John **Fullilove**, Abner **Tatom**, Abel **Tatom**, Luke Carrol.
Jane, wife of Ezekiel **Hampton**, relinquishes her dower right.

214- Sept. 7, 1768- William **Jones** to Littleton **Mapp** for 55 pds. 200 acres being part of tract granted to **Jones** Nov. 9, 1760 from Granville at **Ross**'s line (**Rose**'s) on Franks creek at **Jones**'s back line, **Green**'s line.
Wts: Peter **Nowland**, James **Caudill**.

215- Aug. 2, 1774- Miles **Williams** of Wake Co., N.C. to Frederic **Wiggins** of Granville Co. for 100 pds. 151 acres on both, sides of Indian creek on **Robinson**'s line, Reuben **Morse**'s line on corner of **Williams**'s and Evan **Ragland**'s lines.
Wts: none.

216- Mar. 14, 1774- Richard **Henderson** to Bartlet **Searcy** for 39 pds. 38 acres on NutBush creek on **Searcy**'s branch.

Wts: Thos. **Satterwhite**.

216, 217 [blank left for date] 1774- George **Tilman** to Samuel **Morse** for 60 pds. 10 shillings 200 acres at Lend **Linsey**'s corner to **Vanlandingham's** corner.
Wts: none ([Goodith], wife of George **Tilman**, relinquishes her dower.

217, 218- July 30, 1774- John **Bolin** to Jacob **Cozart** for 50 pds. 200 acres on a branch of Nap of Reeds creek.
Wts: Joseph **Manggum**, James **Langston**.

218, 219- Nov. 4, 1773- Richard **Clanton** to Bromfield **Ridley** for 160 pds. 489 acres on the south side of Flat creek whereon, **Clanton** now lives at Leonard **Linsey**'s corner, on **McLemore**'s line.
Wts: John **Keeling**, David **Clanton**.
Susanna wife of Richard **Clanton** relinquishes her dower right.

219, 220- Oct. 8, 1773- John **Taylor**, Jr. paid to James **Henderson** and wife Ann, 140 pds. 200 acres(?) on John **Taylor**'s line.
Wts: John, William, Joseph **Taylor**.

220, 221- Jan. 15, 1772- William **Brown** to Simon **Williams** for 65 pds. 120 acres on **Anderson**'s swamp at Joseph **Linsey**'s line.
Wts: William **Brown**, Jr., Nathan **Sims**.
Signed by William and Marget **Brown**.

221, 222- Apr. 3, 1773- James **Scarlet** of Orange Co., N, C. to James **Veazey** of Orange Co., N.C. for 65 pds. 94 acres on E side of Nap of Reed creek.
Wts: James **Bennitt**, Thomas **Manning**.

208

222, 223- Jan. 25, 1774- Ansil **Parish** (**Parrish**) and wife Elizabeth to Thomas **Goodwin** for 130 pds. 200 acres on **Anderson** Swamp at **Eaton**'s line, Thos. **Parrish**'s line, Drury **Kimball**'s.
Wts: Mathew **Goodwin**, Elijah **Parrish**, Older **Neal**.

223, 224- May 11, 1774- John **Hawkins** of Bute Co., N.C. to Duncan **Campbell** and Co., merchants, of Granville Co., N.C. for 50 pds. 100 acres formerly belonging to Christopher **Johnston** on S side of Little Ruing creek at mouth of Great Branch to Brissiah **Parrish**'s line.
Wts: Len Henley **Bullock**, Robert **Reid**.

224, 225- Jan. 27, 1774- Robert **Harris** to Thomas **Harris** for 100 pds. 150 acres in Granville Co., N.C.
Wts: Sherwood **Harris**, Turner **Harris**.

225, 226- Feb. 4, 1775- Samuel **Pittard** and wife Mary to Lataney Mountague for 100 pds. 180 acres in Wm. **Graves**'s line on N. side of Lick branch.
Wts: John **Young**, Humphrey **Davis**, Jacob **Mitchell**, Samuel **Pittard**, Jr., Samuel **Smith**- -Mary, wife of Samuel **Pittard** relinquishes her dower right.

227, 228- Nov. 20, 1773- Howell **Moss** to Vinkler **Jones**. for 88 pds. 138 acres in the head of Little Island creek at Joseph **Davenport**'s line.
Wts: David **Mitchel**, Joseph **Williams**.

228, 229- Jan. 23, 1773- William **Traylor** to Daniel **Williams** for 50 pds. 220 acres which is land **Traylor** purchased of Richd **Johnston** and bounded by land of Fennl **Marks**, William **Sprunt**, Will **Kinnon**, Joseph **Waldrop** and John **Hargrove**.
Wts: Zach **Bullock**, Fennel **Marks**.

229, 230- Jan. 6, 1775- John **Baynes** and wife Mary to Thomas **Muller** for 150 pds. 228 acres on S fork of Mountain Fork of Jonathan's creek on Jas. **Yancey**'s Jr.,'s line, at Saml **Whitehead**'s line.
Wts: Hugh **Galt**, Danl **Grant**.

231, 232- Jan. 27, 1775- Charles **Williams** to John **Williams** for 15 pds. 150 acres on N. side of Ruin creek at John **Williams**'s line which is the 150 acres sold by Charles **Williams** to William **Ford** who held a bond for same and **Ford** assigned to Clement **Hancock** who assigned to John **Williams**-
Wts: Bromfield **Ridley**, William **Campbell**.

232, 233- May 14, 1774- Mathew **Cabiness** of Mecklinburg Co., Va. to John **Collins** of Halifax Co., Va. for 55 pds. 205 acres in Granville Co., N.C. between land of Thomas **Banks**, John **Hargrove**, Daniel **Williams** at county line on branches of **Taylor'**s Mill creek.
Wts: Edmund **Taylor**, Thomas **Brown**, Sr., Thomas **Brown**.

233, 234- Dec. 17, 1772- Thomas **Lanier** to John **Williams** for 310 pds. 305 acres on both sides of Hico road on branches of Nut Bush creek and Little Island creek known as ***Lanier'**s Ordinary Lands*, along Vinkler **Jones**'s line, William **Potter**'s line, at line of land formerly property of Josiah **Mitchel**, and is same land, excepting 5 acres, heretofore sold to **Williams** by **Lanier** which David **Mitchel** sold to **Lanier** Apr. 22, 1763- which was then called *Daugherty's Lott*.
Wts: Daniel **Williams**.

234, 235- Nov. 10, 1774- David **Daniel** to William **Bagley** (**Bagly**) for 20 pds. 237 acres at Phillip **Burford**'s line.
Wts: Nathaniel **Peebles**, Henry **Bagley**, Thos. **Davis**.

235, 236- Feb. 4, 1775- Edmund **Taylor** of Mecklenburg Co., Va. gave to his son Richard **Taylor**, 1,820 acres in Granville Co., N.C. which is the land I purchased of Mrs. Elizabeth **Kennon** for 600 acres and the land I purchased of Robert **Gilliam** of 1220 acres adjoining each other.
Wts: Joseph **Taylor**, Thomas **Beech**.

236, 237- Jan. 6, 1775- Thomas **Mutter** and Co., merchants, to Thomas for 150 pds. 250 acres at line of James **Yancey**, Sr. which was conveyed by deed of trust from John **Baynes** to Thomas **Mutter** and Co.- Jan. 22, 1772.
Wts: Thornton **Yancey**, Hugh **Galt**.

209

237, 238- Oct. 3, 1774- Richard **Harris** and wife Priscilla (Preciller) to John **Young** for 256 pds. 10 shls. 342 acres on both sides of Spewmarro creek whereon **Harris** now lives and holds by deeds from Phillemon **Hawkins** and Jonathan **Knight** on Ridge path at **Young**'s line, Drury and William **Allen**'s lines, Henry **Graves**'s line, on Lick branch at Samuel **Pittard**'s line and along Samuel **Smith**'s line, to Plum Tree branch in Humphrey **Davis**' line and down to McCall Elliot and Co.'s line, Jonathan **Knight**'s line.
Wts: Wm. **Webb**, Benjamin **Beardon**, Richard **Harris**.

239- Feb. 6, 1775- Christopher **Harris** and wife Caty to George **Harris** for 105 pds. 144 ½ acres at John **Tatom**'s line.
Wts: none.

240- Feb. 7, 1775- James **Downey** to Josiah **Daniel** of Albemarle Co., Va. for 300 pds. 520 acres on both sides of Grassy creek to mouth of Hay Meadow branch.
Wts: Chesley **Daniel**, James **Daniel**.

241- Feb. 8, 1775- James **Willis** to John **Hogan** for 125 pds. 150 acres on **Hogan**'s line along **Smith**'s and **Benton**'s lines to Spring Branch down Reedy Branch to beginning (Elizabeth, wife of James **Willis**, relinquished.
Wts: Wm. **Watson**, Dudley **Jeter** (her dower right.

242- Nov. 3, 1774- John **Layton** and wife Jeaney to Drury **Smith** of Mecklenburg Co., Va. for 30 pds. 100 acres in Granville Co. on **Smith**'s line and **Hunt**'s line. Signed John and Jeaney **Layton**.
Wts: Anderson **Smith**, Claud **Muirhead**.

243- Jan. 24, 1775- Julius **King** to James **Dyar** for 41 pds., 10 shs. 120 acres on both sides of Ledge of Rock creek at edge of a pond and on Thomas **Yates**es line, being part of tract purchased by George **Miller** from Henry **McCulloch** and sold to Julius **King**.
Wts: George **Wright**, Roger **Phillips** (wife of **King** relinquishes her dower.

244- Jan. 31, 1775- Henery **Greaves** (Henry **Graves**) to his son Lewis **Yancey**, a gift of 227 acres that Lewis **Yancey** lives at Lovat **Gates** line to Lick branch on Henry **Graves**' line.

245, 246- Dec. 29, 1774- Richard **Henderson** to Bartlet **Searcy** for 40 shillings 2 1/4 acres on Nut Bush creek at Searcy's line.
Wts: Nathaniel **Harris**.

246, 247- Jan. 7, 1774- Michael **Wilson** to Thomas Welmon **Culverhouse** of Orange Co., N.C. for 100 pds. 225 acres on both sides of Picter branch in Granville Co. (signed by Michael and Margaret **Wilson**).
Wts: John **Ross**, James **Dyar**, William **Jones**.

247- Feb. 1, 1775- Jeremiah **Mize** to Howel **Mize** for 5 shls. 100 acres on S side of Tar river and mouth of Reedy Branch.
Wts: Jesse **Meadows**, Mary **Justis**.

248, 249- Feb. 8, 1775- Micajah **Bullock** to McCall **Elliott** and Co. of same county and State, for 58 pds. 3 shls. 4 pence- mortgages a negro wench named **Rose** and a man's hat.
Wts: James **McCallum**, Robert **Kennon**, Jonath **Parker**, Jr.

249, 250- Feb. 8, 1775- Henry **Lyne** from William **Kennon** for 400 pds. paid by Henry **Lyne**, two tracts of land in Granville Co.- 530 acres bought of Robert **Gilliam** by **Kennon** Nov. 11, 1769 and 275 acres bought of William **Potter** Oct. 17, 1770 and together containing 805 acres.

250, 251- Jan. 17, 1775- William **Cooper** to Ebenezar **McHarg**, factor for Alexander Donald and Co., merchants in Glasgow, Great Britain for 44 pds. 176 acres on Joseph **Taylor**'s line, James **Mitchell**'s, Reuben **Piles** line.
Wts: Edmund **Taylor**, Noah **Dortch**, Wm. **Brown**.

251, 252- Nov. 22, 1774- Simon **Williams** to Benjamin **Thomas** for 38 pds. 100 acres on **Anderson**'s swamp at Robert **Williams**'s line.
Wts: Samuel **Hammond**, Job **Hammond**.

252, 253- Oct. 11, 1770- Edmund **Taylor**, William **Kennon** and Charles **Kennon** to John **Keeling** for 175 pds. 125 acres at David **Mitchel**'s line, formerly and on John **Williams**' line, Joseph **Glover**'s line to branch of Island creek.
Wts: Will **Potter**, Stephen **Wilson**.

210

254, 255- May 14, 1774- Thomas **Bradford** and wife Mary to Thomas **Banks**, for 58 pds., 16 shillings 490 acres adjoining land **Banks** lives on being on both sides of Quicksand creek granted to Philemon **Bradford** by Lord Granville Aug. 1762.
Wts: Jones **Fuller**, John Bridges.

255, 256- Jan. 7, 1775- William **Cooper** to James **Mitchel** for 18 pds. 6 shls. 3 pence, 73 ¼ acres in James **Mitchel**'s line, Reuben **Pyles**' line.
Wts: Wm A **Potter**, David **Mitchel**, John **Hunt**.

256, 257- Dec. 17, 1772- James **Butler** to Roland **Gooch** of Mecklenburg Co., Va. for 50 pds. 100 acres on E side of **Howlet**'s creek, a branch of Island creek to Zacheriah **Hester**'s line.
Wts: James **Terry**, John **Minter**, William **Terry**.
signed by James and Winafred **Butler**.

257, 258- Apr. 19, 1773- William **Crag** to Roland **Gooch** 66 pds. 13 shls 8 pence- 234 acres on both sides of **Howlet**'s creek at **Harris**'s line on **Easter**'s line, 25, being half of tract Henry **Melton**, Sr. took up from Granville June 25, 1761 and also being the land Benjamin **Whicker** lived on.
Wts: Jno. **Minter**, William **Terry**, Obadiah **Clement**.

258, 259- Feb. 27, 1775- Thomas **Person** to William **Ford** for 50 pds. 100 acres on **Aaron**'s creek bought by **Person** from Augustine **Bates**.

Wts: Memucan **Hunt**

259, 260- Oct. 15, 1774- Carter **Partee** and Edmund **Partee** to Abraham **Potter** for 100 pds. 200 acres being remaining part of 625 acres **Potter** purchased, of Charles **Partee** on N. side of **Hampton**'s creek.
Wts: Benja **Partee**, Peter **Akin**.
signed by Edmd., Chas., Barshaba **Partee**.

260, 261- Oct. 23, 1773- John **Cozart** to George **Thompson** for 30 pds. 10 shls. 30 1/2 acres at a branch in **McCulloch**'s line.
Wts: Reuben **Searcy**, William **Jones**.

261, 262- Oct, 18, 1773- Joseph **Fletcher** to William **Bowden** for 10 pds. 50 acres at John **Craft**'s line, **Wiggins**' line.
Wts: Alexa **Muirhead**, Chas. **Galbreath**, John **Craft**.

262, 263- July 25, 1773- Francis **Kinner** to **Dickens** and **Parker**, merchants of Orange Co., N.C. for 106 pds. 13 shls. 9 pence mortgages 75 acres in Granville Co., N. C. part of land formerly belonging to **John Cragg**, also crop on land, furniture, household goods, stock-
Wts: Bennett **Nallee**, Nathl **Rogers**, Henarey **Ford**.

264- Apr. 7, 1773- Edmund **Taylor** of Mecklenburg Co., VA. gave to his son Lewis **Taylor** 621 acres in Granville Co., N.C. which was. bought of Isaac **Mitchell**-
Wts: Ro. **Lewis**, Howel **Lewis**.

264, 265- Mar. 11, 1775- Absalom **Davis** to Rowland **Terry** for 22 pds. 100 acres on E side of **Michael**'s creek at **Terry**'s own line, Robert **Lanier**'s.
Wts: William **Byars**, Richd **Davis**, Cheslee **Davis**.

265, 266- Oct. 20, 1773- Thomas **Rose** to James **Dunlap** for 100 pds. 404 acres on Nappy Reed creek on **Townsend**'s line, Joseph **Walker**'s line.
Wts: James **Langston**, John **Blake**, Robert **Dickens**.

267- Mar. 30, 1775- Absalom **Davis** to Augustin **Davis** his son, a gift of 100 acres on **Michals** creek at John **Penn**'s line at Absalom **Davis**'s line.
Wts: Cheslee **Davis**, Richard **Davis**.

268- Dec. 31, 1774- James **Hunt** to Thomas **Mutter** for 150 pds. 667 acres at **Mutter**'s line.-
Wts: Hugh **Galt**, John **Hunt**, Gedeon **Crenshaw**.

269- Feb. 4, 1775- Nathaniel **Robinson** and wife Elizabeth to Nicholas **Robinson** for 30 pds. 275 acres in **Dickerson**'s line, **Ballard**'s line on Sandy creek.
Wts: none.

271- 272- Mar. 9, 1775- Augustine **Davis**, Sr to Richard **Wilkins** for 125 pds. 250 acres on Little Island creek, both sides.
Wts: Wm. **Potter**, Solomon **Walker**, Moses **Potter**.

271, 272- repeated)- Aug. 2, 1775- Richard **Wilkins** to William **Potter**, David **Mitchel**, John **Potter**, John **Coleman** mortgages land, tools, livestock etc.
Wts: Thos **Satterwhite,** Adam **Potter**, Wrn. **Kennon**, M. **Hunt**, William **Farrar**.

273, 274- Aug. 1, 1775- Nathaniel **Jarrott** of Bute Co. to Isaiah **Paschal** for 40 pds. 200 acres whereon **Paschal** lives-
Wts: Samuel **Fuller**.

211

Granville Co NC record of deeds
Book L 1775-1778
preceded by Index John **Hunt**, Register

1- July 31, 1775- Crawford **Buckanon** to Stephen **Turner** for 20 pds. 100 acres on Little Deep Creek up Wolf Branch at John **Chadwick**'s line, Elisha **Paschal**'s line.
Wts: Dennis **Paschal**. John **Paschal**, (El)izabeth **Paschal**.

2- May 27, 1768- Benjamin **Hardy** of Johnston Co., N.C. to Samuel **Despain** of Granville Co., N. C. for 37 pds., 10 shls. 180 acres on waters of Nuce river and on Horse creek being land Samuel **Despain** occupies.
Wts: Robert **Goodloe**, Jr, James **Wade**.

3- Aug. 1, 1775- Samuel **Fuller** to Nathaniel **Jarrett** of Bute Co., N.C. for 10 shls.- 10 acres in Granville Co. on Buffaloe creek at **Fuller**'s line.
Wts: Isaiah **Paschal**.

4- Nov. 15, 1773- James **Williams** and wife Mary to Joseph **Williams** for 400 pds. 438 acres on Great Island creek on N. side of Grassy creek.
Wts: William **Taylor**, John **Hunt**, Richd **Harrison**.

5- Nov. 15, 1773- James **Williams** and wife Mary to Joseph **Williams** for 200 pds. 425 acres on Great Island creek at Isaac **Mitchel**'s corner.
Wts: William **Taylor**, Richd **Harrison**, John **Hunt**.

6- Oct. 3, 1775- Thomas **Bridges** to Moses **Bridges** of Orange Co., N.C. for 65 pds. 250 (?) acres being land granted to Liddia **Lashley** and from said Liddia and James **Bridges** by deed Nov. 12, 1774 on both sides of Tar river (granted to Liddia **Lashley** Dec. 3, 1760-)
Wts: Gabriel **Davey**, Alexander **Davidson**.
Ann, wife of Thomas **Bridges**, relinquishes her dower right.

7- May 18, 1775- Reuben **Searcy** and wife Susanna, to John **Potter** of Mecklinburg Co., Va. for 1200 pds. 580 acres on Tar river near the Beaver house on Sherwood **Harris**'s corner.
Wts: Willm **Potter**, John **Searcy**, Jr., Asa **Searcy**.

8, 9- July 18, 1772- John **Searcy** to Richard **Henderson** for 200 pds. 141 acres on **Searce**y's Branch at his back line within fenced lands of Richard **Henderson**'s land which was granted to **Searcy**-
Wts: James **Wallace**, Joseph **Linsey**, Tho **Henderson**.

9, 10- Oct. 8, 1773- Abraham **Cook** to John **Walker** for 50 pds. 75 acres c on Little Island creek on Lick Branch.
Wts: Reuben **Searcy**, Ed **Harrison**, Joseph **Williams**.

10, 11- Nov. 7, 1775- Jonathan **Kittrell**, Sr. to Jonathan **Kittrell**, Jr. for 5 shls. 360 acres at head of **Norris** creek which was granted to Jonathan **Kittrell**, Sr. July 2, 1761 by Granville.
Wts: Robert **Bell**, John **Pulliand**.

11, 12- Nov. 6, 1775- John **Stovell** to Owen **Griffin** for love etc for Owen **Griffin**; a gift of land whereon he lives on Grassy Creek at John **Young**'s and Jonathan **Knight**'s line.
Wts: John **Young**, Joseph **Landers**, Drury **Allin**.

12, 13- Oct. 21, 1775- Joel **Chandler** to Thomas **Mutter**, merchant, for .[6] . pds. 15 shls. 6 3/4th acres on N. side of Jonathan creek on Thomas **Mutter**'s former line.
Wts: Danl **Grant**, Hugh **Galt**.

13, 14- Mar. 14, 1775- David **Lewis** of Craven Co., South Carolina to Henry **Graves** for 64 pds. 300 acres on S side of Pear (Tarr) river on John **Mize**, Jr.'s line being land I bought of Charles **Williams**.
Wts: Lewis **Yancey**, Mary **Yancey**, Lovet **Gates**.

14, 15- May 6, 1775- Thomas **Bridges** to William **Glass** for 175 pds. 465 acres on **Aaron**'s creek including all land

purchased by Thomas of James **Bridges** on **Harris**'s line.
Wts: Thomas **Person**, Anthony **Peeler**.
Ann, wife of Thomas **Bridges**, relinquishes dower right.

212

15, 16- July 16, 1772- William **Cooper** and wife Mary to Richard **Henderson** for 75 pds. 155 acres on Nut Bush creek at Robert **Mitchel**'s.
Wts: Len H. **Bullock**, Thos. **Rice**.

17, 18- Dec. 9, 1773- Thomas **Burden** to Richard **Henderson** for 150 pds. 363 acres on both sides of **Anderson** Swamp at James **Daniel**'s line, Guilelmus **Smith**'s and Richard **Henderson**'s lines and by land claimed by Len Henley **Bullock** whereon **Burden** now lives.
Wts: Samuel **Henderson**, Sarah S.

18, 19- Jan. 17, 177- Gillam **Harris** to Robert **Reed** and Co., merchants for 176 pds. 12 shls. mortgages 418 acres on both sides of **Newby** creek on Israel **Fuller**'s corner on John **Bridges**' line and also cattle and other live stock etc- to secure debt.
Wts: Reuben **Searcy**, Thos. **Bradford**, James **Stewart**.

20- Feb. 6, 1776- James **Hunt** and wife Sarah to John **Hunt** for 100 pds. 500 acres on lines of **Lewis**, **Parkman** and **Cobb**.
Wts: M. **Hunt**.

21- Feb. 3, 1776- James **McMurrey** of Bedford Co., VA. to William **Taylor** of Granville Co. for 20 pds. 216 acres on Josiah **Mitchell**'s line, **Winston**'s and William **Taylor**'s lines.
Wts: Thomas **Banks**, John **Brown**, John **Lynch**.

22, 23- Jan. 5, 1776- Thomas **Boyd** to John **Gwin** of Mecklenburg Co., VA for 500 pds. 300 acres on both sides of Tarr river about 3 miles above Trading path- being land whereon Robert **Boyd** now lives.
Wts: Thornton **Yancey**, James **Jones**.

23, 24- Dec. 12, 1775- John **Weaver** and wife Ann to Thos. **Roland** for 12 pds. 65 acres on Nut Bush creek on Evan **Ragland**'s line, at mouth of Frederick **Weaver**'s spring branch.
Wts: Edward **Weaver**, William **Neal**.

24, 25- Nov. 24, 1773- Charles **Kennon** to Robert **Monford** of Mecklenburg Co., VA. for 800 pds. 675 acres on Hyco Path.
Wts: Thomas **Person**, Robert **Dickins**.

25, 26- Sept. 20, 1767- Joseph **Rogers** to Jonathan **Kittrell** for 2 pds. 10 shls. 50 acres being part of 357 acres granted **to Rogers** June 1, 1762 on **Martin**'s creek, at **Rogers**' line.
Wts: Samuel **Fuller**, John **Roland**.

27, 28- Dec. 4, 1775- Henry **Parkman** and wife Hannah to John **Howard** Sr for 5 pds. 220 acres on Butchers' branch at **Cooke**s corner, on **Harris**'s line, **More**s line granted to **Parkman** Dec. 4, 1775.
Wts: Benjamin **Howard**, Frances **Parkman**.

28, 29- Oct. 14, 1774- Thomas **Person** to Robert **Monford** of Mecklenburg Co., VA. for 100 pds. 100 acres on N side of Fox creek on **Montford**'s In line.
Wts: None.

30, 31- Nov. 24, 1773- William **Kennon** to Robert **Monford** of Mecklenburg Co., VA. for 25 pds. 125 acres on **Kennon**s corner and on **Person**'s line.
Wts: Thomas **Person**, Ro. **Lewis**.

31, 32- Feb. 7, 1774- Richard **Searcy** and wife Mary to Peter **Fleming** for 35 pds. 128 acres on **Anderson**'s swamp in John **Fleming**'s line and at James **Daniel**s' line.

Wts: Wm. **Daniel**, Wm. **Gilliam**.

32, 33- Feb. 6, 1776- John **Hogan** to James **Willis** of Chatham Co., N. C. for 166 pds. land in Granville Co. containing 150 acres on John **Hogan**'s line, **Smith**'s line, **Benton's** corner on Reedy branch.
Wts: none (Keziah, wife of John **Hogan** relinquishes dower.

34, 35- May 7, 1776- James **Dyar** to Benjamin **Wade** for 60 pds. 120 ac acres on Thomas **Yates** line being part of land bought of George **Boyers**.
Wts: Demsy **Moore**, Bartlet **Williams**.
Wife (unnamed) relinquishes dower.

35, 36- May 9, 1776. John **Dickerson**, merchant, to John **Boddie** for 106 pds. 300 acres on Cedar creek, both sides, at **Pope**'s Quarter which land was granted by Granville Mar. 11, 1760 for 600 acres to Richard **Bridges** and sold by him to James **Winningham** and be sold to **Dickerson**.
Wts: Thos. **Banks**, George **Nicholson**.

213

36, 37- Dec. 26, 177- (Registered- May 1776) Nathan **Sims** of Colleton County, South Carolina to John Williams **Daniel** of Granville Co., N. C. for 70 pds. 140 acres on branches of **Anderson**'s swamp at Len H. **Bullock**'s line in Simon **Williams**' line.
Wts: Guilielmus **Smith**, James **Daniel**.

37, 38- Oct. 16, 1775- John **Mitchel** and wife Martha to James **Hunt** for 350 pds. - - - acres of land on roadside at William **Bullock**'s line and David **Mitchel**'s and Thomas **Lanier**'s line on Little Nut Bush creek at Robert **Williams**' line.
Wts: Anne, Mary and Samuel **Smith**.

39- Apr. 30, 1776- Minues **Griggs** to John **Boyd** for 125 pds. 312 acres on branches of Tar river.
Wts: Jonathan **White**, John **Mathews**, Richd **Harris**.

40, 41- Nov. 15, 1773- Thomas **Rose** and wife Lyddia to Ellis **Drewry** for 225 pds. 200 acres on N. side of Tar river at **Russel**'s corner.
Granted 1753 April-
Wts: James and Solomon **Langston**, John **Hogins**.

41, 42- Nov. 27, 1766- John **Hogan** to Michael **Wilson** for 50 pds. 108 acres at **Benton**'s line, on Reedy Branch, **Caudle**'s line.
Wts: John **Hamilton**, Edwd **Moore**.
Kezia, wife of John **Hogan** relinquishes dower.

42, 43 - Sept. 30, 1771- Wm. **Hendley** to Winfield **Wright** for 40 shls. part of tract Wm. **Hendley** bought of John **Pope** and the whole land he has on S side of Peter **Cawley**'s branch.
Wts: Elizabeth and Benjamin **Wright**, Samuel **Pitman**.

43, 44- Apr. 6, 11772- Joshua **Moss** and wife Elizabeth of Mecklenburg Co., VA. to John Williams **Daniel** for 20 pds. 40 acres on branches of **Anderson** Swamp at lines of Len Henley **Bullock** and at John Williams **Daniel**'s line.
Wts: Thomas **Rice**.

45- Joshua **Moss** and wife Elizabeth of Mecklenburg Co., VA. for 40 pds. from John Williams **Daniel**, sold 300 acres on branches of Great Nut Bush creek at Nimrod **Williams**' corner.
Wts: Thos. **Rice** Registered- Apr. 6,1772

46 thru 48- Grant from Lord Granville to Egbert **Haywood** of Edgecombe Co., N. C. for 610 acres in Granville Co., N. C. on Mountain creek on **Haywood** and Phillip **Pryor**'s lines- -1758-
signed by Joseph **Bodley**, Francis **Corbin**.

49, 50- Feb. 1, 1764- Egbert **Haywood** and wife Sarah, John **Hardy** and wife Deborah all of Halifax County, N. C.

to Chesley **Daniel** of Lunenburg Co., VA for 500 pds. 1250 acres in Granville Co., N. C. on both sides of Mountain creek on Phillip **Pryor**'s and Edward **Roberts**' lines.
Wts: Markham **Ware**, Wm. **Branch**, Chris **Dudley**.

51, 52- Jan. 6, 1777- Joseph **Johnston** to Sarah **Hayes** for 20 pds. 100 acres on a branch in Granville Co.
Wts Samuel **Fuller**, Samuel **Huckabay**, Ferehy **Fuller**.

52, 53- Aug. 6, 17- - Moses **Briges** (**Bridges**) to George **Roberts** for 113 pds. 13 shls. 4 pence 250 acres on both sides of Tar river at Crooked Run.
Wts: John **Oliver**, James **Langston**, Richd **Harris**.

53 thru 55- Jan 29, 1777- Henry **Lyne** to James **Mitchel** for 105 pds. 2 1/4 acres near Little Nut Bush creek at **Lyne**'s corner and a tract of 103 acres near said creek at **Mitchell**'s and **Lyne** s lines.
Wts: John **Penn**, George **Terry**, Robt. **Crawley**, R. **Mumford**.

55, 56- Jan. 1, 1777- Richard **Harris** to Daniel **Stanard** for 110 pds. 185 acres on both sided of Poplar creek (**Stanard** also spelled **Standard**).
Wts: William **Hicks**, George **Harris**.

56 thru 58- Feb. 1, 1777- Christopher **Harris** and wife Caty to Ransone **Sutherland** for 439 pds. 490 acres on Poplar and Tabb creek whereon **Harris** lives on **Hudson**'s corner.
Wts: William T. **Hughlett**, Darwin **Harris**.

58 thru 60- Jan. 29, 1777- Michael **Redwine** to Robert **Harris**, Jr. for 80

214

pds. 200 acres on Ledge of Rocks creek, which is all land bought by Francis **Faulks** of Chauncey **Townsend**, as agent of **McCulloch**, on George **Boyers** corner, George **Miller**'s line.
Wts: Thos. **Harris**, David **Harris**.

60, 61- Feb. 9, 1776- John **Dickerson** to John **Peace**, Jr. for 50 pds. 225 acres on both sides of Fort creek.
Wts: Pomprett **Herndon**, Wm. **Byram**.

61, 62- Nov. 21, 1775- George **Alston**, late of the county of Granville, to John **Ross** for 47 pds., 18 shls., 8 pence, 200 acres which was conveyed by John **Ross** to **Alston** on Mar. 18, 1773 registered in Book K- folio 132-
Signed by Andrew **Miller**, attny for George **Alston** in Halifax Co., N. C.
Wts: James **Stuart**, Henry **Joyner**.

63- Mar. 8, 1776- John **Weaver** to Thomas **Roland** for 113 pds., 6 shls. 8 pc 100 acres on Ready Fork at **Kimbell**'s line to his Spring Branch.
Wts: Frederic **Wiggins**, Aramanus **Weaver**.

64- May 4, 1774- Peter **Vincent** to John **Dickerson** for 50 pds. 150 acres on Fort creek at Peter **Vincent**'s line.
Wts: Jno. **Peace**, Jr., Simon **Secra**.

65- Jan. 5, 1777- Len Henley **Bullock** to Thomas **Bell** for 20 pds. 200 acres in Bute Co., N. C. in Joab **Mitchell**'s old line on Thomas **Person**'s line.
Wts: none.

66- Sept. 23, 1776- John **Weaver** to Aramanus **Weaver** for 32 pds. 1 shl 3 pence, 75 acres on E side of Nut Bush creek on Thomas **Roland**'s corner.
Wts: Merryman **Barns**, Frederick **Weaver**.

67, 68- Dec. 2, 1776- William **Howell** and wife Nancy to Nicolas (Nicholas) **Tally** for 80 pds. 140 acres on S side of Fishing creek being part of 280 acres granted by deed from Thomas **Howell** to his son William **Howell** on John **Varner**'s spring branch.
Wts: Barnet **Pulliam**, Gideon **Crews**, Thomas **Crews**.

68, 69- Jan. 1, 1776- John **Ross** to Solomon **Staton** for 100 pds., 200 acres being land conveyed from George **Byers** to John **Ross** crossing the Trading Path- deed dated Jan. 1771 registered in Book I folio 150.
Wts: Robert **Bell**, George Lane **Moore**.

69, 70- Jan. 4, 1777- Thomas **Person** to Lewis **Anderson** for 30 pds. 75 acres on N. side of Fishing creek at line formerly **Bradford**'s corner at **Anderson**'s, **White**'s, **Tatom**'s lines.
Wts: M. **Hunt**, John **Hunt**.

71, 72- Oct. 14, 1776- Henry Eustace **McCulloch** to Charles **Merryman** of Granville Co. for 20 pds. 200 acres being part of land known as *Tract No. 12*, in Granville Co. at Michael **Wilsons** corner and is part of land granted to Henry **McCulloch** by King George of Great Britain and deeded to Henry **Holtsclaus** July 4, 1763 and by him to Henry Eustace **McCulloch**.
Wts: John **Hinchen**, Jas. **Burges**, Wm. **Johnston** (signed by Thos. **Frohock** attny)

73, 74- Apr. 15, 1777- William **Willingham** to Daniel **Grant** for 133 pds. 6 shillings, 8 pence, 229 acres on **Gill**'s line.
Wts: Richard **Davis**, Nathaniel **Malone**, Isabell **Davis**.

74, 75- Jan. 10, 1775- William **Cooper** and wife Mary to Joseph **Taylor** for 50 pds. 118 acres on Meeting House Road where Capt. James Mit .[1] . line crosses at corner of **Donald**'s land.
Wts: John **Taylor**, Elijah **Mitchel**.

75, 76- Mar. 11, 1776- William **Corder** and wife Febby to Peter **Akin** for 70 pds. 50 acres on **Graves**' corner on **Corder**'s line, Henry **King**'s line.
Wts: Isham **Caudle**, Richd **Foster**.

76, 77- July 29, 1775- William **Hudspeth** and Giles **Hudspeth**, Jr. to Reuben **Searcy** for 300 pds. 600 acres on both sides of Hatcher's creek which land was given to William and Giles **Hudspeth**, Jr., by their father Giles **Hudspeth**, Sr. at John **Hamilton**'s line at Giles **Hudspeth**s Sr.'s old line.
Wts: Sherwood **Harris**, Wm. **Reardon**.

78- May 5, 1777- Justus **Parish** to Elijah **Parish** for 26 pds. 13 shls, 4 pence 50 acres on Maple Spring branch, south side of Tabbs creek to

215
the mouth of Cabin Branch to the old line.
Wts: Sherwood **Parrish**, Lewis **Parrish**.

79- May 3, 1777- in the first year of our Independency- William **Hicks** gave to his son William **Hicks**, Jr. 293 acres on both sides of Tabbs crk on **Mattock**'s line, William **Hicks** line, at land formerly belonging to Robert **Hicks**.
Wts: Timothy **Cooper**, Thos. **Norman**.

80- Nov. 1, 1776- Drury **Kimball** and his wife Sarah to Bartholomew **Kimball** for 50 pds. 100 acres on **Anderson**'s swamp at dividing line between Thomas **Parrish** and George **Rodes**.
Wts: John **Williams**, John **Mitchell**, Michael **Mauzy**.

81, 82- Mar. 13, 1773- John **Keeling** to John **Williams**, attny at law; for 175 pds. 125 acres including the forks of the road where **Cannon** and **Taylor** formerly kept a store, on both sides of Hico road at David **Mitchell** line on the Long Branch at Joseph **Glover**'s former line to a branch of Little Island creek adjoining William **Potter**'s, formerly Joseph **Glover**'s line.
Wts: Thos. **Satterwhite**, Willm **Farrer**, Sr.

82, 83- Jan. 22, 1777- Thomas **Key** to Benjamin **Guy** for 30 pds. 100 acres on E side of **Jefferson**'s road near Little Deep creek at Elisha **Paschal**'s line-

---

[1] Name caught in binding of book.

signed by Thomas and Mary **Key**.
Wts: William **Key**, William **Todd**, Dennis **Paschal**.

84- May 1, 177- - Michael **Redwine** to Boling **Adcock** for 50 pds. land on Little Branch containing 60 acres.
Wts: Thomas **Harris**, Michael **Redwine**, Jr.

85- May 6, 1777- John **Stovall** to Benjamin **Stovall**, his son, for 50 pds. the land whereon Benjamin **Stovall**. now lives on Jonathan's creek at John **Stovall**'s line to the dividing line made by him- 225 acres.
Wts: Reuben **Searcy**.

86, 87- Dec. 25, 1776- Baxter **Ragsdale** to Volentine **White** for 33 pds. 6 shls. 8 pence, 100 acres between Tabbs creek and Long Creek, **Dickerson**'s line.
Wts: Zachariah **Higgs**, Thommy **White**.

88- May 6, 1777- Elisha **Paschal** and wife Ann to Dennis **Paschal** for 40 pds. 200 acres on E side of Deep creek at Samuel **Paschal**'s line.
Wts: Thomas **Key**, William **Key**, Benjamin **Guy**.

89, 90- May 6, 1777- Robert **Hester** and wife Mary to John **Whicker** for 25 pds. 100 acres on a prong of Fishing Creek at **Hicks**'s line, **Bruce**'s line to Nathan **Bass**es corner.
Wts: Benjamin **Hester**.

90, 91- Mar. 6, 1776- John **Griggs** of Roan (Rowan) Co., N. C. to Richard **Harris** of Granville Co., N. C. for 160 pds. 300 acres in Granville Co. on John **Boyd**'s line and on both sides of **Owen**s Creek, at **Gwin**'s corner to Sherwood **Harris**'s line which land was granted to Minus **Griggs** by Earl Granville Nov. 9, 1757 (1757).
Wts: John **Oliver**, Geo. **Roberts**, John **Hampton**.

92- May 20, 177- - Sherwood **Harris**, son of Sherwood **Harris**, deceased, to Thomas **Harris** for 80 pds. 160 acres which is the tract of land given Sherwood **Harris** by his father Sherwood **Harris**, Sr., deceased by his last will and testament which land he bought of Jonathan **White** and including the plantation whereon Henry **White** lived.
Wts: John **Gwinn**, Sherwood **Harris**.

93- Mar. 13, 1777- John **Tatom** to Robert **Hester** for 213 pds. 6 shls. 8 pence, 200 acres on both sides of Fishing creek.
Wts: William **Mackenzie**, Donald **Galbreath**, Benjamin **Hester**.
Wife (unnamed) relinquishes dower right.

94, 95- Dec. 2, 1776- George **Miller** and wife Mary to Nathan **Okey** for 15 pds. 50 acres, 10 poles on Ledge of Rocks creek being part of 320 acres purchased by George **Miller** from Henry **McCulloch**.
Wts: George **Wright**, Michael **Redwil** (**Redwine**).

95, 96- Feb. 22, 1777- David **Bridges** of Wake Co., N. C. to John **Lunsford** of Granville Co., N. C. for 20 pds., 350 acres on branches of Newlight creek at **Harris**'s line being part of tract granted to John **Bridges**.

216
July 25, 1761 and deeded to David **Bridges**.
Wts: John **Bridges**, Elisha **Lunsford**.

97, 98- Jan. 21, 1771- James **Yancey** to John **Wicker** for 12 pds. 60 acres at George **Anderson**'s corner to Mirey branch and down branch to John **Wicker**'s corner line.
Wts: Michael **Wilson**, Saml **Hopkins**, Jr., Cutbird **Hudson**.

98, 99- May 7, 1776- Joseph **Landis**h and wife Sarah to Sherwood **Harris** for 60 pds. 200 acres in Granville Co., on branches. of Tar river.
Wts: Richd D. **Cooke**, Robert **Harris**, Jr. (signed Joseph **Landiss**.

99, 100- Jan. 29, 1777- Robert **Harris**, Jr. to Michael **Redwine** for 80 pds. 360 acres as per deed from Chauncey

Townsend Aug. 7, 1763.
Wts: Thos. **Harris**, David **Harris**.

100, 101- Dec. 11, 1776- Charles **Parrish** to Charnick **Cox** far, 47 pds. 120 acres on E side of Nut Bush creek on Frederick **Wiggins**' line, Evan **Ragland**'s line, Edward **Weaver**'s line and Thomas **Wiggins**' line.
Wts: Sherwood **Parrish**, Shadrack **Parrish**, Frederick **Wiggins**.
signed by Charles and Elishaba **Parrish**.

102, 103- May 1, 1776- John **Kittrell** to Joseph **Peace**, Jr. for 26 pds. 13 shls. 4 pence, 200 acres on W side of Tabbs creek at Christian **Thomas**' line, Alex **Shelling**'s line, being part of tract granted Dec. 1, 1760 to George **Moore**-
Wts: John, Samuel and Ben **Smith**.

103, 104- Dec. 30, 1776- Miles **Wells** and wife Suzan to William **Howell** for 133 pds. 270 acres on Fishing creek at **Frazier**'s line and **Taylor**'s and Robert **Duke**'s lines.
Wts: James **Norvell**, Barnett **Pulliam**, John **Whicker**, George **Hunt**.

104, 105- Mar. 6, 1776- Frederick **Weaver** and wife Elizabeth to Bartholomew **Kimball** for 130 pds. 50 acres on Reedy Fork.
Wts: Mathew **Goodwin**.

105, 106- Mar. 7, 1777- Philemon **White** to Thomas **Rice** for 60 pds. 100 acres near the road.
Wts: William **Reeves**, William **Hicks**, Jr.

106 thru 108- Oct. 26, 1776- Jonathan **Kittrell**, Jr. to Cader **Parker** for 30 pds. 360 acres on **Harris**'s creek at **Hill**'s line, granted to **Kittrell**, Sr. on July 24, 1761.
Wts: John **Jones**, Jemima **Parker**.

108, 109- Mar. 29, 1776- Samuel **Pittard** wand wife Mary to John **Pittard** for 115 pds. 180 acres on Spewmarrow creek at dividing line in **Graves** Corner and on **Harris**'s line.
Wts: Jesse, Frances, and Robert G. **Harper**, Samuel **Smith**.

110, 111- Oct. 27, 1773- John **Davis** to John **Powell** of Accomack Co., VA. for 100 pds. 202 acres on N. side of Grassy creek along **Grant**'s line, **Busbee**'s and **Willingham**'s lines.
Wts: Thomas **Person**, John **Ballard**.

111, 112- May 20, 1777- Thomas **Person** to William **Liles** for 300 pds. 1250 acres being the whole of two tracts that was taken up by **Person**'s adjoining land now property of Robert **Goodloe** on both sides of Horse creek on Robert **Goodloe**'s line.
Wts: Alex **Campbell**, John **Hunt**.

113, 114- July 29, 1777- William **Liles** to Robert **Goodloe** of Bute Co., N. C. for 42 pds. 15 shls. 2 tracts of land on both sides of Horse crk of which one is 45 acres which **Liles** purchased of Thos. **Person**'s on **Goodloe**'s line, and the other tract on W side of creek on **Goodloe**'s line containing 65 acres-
Wts: Nancy **Liles**, Nathan **Jackson**.

114, 115- Mar. 9, 1776- John Henry **Wideman** to Robert **Allison**, Jr. for 150 pds. 374 acres on both sides of **Adcock**'s creek whereon **Wideman** now lives at David **Harris**'s line.
Wts: Wm. **Ogelvie**, Robert **Harris**, Jr.
Wife relinquishes her dower right.

217

115, 116- Jan. 25, 1777- Jacob **Rictwiel** and John **Rictweil** to Miles **Wells** for 50 pds. 233 acres in Granville Co. on Michael **Fulers** and on **Shelton** creek, being part of tract taken up by William **Meadows** on **Slaughter**'s line.
Wts: Thomas **Person**, Jno. **Stone**.

116, 117- Apr. 14, 1777- Edmund **Taylor** of Mecklenburg Co., VA. to Samuel **Hunt** of Granville Co., N. C. for 80 pds. 200 acres between lines of Jonathan **Parker**, Mourning **Hunt** and **Goodloe**'s orphan's lands.

Wts: John and Howel **Taylor**, Ro. **Lewis**.

117, 118- Aug. 5, 1777- Wm. **Liles** to Mathew **Lowery** for 50 pds. 200 acres on S side of Buffalo creek being part of tract bought of Thomas **Person**.
Wts: Samuel **High**, Nathan **Jackson**.

118, 119- July 30, 1777- James **Moore** of Wake Co., N, C. executor of Edward **Moore** deceased, late of Granville Co., to Edward **Moore** for 410 pds. 385 acres on both sides of Mill creek a branch of Tar river at William **Crag**'s line.
Wts: Jas. **Stainback**, James **Jett**.

120, 121- Sept. 9, 1775- Joseph **McDaniel** to Gibbe **Chavers** for 45 pds. 8 shls. 10 pence, 300 acres on N. side of Tar river, and live stock
This is a deed of trust, or mortgage-
Wts: Jonathan **Kittrell**, Zacharias **Higgs**.

122- Aug. 7, 1777- Edmund **Taylor** of Mecklinburg to Thomas **Brown**, Jr. for 15 pds. 175 acres in Granville Co at Henry **Freeman**'s corner and on John **Hargrove**'s line, the county line, at Edward **Pages**.
Wts: Henry **Freeman**, Lewis **Taylor**.

123- Aug, 1777- Edmund **Taylor** of Mecklenburg Co., VA. to Henry **Freeman** for 15 pds. 175 acres at Thomas **Brown**, Jr.'s and Edward **Pages** lines, on **Hargrove**'s line.
Wts: Thomas **Brown**, Lewis **Taylor**.

124- Nov. 5, 1777- William **Washington** to his son John **Washington** for a deed of gift, 48 acres on **Merritt**'s corner.

125- . . . . . 1777, Mordica **Moore** to Robert **Russel** for 66 pds. 265 acres on **Jones**'s line at **Hamton**' and **Thompson**'s lines.
Wts: Thomas **Fowler**, Mordica **Moore**, Jr.

126- July 26, 1776- Reuben **Searcey** and wife Susanna to Richard **Searcy** for 100 pds. 320 acres on both[e] sides of **Boling** creek.
Wts: Joseph **Moore**, George **Searcy**.

127- Feb. 6, 1777- Lewis **Anderson** to Winf **Wright** (Winfield **Wright**) for 60 pds. 265 acres on Beaver Dam creek which **Anderson** bought of Philemon **Bradford**.
Wts: Israel **Judge**, Chas. **Bowling**, Benjamin **Wright**.

128- Sept. 6, 1777- Thomas **Fowler** and wife Jean to John **Kelley** for 220 pds. 155 acres on Tarr river on **Blant**'s formerly **Davenport**'s line.
Wts: Reuben **Searcy**, James **Norvell**, Miles **Wells**.

129- Feb. 5, 1777- William **Washington** to his son John **Washington** a gift of 50 acres at **Merritt**'s line on Tar river to Thomas **Person**'s line.
Wts: James **Langston**, Stephen **Merritt**.

130, 131- May 9, 1777- John **Oliver** and wife Fanney to Thomas **Bradford** for 100 pds. 62 1/4 acres on Tar river, which is land he bought of Peter **Nowlan** at Isham **Caudle**s corner.
Wts: Isum **Caudle**, James **Gunter**.

131, 132- Aug. 7, 1777- Cutbert **Hudson** to Ransons **Southerland** for 54 pds. 13 shls. 4 pence, 20 ½ acres on S side of Tabbs creek on Glebe road at dividing line between **Hudson** and Christopher **Harris**.
Wts: William **Hughlet**, Turner **Harris**.

132, 133- Oct. 1, 1777- Daniel **Grant** to John **Owen**, Jr. his son-in-law

218
a deed of gift of 64 acres on Grassy creek.
Wts; Stephen **Gafford**, Gideon **Johnson**, Fanny **Owen**.

133, thru 135- July 26, 1777- John **Walker** to William **Potter** for 150 pds. 292 acres on **Wheeler**'s corner, on Island creek to William **Potter**'s line-
Wts: Joseph **Taylor**, David **Mitchell**, Vinkler **Jones**.

135, 136- Nov. 5, 1777- William **Buchannon** to Elisha **Paschal** for 15 pds. 150 acres on branches of Deep creek in **Paschal**'s old line.
Wts: Samuel **Hammond**, John **Bait**.

136, 137- Sept. 29, 1777- Stephen **Beckham** and wife Rachel **Beckham** of Bute Co., N. C. to Samuel **Hammond** of Granville Co. for 45 pds. 119 acres on Deep creek at John **Hawkins**' old line.
Wts: Elisha **Paschal**. John **English**.

137, 138- Feb. 6, 1777- Tobott **Cockleree** and Michael **Cockleree** and Mary **Moyars** of Granville Co., N. C. to Thomas **Person** for 350 pds. 500 acres on both sides of **Shelton**'s and **Potts** creek at **Shearmon**'s line on Staney creek.
Wts: William **Palmer**, Samiel **Dyer**.

138, 139- Jan. 2, 1777- James **Wallace** and wife Mary to Philip **Burford** of Bute Co., N. C. for 80 pds. 140 acres which **Wallace** bought of Robert **Mitchall** at Bromfield **Ridley**'s and Sherwood **Sims**'s lines.
Wts: Wyatt **Hawkins**, Saml **Paschal**, Billey **Gooch**, John **Kendrick**.

139 thru 141- Nov. 5, 1777- James **Walker** and wife Elizabeth to William **Graves** for 400 pds. 450 acres whereon **Walker** now lives at Mountain fork of Grassy creek on Daniel **Malone**'s line, Jospeph **Roberts**, Daniel **Grant**'s lines, John **Daniel**'s' line. . and line of land bought of Isham **Malone** by **Walker**.
Wts: John **Stovall**, John **Kibbe** (**Kelle**)

142- . . .1777- Mordaci **Moore** to Robert **Russel** for 20 pds. 60 acres on William **Jones** and Thomas **Person**'s lines.
Wts: Thomas **Fowler**, Mordeca **Moore**, Jr.

143- Nov. 5, 1777- James **Walker** and wife Elizabeth to Daniel **Grant** for 200 pds. 525 acres on Grassy creek at Daniel **Malone**'s and at **Walker**'s lines, to Robert **Bailey**'s line, William **Allen**'s line.
Wts: Thomas and John **Owen**.

144- Oct. 20, 1777- Thomas **Person** to John **Owen**, Jr. for 211 pds. 631 acres being part of tract granted to **Person**'s, at **Owens** line, near Grassy creek on **Howard**'s and **Owen**'s lines.
Wts: Thomas **Owens**, Thomas **Grant**

145- Dec. 16, 1776- Laurence **Pettyford** to Benja **Wright** for 50 pds. 300 acres on Philemon **Bradford**'s line on Beaver Dam creek, which is land **Pettiford** bought of Philemon **Bradford**, on line of Reuben **Bass** and **McCulloch**.
Wts: Wm. **Henley**, Wm. **Cooper**.

146, 147- Apr. 5, 1777- Jesse **Landers** (**Sanders**?) to Henry **Graves** for 36 pds. - - **Landers** indebted to **Graves**– - this is mortgage on 150 acres adjoining lands of Joseph **Farmer**, George **Newton**, Lewis **Yancey** and Thomas **Mutter**-
Wts: Joseph **Walker**, William **Graves**.

147, 148- Nov. 4, 1777- Israel **Eastwood** to Jesse **Meadows** for 200 pds. 326 acres on both sides of Mountain creek at Hill **Langston**'s corner.
Wts: Stephen **Merritt**, Robert **Russel**.

148, 149- Apr. 29, 1777- Drury **Allen**, and, wife Elizabeth to John **Young** for 250 pds. 400 acres whereon **Allen** Now lives at William **Allen**'s line and on county line, to Richard **Yancey**'s line.
Wts: David **Allen**, Benjamin **Beardon**, James **Wade**.

149, 150- Mar, 15, 1777 Jonathan **White**, to Hugh **Currin** Jr. for 60 pds. 140 acres on Tabbs creek, on **Person**'s line, **Bell** and **Mattock**'s line.

Wts: James and William **Currin**- - signed Jonathan and Matthew **White**).

150, 151- Jan. 20, 1777- Ephraim **Jones** to Richard **Jones** for 25 pds. 100 acres on S side of Tar river on John **Rust**'s line and **Nevell**'s corner.
Wts: John **Neville**, Nathaniel **McGehee**.

219

152- Jan. 21, 1777- William **Mills** to Nathaniel **McGehee** for certain amount, 19 acres at **Cooper**'s corner on Ford branch of Tar river.
Wts: Nathan **McGehee**, John **Neville**.

153- Aug. 30, 1777- William **Potter** to David **Mitchel** for 18 pds. 13 shls and 3 pence, 14 acres adjoining land whereon Joseph **Glover** and Joseph **Winston** formerly lived.
Wts: Samuel **Sneed**, Daniel **Williams**.

154, 155. 1777- Augustine **Davis** to George **Newman** for 120 pds. 250 acres being part of larger tract granted Nov. 27, 1760 to John **Bird** on both sides of **Michael**'s creek.
Wts: Augustine **Davis**, Jr., Absalom **Davis**.

155, 156- Jan. 1, 1777- Thomas **Parrish** to William **Godfrey** for 59 pds. 60 acres on **Anderson**'s swamp at **Eaton**'s corner.
Wts: Zacherias **Higgs**, Michael **Mauzey**.

156, 157- Dec. 1775- Augustine **Davis** from Richard **Wilkins** for 100 pds. 250 acres on both sides of Little Island creek being part of tract granted to John **Bird** Nov. 7, 1760.
Wts: Augustine **Davis**, Jr.

157, 158- Oct. 29, 1777- Sarah **Williams** executrix, Robert **Williams**, Richard **Harrison**, Thomas **Lanier**, Joseph **Williams** executors of will of Joseph **Williams** deceased, to Argill **Hanks** for 65 pds. 125 acres in Granville Co., being land of Joseph **Williams**, Sr. deceased which was conveyed to him by Nathaniel **Robertson** Oct. 7, 1772 and registered Jan. 5, 1772- - Joseph, Sr. sold to **Hanks** during his life-
Wts: James **Frazer**, Bartlet **Searcy**, [Thomas **Rice**], and John **Rice**.

158, 159- Jan. 7, 1777- Alexander **Gray** of Amelia Co., VA. to Auther **Moore** of Orange Co., N. C. for 80 pds. 238 acres on Nap of Reeds creek at William **Bennett**'s corner.
Wts: John **Gwinn**, Wm. **Tapp**.

160, 161- Nov. 1, 1773- John **Dickerson** to Leonard Clark **Higgs** for 80 pds. 100 acres on S side of Ruin Creek on John and Solomon **Blackman**'s line and George **Woodlief**'s line.
Wts: Jno. **Peace**, Zacharias **Higgs**.

161, 162- Oct. 10, 1777- Solomon **Langston** to William **Philpot** for 133 pds. 6 shls. 8 pence 180 acres on Stephen **Merritt**'s line, **Langston**'s line and on **Washington**'s line.
Wts: James **Langston**, Howel [**How**].

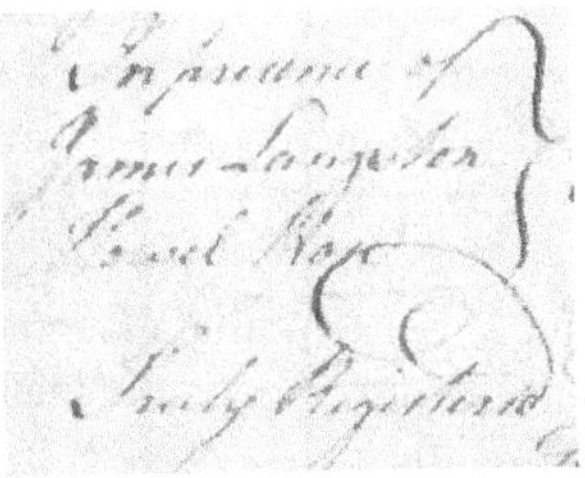

162, 163- Nov. 3, 1777- Elijah **Hanks** and wife Ann to John **Brame** of Mecklinburg Co., VA. for 164 pds. 6 shls. 8 pence, 200 acres on both sides of Crooked Run Creek at James **Brame**'s line.
Wts: James **Brame**, Thomas **Craft**, Lewis **Roffe**.

163, 164- Nov. 1, 1777- Robert **Fleming** and wife Mary to John **Craft** for 120 pds. 152 acres on Nut Bush creek at Miles **Williams**' and Reuben **Morris** and Thomas **Wiggins**' lines.

Wts: James **Hague**, Charnick **Cox**.

165- Aug. 30, 1777- John **Williams** to David **Mitchel** for 6 pds. 13, shls and 4 pence, 25 acres on Chrismas Ray's Spring branch.
Wts: Daniel **Williams**, Ro. **Lewis**.

166, 167- Nov. 3, 1777- Thomas **Craft** and wife Elizabeth to James **Brame** of Mecklinburg Co., VA. for 200 pds. 221 acres on both sides of Crooked Run in **Linsey**'s line-
Wts: James **Hague**, Dennis **Driskill**.

167, 168- Nov: 22, 1776- Edmund **Partee** to James **Cozart** for 50 pds. 100 acres on **Cozart**'s old line being all the land Anthony **Cozart** Sr sold to Edmund **Partee**.
Wts: James **Gunter**, Robert **Alsion**, Benjamin **Partee**.

168, 169- Aug. 6, 1777- Michael **Satterwhite** to James **Satterwhite** for 100 pds 572 acres on **Harris**'s line on both sides of **Michael**'s creek on Mitchel **Murray**'s line, at **Davenport**'s corner.
Wts: Jno. **Tarver**, Randal **Mitchel**.

220

169, 170- Nov. 4, 1777- James **Willis** to Ambrose **Barker** for 200 pds. 150 acres at John **Hogan**'s line, **Smith**'s and **Benton**'s lines, on Reedy Branch.
Wts: none- - Elizabeth, wife of James **Willis** relinquishes her dower.

170, 171- Sept. 6, 1777- Thomas **Fowler** and wife Jean to John **Kelley** for 220 pds. 303 acres on Tar river in Granville.
Wits: Reuben **Searcy**, Miles **Wells**, James **Norvell**.

171, 172- Jan. 13, 1776- William **Bullock** to **eek** (?)[**Peck**] for 100 pds. 142 acres on forks of Neuse river on Nap of Reeds creek at Tyree **Harris**'s corner. out of ***McCulloch** tract.*
Wts: Robert **McCulloh**, Catherine **Bullock**.

172, 173- Oct. 7, 1776- Leuroy **VanLandingham** to Samuel **Morse** for 53 pds. 13 shls. 4 pence, 150 acres on Ruin creek at **Bodine**'s line, John **Hayes'** line, John **Craft**'s, Abraham **Morse**'s line.
Wts: James **Stark**, David and Elijah **Mitchel**, Thos. **Satterwhite**.

173, 174- Nov. 4, 1777- Michael **Wilson** to Ambrose **Barker** for 100 pds. 108 acres at **Benton**'s line on Reedy Branch at **Caudle**'s line.
Wts: none (Amey, wife of Michael **Wilson** relinquishes her dower right.

175 thru 177- Oct. 11, 1777- William **Barton** mortgages to William **Johnston** one of execrs of Darwin **Elwick**, deceased, of Orange Co. N. C. for 300 pds. 700 acres in Granville Co., N. C. on both sides of Tar river including Moses **Linsey**'s and James **Gowan** improvements on land, one moiety of a tract of 200 acres on Tabbs creek adjoining **Dickerson**'s land as per deed from Samuel **Weaver** to Darwin **Elwick** Nov. 10, 1763, and one moiety of 500 acres on Poplar creek granted to Darwin **Elwick** Oct. 23, 1754 and one moiety of tract on Poplar creek of 420 acres granted to **Elwick** July 29, 1761,and one moiety of tract on Tabbs creek granted to **Elwick** for 680 acres Dec. 2, 1760- one other moiety of 525 acres granted to John **Mauldin** Dec. 5, 1761 and sold to **Elwick**- - also two negroes mortgaged.

177- Nov. 3, 1777- William **Barton** one of heirs of Darwin **Elwick** late of Granville Co. appoints William **Johnston** of Orange Co. as attorney to handle interest in above tracts of land.
Wts: Bromfield **Ridley**.

178- Jan, 10, 1777- John **Warmouth** to Edward **Homes** for 40 pds. 100 acres on **Downey**'s line and on Norris creek.
Wts: James **Walker**, George **Head**.

179- Aug. 20, 1777- Giles **Hudspeth** of Surry Co., N. C. to Abel **Tatom** of Granville Co., N. C. for 150 pds. 300 acres at Aquila **Snelling**'s line taking in plantation whereon Rody **Bramit** now lives and part of land bought by Gibbe

Chavis of John **Mitisock**.
Wts: Ralph and John **Hudspeth**.

180- Nov. 3, 1777- Sherwood **Harris** to James **Johnson** for 100 pds. 200 acres on W side of Cattail branch.
Wts: Reuben **Searcy**, Henry **Tuder**.

181- Aug. 1, 1777- Giles **Hudspeth**, of Surry Co., N. C., to his son John **Hudspeth** of Granville Co., N. C. for 75 pds. 200 acres on S side of Fishing creek on William **Douglas**'s line.
Wts: Isaia **Cox**, Ralph **Hudspeth**.

182- Oct. 15, 1777- Nicholas **Metlock** to James **Thompson** of Louisa Co., VA. for 300 pds. 200 acres on S side of Tabbs creek where old Trading path crosses (Mary, wife of **Metlock**, relinquishes her dower right).
Wts: Abner **Tatom**, John **Thompson**, James **Jett**.

183- Aug. 8, 1775- John **Hamilton** late of Nansemond Co., VA. to Reuben **Searcy** for 25 pds. 100 acres on both sides of Hatcher's creek at John **Morris**'s corner.
Wts: John **Williams**.

184- Nov. 22, 1776- Anthony **Cozart**, Sr. to James **Cozart** for 25 pd. 50 acres in Granville Co. at mouth of Persimmon Branch at **Cozart**'s old line.
Wts: John **Mise**, James **Gunter**.

185- May 6, 1777- Thomas **Rice** to Edward **Bullock** for 60 pds. 100 acres on Fishing creek.
Wts: Reuben **Searcy**, Richard **Searcy**.

221

186- Feb. 1, 1773- John **Dickerson** to Zacharias **Higgs** for 27 pds. 150 acres on W side of Tabbs creek on Justus **Parrish**'s line.
Wts: John **Peace**, Jr.

187, 188- Aug. 5, 1777- Isham **Cordel** (**Caudle**) and Elizabeth his wife to Thomas **Bradford** for 85 pds. 100 acres on S side of Tar river on **Jones**' line-
Wts: Thos. **Veases**, Wm. **Burford**, Robert **Allison**.

188, 189- Oct. 5. 1777- Littleton **Mapp** and wife Elizabeth to John **Oliver** for 133 pds. 415 acres on both sides of Cub Creek whereon **Mapp** lives.
Wts: James **Langston**, John **Washington**, James **Benton**.

189, 190- Jan. 30, 1776- Robert **Allison** to Absalom **Foard** for 46 pds. 6 shls. 8, pence, 150 acres on W side of Tar river being part of a grant to William **Tonily** (?) Nov. 29, 1760.
Wts: Richard **Harris**, Margret **Boyd**, John **Oliver**.

190, 191- Nov. 3, 1777- Solomon **Langston** to Thomas **Goss** for 303 pds. 6 s shls. 8 pence 400 acres on S side of Tar river at mouth of Mountain Creek at **Langston**'s corner.
Wts: James **Langston**, Wm. **Philpott**.

191, 192- Oct. 7, 1777- Daniel **Williams** to Benjamin **Roberson** for 100 pds. 220 acres being land Daniel **Williams** purchased of William **Taylor** adjoining land of James **Taner**, John **Collins**, William **Duncan**, Richd **Taylor** and John **Hargrove**.
Wts: Leonard and William **Sims**.

193, 194- Oct. 1, 1777- Robert **Williams** and wife Sarah to Robert **Wooding** of Halifax Co., VA. for 3000 pds. 734 acres in Granville Co. on W side of Hico road at lower end of Nut Bush old race path, on Col. William **Bullock** line and lands of James **Hunt**, Thomas **Lanier** and that that forrmerly belongs to Joseph **Winston**, being land **Joseph Williams**, deceased, gave to the aforesaid Sarah in his last will which now belongs to Robert **Williams** by marriage to Sarah, wife and widow of Joseph **Williams** decd.
Wts: John **Lain**, John **Rice**, Mary **Lain**, Bartlett **Searcy**.

195, 195- Feb. 3, 1776- Thomas **Norman** to Mourning **Hunt** for 150 pds. 190 acres on Ruin creek at Len Henley **Bullock**'s corner.
Wts: Sherwood **Harris**, John **Washington**.

195, 196- Dec. 4, 1778 Ambrose **Barker** to Len H. **Bullock** for 300 pds. land on **Benton**'s old line, **Hamilton**'s line, **Smith**'s line including all land bought of James **Willis** and Michael **Wilson** by **Barker**, Nov. 4, 1777.
Wts: none.

196, 197- Oct. 5, 1764- William **Bullock** to Len Henley **Bullock** for 500 pds. 580 acres on **Anderson**'s swamp at **Daniel**'s branch on **Daniel**'s line near the road, in **Searcy**'s line, on John **Wade**'s corner.
Wts: George **Sims** and William **Sims**.

198 - Feb. 5, 1777- Robert **Harris**, Sr. to Elisha **Linsey** for 65 pds. 215 acres on Meadow Spring Branch in Luke **Carrol**'s old line.
Wts: Reuben **Searcy**, David **Harris**.

199, 200- Dec. 9, 1777- Littleton **Mapp** to Peter **Noland** for 68 pds. 15 shls. 200 acres being part of tract granted to William **Jones** Nov. 29, 1760 at **Rose**'s line, to Frances' creek on **Green**'s line.
Wts: James **Gunter**, Sampson (Samson) **Noland**.

200, 201- Jan. 1778- William Hargraves **Searcy** to Henry **Reardon** for 10 pds. 7 3/4ths acres on **Boling**'s creek and another tract of 1 ½ acres.
Wts: Richard **Searcy**, Reuben **Searcy**.

201, 202- Sept. 30, 1771- Lewis **Thomas** of Bertie Co., N.C. to Len. Henley **Bullock** for 50 pds. 150 acres on Fishing creek in Granville Co. on Robert **Hicks**'s line which was formerly held by John **Lewis** and deeded to Lewis **Thomas** Oct. 22, 1760.
Wts: John **Bullock**, Jr., William **Sims**, Joseph **Smith**, Turner **Jordan**.

202, 203- Oct. 10, 1777- William **Jones**, Sr. and wife Elizabeth to Henry **Green** for 150 pds. 202 acres on both sides of Nap of Reeds creek on **Townsen**'s line, Capt. **Hampton**'s corner, John **Walker**'s corner.
Wts: George **Wright**, William **Jones**, Jr., William **Merryman**.

222

203, 204 . . . 1778- John **Searcy**, Sr. to Henry **Reardon** for 100 pds. 165 acres at Richard **Searcy**'s corner.
Wts: Reuben and Richard **Searcy**.

204, 205- Feb. 3, 1778- William **Moore** and James **Moore** execrs. of the last will of Edward **Moore** deceased, to John **Mitchel** for 800 pds. 385 acres on both sides of Mill creek at William **Gragg**'s former line.

205, 206- Feb. 2, 1778- Len Henley **Bullock** to Charles Rust **Eaton** for 170 pds. 488 acres along **Eaton**'s line, **Spivey**'s line including Bare Pond.
Wts: M. **Hunt**, Wm. **Taylor**.

206, 207- Jan. 12, 1778- John **White** to Robert **Allison**, Sr. for 275 pds. 292 acres on both sides of Fishing creek which was granted Aug. 3, 1759 to Robert **Harris** by Earl Granville (signed John,and Mary **White**, his wife.).
Wts: Sherwood **White**, John **Allison**.

208, 209- Feb. 1, 1778- Robert **Hicks** to Thomas **Hicks**, his son, for 75 pds. 300 acres which Robert **Hicks** purchased of George **Morris** Feb. 3, 1755, and also two negroes. If Thomas **Hicks** die without bodily heirs then the land and negroes to go to Robert **Bell**, son of Thomas **Bell** and Sarah **Bell** his wife, and grandson of Robert **Hicks**.
Wts: Robert **Hester**, Benjamin **Hester**.

209, 210- Nov. 6, 1777- William **Moore** of Caswell Co., N. C. to George **Howard** of Granville Co., N. C. for 150 pds. 200 acres on Tar river in **Taylor**'s line-
Wts: Wm. **Kennon**, A. **Tatom**.

210, 211- Sept. 12, 1775- Jeremiah **Bailey**, Sr. to William **Bailey** for 20 pds. 150 acres on both sides of Newlit creek in **Man**'s and **Fuller**'s lines-
Wts: William **Jones**, John **Baley**, Jones **Fuller**.

211, 212- Jan. 26, 1778- Rowland **Terry** and wife Henritta to Joseph **Winston** of Surry Co., N. C. for 200 pds. 200 acres on N. side of Little Nut Bush creek at Joseph **Winston**'s line formerly James **Terry**'s.
Wts: Thos. **Satterwhite**, John **Walker**, William **Byars**, Robert **Williams**.

212, 213- Sept. 16, 1777- Reuben **Piles** to Joseph Acin (Akin) of the Colony of Virginia, for 200 pds. 460 acres on waters of **Gilliam**'s branch in Granville Co., N. C. at Richard **Taylor**'s line, **Hargrove**'s line.
Wts: John **Tarver**, Randal **Mitchell** (also spelled Randolph.)

213, 214- Dec. 1, 1777- Mourning **Hunt** to Robert **Hester** for 50 pds. 100 acres on both sides of Fishing creek on east side of New Road.
Wts: James **Currin**, Benjamin **Hester**.

214, 215- July 23, 1776- Nathaniel **Snipes** to James **Simple** for 77 pds. 200 acres on branches of **Hatcher**'s Run being the land **Hamilton** and Co. sold to John **Hogan** Nov. 7, 1766.
Wts: Abraham **Potter**, Alexa **Campbell**.

215, 216- Nov. 21, 1777- James **Yancey** to Phillip **Yancey** for 50 pds. 200 acres at Thornton **Yancey**'s upper corner in the country line.
Wts: Thornton **Yancey**, John **Smith**, John **Baynes**.

217, 218- Jan. 17, 1778- Augustine **Davis** and wife Molley. and Absalom **Davis** to John **Penn** for 110 pds. 150 acres on N. side of Michal's creek on Rowland **Terry**'s line- Absalom **Davis** exchanged part of the land with his son Augustine **Davis** for other lands in lieu thereof, and no deed having been made, this deed is made with consent of al. parties.
Wts: John **Taylor**, Jr., Rowland **Terry**, John **Trainham**.

218, 219- Feb. 5, 1778- Sherwood **Harris** and wife Ann to John **Hawkins** for 450 pds. 225 acres on Tar river on Nicholas creek.
Wts: none.

219, 220 - Nov. 24, 1769- Joseph **Miller** and wife Nancey to John **Hammock** for 25 pds. 200 acres on **Hill**'s line to the path leading from Phillip **Taylor**'s Race paths towards George **King**'s to a line of Jonathan **Parker**'s which land was taken up by Jonathan **Parker** and sold to Joseph **Miller**.
Wts: David **Knott**, John **Knott**.

221, 222- Nov. 4, 1777- in the 2nd year of our Independence, William and James **Moore** of Wake Co., N. C. executors of last will of Edward **Moore** dec'd and Edward **Moore** of Granville Co., N. C. to Samuel **Smith** of Granville Co.

223
for 153 pds. 6 shls. 8 pence, 200 acres on bothe sides of Beaverdam crk. in Granville Co., as per deed made by Henry **McCulloch** to Edward **Moore** Aug. 15, in the third year of the Reign of George the third of Great Brtn.
Wts: John **Oliver**, Elijah **Moore**, Reuben **Searcy**, Philip **Yancey**.

222, 223- Feb. 4, 1778- John **Hawkins**, Jr. of Bute Co., N. C. to Joseph **McDaniel** of Granville Co., N. C. for 133 pds. 6 shls. 8 pence 80 acres on S side of Ruin creek at what is called **Campbell**'s line. which is all **Hawkins** owns on South side of Ruin creek.
Wts: Phil **Hawkins**, Ben **Wade**, Samuel **Fuller**.

223, 224- Nov. 3, 1777- John **Hooker** to Joshua **James** for 200 pds. 200 acres being part of the 100,000 acres formerly belonging. to Henry **McCulloch** commonly called *Tract. No. 12*- on Andrew **Hampton**'s line on middle fork of Beaverdam creek.
Wts: John **Dickerson**, Jonathan **Rives**.

224, 225- Feb. 2, 1778- Bailey **Fleming** and wife Ann of Bute Co., N. C. to Charles **Wortham** of county and State aforesaid, for 37 pds. 37 acres on E side of Middle fork of **Anderson** Swamp at **Daniel**'s corner in Granville County, N. C.- signed Bailey and Ann **Fleming**.
Wts: Jno. **Fleming**, James **Baley**, Phil **Hawkins**, Jr.

226- Nov. 26, 1777- Luke **Harp** to Frederick **Wever** for 100 pds. 100 acre on S side of Middle creek to John **Rust**'s line along **Shappard**'s line.
Wts: John **Nevill**, John **Cook**.

227- Feb. 12, 1777- Peter **Vinson** to Robert **Jones** of Bute Co., N. C. for 120 pds. 226 acres on branches of Cedar creek and Middle creek at what formerly was Arthur **Fuller**'s line at dividing line between his land and that of John **Cape** along **Marshall**'s line (name spelled **Vincent** also).
Wts: Thos **Cook**, Daniel **Jones**.

228- Jan. 1, 1778- Michael **Redwile** to Richard Donaldson **Cooke** for a negro named Harry, a tract of land in Granville Co. purchased of Robert **Harris**, Jr. reserving 60 acres out of tract which **Harris** sold to Boling **Adcock** at the boundary line of Lord Granville and **McCulloch**'s lands and containing 360 acres excepting the 60 acres afore mentioned. Cresa **Redwile**, wife of Michael **Redwile** relinquishes her dower right).
Wts: Francis **Ross**, James **Hawkins**.

229, 230- Aug. 17, 1777- James **Yancey**, Sr. to Lewis **Yancey** for 100 pds. land on both sides of Mountain creek of Jonathan creek along part of tract bought by James **Yancey** Sr of Robert **Jones**, attny, as per deed Mar. 6, 1753 on Thos. **Mutter**'s line at Jesse **Landers** corner, George **Newton**'s line to the Country line containing 500 acres.
Wts: James **Yancey**, Jr., Thomas **Taylor**.

231, 232- Jan. 16, 1776- Thomas **Critcher** and wife Esther to Memucan **Hunt** for 60 pds. 143 acres on N. side of Tar river being land whereon Elizabeth **Williams** now lives and was bequeathed by will of William **Williams**, deceased, to his son Stephen **Williams** and by him transferred to Thomas **Critcher** by deed of trust.
Wts: Robert **Reid**, John **MacIver** (signed Thomas and Easter **Critcher**.

232, 233- Dec. 6, 1777- John **Morgin** to Richard **Head** for 25 pds. 25 acres at the county line on Grassy creek to mouth of Cedar branch.
Wts: Henry **Graves**, Nicholas **Newport**, Jacob **Owens**.

233, 234- Dec. 15, 1777- John **Chandler**. to William **Wright** of Mecklenburg Co., Va. for 110 pds. 50 acres on S side of Jonathan's creek in Granville Co., N.C. between **Larkins**, **Johnston**'s and William **Clayton**'s lines.
Wts: Nathl **Brown**, Ransom **Boswell**, Owen **Griffin**.

234, 235- Oct. 27, 1779 (1769) Henry **Fuller** to James **Moore** for 20 pds. 98 acres on Tabs creek at Ezekiel **Fuller**'s corner at old Ridge path to Edward **Harris**'s line.
Wts: Robert **Moore**, William **Askew**.

235, 236- Dec. 19, 1777- Sarah **Williams**, execrx., Robert **Williams**, Joseph **Williams**, Thomas **Lanier** and Richard **Harrison** excrs. of Joseph **Williams** deceased, to Lewis **Taylor** for 550 pds. 797 acres on Island creek in Granville Co. which was bought by Joseph **Williams** deceased, from his brother James **Williams**.
Wts: William **Bullock**, Jno. **Henderson**, Henry **Pattillo**, John **Tanner**.

224

237- Feb. 3, 1778- George **Roberts** to James **Daniel** for 226 pds., 13 shls. 4 pence, 250 acres on both sides of Tar river.

238- Mar. 27, 1775- Joseph **Waldrop** to Edmund **Taylor** of Virginia for 40 pds. 200 acres in Granville Co., N.C. on **Gillam**'s creek between lands of Edmund **Taylor**, Reuben **Pyles**, John **Hargrove** and vacant land.
Wts: John **Williams**, Francis **Taylor**.

239- Aug. 13, 1777- Archibald **Hamilton** and Co., merchants, to Richard **Posey** for 27 pds. 10 shls. 50 acres on **Anderson** Swamp at West **Harris**'s line in Granville Co., N.C.

Wts: Thomas **Person**, Will **Ross**, Stephen **Jett**.

240- Oct. 26, 1777- John **Body** to John **Whitfield** for 160 pds. 300 acres on Cedar creek at James **Blackwell**'s line, **Ledbetter**'s line being part of land granted to Richard **Bridges** who deeded to **Winningham** and he to **Dickerson** and he to **Boddie** signed John **Boddie**.
Wts: James **Blackwell**, James **Weathers**.

241- [243]- Jan. 30, 1768- Shem **Cook** to Harris **Gilliam** for 266 pds., 13 shls., 4 pence, 111 acres on both sides of Fort creek being part of land granted by Granville to James **Young** at dividing line between me and John **Heffelin** (**Heffellin**) and to line between **Cook** and Harris **Gilliam**.
Wts: John **Rust**, Frederick **Wever** Registered- Feb. 1778 acknowledged by Shem **Cook** as his act and deed-

243, 244- Dec. 23, 1777- Benjamin **Roberson** to Daniel **Williams** for 100 pds. 220 acres whereon Stephen **Hargrove** now lives that William **Traylor** sold to Daniel **Williams** at lines of James **Lane**, John **Collins**, Wm. **Dunkon**, Richard **Taylor** and John **Hargrove**.
Wts: John Smith **Hurt** [Jurat], Benja **Goodman**.

244, 245- Feb. 2, 1778- John **Hawkins** to James **Downey** for 900 pds. 350 acres on both sides of Island creek opposite upper Beaver ponds.
Wts: none.

245, 246- Jan. 29, 1768- Joseph **Wade** to Shem **Cook**, Sr. for 266 pds: 13 shillings, 4 pence, land on both sides of Fort creek being part of land granted by Granville to James **Young** at dividing line between me and John **Heffellin** and between me and Harris **Gilliam** containing 111 acres.
Wts: Joseph **Hill**, John **Heffellin**.

247- Feb. 2, 1778- John **Fleming** and wife Mary to Charles **Wortham** of Bute Co., N.C. for 99 pds. 15 shls. 99 3/4ths acres on E side of middle fork of **Anderson**'s swamp at **Daniel**'s corner to **Bullock**'s line.
Wts: Phil **Hawkins**, Jr., John **Fleming**.

248, 249- July 25, 1774- Leonard Henley **Bullock** to William **Bullock** for 500 pds. 435 acres at Bartlet **Searcy**'s line along William **Cooper**'s line, at Elisha **Sims** and Leonard **Sims** line on Nut Bush creek.
Wts: Daniel **Williams**, Sherwood **Sims**.

249, 250- Dec. 16, 1774- Benjamin **Ragland** and wife Ann to Christopher **Harris** for 250 pds. 250 acres on Island creek and Nut Bush creek at **Davenport**'s old line, on Little Island creek.
Wts: Wm. **Wilson**, James **Stainback**, Burges **White**.

250, 251- Dec. 10, 1774- Benjamin **Ragland** and wife Ann to Christopher **Harris** for 100 pds. 212 acres on both sides of Hico road and on Little Island creek at **Clanton**'s, **Syms** and **Glover**'s lines, **Mitchel**'s and **Davenport**'s.
Wts: Wm. **Wilson**, James **Stainback**, Burges **White**.

251, 252- Jan. 8, 1778- Michal **Peeler** (**Pealor**) of Rowan Co, N. C. to James **Daniels** of Granville Co., N.C. for 5 shillings, 233 acres on N., side of Crooked Run-
Wts: Absalom **Davis**, Wilm **Cocke**, George **Roberts**.

252, 253- Apr. 19, 1774- Thomas **Pope** to James **Blackwell** for 210 pds. 388 acres in Granville and Bute Co., N.C. on Cedar creek at [Shemuel **Kerney**'s] line once Joseph **Fuller**'s line, on **Jones** creek, being part of tract granted by Lord Granville to Philemon **Bradford**, Sr. Nov. 13, 1756 and deeded to James **Vincent** who sold to Britain **Fuller** and he deeded to Solomon **Fuller** Jr: who sold to John **Pope**, Esq. and from him to Thomas **Banks** and **Banks** to John **Pope**, Esq. again and he deeded to Thomas **Pope**.
Wts: Thomas **Banks**, Jr., Thomas **Banks** Sr.

225

254, 255- Feb. 2 1778- Bailey **Fleming** (signed Bly **Fleming**) of Bute Co., N.C. to Jno. **Fleming** of Granville Co., N.C. for 100 pds. 50 acres on middle fork of **Anderson**'s swamp at **Person**'s line.
Wts: Phil **Hawkins**, Jr., Charles **Wortham**.

255, 256- Feb. 3, 1778- Joseph **McDaniel** and wife Sarah to John **Tatom** for 70 pds. 300 acres on N. side of Tar river in **Hudspeth**'s line and on **Chavers** line.

256, 257- Oct. 20, 1777- Archibald **Hamilton** and Co. of Halifax Co., N.C. merchants, to Edward **Moore** of Granville Co., N.C. for 640 pds. 640 acres in Granville Co. on both sides of Tar river.
Wts: Stephen **Jett**, Jno. **McDowall**, Wm. **Hamilton**.

258, 259- Oct. 20, 1777- Archibald **Hamilton** and Co. of Halifax Co., N.C. to Edward **Moore** for 1100 pds. 1203 acres in Granville Co. on Fishing creek at Michael **Wilson**'s corner in **Benton**'s line, **Willis** line.
Wts: Stephen **Jett**, Jno. **McDowall**, Wm. **Hamilton**.

259, 260- Oct. 20, 1777- Archibald **Hamilton** and Co. of Halifax Co., N.C. to Edward **Moore** for 200 pds. 200 acres in Granville Co. at Nathaniel **Henderson**'s line.
Wts: Stephen **Jett**, Jno. **McDowall**, Wm. **Hamilton**.

260, 261- Oct. 20, 1777- Archibald **Hamilton** and Co. of Halifax Co., N.C. to Edward **Moore** of Granville Co., N.C. for 500 pds. 500 acres at John **White**'s line on Sarah **Arnold**'s line.
Wts: Stephn **Jett**, Jno. **McDowall**, Wm. **Hamilton**.

262, 263- Oct. 20, 1777- Archibald **Hamilton** and Co. of Halifax Co. to Edward **Moore** for 200 pds. 200 acres which is part of land deeded William **Jordan** by Augustine **Bates** of branches of Fishing creek, in 1762, on **Bass**'s line.
Wts: Stephen **Jett**, Jno. **McDowall**, Wm. **Hamilton**.

263 thru 265- Apr. 4, 1770- Leonard Henley **Bullock**, Esq., sheriff of Granville Co., N.C. to Ishum **Parham**- Debt owed by Phillip **Pryor** to William **Tryon**, Esq. and court orders property of **Pryor** sold to pay debt. 600 acres on both sides of Reedy creek at **Smith**'s, **Willis**'s lines sold to highest bidder who was Isham **Parham**.
Wts: Jno. **Campbell**, Thomas **Mutter**.

265 thru 267- July 19, 1777- Sheriff Len Henley **Bullock** of Granville Co., N.C. sold at public sale the property of Robert **Eyre** and William **Jackson** for debt due, to [Zachariah] **Bullock** land in Granville Co. 640 acre.
Wts: Thos. **Henderson**.

268, 269- May 4, 1778- John **Lewis**, Jr. to Howel **Lewis** of Halifax, Va. for 2500 pds. 2311 acres in Granville Co., on a branch of Grassy creek whereon John **Lewis**, Jr., now lives bounded by estate of Phillip **Taylor**, deceased, and lands of Thomas **Persons** known as *The Mountain tract*, and also by land of Robert **Lewis**, James **Downey**, James **Johnston**, and vacant land-
Wts: none (Catherine wife of John **Lewis** relinquishes dower right.

269, 270 Apt. 16, 1778- John **Roe** to Thomas **Pool** for 130 pds. 100 acres on N. side of Grassy creek at mouth of HayStack branch to Robert **Beasley**'s line-
Wts: Daniel **Grant** (Judith **Roe**, wife of John **Roe**, relinquishes her dower right in land).

270, 271- Mar. 28, 1778- Robert **Busley** (**Burley**) of Lunenburg Co., Va. to Thomas **Pool** of Granville Co., N.C. for 28 pds. 56 acres on Grassy creek on Daniel **Grant**'s line-
Wts: Thomas **Grant**, Benja **Crenshaw**, Danl **Grant**.

271, 272- Aug. 22, 1771- John **Verner** to Len Henley **Bullock** for 40 pds. 10 acres on **Mead**'s line.
Wts: Daniel **Williams**, Wm. **Burford**.

272, 273- Mar. 2, 1778- Reuben **Pyles** and wife **Hester** to John **Baggit** for 20 pds. 300 acres on N. side of Tar river (signed Reuben and Esse **Pyles**).
Wts: John **Mitchell**, Richard **Featherstone**, William **Davenport**.

274- Mar. 5, 1776- Zachariah **Boughan** from Robert **Allison** for 133 pds. 265 acres on **Thompson**'s line at **McCullock**'s line along **Williams** line, on **Jones**'s line.
Wts: Wm. **Ogelvie**, George **Thompson**, Wm. **Howel**.

226

275- May 6, 1778- John **Smith** to Benjamin **Smith** for 50 pds. 160 acres on both sides of Little Creek on Solomon **Smith**'s line at **Chavis**'s line.
Wts: none.

276- Jan. 5, 1778- John **Oliver** and wife Fanney to Joseph **Gooch** of Amelia Co., Va. for 800 pds. 400 acres in Granville Co., N. C, on both sides of Tar river at John **Landess**'s line, **Gwin**'s line, at Peter **Noland**'s line.
Wts: Gideon **Gooch**, James **Hunt**, George **Hunt**.

277, 278- Apr. 5, 1778- David **Fuller** to John **Champion** for 40 pds. 40 acres on both sides of Cedar creek at **Champion**s own line.
Wts: Richd **Champion**, John **Dent**.

278, 279- Apr. 4, 1770- Isham **Parham** to Leonard Henley **Bullock**, Esq. for 23 pds. 4 shillings 600 acres on both sides of Reedy Branch at **Smith**'s corner.
Wts: Absalom **Tatom**, Thomas **Mutter**.

279, 280- Mar. 13, 1776- Solomon **Langston** to Thomas **Person** for 60 pds. 200 acres on both sides of Ledge of Rocks creek at Lodowk **Ingle**'s corner on **Beck**'s line.
Wts: Stephen **Maritt**, Robert **Dickens**.

280, 281- Feb. 10, 1777- Christian **Pealor** (**Pealer**) to Thomas **Person** for 200 pds. 450 acres on both sides of **Shelton**'s creek including the plantation of sd. **Pealor** and Anthony **Pealor** (**Pealer**) on **Person**'s corner, **Slaughter**'s line.
Wts: David **Witherspoon**, John **Wilkerson**.

281, 282- May 21, 1777- Thomas **Person** to John **Guinn**, both of Granville Co., N.C. for 50 pds. 100 acres on fork of Mill creek and Tar river, being part of tract granted formerly to Andrew **Hampton** by Granville at **Phipps** corner, **Bradford**'s and **Knowland**'s lines.
Wts: William **Jones**, Mathew **Dewty**.

283- Jan. 22, 1776- John [**Boddie**] and wife Hannah to George **Nicholson**, Jr. for 100 pds. 200 acres being part of larger tract granted to Richard **Bridges** Mar. 11, 1760, on Cedar creek for 600 acres and deeded to James **Winningham** and by him to **Boddie**.
Wts: John **Pope**, Osborn **Pope**.

284, 285- Dec. 15, 1777- George **Thompson**, Sr. and wife Lucy to Simon **Clement** of Amelia Co., Va. for 650 pds. 500 acres on N. side of **Thompson**'s mill creek at **McCulloch**'s old line along Charles **Partee**'s line.
Wts: Gideon **Gooch**, Zepheniah **Clement**, James **Satterwhite**.

285, 286- Jan. 14, 1778- John **Oliver** and wife Fanney to Miles **Wells** for 300 pds. 415 acres in Granville and Caswell counties, N.C. on, N, side of Cub creek.
Wts: John **Washington**, John **Clement**, Daniel **Gooch**.

286, 287 Jan, 1, 1778- Thomas **Bradford** and wife Mary to John **Oliver** for 250 pds. 162 acres on S side of Tar river on **Landess**'s line, **Guinn**'s line and **Noland**'s line being part of land granted Isaac **Reeks** July 21, 1743.
Wts: John **Massay**, Thos **Bradford**, Jr., Philemon **Bradford**.

288- Dec. 16, 1777- William **Parrel** (**Parral**) to John **Withers** for 160 pds. 350 acres on both sides of Beaverdam creek at **McCulloch**'s line granted to Philemon **Bradford** Aug. 1, 1762 and he deeded to **Parrel**.
Wts: Joshua **Pope**, Osborn **Pope**.

289, 290- May 4, 1778- Thomas **Person** to Richard **Bennit** for 400 pds. 550 acres on both sides of Grassy creek purchased of Thos **Tarry** and William **Wharton** on lines of land of **Daniels**, **Wilkerson**, **Kennon**.
Wts: Peter **Bennet**.

290, 291- Sept. 19, 1775- Julius **Nichols** of Bute Co., N.C. to Leonard Henley **Bullock** of Granville Co., N.C. for 100 pds. 631 acres on both sides of the Main road on branches of deep creek in **Bird**'s line.
Wts: Richd **Henderson**, Mary **Goodloe**.

291, 292- Apr. 4, 1778- James **Hunt** to James **Raven**, a deed of gift of 200 acres, being part of tract I live on at Drury **Smith**'s line of land purchased of Nathl **Patterson** on Wm. **Amies** line including land whereon Hezekiah **Chiles** has lived for some time.
Wts: Reuben **Searcy**, Daniel **Williams**.

292, 293- Jan. 7, 1775- Richard **Henderson** to Len Henley **Bullock** for 70 pds. 156 acres bounded by lands of Bartlet **Searcy**, Elisha **Sims**, **Bullock**'s, Daniel **Williams** and John [**Searcy**'s] lands.
Wts Jno. **Williams**.

227

293, 294- Feb. 12, 1778- Edward **Bullock** to William **Wright** of Louisa Co., VA. for 120 pds. 100 acres in Granville Co. near the road.
Wts: Wm. **Hicks**, Thomas **Thompson**.
Winifred, wife of Edward **Bullock**, relinquishes dower right.

294, 295- Mar. 20, 1778- Richard Donaldson **Cooke** to Robert **Harris**, Sr. for 300 pds. 360 acres reserving 52 acres out of tract which Robert **Harris**, Jr. sold to a certain Boling **Adcock**, at the boundary line between Lord Granville's and **McCulloch**'s land.
Wts: John **Potter**, John **Hawkins**.

295, 296- May 5, 1778- Nathan **Childs** and wife Elizabeth to John **Thorp** of Amelia Co., VA. for 277 pds. 10 shls. 302 acres in Granville. Co., N. C. on W side of Island creek on **Minter**'s corner in **Lewis** Line.
Wts: John **Oliver**, Gideon **Gooch**, Benjamin **Hester**.

296, 297- Feb. 8, 1778- Thomas **Person** to John **Smith** for 100 pds. 480 acres on both sides of Little creek at **Chavers** line.
Wts: Memucan **Hunt**, Benja **Goodman**.

297, 298- Mar. 22, 1778- Robert **Harris** to Samuel **Harris** for 100 pds. 584 acres near head of Mirey branch.
Wts: Thos. **Harris**, Jemima **White**.

298, 299- Aug. 3, 1778- William **Burford** gave to his son William **Burford**, Jr. 200 acres on both sides of Ledge of Rocks creek whereon William, Jr. now lives at Frederick **Peeks** line.
Wts: Danl **Burford**, Richard **Clements**.

299, 300- Aug. 3, 1778- George **Stovall** (**Stovaul**) and wife Ann of Mecklenburg Co., VA. to William **Pool** of Granville Co., N. C. for 72 pds. 320 acres on N. side of Grassy creek, both sides of Rattle Snake branch being one half land **Stovall** now lives on (that is Josiah **Stovall**).
Wts: none.

300, 301- Aug. 4, 1778- Henry **Fuller** to John **Edwards** for 30 pds. 263 acres at Samuel **Fuller**'s line, Henry **Fuller**'s line, Littleton **Fuller**'s line on Long creek and up Great Branch.
Wts: Wm. **Hornsby**, Wm. **Roberts**.

301, 302- May 12, 1778- Richard **Yancey**, Sr. of Mecklenburg Co., VA. to gave to his son Charles **Yancey** 240 acres in Granville Co., N. C. on both sides of Beach creek on Jonathan's creek on John **Young**'s line, **Stovall**'s line.
Wts: Thomas **Grant**, James **Smith**, John **Young**.

302, 303- July 5, 1777- **Reuben Searcy** to Henry **Straider** for 110 pds. 136 acres on both sides of **Hampton**'s creek at Nicholas **Holsteins**, Ephraim **Hampton**'s lines-
Wts: Robt. **Harris**, William **Jacobs**.
Susanna, wife of Reuben **Searcy**, relinquishes her dower right.

303, 304- June 27, 1778- Mathew **Flournoy** and wife Elizabeth of Charlotte Co., VA, to Lemuel **Smith**, Pittsylvania Co., VA. for 200 pds. land which was deeded to Elizabeth **Smith**, widow, by Lord Granville.
Wts: Samuel and Robert **Flournoy**, John P. **Smith**.

304, 305 . . .1778- Francis **Howard** to Thomas **Owen** for 50 pds. 15 acres on Grassy creek at **Owen**'s line, **Howard**'s line.
Wts: Danl **Grant**, Charles **Edwards**.

306, 307- Oct. 1, 1778- Edward **Silva** to John **Dickerson** for 30 pds. 170 acres on N. side of Tar river on old Ridge Path.
Wts: John **Easter**, John **Moore**.

307, 308- Jan. 1778- Henry **Reardon** to William Hargraves **Searcy** for 10 pds. 7 3/4ths acres-
Wts: Reuben **Searcy**, Richard **Searcy**.

308, 309- Oct. 1, 1777- James **Stark** and wife Jane to Robert **Fleming** for 80 pds. 152 acres at Reuben **Moss**es line on Nut Bush creek.
Wts: Reuben **Morse**, Charnick **Cox**, Joshua **Denton**.

309, 310- May 5, 1778- Jane **Newton**, George **Newton** and Ursley his wife, to John **Young** for 100 pds. land on Mountain fork of Jonathan's creek including the plantation whereon **Newton**'s now live at James **Yancey**'s line containing 100 acres.
Wts: James **Langston**, Wm. **Webb**, Jona **Knight**.

228

311- Sept. 17, 1777- Abraham **Potter** to Charles **Partee** for 14 pds. 10 shls., 15 acres at mouth of Edmund **Partee**'s spring branch whereon **Potter** now lives-
Wts: Edmd **Partee**, John **Finley**.

312. 1778- George **Newman** and William **Vickery** to Thomas **Lanier** for 900 pds. 450 acres on both sides of **Michael**'s creek being part of land granted by Lord Granville to John **Bird** Nov. 27, 1760.
Wts: Ben **Wade**, James **Daniel**.
Elizabeth, wife of William **Vickery** relinquishes her dower right and Frances wife of George **Newman** relinquishes her dower right in land. Ann wife of Augustine **Davis**, relinquishes her dower right.

313- Dec. 25 1777- William **Jacob** to Robert **Russel** for 3 pds. 100 acres on N. side of Mill creek.
Wts: Henry **Straider**, George **Straider**.

314- Dec. 29, 1774- Joseph **Cooper** to John **Dickerson** for 10 pds. 50 acres on S side of Tar river at **Nevell**'s corner on the Ford branch.
Wts: John **Peace**, Jr., Samuel **Brumitt**.

315- Feb. 6, 1777- Reuben **Bass** to Ben **Wright** for 8 pds. 50 acres on Beaverdam creek which **Bass** bought of Lawrence **Peteford** near **McCulloch**'s line-
Wts: Charles **Nowlin**, Daniel **Nowlin**.

316- May 13, 1778- Benjamin **Howard** to William **Hickman** for 100 pds. 164 acres on both sides of Hay Meadow branch at line that formerly was **Mitchel**'s-
Wts: David **Howard**, Benjamin **Beardon**.
Lucy, wife of Benjamin **Howard**, relinquishes her dower right.

317- May 15, 1778- David **Fuller** to Charles **Knowlin** (**Nowland**) for 51 pds., 3 shls. 4 pence, 100 acres on Cedar creek on road. at **Fuller**'s line,**Pope**'s corner.
Wts: James **Blackwell**, James **Weathers**.

318- July 31, 1778- Moses **Overton** of Mecklenburg Co., VA and wife Elizabeth to Robert **Burton** of Granville Co., N. C. for 60 pds. 360 acres in Granville Co., N. C.-
Wts: Peter **Oliver**, James **Pool**, Thos. **Young**.

319- Sept. 26, 1774- Joseph **Cooper** to Thomas **Person** for 100 pds. 175 acres on S side of Tar river along **Rust**'s line, **Jones**'s line.

Wts: William **Kennon**, John **Kennon**.

320- May 30, 1778- Reuben **Pyles** to Robert **Gillespie** for 133 pds. 14 shls.land on both sides of **Taylor's** road at John **Hargraves** line and Jos. **Taylor**'s line.
Wts: Joseph **Akin**, Howell **Taylor** (Esse, wife of **Pyles**, relinquishes dower.

321- May 14, 1778- Thomas **Person** to Francis **Howard** for 60 pds. 150 acres on Grassy creek at **Howard**'s corner, at **Duty**'s Spring branch.
Wts: Rowland **Thomas**.

322- Jan. 18, 1769- John **Hamilton** of Halifax Co., N. C. to John **Dickerson** of Granville Co., N. C. for 10 pds. 170 acres on N. side of Tar river.
Wts: Stephen **Jett**, Henry **Fuller**.

323- May 30, 1778- Reuben **Piles** (**Pyles**) to James **Akin** of Chesterfield Co., VA. for 216 pds. 6 shls. 320 acres in Granville Co., N. C. on **Gilliam's** branch being residue of larger tract of which tract he sold parts to Joseph **Akin** and to Robt. **Gillespie** being all lands between lands of Joseph **Akin**, Robert **Gillespie**, Joseph **Taylor**, Ebenezar **McHarg** and Philemon **Hawkins** (Essey, wife of said **Pyles**, relinquishes dower.
Wts: Robt. **Gillespie**, Joseph **Akin**.

324- Aug. 4, 1777- Abraham **Potter** and wife Sarah to William **Webb** for 800 pds. 800 acres adjoining lands of Len. **Adcock**, Wm. **Bullock**, Charles **Partee** and Michael **Cockleree** which was purchased by **Potter** of Charles **Partee**, Edmd **Partee** and Robt. **Boyd**.
Wts: Danl **Grant**, John **Young**.
Sarah, wife of Abraham **Potter** relinquishes her dower right.

325- Aug. 1, 1778- Joseph **Winston** and wife Elizabeth of Surry Co., N. C. to Robert **Williams** of Granville Co., N. C. for 453 pds. 15 shls. land on NW side of Little Nut Bush creek containing 40 acres, at William **Taylor's** corner, being land bought of James and Rowland **Terry** and James **Mitchel**.
Wts: Robert **Hyde**, James **Merritt**, Jacob **Price**, Wm. **Masters**.
Signed by Joseph and Bettey **Winston**.

229

326, 327- Aug. 4, 1778- John **Smith** to Solomon **Smith** for 20 pds. land of 150 acres which was deeded from Thomas **Person** to John **Smith** on the road on Pimple Hill-
Wts: none.

327, 328- Oct. 19, 1767- William **Chavers**, Jr. to Edward **Silvey** for 30 pds., 170 acres on N. side of Tar river on old Ridge road.
Wts: William **Phillips**, Antho **Phillips**.

328, 329 July 29, 1761- Grant to Abraham **Cook** for 700 acres on Island creek at **Mitchel**'s, **Ford**'s, **Glover**'s, **Harris**'s, **Satterwhite**'s and on **Cook**'s own line, in Granville Co., N. C by Lord Granville.
Signed by Thos **Child** as agent-

329, 330- Nov. 27, 1760- Grant to James **McGehee**, from Lord Granville for 600 acres in Granville Co., on both sides of **Taylor**'s creek.

330, 331- May 22, 1776- Benjamin **Ragland** to Evan **Ragland** for 50 pds. 320 acres in Granville Co., N. C. on Flat creek.
Wts: Thomas **Critcher**, Elijah **Mitchel**, Thomas **Critcher** Jr.

331, 332- Aug. 4, 1778- Evan **Ragland** to Benjamin **Ragland** for 50 pds. 320 acres on N. side of Flat creek on old courthouse road.
Wts: Bromfield **Ridley**, Chesley **Daniel**.

END OF BOOK*L**

Granville Co., N. C. Record of Deeds
book M

230-----
Index precedes--

Page 1-thru 3- May 10,1755- Grant from Lord Granville to William **Eaton** for 630 acres on both sides of Tabbs creek at corner of **Eaton**'s old land.

3 thru 6- May 10,1755- Grant from Lord Granville to William **Eaton** for 213 acres on both sides of Tabbs creek on **Chavers** lines, at his own line.

6 thru 8- May 10,1755- Grant from Lord Granville to William **Eaton** for 190 acres on Ea side of Ruin creek at **Eaton**'s old line.

8 thru 11- May 10,1755- Grant to William **Eaton** for 479 acres on east side of Ruin creek at his own corner

11 thru 14- May 10, 1755- Grant to Francis **Mabry** for 265 acres on his own line on both sides of Tar river

14 thru 17- Oct. .23, 1754- Grant to Darwin **Elwick** for 500 acres on both sides of Poplar creek

17 thru 20- May 9,1755- Grant to Col. John **Haywood** for 449 acres on both sides of Tabbs creek.

20, 21- May -1755- John **Haywood** of Edgecombe Co.,N. C. to William **Chavers** for 5 shillings, 449 acres of a grant transferred to **Chavers**.
Wts: Sher **Haywood**, A. **Smith**.

21 thru 23- May 10,1755- Grant to Col. John **Haywood** of Edgecombe Co N. C. for 637 acres in Granville Co. on S side of Little creek

24- May-- 1755- John **Haywood** of Edgecombe Co.,N. C. to William **Chaver** of Granville Co. deeds the 637 acres above granted--

24 thru 27- May 7; 1755- Grant to John **Dosier** of Granville Co., N. C. for 557 acres on E side of Mill creek at head of Alexanders branch at Henry **King**'s line.

27 thru 30- Mar. 25, 1749- Grant to Gideon **Macon** of Granville Co. for 500 acres on both sides of Hub Quarter creek on Benjamin **Kimbal**'s line.

31 thru 33- Apr. 8, 1753- Grant to Philemon **Hawkins** for 560 acres on his own old line in Granville Co. N. C.

34 thru 36- Apr,28,1753- Grant to Phileomon **Hawkins** for 325 acres on both sides of Ashley's creek.

37 thru 39- Oct.24, 1754- Grant to Claborn **Harris** for 300 acres on Little Ruin Creek in Granville Co.

40, 41- Mar. 21, 1778- Abraham **Cook** and wife Amey to Sherwood **Harris** for 375 pds. 435 acres in Granville Co. on Tar river on Elisha **Linsey**'s line on Cattail creek.
Wts: Robert **Allison**, Thos. **Wilburn**.

41, 42- Feb. 5, 1777- Abraham **Cooke** and wife Amey to Elisha **Linsey** for 15 pds. 50 acres on E side of Tar river on Spring branch.
Wts: David and Sherwood **Harris**.

42, 43- June 6, 1778- William **Jacob** to William **Jones** for 50 pds. 100 acres on S side of Mill creek.
Wts: John **Gwin**.

43, 44. 45- Oct. 1,1778- William **Phillips** to John **Dickerson** for 22 pds. 170 acres on N. side of Tar river.
Wts: John **Easter**, Charles **Moore**.

45, 46- Mar. 9, 1778- John **McKesock** of Bute Co., N. C. to John **Dickerson** for 40 psis. 198 acres on both sides of Little

creek.
Wts: Jno. **Peace** Jr., Wm. **McKissock**.

46, 47- Dec. 30, 1777- William **Cockrel** (**Cockrill**) to [Malaehy **Frazier**] for 50 pds. 65 acres on Grassy creek in **Frazier**'s old corner, **Person**'s line where William **Cockrell** now lives.
Wts: John **Dunkin**, Catron **Cockrell**.

47, thru 49- Aug. 12, 1778- William **Jones** to Peter **Knowland** for 50 pds. 300 acres on N. side of Frank's creek on Peter **Knowland**'s old line and

231
whereon **Knowland** now lives.
Wts: Henry **Green**, Jacob **Brantlon**, Job **Green**.

49, 50- Oct. 1, 1778- John **Potter** and wife Mary to John **Hawkins** and Abraham **Potter** for 2600 pds. 580 acres in Granville Co., N. C. on Tar river near the Beaver house at **Harris**'s line and on Nicholas's creek.
Wts: Reuben **Searcy**, Sherwood **Harris**.

50, 51- Dec. 26, 1777- Robert **Downey** to William **Frazier**, for 100 pds. 100 acres on Grassy creek in **Lewis**'s line, **Frazier**'s line whereon Robert **Downey** now lives.
Wts: David **Knott**, James **Downey**, Robert **Malone**.

52, 53- Nov. 3, 1778- Richard **Posey** to Ralph **Neal** for 60 pds. 30 acres on Isham **Harris**'s line, Arthur **Jordan**'s line, Green **Dukes** line, **Neal**'s line.
Wts: Phil **Hawkins**, Major **Mitchel**.

53 thru 55- Nov. 24, 1777- Thomas **Yates** to James **Bullock** for 236 pds. two tracts of land on North side of Ledge of Rocks creek one tract bought of George **Byars** by **Yates** Sept. 19, 1770 and the other tract George **Byars** bought of Henry **McCulloh** Sept. 3, 1759 at George **Miller**'s corner containing 271 acres and the other tract containing 200 acres also at **Miller**'s line- In both tracts 471 acres (signed Thomas and Elizabeth **Yates**).
Wts: Jeremiah **Bullock**, Solomon **Staton**, William **Ogelvie**.

55 thru 57- Oct. 30, 1778- John **Lunsford** to John **Bridges** for 53 pds. 7 shillings, 150 acres on branches of New Light creek on the Ridge path at **Harris**'s corner being part of tract granted to John **Bridges** July 25, 1761 and deeded to David **Bridges** who sold to John **Lunsford**.
Wts: John **Husketh**, Gilliam **Harris**.

57 thru 59- Apr. 6, 1772- John **Bridges** to Thomas **Banks**, Jr. for 25 pds. 200 acres being part of grant to **Bridges** July 25, 1761 on **Ricks** line.
Wts: John **Bradford**, Joseph **Parker**.

59, 60- John **Taylor**, the elder, gave to his son William **Taylor**, 328 acres on both sides of **Taylor**'s Ferry Road on **Michel**'s line to Spring branch Apr. 10, 1776.
Wts: Jno. **Rawlins**, Jr., Charles **Lewis**, Joseph **Taylor**.

60, 61- Sept. 12, 1778- George **Miller** and Susanna **Miller** to Michael **Redwile** for 450 pds. 320 acres excepting 50 acres sold to Nathan **Okey** being land whereon **Miller** lives.
Wts: R. D. **Cooke**, Francis **Ross** (Mary wife of George **Miller** relinquishes her dower right in land.)

62, 63- Dec. 18, 1776- Egbert **Haywood** to Thomas **Person** for 10 pds. (**Haywood** of Halifax Co., N. C.) 100 acres in Granville Co. on Grassy creek including all land bought of Richard **Briggs** at lines of land of **Person**, **Daniel**, and **Kennon**-
Wts: John **Hunt**, Wm. **Bradford**.

63, 64- Sept. 22, 1778- Benjamin **Wade**, Esq. sheriff of Granville Co., N. C. sold, by court order, the property of John **Harris**, deceased, at suit brought for debt by William **Alston** of Hillsborough district. 150 acres at former line of Thomas **Lewis**, in Granville Co., sold to Sherwood **Harris**.

Wts: Abram **Potter**, John **Potter**.

65, 66- Apr. 2, 1765- Edward **Palmer** to William **Cocke** for 500 pds. 200 acres on S side of Island creek which William **Taylor** patented Apr. 20, 1745 and also a tract of 296 acres at fork of Island creek at **Howel**'s line, formerly, which William **Moore** patented Apr. 25, 1754 and also a tract of 224 acres at **Moore**' line to **Read**'s wagon road and at **Easter**'s line being part of land granted to Jno. **Glover** and deeded to Edward **Palmer**- In all 720 acres in Granville Co.
Wts: Rob **Munford**, Henry **Howard**, Drury **Smith**.

68, 69- Nov. 2, 1778- William **Taylor** to Edmund **Taylor** for 3000 pds. (Edmund **Taylor** of Mecklenburg Co. VA.) a tract of land made up of several small tracts in Granville Co on Nut Bush creek and Little Island creek on both sides of the road leading to **Taylor's** ferry being land whereon William **Taylor** now lives containing 1,236 acres adjoining lands of Joseph **Taylor**, Benja **Johnston**, Thomas **Lanier** and Robert **Williams**.
Wts: Bennatt **Goode**, Richard **Taylor**, Joseph **Taylor**, Esq.

232

69, 70- Feb. 5, 1776- Pleasant **Hart** to Thomas **Person** for 65 pds. 300 acres being part of a larger tract granted to Thomas **Person** on SE side of **Aaron**'s creek, [**Harrison**'s line], at dividing line between me and Bryan.
Wts: John **Hunt**.

71, 72- Nov. 3, 1778- James **Hunt** and wife Sarah to Thomas **Satterwhite** for 1106 pds. 13 shls. 4 pence, 415 acres on road at William **Bullock** line in David **Mitchel**'s line, **Lanier**'s line on Little Nut Bush creek at Robert **Williams**' line.
Wts: Reuben **Searcy**.

72, 73- Oct. 31, 1778- John **Huskey** to John **Huskey**, Jr. for 50 pds. 240 acres on Beaver Dam creek on James **Weather**'s line.
Wts: James **Winningham**, Jr., Sharod **Winningham**, John **Bridges**.

74, 75- July 17, 1778- George **Brack** to Richard **Stringfellow** of Bute Co., N. C. for 400 pds. 210 acres on John **Weaver**'s line on Nut Bush creek. signed by George **Brack**, Elizabeth **Brack**.
Wts: Merryman **Barns**, John **Weaver**.

76, 77- Aug. 20, 1778-. Israel **Eastwood** to Ephraim **Frazier** for 100 pds. 267 acres at mouth of Spring branch, N. side of **Shelton**'s creek at **Person**'s and **Sherman**'s lines.
Wts: James **Langston**, Jeremiah **Frasier**.

77 thru 79- Nov. 2, 1778- Daniel **Malone** and wife Elizabeth to David **Smith** of Mecklenburg Co., VA. for 500 pds. 267 acres, whereon **Malone** now lives at mouth of Church Spring Branch to William **Graves**' line, Daniel **Grant**'s line.

79 thru 81- July 4, 1778- Samuel **Jeter**, Cutbird **Hudson** and William **Huckaby**, executors of the Will of Samuel **Huckaby**, deceased, to George **Brister**, 101 pds. 240 acres at Samuel **Jeter**'s line to mouth of **Worley**'s creek to mouth of **White** Dirt Branch reserving 1/3rd part as dower of Elizabeth **Brister**, widow of Samuel **Huckaby** for her lifetime.
Wts: Edward **Bullock**, Reuben **Talley**, Reuben **Pyles**, Samuel **Kittrell**, and William **Barton**.

81, 82- Oct. 26, 1778- Robert **Munford** of Mecklenburg Co., VA. to William **Palmer** of Granville Co., N. C. for 1105 pds. land on Fox creek being the land purchased of Charles **Kennon**, Thomas **Person** and William **Kennon**.
Wts: Thomas **Brissie**, Jr., Edward **Lewis**, Sr., Wm. **Hepburn**.

83, 84- Nov. 4, 1778- Christopher **Harris** and wife Catherine to Thomas **Critcher** for 100 pds. 100 acres on the road at Henry **White**'s line.
signed Christopher **Harris**, Cathron **Harris**.

84, 85- Nov. 6, 1774- Joshua **Hays** to Noel **Johnston** for 15 pds. 150 acres at **Hays** line on Tabbs creek on John **Parham**'s line.
Wts: John **Mauldin**, Blake **Mauldin**.

86, 87- Apr. 28, 1773- William **White** and wife Mary to Christopher **Harris** for 35 pds. 100 acres conveyed to William **White** by the will of Jonathan **White**, deceased, his father in 1772 at Henry **White**'s corner.

Wts: Cutbird **Hudson**.

87, 88- Feb. 3, 1778- Thomas **Goss** to George **Roberts** for 133 pds. 6 shls. 1 pence, 280 acres on both sides of Stony Creek a fork of Tar river at the road near **Sherman**'s Meeting house on Thos. **Phillpot**'s line, John **Williams**' line to **Eastwood**'s line.
Wts: John **Guin**, George **Brister**.

89 thru 91- July 30, 1778- Robert **Harris** to Christopher **Harris** for 37 pds. 309 acres at Sherwood **Harris**'s line, Samuel **Harris**'s line along the road to William **Ogelvie**'s corner at Nicholas **Holston**'s line.
Wts: Benjamin **Wade**, Davis **Mitchel**.

91, 92- Nov. 3, 1778- Walter **Ownbey** of Bute Co., N. C. to William **Going** of Granville Co., N. C. for 100 pds. 150 acres granted by Granville on Mar. 13, 1760 to William **Mackby** and deeded to Randolph **Sandling** and from him to **Owenby** at Poplar Branch.
Wts: John **Going**, Bird **Driver**.

92, 93- Oct. 24, 1774- Robert **Lewis** of Goochland Co., VA. to John **Henderson** Granville Co., N. C. for 500 pds. certain land in Granville Co., N. C. Robert **Lewis** in 1771 purchased of Solomon **Alston** the land whereon **Alston** lived in Granville Co. called ***Alston**'s Low Ground* and also all high land

223
adjoining thereto, containing 2,640 acres for 1200 pds. for which a deed was to be made by Solomon **Alston** who gave his bond for such, delivered on or before Dec. 1, 1771- Solomon **Alston** died before deed was made and in his Will gave the land to said Robert **Lewis** but failed to mention his heirs and assigns forever and since Howel **Lewis**, brother of Robert was co-purchaser of said land and was contracted to pay 1/3rd part of cost of land and Howel **Lewis** sold his 1/3rd of the land to John **Henderson** for 500 pds. and now Robert **Lewis** deeds that part of land to **Henderson** land whereon he, said **Henderson**, lives.
Wts: Edmund **Taylor**, Robert **Lewis**, Wm. **Mallory**.

95, 96- Nov. 10, 1778- Isaac **White** to John Williams **Graves** for 360 pds. 296 acres on Grassy creek at James **Williamson**'s line, being part of tract deeded by Samuel **Reed** to me whereon I now live.
Wts: Gideon **Crenshaw**, Henry **Spalding**, Charles **Spalding**, John **Hart**.

96, 97- Jan. 21, 1779- Bartholomew **Kimball** to Thomas **Rowland** for 400 pds. 51 acres on Stone branch.
Wts: Wm. **Gilliam**, James **Mitchell**.

97, 98- Jan. 22, 1779- John **Jones** of Mecklenburg Co., VA. to Daniel **Malone** of Granville Co., N. C. for 1000 pds. 312 acres on William **Gill**'s line, Thomas **Appling**'s line, Wm. **Royster**'s line in Granville Co.
Wts: Thomas **Mutter**, James **Downey**, Joseph **Hart**.

98, 99- Nov. 17, 1778- Richard **Clapton** (**Clopton**?) of Bute Co., N. C. to Baxter **Ragsdale** for 80 pds. 180 acres on both sides of Long Creek in **Chavis** line on old Ridge Path.
Wts: David **Ragsdale**, Jas. **Hornsby**, Anthony **Cole.**

99, 100- Dec 5, 1778- John **Huskey**, Jr. to Thomas **Bridges** for 200 pds. 240 acres on **Weather**'s line, Beaverdam creek.
Wts: James **Claxton**, Benjamin **Spain**, James **Winnenham**.

100, 101- Jan. 30, 1779- Abraham **Potter** and wife Sarah to William **Webb** for 800 pds. 800 acres adjoining land of Leonard **Adcock**, James **Bullock**, Charles **Partee** and Michael **Vockleree** which was purchased by **Potter** from Charles **Partee** and Edmund **Taylor**, Robert **Boyd** on **Adcock**'s creek.
Wts: Samuel **Smith**, John **Young**, Cutbird **Hudson**.

102- Dec. 3, 1778- Robert **Boyd**, Sr. and wife Lucretia to Abraham **Potter** for 100 pds. 200 acres adjoining lands of Leonard **Adcock**, James **Bullock**, and lands of Abraham **Potter** purchased of Charles **Partee**.
Wts: Sherwood **Harris**, John **Hawkins**.

103- May 13, 1776- Thomas **Person** to Chesley **Daniel** for 5 pds. 50 acres being the land in dispute between Egbert **Haywood** and myself as it was deeded to both of us and in on Grassy creek at **Roberts**' line, **Daniel**'s line.
Wts: M. **Hunt**, Wm. [**Blank**].

104, 105- Nov. 17, 1778- Sampson **Wiggins** of Bute Co., N. C. to James **Stark** for 536 pds. 200 acres in Granville Co.
Wts: Charles **Daniell**, John **Tabor**, William **Tabor**.

105- Dec. 26, 1778- Abraham **Potter** to John **Hawkins** for 1500 pds. ½ of a tract of land and Mill, being land Abraham **Potter** and John **Hawkins** bought of John **Potter**.
Wts: David **Harris**, Jno. **Potter**.

106- Jan. 21, 1779- John **Weaver** (**Wever**) to Thomas **Roland** for 400 pds. 150 acres on Ready Fork to head of Spring Branch to Great Branch.
Wts: Wm. **Gilliam**, James **Mitchell**.

107- Nov. 30, 1777- Peter **Akin** to Chas. **Partee** for 40 pds. 80 acres which Rudy **Buzzard** once owned at John **Mize**'s corner, John **Corder**'s line.
Wts: John **[Tenstey]** (?), Benja **Partee** (signed Peter and Mary **Akins**.)

108- Nov. 18, 1778- John **Calley** (**Kalley**, **Kelly**) and wife Ann to William **Cocke** (**Cooke**) for 533 pds. 313 acres on Tar river, also 155 acres at **Davenport**'s line.
Wts: David **Webb**, James **Daniel**, Bennett **Williams**.

234

109, 110- Nov. 17, 1778- John **Cragg** to William **Cocke** for 20 pds. 75 acres on branches of Tar river being part of tract **Cragg** bought of Richrd **Fowler**-
Wts: David **Webb**, James **Daniel**.

110, 111- Nov. 21, 1775- John **Griggs** to John **Corder** for 5 shls. 11 acres along **Griggs** line on a branch of Tar river where the old trading path crosses to Jno. **Boyd**'s line.
Wts: Jonathan **White**.

111, 112- Jan. 30, 1779- Miles **Wells** to William **Allen** for 150 pds. 233 acres on **Shelton**'s creek being part of survey taken up by William **Meadows** in Jacob **Slaughter**'s line.
Wts: James **Daniel**, Benit **Williams**.

112, 113- Feb. 2, 1779- Robert **Hester** to Reuben **Talley** for 200 pds. 100 acres at James **Currin**'s line, Edward **Bass**'s line, Robert **Hicks** line on south side of Fishing creek at mouth of Little Branch.
Wts: Benjamin **Hester** (signed Robert and Mary **Hester**.

113, 114- Jan. 1, 1779- Jesee **Landers** (**Landess**) of Mecklenburg Co., VA. to William **Cox** of Granville Co., N. C. for 200 pds. land at mouth of a small branch, South side of Mountain fork of Jonathan's creek to Thomas **Mutter**'s line, Joseph **Farmer**'s line at dividing line between William **Cox** and Joseph **Farmer**, purchased by **Landers** of James **Yancey**, Sr. whereon said **Landers** formerly lived containing 150 acres.
Wts: Henry **Graves**, Stephen **Haston**.

115- Nov. 23, 1778- John **Potter** bought of John **Gwinn** (**Gwin**) for 1500 pds. 300 acres on S side of Tar river.
Wts: Thos. **Wilburn**, William **Jones**.

115, 116- Nov. 23, 1778- John **Gwinn** to John **Potter** for 500 pds. 100 acres on **Phipps**' corner, **Bradford**'s line, **Nowlin**'s line.
Wts: Thos. **Wilburn**, William **Jones**.

116, 117- Feb. 4, 1778- Thomas **Bradford**, executor of the Will of Jonathan **White**, deceased, to Thomas **Critcher** for 561 pds. 200 acres on Fishing creek at George **Alston**'s line, Thomas **Critcher**'s line, Lewis **Anderson**'s line.
Wts: Ro. **Lewis**, Wm. **Ogelvie**.

118, 119- Feb. 2, 1779- James **Williamson** and wife Sarah to Samuel **Pittard** for 280 pds. the land whereon **Williamson** lives and bought of Gideon **Crenshaw** of 200 acres.
Wts: Henry **Graves**, Humphrey **Davis**.

119, 120- Jan. 15, 1779- John **Minter** of Ninety Six District, South Carolina to Gideon **Gooch** of Granville Co., N.C. for 225 pds. 200 acres on both sides of Island creek at **Holley**'s line, **Howlet**'s line and also 200 acres at Nathan **Halley**'s line on Island creek.
Wts: Rowland **Gooch**, John **Terrell**, Zepheniah **Clement**.

120, 121- Dec. 31, 1778- Robert **Allison**, Sr. to William **Allison** his son, for 10 shls. 272 acres on both sides of Low Ground Creek near **Wilkerson**'s path at his line reserving ½ to himself for life.
Wts: William **Barber**, John **Henderson**.

122- Dec. 1, 1778- Robert **Allison**, Sr. to his son John **Allison** for 400 pds. 220 acres on [E] side of Fishing creek reserving ½ to himself for life.
Wts: William **Berton**, John **Henderson**.

123- Dec. 31, 1778- Robert **Allison**, Sr. to his son James **Allison** for 100 pds. 292 acres on [both] sides of Fishing creek [beginning on the east side] reserving ½ to himself for his lifetime.
Wts: William **Barton**, John **Henderson**.

124, 125- May 19, 1775- Robert **Lanier** (**Lanear**) to Richard **Davis** for 50 pds. 300 acres on both sides of Great Watry Branch on Roland **Tarry**'s line to Richard **Claton**'s line at head of Mirey Branch along **Vicker**'s line to Absalom **Davis**'s line.
Wts: Christopher **Harris**, Jesse **Benton**, Elijah **Mitchel**.

125, 126- Nov. 18, 1778- Nathan **Okey** and Mary **Okey** to William **Jones** for 70 pds. 50 acres and 10 poles on Ledge of Rocks creek being part of tract George **Miller** bought of Henry **McCulloh** containing 320 acres.
Wts: George **Wright**, William **Jones**, Sr., Mary **Phillips**.

235

126, 127- Dec. 9, 1778- William **Pool** and wife Elizabeth to Josiah **Stovaul** (**Stovall**) for 400 pds. 326 acres on N. side of Grassy creek and on both sides of [Tattle] Snake Branch whereon **Stovall** now lives.
Wts: John **Culbreath**, Owen **Griffen**, Wm, **Dunkan**.

127 thru 129- May 25, 1778- William **Gooch** Sr. of Caswell Co, N.C. to Philemon **Holland** of Granville Co., N.C. for 100 pds. 700 acres on both sides of Whitstone Branch, at **Hawkins** corner.
Wts: William **Gooch**, Billy G. **Gooch** (signed William & Frances **Gooch**).

129, 130- Jan. 2, 1779- Philemon **Hillard** to Billey Gosling **Gooch** of Caswell Co., N.C. for 500 pds. 700 acres being land taken up by John **Paschal** Mar. 1, 1762 in lower end of Granville Co. on both sides of Whit Stone Branch at **Hawkins** corner.
Wts: None.

130, 131- Feb. 3, 1779- John **Mauldin** and wife Sarah to Thomas **Norman** for 325 pds. 520 acres which was granted Nov. 28, 1760 to Thomas **Lowe**; on Tabbs creek at **Loyd**'s corner, **Eaton**'s line.
Wts: Bartlet **Searcy**.

132- Nov. 2, 1778- John **Dickerson** to John **Dickerson**, Jr. for 10 pds. 170 acres on Tar river and Ridge Path.
Wts: John **Peace**, Jr., Jos. **Peace**, Jr.

133- Dec. 28, 1778- Unity **Goodwin** and Mathew **Goodwin** of Granville Co to Roger **Thornton** of Bute Co., for 600 pds. 200 acres at **Eaton**'s corner on **Anderson**'s swamp at Drury **Kimball**'s line.
Wts: William **Thornton**, Phillemon **Beckham**.

134, 135- Jan. 1, 1779- William **Myrick** and Sary (Sarah) his wife of Bute Co., N. C. to Philemon **Hawkins**, Jr. for 1200 pds. 596 acres on **Anderson** swamp at **Kimball**'s corner, Geo. **Jordan**'s line which was granted to **Myrick** Aug. 26,

1760 in Granville Co.
Wts: Robert **Jones**, John **Hawkins**.

135, 136- Feb. 1779- John **Corder** of Caswell Co., N. C. to James **Cozart** for 250 pds. 150 acres on S side of Tar river.
Wts: none.

136, 137- Nov. 19, 1778. Baxter **Ragsdale** to James **Fowler** for 25 pds. 100 acres at Valentine **White**'s and John **Earl**'s line, Daniel **Hunter**'s line.
Wts: Jas. **Hornsby**, Baxter **Ragsdale**, Jr.

137, 138- Feb. 2, 1779- Richard **Wilkins** and wife Rebecca, David **Mitchel**, and John **Potter** to Henry **Pattillo** and Richard **Harrison** for [1533] pds. 6 shls. 8 pence 200 acres on both sides of **Michael**'s creek in Granville Co.
Wts: Micajah **Bullock**.

138, 139- Nov. 2, 1778- Samuel **Paschal** of Bute Co. to Elisha **Paschal** of Granville Co. for 4 pds. 8 acres on Maypole Branch at Samuel **Paschal**'s own corner.
Wts: Bartlet **Searcy**, Samuel **Hammond**.

139, 140- Jan. 1, 1779- Richardson **Owen** of Guilford Co., N. C to Joseph **Gill** of Granville Co. for 200 pds. 577 acres on both sides of **Andrews** branch.
Wts: John and Thomas **Owen**, David **Wilkerson**.

140, 141- Jan. 15, 1779- Benjamin **McCulloh** of Halifax Co., N. C. to James **McLemore**, Jr. of Granville Co. for 50 pds. 225 acres at Michael **Wilson**'s corner, in Granville Co.
Wts: Robt. **Harris**, James **Claxton**.

141, 142- Sept. 15, 1778- Richard **Davis** to Augustine **Davis** for 100 pds. 300 acres on Thomas **Lanier**'s line, on Mirey Branch at lines of Robert **Burton** and Thomas **Person**.
Wts:- Augustin and Wiley **Davis**, Absalom Davis **Young**, [Jurat]

142, 143- Sept. 15, 1778- Absalom **Davis** and Richard **Davis** to Augustine **Davis** for 100 pds. 120 acres in Granville Co. on Little Watry Branch on Thomas **Lanier**'s line.
Wts: Augustine and Wiley **Davis**, Absalom Davis **Young**.

143, 144- Nov. 2, 1778- Dennis **Paschal** to Elisha **Paschal** for 35 pds. 41acres on E side of Deep creek at Samuel [**Paschal**]'s and James **Paschal**'s lines.
Wts: Bartlet **Searcy**, Saml **Hammond**.

236

144, 145- Feb. 1, 1779- John **Ross** to James **Claxton** for 100 pds. 206 acres which was laid off for **Ross** out of Henry **McCulloh**'s *tract No. 12* on Ledge of Rocks creek.
Wts: Solomon **Staton**, Samuel **Adams**, William **Jones**, Abraham **Glimpp**, Jas. **Ross**.

145, 146- Feb. 3, 1779- John **Mitchel** to Jacob **Mitchel** for 200 pds. 220 acres on Beaver Pond creek on **Potter**'s line.
Martha, wife of John **Mitchel**, relinquishes her dower right.
Wts: none.

146, 147- Feb. 3, 1779- John **Mitchel** to Jacob **Mitchel** for 200 pds. 225 acres in Granville Co.
Wts: none. (Martha, wife of John **Mitchel**, relinquishes dower in land.

147, 148- Nov. 16, 1778- Abram **Cook** to Thomas **Barnett** for 10 pds. 25 acres on Indian fork of Little Island creek at Thomas **Barnett**'s line, and Robert **Burton**'s line.
Wts: Daniel **Clayton**, William **Ogelvie**.

148, 149- Mar. 10, 1778- Richard **Searcy** and wife Mary to John **Warmoth** for 500 pds. 320 acres on both sides of

Boling creek at William Hargrove **Searcy**'s corner.
Wts: Reuben **Searcy**, Banjamin **Howard**.

149, 150- Mar. 5, 1779- Henry **Reardon** and wife Mary to John **Warmoth** for 500 pds. 166 ½ acres on **Bolling** creek at Richard **Searcy**'s corner, William Hargrove **Searcy**'s line.
Wts: Ozwell **Towns**, William H. **Searcy**.

150, 151- May 3, 1779- John **Brame** and wife Mary of Mecklenburg Co., Va to Thomas **Brame** for 230 pds. 200 acres on both sides of Crooked Run at John **Brame**'s line, Wm. **Hanks**'s line, Traverse **Bowdon**'s and Geo. **Brack**'s lines.
Wts: James **Brame**, Merryman **Barns**.

151, 152- Jan. 26, 1779- Richard **Young**, Sr, and wife Mary of Mecklenburg Co., Va. to Charles **Yancey** for 300 pds. 20 acres on Buck creek at county line, Charles **Yancey**'s corner.
Wts: John **Young**, Joshua **Coffee**.

152, 153- Apr. 5, 1779- Chas. **Partee** to Isaac **Head** for 50 pds. 80 acres on John **More**'s line, James **Cozart**'s line.
Wts: Samuel **Slawter**, John **Tinsley**.

153, 154- Jan. 14, 1779- Richard **Henderson** to William **Todd** for 20 pds. 200 acres on **Paschal**'s line, Sherwood **Sims**'s line.
Wts: George **Gayden**, Howel **Moss**.

154, 155- Mar. 4, 1779- Thomas **Ring** to William **Kennon** for 3000 pds. 680 acres on **Person**'s line, **Hill**'s line, both sides of Fox creek.
Wts: John **Ring**, Hugh **Greenwood**.

155, 156- Apr. 9, 1779- Charles **Merryman** and wife Elizabeth to William **Jones** for 400 pds. 200 acres at Michael **Wilson**'s corner which land was sold by Henry **McCulloh** July 4, 1763 to Henry **Holtslaus**.
Wts: George **Wright**, William **Merryman**, Sarah **Wright**.

157, 158- May 4, 1779- Josiah **Mitchel**, David **Mitchel**, John **Mitchel** and Michael **Satterwhite**, executors of James **Mitchel** deceased, to Len Henley **Bullock** for 8,512 pds. 607 acres on W side of Little Nut Bush creek where James **Mitchel** lived, on lines of land of Robert **Williams**, Josiah **Mitchel** and Joseph **Taylor**, at land whereon Michael **Satterwhite** lives, on Henry **Lyne**'s line-
Wts: Solo **Mitchel**, Bromfield **Ridley**.

158, 159- May 3, 1779- Josiah **Mitchel**, David **Mitchel**, John **Mitchel** and Michael **Satterwhite** executors of James **Mitchell** deceased to **Colclough** for 150 pds. 300 acres on both sides of **Michel**'s creek at James **Satterwhite** corner, on Hico road.
Wts: Granville **Davis**, James **Mitchel**, John **Mitchel**.

159- Apr. 21, 1779- David **Howard** to Peyton **Wood** for 500 pds. 220 acres on Butchers branch adjoining the land of John **Hunt**, Samuel **Clay**, Peyton **Wood** and Col. Edmund **Taylor**.
Wts: Mary **Howard**.

160, 161- Dec. 1, 1778- Robert **Harris** to Thomas **Jenkins** for 400 pds. 360 acres on Ledge of Rocks creek at boundary line between Lord Granville and **McCulloh** which Robert **Harris** formerly sold to Boling **Adcocks**, reserving

237
reserving 52 acres which Robert **Harris**, Jr. sold to Bolling **Adcock**.
Wts: Abram and John **Potter**, Reuben **Searcy**.

161- Nov. 28, 1778- James **Mitchel** to Josiah **Mitchel** for 200 pds. 204 acres on Nut Bush creek on Mathew Branch.
Wts: John **Morris**, Rawley **Hammond**.

162- Mar. 23, 1779- Len H. **Bullock** to Samuel **Hammond** for 120 pds. 231 acres on Deep Creek on John Williams **Daniel**'s line.

Wts: Job **Hammond**, John **Tilley**.

163- May 4, 1779- Pomfrett **Herndon** to Jonathan **Kittrell**, Jr. for 500 pds. 216 acres on both sides of Tabbs creek and on Ruin Creek at Daniel **Hunter**'s corner.

164, 165- Dec. 26, 1778- William **Webb** and wife Frances to John **Lewis** and Samuel **Smith**, trustees appointed by the United Presbyterian congregation of Grassy Creek and Nut Bush creek, on behalf of their congregation for 400 pds. 225 acres on Grassy creek on West side of Drury **Smith**'s land, on South by William **Amis** and Samuel **Smith**, on East by Samuel **Smith** and on North by Samuel **Smith**.
Wts: Lewis and Hannah **Amis**, John **Ravens**.

165, 166- Nov. 27, 1777- Nathaniel **McGehee** to John **Rogers** of Pitt Co., N.C., for 100 pds. 100 acres at **McGehee**'s corner on **Taylor**'s creek which was granted to James **McGehee**, father of Nathaniel **McGehee**, Mar. 1761.
Wts: Joseph **Webb**, William **Smith**, John **Nevill**.

166, 167- Mar. 27, 1779- James **Veazey** of Orange Co., N.C. to Zebulon **Veazey** for 80 pds. 94 acres in Granville Co. on Nap off Reeds creek at James **Bennett**'s corner, William **Bennett**'s line.
Wts: William **Gallimore**, Joseph **Justice**.

167, 168- Mar. 27, 1779- James **Veazey** of Orange Co., N.C. to Zebulon **Veazey** for 200 pds. 101 acres on Nap of Reeds creek at James **Bennett**'s.
Wts: Wm. **Gallimore**, Joseph **Justice**.

168, 169- Apr. 7, 1770 David **Parrish** to William **Bell** for 26 pds. Virginia currency evaluated at 32 pds. 10 shillings proclamation money, 182 acres which David **Parrish** bought of Jacob **Gray** Aug. 10, 1761 at **Bell**'s line on Buffalo branch at Samuel **Jeter**'s line on main road from **Taylor**'s Ferry to Harrisburg, N.C-
Wts: George, Betty and Sarah **Bell**.
Judith, wife of David **Parrish**, relinquishes her dower in land.

170, 171- Feb. 5, 1779- Philip **Chavis** of Bladen Co., N.C. to Zorabable **Williamson** of Granville Co. for 270 pds. 270 acres on **Colling** creek in Granville Co. on **Moore**'s line.
Wts: James **Hornsby**, Charles **Moore**, John **Hays**.

171, 172- Aug. 6, 1778- Robert **Dickens**, surviving partner of Jno. **Parker** deceased, to [Michl] **Cocklereece** for 500 pds. 320 acres on S side of Indian Field branch at line of land formerly **McCulloh**'s to **Thompson**'s and **Person**'s line. (Mary, wife of Robert **Dickens**, relinquishes dower right).
Wts: Osborn **Jeffreys**, Jr., Henry **Streader**, Wm. **Waite**.

172, 173- Aug. 1, 1762- Grant from Lord Granville to James **Moore** for 650 acres on N. side of Tar river at **Harris**'s line, along **Carrill**'s line.

173, 174- May 3, 1779- Robert **Williams** and wife Sarah deeded to Robert **Wooding** 734 acres in Granville Co. and since Sarah **Williams** is a resident of Pittsylvania Co., Va., her deposition is taken as to her willingness to sell land and relinquish her dower right. Stephen **Coleman**, William **Short** and Reuben **Pain** of Pittsylvania County, Va. take deposition June 22, 1779.

174, 175- Aug. 3, 1779- Isaac **Williams** and Jesse **Williams**, administrators of James **Moore** of Southampton County, Va. to Wiatt **Wilkerson** of Granville Co., N.C. for 1665 pds., 650 acres in Granville Co. on N. side of Tar river at **Harris**'s line, **Carrell**'s line.
Wts: Thomas **Person**, Wm. **Hornsby**.

175, 176- Aug. 3, 1779- William **Colclough** to Thomas **Person** for 600 pds. 300 acres on **Michael**'s creek at James **Satterwhite**'s corner on Hico Road.
Wts: Patrick **Duffy**, Charles Rust **Eaton**.

238

176, 177- Oct. 8, 1777- William **Wilkerson** to William **Hornsby** for 35 pds. 100 acres on S side of Tar river at

Thomas **Banks**' line.
Wts: Thos. **Banks**, William **Hewit**.

177, 178- Apr. 20, 1779- Robert **Wooding** of Halifax Co., Va. to Richard **Henderson** for 550 pds. 734 acres on E side of Hico Road on the Nut Bush old race path to Col. William **Bullock**'s line, James **Hunt**'s and Thomas **Lanier**'s and Robert **Williams**' line which is land bought of Robert **Williams**-
Wts: Abra. **Shelton**, Robert **Williams**.

178, 179- Aug. 2, 1779- Joseph **Rogers** to Samuel **Kittrell** for 5 pds. 50 acres on **Rogers**' line, Jon **Kittrell**'s line.
Wts: none.

179, 180, 181- Aug. 3, 1779- Benjamin **Wade**, Esq, sheriff of Granville Co. to Charles **Yarbrough** of Franklin Co., N.C. [for 25 pds], land that was property of Michal **Gowing** for debt due and by suit brought in Bute Co. against him and sold tract of 100 acres on **Taylor**'s creek which Michael **Gowing** let his brother Edward **Gowing** live on adjoining lands of John Simmons **Person** and Randolph **Sandland**'s land.

181, 182- Aug. 3, 1770- Robert **Wallace** of Chatham Co., N.C. to Solomon **Staton** of Granville Co., N.C. for 300 pds. 200 acres in Granville Co. near Trading Path at John **Ross**'s corner.
Wts: Jeremiah **Bullock**, George Lane **Moore**.

182, 183- Aug. 3, 1779- Len Henley **Bullock** and wife Susanna to John **Walker** for 3000 pds., 1880 acres on Fishing Creek in Granville Co., N.C. including the court house, at **Person**'s line, on **Hester**'s line and at his own corner and at **Campbell**'s line, **Bell** and Co. line.
Wts: Joseph **Taylor**, Reuben **Searcy**.

183, 184- Aug. 2, 1779- James **Daniel** to Joseph **Daniel** for deed of gift to said Joseph, 245 acres of land on W side of **Anderson**'s swamp in Granville Co. on **Glover**'s road.
Wts: none.

184, 185- Mar. 8, 1779- Robert **Robinson** and Lucretia **Robinson** to Arthur **Jordan** for 1000 pds. land on both sides of Indian Creek-
Wts: Samuel **Henderson** Jr., William **Gilliam**, Jr. (name also spelled **Roberson**).

185, 186- Oct. 3, 1778- Francis **Ross** to Ralph **Williams** for 350 pds. 202 acres on Ledge of Rocks creek at James **Bullock**'s line.
Wts: Joseph **Taylor**, Ben **Wade** (signed Francis and Mary **Ross**.
End of Book- - M--

Granville Co., N.C. Record of Deeds Book O 1779-1790

[Book O appears before book N in page order]

239

1- Registered- Nov. term. 1779- Thomas **Harris** to Sherwood **Harris** for 100 pds. 160 acres whereon Henry **White** formerly lived and which was purchased of Jonathan **White** by Sherwood **Harris**, Sr, deceased and willed to Sherwood **Harris**, Jr.
Wts: Ephraim **Hampton**, John **Miner**.

1, 2- Aug. 21, 1779- Robert **Robinson** and wife Lucretia to Frederick **Wiggins** for 80 pds. 80 acres on both sides of Indian Creek at **Morse**'s line.
Wts: John **Fleming**, Isham **Harrison**.

2, 3- May 4, 1779- Zachariah **Boughan** and wife Drucilla to Simon **Clement** for 160 pds., 20 acres on **Hampton**'s Mill creek along Robert **Russel**'s line, at Simon **Clement**'s line.
Wts: Obadiah **Clement**, Daniel **Gooch**, Samuel **Clement**.

3, 4- Nov. 20, 1778- Phillip **Chavis** of George Town District, South Carolina to Hugh **Snelling** of Granville Co., N.C. for 2000 pds., 600 acres on N. side of Tar river on both sides of **Collins** creek and Tabbs creek in Granville Co. on **Clapton**'s line at county line and on **Harris**'s line.
Wts: John **Nevill**, Thos. **Carrell**, Charles **Moore**.

4- Mar. 1, 1779- Christopher **Harris** to Richard **Wilkins** for 150 pds. 15 acres on branches of Mill creek at John **Hawkins**' line at line of land that was Sherwood **Harris**'s, to Henry **Straton**'s line.
Wts: Sherwood **Harris**, Robert **Harris**, Jr., Darwin **Harris**.

5- Nov. 3, 1779- John **Hawkins** to Richard **Wilkins** for 1000 pds. 225 acres on S side of Tar river on Nicholas creek.

5, 6- Nov. 1, 1779- Sherwood **Harris** and Jane **Hedspeth** (relict and widow of Sherwood **Harris**, Sr., deceased) to John **Duncan** of Amelia Co., Va. for 2000 pds. 160 acres in Granville Co., N.C. which land was willed to Sherwood **Harris**, Jr. by his father Sherwood **Harris**, Sr., deceased, which land he had purchased of Jonathan **White** together with the plantation whereon Henry **White** formerly lived.
Wts: George **Briston**, Sr., James **Briston**.

6- Aug. 2, 1779- Arthur **Jordan** produced a deed from Robert **Robinson** and Lucretia his wife in Granville Co., and Lucretia was questioned by Bartle **Searcy** and Charles **Eaton**, as to her willingness to relinquish her dower-

6, 7- Oct. 31, 1779- John **Warmoth** and Willey his wife, to John **Hawkins** for 4000 pds. (name may be Willey instead of Milley[2]) 486 ½ acres on both sides of **Bolling**'s creek.
Wts: Reuben **Searcy**, John **Potter**.

7, 8- Nov. 1, 1779- Richard **Bennett** to Peter **Bennett** for 20 pds. 275 acres which was bought of Thomas **Person** adjoining lands of **Daniels**, **Roberts**, **Wilkerson**, on both sides of Grassy creek.
Wts: Lewis **Bennett**, Jos. **Gill**.

8- Oct. 29, 1779- Richard **Bennett** to Lewis **Bennett** for 500 pds. 275 acre which sd. Richard bought of Thomas **Person** on both sides of Grassy creek adjoining **Daniel**'s, **Kennon**'s lines.
Wts: Jos. **Gill**, Peter **Bennett**.

9- Nov. 1, 1779- Joseph **Allen** to John **Chadwick** for 800 pds. 100 acres at Charles **Caller**'s line at mouth of **Melon**'s branch, **Buchannon**'s line, Wyatt **Hawkins'** and **Paschal**'s line.
Wts: George **Taylor**, Dennis **Paschal**.

9, 10- Oct. 14, 1779- William **Hickman** to John **Heath** for 500 pds. 164 acres on both sides of Hay Meadow branch

---

[2] Name is Willey.

on **Howard**'s line, **Mitchell**'s line.
Wts: David **Howard**, John **Howard**, Thos **Pool**.
Avarilla, wife of William **Hickman**, relinquishes her dower right.

10- Aug. 28, 1779- Thomas **Pool** to John **Blackwell** of King William Co., Va. for 900 pds. 156 acres in Granville Co., N.C. on N. side of Grassy cre[ek] at Robert **Beasley**'s corner and down creek to mouth of Hay Stack branch.
Wts: Danl **Grant**, Saml **Crafton**, Lewis **Bennett**

240
Obedience, wife of Thomas **Pool**, relinquishes her dower right in land.

11- Aug. 24, 1779- John **Ware** of [Pitsilvania] Co., VA. to John **Rust** of Granville Co., N. C. for 500 pds. 225 acres on branches of Fort creek and of Middle Creek adjoining **Sheapherd's**, **Ballinger**'s mill path, **Gilliam**'s, **Weaver**'s lines, being part of tract granted to Samuel **Ware** deceased, father of John **Ware**, by Lord Granville July 27, 1761.
Wts: Harris **Gilliam**, John **Nevell**, George **Rust**.

12- Oct. 3, 1778- Joshua **James** to John **Hooker** for 330 pds., 200 acre being part of the 100,000 acres granted to Henry **McCulloh** by King George of Great Britain on Andrew **Hampton**'s corner on Beaver Dam creek the Middle fork.
Wts: John **Hooker**, Jr., Doshe **Patterson**.

12, 13- Oct. 30, 1779- Samuel **Glaze** to Benjamin **Glaze** for 50 pds. 300 acres at Memucan **Hunt**'s line, Jonathan **Knight**'s line, William **Knight**'s and Samuel **Smith**'s line, Drury **Smith**'s line.
Wts: Samuel **Smith**, William **Cockrell**.

13- Sept. 30, 1779- Benjamin **Bonner** and Frances **Bonner** to Joseph **Okey**, Jr. for 800 pds. 130 acres being part of 555 acres sold by Michael **Wilson** from Henry **McCulloh** July 11, 1763 on S side of Picture branch at James **Boyd**'s corner.
Wts: George **Wright**, Christian **Walker**.

14- Oct. 29, 1779- John **Chadwick** to George **Taylor** for 2000 pds. 200 acres on Deep creek at **Allen**'s line, **Gutrey**'s line, **Turner**'s line.
Wts: Jno. **Twitty**, William **Key**.

14 15- Aug. 4, 1779- John **Dickerson** to Samuel **Dispain** for 108 pds. 12 shillings, 180 acres on both sides of Horse creek.
Wts: John **Pope**, Jno. **Peace**, Jr.

15- Aug. 16, 1779- William **Wright** and wife Drucilla to William **Stovall** for 800 pds., 50 acres on S side of Jonathan's creek on Ransom **Boswell**'s line-
Wts: Josiah **Stovall**, Owen **Griffin**.

16- May 1, 1779- Luke **Landers** to Thomas **Bond** for 100 pds.- 9 acres on Grassy creek on **Bond**'s line.
Wts: Henry **Spaulding**, Charles **Spaulding**.

16, 17- Oct. 2, 1779- William **Wortham** of Warren Co., N. C. to William **Vanlandingham** of same Co. for 1600 pds., 136 3/4ths acres on **Anderson**'s swamp at **Daniel**'s corner, on **Person**'s line.
Wts: John **Flemmin** [Jurat], James **Baley**.

17, 18- Mar. 1, 1779- Christopher **Harris** to Sherwood **Harris** for love of him, a gift of 294 acres on Tar river at Samuel **Harris**'s line and at William **Ogelvie**'s corner, on Nicholas **Holstein**'s line, on Sherwood **Harris**'s line.
Wts, Darwin, Sherwood and Robert **Harris**, Jr.

18- Oct. 28, 1779- William **Bullock** to Washington **Salter** (?), son of Robert **Salter**, deceased, of Pitt Co., N. C., for 8000 pds. 844 acres in Granville Co on Nut Bush creek and Flat creek on **Mitchel**'s line, David **Mitchel**'s line.
Wts: John and Richard **Taylor** and Thomas **Satterwhite**.

19- Nov. 2, 1779- Robert **Roberson** and wife Lucretia to Thomas **Person** for 84 pds. 126 acres on both sides of

Indian creek in Granville Co at **Person**'s corner, and on **Williams**' and **Hawkins**' lines.
Wts: David **Mitchel**, Richd **Harrison**.

19, 20- July 27, 1761- Grant from Granville to Samuel **Ware** for 425 acres on both sides of Flat creek adjoining **Moxley**'s, **Shepherd** and **Ballinger**'s lines.

20, 21- Aug. 18, 1779- Richard **Henderson** and wife Elizabeth to Abner **Nash** of Craven Co., N. C. for 20,000 pds. 900 acres on Nut Bush creek in Granville Co., N. C. at William **Taylor**'s line, to Little Nut Bush crk on Daniel **Williams**' line on Ridge Path north of Nut Bush low ground on road leading from **Taylor**'s Ferry to NutBush Church past the place that Joseph **Williams** lived at time of his death, at Thomas **Satterwhite**'s line including all plantation whereon Robert **Williams** and Joseph **Winston**

241
formerly lived and **Henderson** purchased of Robert **Williams**.
Wts: Howel **Moss**, R. **Hyde**, Samuel **Henderson**, Jr.

21, 22- Oct. 20, 1779- Abner **Nash** and wife Mary of Jones Co., N.C. to John **Somerville** of Halifax Co., N.C. for 20,000 pds., 900 acres on both sides of Little Nut Bush creek at William **Taylor**'s corner at Daniel **Williams**' line to Ridge path on road leading from **Taylor**'s Ferry to NutBush Church by the place whereon Joseph **Williams** formerly lived at time of his death, on Thomas **Satterwhite**'s line including plantations whereon Robert **Williams** and Joseph **Winston** formerly lived which **Henderson** bought of Robert **Williams** and sold to Abner **Nash**.
Wts: none) Mary **Nash** relinquishes her dower right.)

22, 23- Jan. 27, 1776- John **Hampton** and Kiturah of Rowan Co., N.C. to Robert **Reid** of Granville Co., N.C. for 100 pds. 340 acres in Granville Co. on **Arnold**'s and **Harris**'s lines.
Wts: James **Stainback**, Thos. **Rice**.

23- Feb. 7, 1780- Ro. **Lewis** to John **Kennon** for 8000 pds. land on both sides of Island creek adjoining Gideon **Gooch**, John **Thorp** and John **Ferrill** and James **Downey**'s lands, Edward **Taylor**'s James **Terry**'s & Nicholas **Burch**'s lines.. being 2 tracts purchased by **Lewis** of Thomas **Whicker**. Sr. and John **Oliver**-
Wts: Nicholas **Burch**, James **Lewis**.

23, 24- Dec. 27, 1779- Robert **Hicks**, Sr. to Isaac **Hicks** of Wake Co: N.C. for 3000 pds. 500 acres (and his heirs of his body, but failing to leave heir, then the land to George **Bell**, son of Thomas and Sary **Bell**, my grandson) on Edward **Bass**'s corner, John **Wicker**'s corner, Robert **Hicks**, Jr.'s and, Sr.'s lines- Robert **Hicks**, Sr; reserving right to cut timber on land for his lifetime- which is part of 700 acres granted to Hicks- Nov. 28, 1760 and also part of a tract granted to **Hicks** Oct. 26, 1752.
Wts: Robert **Hester**, William **Hester**.

24, 25- Dec. 1, 1779- Zacharias **Higgs** to Joseph **McDaniel** for 150 pds. 150 acres on mouth of branch adjoining Justice **Parrish**'s land on Tabbs creek.
Wts: William **Walker**, James **McDaniel**.

25, 26- Nov. 12, 1778- Absalom **Davis** to Thomas **Lanier** for 1,080 pds. 210 acres whereon he now lives at Augustine **Davis**'s, Jr. corner, **Lanier**'s line on Island creek, Rowland **Terry**'s and John **Person**'s corner.
Wts:- Augt **Davis**, Jr., Nathl **Norwood**, William **Byars**.

26- Feb. 4, 1780- James **Langston** to his son William **Langston** for love and valuable consideration 274 acres on S side of Tar river at **Langston**'s old corner on Mountain Creek Hill to **Eastwood**'s line on Reedy Branch.
Wts: John **Wood**, Jesse **Langston**.

26, 27- Feb. 5, 1780- James **Langston** to his son-in-law John **Wood**, a gift of 200 acres on S side of Tar river on Mountain creek except to reserve to myself any mine found thereon and also stone[?] for my use.
Wts: Elinor **Rose**, Jesse **Langston**.

27, 28 . . . 1780- John **Hawkins** to John **Potter** of Mecklinburg Co., Va. for 10,000 pds. 580 acres on Tar river in Granville Co., N. C. near the Beaver house at **Harris**'s line, on Nicholas creek, at Sherwood **Harris**'s.

Wts: Thos. **Wilburn**, Ralph **Williams**.

28- Sept. 4, 1779. James **Fowler** to Mark **White** for 480 pds. 100 acres on N. side of Tabbs creek on Valentine **White**'s line, John **Earl**'s line.
Wts: Thos. **White**, Augustine **Woodlief**.

28, 29- Feb. 7, 1780- Gideon **Gooch** to William **Burch** for 200 pds. 30 acres on Island creek adjouning Nicholas **Burch** Sr.'s line, adjoining Roling **Gooch** and Zachariah **Hester**'s land.

29, 30- Feb. 9, 1780- Michael **Cockleree** to Francis **Bressie** of Mecklenburg Co., Va. for 2000 pds. 320 acres on S side of Indian Creek, on **Person**'s and **Harris**'s lines- signed by Michael and Rebecah (wife) **Cockleree**.
Wts: None.

30- Jan. 2, 1772- John **Walton**, Jr. of Louisa Co., Va. to Len Henley **Bullock** of Granville Co. for 250 pds. 259 acres in Granville Co., N. C.

242
on **Anderson**'s swamp adjoining **Fleming**'s line and that formerly **McGregor**'s land on Rays Branch.
Wts: Ann **Keeling**, John **Williams**.

30, 31- Feb. 8, 1780- Samuel **Sneed** to Stephen **Sneed** for 1000 pds. 300 acres on **Person**'s line, Ephraim **Hampto**n's line, **Landes**'s line near the School House Spring, **Fips** line and on Mill creek.

31, 32- Nov. 27, 1779- Robert **Hicks**, Sr. to Robert **Hicks**, Jr. for 1500 pds. 230 acres to him and the heirs of his body but failing to leave an heir then to Isaac **Hicks** and his heirs of his body- on East side of Fishing creek, at Thomas **Person**'s line, reserving to self the freedom of cutting wood and timber for lifetime, being part of the tract of 700 acres granted Nov. 28, 1760 to Robert **Hicks**, Sr. and if Robert have no children to go to Isaac **Hicks** and his heirs.
Wts: Thomas **Hicks**, Francis **Hester**.

32, 33- Dec. 3, 1769- Len Henley **Bullock**, sheriff of Granville Co., N.C. to James **Jett**- the property of John **Roach** which was sold for debt due at suit brought by Stephen **Jett**- 200 acres sold at public sale and James **Jett** became highest bidder- land on Newlight creek at **McCulloh**'s line and **Beckham** Branch.
Wts: Jo. **Hawkins**.

33- 34- Nov. 12, 1779- James **Currin** to Ambrose **Barker** for 500 pds. 50 acres on Tabbs and Fishing Creek at **Person**'s line.
Wts: Ransone **Southerland**, Barnet **Jeter**, Wm. **Currin**.

34, 35- Feb. 8, 1780. Joseph **Rogers** and wife Sarah to Thomas **Garriott** of Warren Co., N. C. for 40 pds. 175 acres on N. side of **Martin**'s creek in **Kittrell**'s line.
Wts: Thomas **Walker**, Joseph **Mangum**.

35- Feb. 9, 1780- James **Johnston** to Samuel **Johnston** for 266 pds. 13 shls., 4 pence, 200 acres on W side of Cattail Branch.
Wts: none (Elizabeth, wife of James **Johnston**, relinquishes her dower right.)

35, 36- Feb. 8, 1780- Joseph **Rogers** and wife Sarah to William **Sauls** of Warren Co., N. C. for 250 pds. 82 acres in Granville Co. on S side of **Martin**'s creek.
Wts: Solomon **Walker**, Joseph **Mangum**.

36, 37- Mar. 6, 1778- Alexander **Douglass** and wife Kezziah to Robert **Burton** for 100 pds. 400 acres on E side of Little Island Creek, adjoining John **Willingham**, Thomas **Barnett**, Jesse **Harper**, Timothy **Driscol**, Benjamin **Johnson** and William **Taylor** lands whereon **Douglass** formerly lived.
Wts: Richard **Henderson**, David **Mitchell**.

37, 38- Feb. 5, 1780- James **Wallace** of Ninety Six District, South Carolina by his attny, John **Williams** appointed Jan. 30, 1775- to Robert **Burton**, Esq. 75 acres in Granville Co, on W. side of Little Island creek adjoining Vinkler **Jones**,

Solomon **Walker**, William **Potter** and John **Walker** alias Robert **Burton**.
Wts: none.

38, 39- July 7, 1779- John **Williams** to Robert **Burton**, for love and affection, a deed of gift of 500 acres in Granville Co., N.C. on Nut Bush and Little Island creeks on both sides of Hico road whereon, Williams Borough now stands on Long Branch between **Williams** and Samuel **Morse**'s plantation- at lines of land of Vinkler **Jones**, William **Potter**, David **Mitchel**, Samuel **Morse** excepting 2 acres whereon, NutBush Church stands.
Wts: John **Keeling**, John **Burton**, Jr.

39- Feb. 9, 1780- John **Walker** and wife Anne to Robert **Burton** for 1520 pds. 369 acres on Little Island creek at Lick Branch, being land **Walker** and wife formerly lived on and bought, of William **Yancey**, Joseph **Davenport** and Abraham **Cook** in Oct. 7, 1765, Nov. 29, 1768, Oct. 8, 1773.
Wts: Demsy **Moore**, John **Henderson**.

40- Feb. 9, 1780- Joseph **Taylor** to John **Brodie** for 1632 pds., 118 acres at Meeting House Road on Capt James **Mitchel**'s line, to corner of **Donaldson** and Company's line including the house on the land on Reuben **Pyles** line.
Wts: none.

243

40, 41- Oct. 20, 1779- Robert **Williams** and wife Sarah of Pittsylvania Co., Va. to Richard **Henderson** for 2000 pds. 400 acres in Granville Co., N.C. on Little Nut Bush creek at William **Taylor**'s corner.
Wts: Ben **Terry**, Janey **White**, G. **Strother**.

41, 42- Dec. 2, 1779- Len Henley **Bullock** and wife Susannah to William **Martin** of Halifax Co., N.C. for 11,000 pds. 670 acres on Little Nut Bush creek in Granville Co., N.C. at **Winston**'s former corner, now **Somerville**'s to Josiah **Mitchel**'s line, **Cockleres** line, **Galispy**'s line, Henry **Lyne**'s line being land formerly belonging to James **Mitchel** deceased, and by him left to be sold to highest bidder and **Bullock** was buyer.
Wts: Mary **Somerville**, James **Harrison**, James **Webb**.

42- Jan. 10, 1777- Simon **Williams** to William **Martin** of Halifax Town, for 400 pds. land on Waters of Wolf Branch at **Anderson**'s swamp, in John **Daniel**'s' and Thomas **Person**'s lines and on Henley **Bullock**'s line, Joseph **Linsey**'s and Francis **Williams**, Ben **Thomas**'s lines, including land formerly bought of said **Williams** of Robert **Williams** and William **Brown**.
Wts: John Smith **Hunt**, Len H. **Bullock**.

42, 43- Jan. 10, 1777- Len Henley **Bullock** to William **Martin** of Halifax Town, N. C. for 350 pds. 350 acres in Granville Co. on **Anderson**'s swamp at John Williams **Daniel**'s corner, adjoining **Sims**'s plantation, on Simon **Williams** corner.
Wts: Simon **Williams**, John Smith **Hunt**.

43, 44- Feb. 4, 1778- James **Cozart** to John **Tailor** for 400 pds. 150 acres as per deed to **Cozart**- on S side of Tar river.
Wts: none.

44- Jan. 28, 1780- Thomas **Addison** of Randolph Co., N. C. to Nathan **McGehee** of Granville Co., N. C. for 1 pd. 10 shillings (dollar money) 100 acres on S side of Tar river being part of tract granted to Robert **Mills**, Sr., now deceased, Dec. 1760- by Granville, Lord Proprietor.
Wts: Cornelius **Cooper**, Zachariah **Yarbrough**.

45- Mar. 1, 1780- Reuben **Searcy** to Richard **Searcy** for 100 pds. 180 acres on Billings creek at John **Tuder**'s corner.
Wts: Asa **Searcy**, John **Good**.

45- Apr. 22, 1780- Micajah **Bullock** to Peter **Cash** for 500 pds. 100 acres at corner of **Bullock**'s and **Landess**'s lines to **Bullock**'s and **Amis**'s corners **Bullock**'s and **Smith**'s corner.
Wts: [Ross] **Hawkins**.

46- Apr. 6, 1780- Henry **Straider** to Samuel **Jackson** for 1000 pds. 136 acres on both sides of **Hampton**'s creek at former line of Nicholas **Holstein**'s, on Ephrain **Hampton**'s line.
Wts: John **Potter**, Field **Rudd**.

46- May 1, 1780- Wyat **Wilkerson** to William **Mallory** for 500 pds. 163 acres on Tar river at John **Guest**'s corner.
Wts: Demsy **Moore**, Richd **Searcy**.

47- Mar. 11, 1780- Elisha **Linsey** to John **Guest** for 1000 pds. 287 acres on E side of Tar river on Meadow Branch at Luke **Carrell**'s line.
Wts: Reuben **Searcy**, John **Green**.

47, 48- [Mar] 8, 1780- Richard **Person** to Bury **Lewis** for 100 pds. 100 acres on Buffalo Creek at **Person**'s line.
Wts: John **Huckaby**, Dorothy **Scribner**.

48- Apr. 30, 1780- James **Haskins** to Brereton **Jones** for 70 pds. 26 acres on **Cooke**'s line. . .
Wts: Micajah **Bullock**, Ben **Wade**.

48, 49- May 1, 1780- Wyat **Wilkerson** to Richard **Searcy** for 100 pds. 26 acres on **Bolling** Creek.
Wts: Demcy **Moore**, Willm **Mallory**.

49, 50- Nov. . 1779- John **Lunsford** to Elisha **Lunsford** for 50 pds. 100 acres on New Light Creek in **Vinenam**'s line.
Wts: Gillum **Harris**, Sr., Wm. **Lunsford**.

244

50- Mar. 8, 1780- Richard **Person** to Dorothy **Scribner** for 60 pds. 20 acres on Buffalo creek at Robert **Harris**'s corner, on Bury **Lewis**'s Spring branch.
Wts: John **Huckaby**, Bury **Lewis**.

50, 51- May 1, 1780- Solomon **Smith** to Thomas **Smith** for 800 pds. 150 acres on E side of the road at Pimple Hill.
Wts: Zacharias **Higgs**.

51- Feb. 5, 1780- Justus **Parrish** to Elijah **Parrish** for 2000 pds. 125 acres on S side of Tabbs creek on the old line.
Wts: Zacharias **Higgs**, Sherwd **Parrish**.

52- Apr. 6, 1780- Thomas **Norman** to John **Gilliam** for 10 pds. 341 acres on both sides of Lick Branch on his own line and on **Loyd**'s line.
Wts: William and Charles **Parrish**.

52, 53- Mar. 17, 1780- William **Glasco** to Bishop **Hicks** for 1000 pds. 550 acres on Poplar creek at **Barton**'s corner, to **Davis**'s old corner, **Sutherland**'s corner, to Glebe Corner.
Wts: George and Claborn **Harris**.

53, 54- Apr. 29, 1780- William **Nailing** to William **White** for 500 pds. 250 acres on Fort Creek at John **Hefferman**'s line, **Nailing**'s line.
Wts: Thos. **Banks** [Jurat], David **Bradford**.

54, 55- Apr. 28, 1780- Samuel **Manning** to Benjamin **Guy** for 4 pds. 4 acres at **Guy**'s line on Little Deep creek.
Wts: James **Paschal** [Jurat],Dennis **Paschal**.

55- Feb. 25, 1780- Julus **Webb** and wife Ruth to George **Brack** for 9 pd 12 shillings, 320 acres at William **Parrish**'s line on **Brack**'s field and at **Critcher**'s line.
Wts: James **Brame**, Richard **Stringfellow**.

56- Apr. 9, 1780- William **Ward** to William **Floyd** for 1280 pds. 53 acres on Samuel **Kittrell**s line on Tabbs creek, on **Rogers**' line.
Wts: Zacharias **Higgs**, Leonard **Higgs**.

56, 57- Oct. 16, 1779- Cutbert **Hudson** and wife Elizabeth to Joseph Pumprett **Davis** for 1500 pds. 379 acres at **Ferguson**'s corner, **Jordan**'s and **Harris**'s old lines, Ransone **Sutherland**'s line, at head of Tabs creek.
Wts: James **Hague**, William Edwd **Cocke** (**Cooke**).

57- Apr. 28, 1780- William **Hicks** to Thomas **Thomson** for 200 pds. 27 acres on Tabbs creek, north side of road from Tabbs creek to the Glebe in George **Harris**'s and Barnet **Tatom**'s line and also a tract of land on **Tatom**'s line on same road at Thomas **Thomson**'s line.
Wts: William **Hicks**, (reserves a spring and 10 square yards, to Wm. **Hicks**.)

58- May 2, 1780- Samuel **Allen** to Samuel **Sneed** for 40 pds. 39 acres at **Sneed**'s old corner.
Wts: Garland **Mackalester**, Saml **Jeter**.

58, 59- Apr. 29, 1780- Julus **Wells** (**Wills**) and wife Ruth to Thomas **Craft** for 466 pds. 13 shls. 4 pence, 320 acres at George **Brack**'s corner on **Critcher**'s line, **Hawkins**' corner on T. **Norman**'s line, **Parrish**'s line.
Wts: James **Brame**, George **Brack**.

59- Apr. 15, 1780- Richard **Person** to George **Mills** for 1600 pds. 150 acres on Buffalow creek at Thomas **Smith**'s line, Joseph **McDaniel**'s and Berry **Lewis**'s lines.
Wts: John **Harp**, John **Huckaby**.

60- Mar. 16 1780- Thomas **Owen** to John **Wilkerson** for 14 pds. 378 acres on Grassy creek at David **Wilkerson**'s line, **Simmons**' line.
Wts: William **Puryear**, John **Owen**.

60- Feb. 28, 1780- Len Henley **Bullock** to George **Hunt** for 300 pds. 10 acres adjoining lands of the **Goodloe** estate (no **Somerville**), **Mead**'s and Samuel **Hunt**'s lines, being land formerly purchased by Christopher **Hunt** of John **Varner** and from **Hunt** deeded to **Bullock**.
Wts: Mary **Somerville**, David **Bullock**.

61- Nov. 30, 1779- William **Martin**, executor of James **Martin**, deceased to Charles **Hammond** for 100 pds. 100 acres on **Paschal**'s line.
Wts: Dennis **Paschal**, John **Hammock**, Len H. **Bullock**.

245

61- Mar. 30, 1780- Bennet **Stacy** to Brereton **Jones** for 600 pds. 225 acres on Ledge of Rocks creek on his other line, to **Cooke**'s line and **Williams** line, to **Stanton**'s and **Harris**'s lines.
Wts: Francis and M. **Bullock**, [Jurat]

62- May 3, 1780- David **Mitchel** to Elijah **Mitchel**, his son, a deed of gift of 640 acres on Flatt creek and on Nut Bush creek being the land whereon David **Mitchel** lately lived which he bought in parcels from Thomas and John **Craft**, Reuben **Moss** as per deed in courthouse.
Wts: Thomas **Hall**, Joseph **Taylor**.

62, 63- Mar. 14, 1780- John **Owen**, Sr. to his son Thomas **Owen**, a gift of 169 acres being part of tract bought of Capt. Henry **Howard** on W side of prong of Grassy creek at Francis **Howard**'s corner, to Daniel **Grant**'s line and on said Thomas **Owen**'s line.
Wts: Jos. **Gill**, Richard **Davis**, William **Duty**.

63- Mar 20 1780- Richard **Glasco** to Daniel **Standard** for 120 pds. 120 acres on Poplar creek at corner of land whereon **Standard** now lives at William **Barton**'s line.
Wts: Claborn and George **Harris**.

64- Mar. 10, 1780- Stephen **Merritt** to William **Philpot** for 400 pds. 50 acres being part of land purchased of William **Washington** by **Merritt** on fork of Cub creek in **Washington**'s line.
Wts: Joseph **Langston**, Archibald **Debman**.

64, 65- Feb. 4, 1780- William **Jones** and Elizabeth **Jones** to Fowler **Jones** for 30 pds. 200 acres at Michael **Wilson**'s

corner.
Wts: Henry and Job **Green**.

65- May 2, 1780- John **Ferrill** to James **Johnson** for 1000 pds. 78 acres at **Mumford**'s corner, in **Johnston**'s line, **Malone**'s line.
Wts: M. **Bullock**.

65, 66- Mar. 25, 1780- Samuel **Paschal** of Warren Co., N. C. to Charles **Hammock** of Granville Co. for 12 pds. 12 shls. 83 acres at **Martin**'s corner, on John **Pascal**'s line.
Wts: James **Paschal**, James **Burchett**.

66- Jan. 28, 1780- Edmund **Taylor** to Leonard **Smith** for 1200 pds. 200 acres the land **Taylor** bought of Joseph **Waldrope** on **Gillam**'s branch between lands of Richard **Taylor**, Joseph **Akin**, John **Hargrove**, Daniel **Williams** and William **Duncan**.
Wts: John **Brodie**, Richard **Taylor**.

66, 67- Mar. 25, 1780- Samuel **Paschal** of Warren Co., N. C. to Samuel **Manning** of Granville for 100 pds. 154 acres on E side of Little Deep creek in **Martin**'s line.
Wts: James **Paschal**, Charles **Hammock**.

67, 68- Apr. 29, 1780- William **Key** to William **Guthrie** for 2000 pds. 350 acres on Little Deep creek at John **Chadwick**'s branch, on James **Pascal**'s line, Thomas **Addams** old line-
Wts: James **Paschal**, William **Sims**.

68- May 2, 1780- Robert **Malone** to Robert **Hester** for 1000 pds. 358 acre on Grassy creek on **Smith**'s line.
Wts: James **Mitchel**, Groves **Howard**.

68, 69- Apr. 15, 1780- Samuel **Paschal** of Warren Co., N. C, to Nathaniel **Roberson** for 100 pds. 200 acres on **Martin**'s line, John **Pascal**'s corner in Granville Co., N.C.
Wts: James and John **Paschal**.

69- Mar. 8, 1780- Robert **Harris** to John **Hatcher** for 20 pds. 300 acres as shown by deed to Robert **Harris** Sept, 4th last, on **Claxton**'s line and at **Haskin**'s corner, **Cooke**'s line.
Wts: Micjah **Bullock**, James **Haskin**.

70- Mar. 10, 1780- Robert **Harris**, Sr. to William **Booth** of Virginia for 500 pds. 500 acres in Granville Co. on N. side of **Adcock** creek at **Allison**'s corner, **Harris**'s line, **Ogelvie**'s line, at head of **Hargrove**'s Spring Branch.
Wts: James **Johnston**, Reuben **Searcy**.

246

70, 71- May 1, 1780- William **Barton** to William **Williams** for 500 pds. 440 acres on both sides of Tar river and on Little creek in **Pridy**'s line-
Wts: John **Henderson**.

71- Feb. 4, 1780- William **Jones** and Elizabeth **Jones** to Edward **Jones** for 30 pds. 202 acres at the subdividing line.
Wts: Henry and Job **Green**.

71, 72- May 2, 1780- William **Allen** to Hazelwood **Wilkerson** for 500 pds. 175 acres at **Gooch**'s corner, **Beasley**'s line, **Daniel**'s line, **Landers** corner.
Wts: Richd **Davis**, William **Cocke**, Jr.

72, 73- Feb. 7, 1780- James **Stark** and wife Jane to James **Brame** for 200 pds. 294 acres at **Brame** s line, **Tillman**'s line, **Williams** line, Nathaniel **Williams**'s line.
Wts: James **Mitchel**, George **Brack**.

73- Mar. 25, 1780- Samuel **Paschal** of Warren Co., N.C. to Izabella **Paschal** of Granville Co., N.C. for 80 pds. 140 acres at **Martin**'s line, on **Robertson**'s line, **Turner**'s line.

Wts: James **Paschal**, Charles **Hammock**.

73, 74- Apr. 15, 1780- Samuel **Paschal** of Warren Co., N.C. to Thomas **Key** of Granville Co. for 30 pds. 207 acres on branches of Nut Bush creek at Wm. **Todd**'s corner, **Sims**'s line.
Wts: James **Paschal**, Jr., Nath **Robinson**.

74- May 1, 1780- Samuel **Walker**, Sr. to Samuel **Walker**, Jr. for 1000 pds. 492 acres on both sides of Fishing creek, in **Hudspeth**'s line.
Wts: none.

74, 75- Jan. 21, 1780- William **Cook** to Robert **Harris**, Esq. for 1000 pds. 640 acres in Granville Co., N.C. on S side of **Adcock**'s creek which was surveyed by Thomas **Grant** deputy surveyor of Thomas **Person**, of said county, on William **Hewit**'s line, **Holston**'s line.
Wts: David **Turner**, Sherwood **Harris**.

75- Apr. 26, 1780- Daniel **Grant** to Richard **Davis**, his son-in-law, a deed of gift of 229 acres on Jonathan's creek, on **Gill**'s line.
Wts: Hazelwood **Wilkerson**, Jr., Terry **Davis**.

76- May 2, 1780- John Petty **Cobb** to Cornelius **Cooper** for 100 pds. 58 acres on N. side of Tar river at **Fuller**'s line.
Wts: John **Peace**, Jr.

76, 77- Mar. 23, 1780- John **Willingham** of Henry Co., Va. to Miles **King** of Granville Co., N.C. for 100 pds. 205 acres on Little Island creek, near **Walker**'s ford, on **Duglass**'s line so as to reserve one acre on west side of creek for use of a Mill-
Wts: John **Cox**, John **Marr**, Hay[o]ns **Morgan**, R. **Williams**, [Jurat].

77- Mar. 10, 1780- Richard **Person** to John **Huckaby** for 3000 pds. 380 acres on Buffalow creek at Joseph **Leaman**'s corner, **Hambleton**'s corner, **Harp**'s corner, Bury **Lewis**'s line, Dorothy **Scribner**'s line.
Wts: Jno. **Person**, Berry **Lewis**.

77, 78- May 2, 1780- Robert **Malone** to James **Downey** for 800 pds. 160 acres on Grassy creek at **Terrell**'s corner.
Wts: Graves **Howard**, James **Mitchel**.

78- Mar. 24, 1780- Mathew **Duty** to Phillip **Voss** for 200 pds. 400 acres on both sides of Grassy creek, on **Howard**'s line, **Owen**'s line, **Bridges**' and **Smith**'s line.
Wts: John and Rachel **Young**, Mildred **Allen**.

79- Feb. 4, 1779- William **Weldon** of Halifax Co., N, C. to Thomas **Person** of Granville Co., N.C. for 112 pds., 302 acres being land purchased by Daniel **Weldon** of William **Smith** and afterwards conveyed to William **Weldon**-
Wts: Robert **Harris**, B. **Hawkins**.

79, 80- May 30, 1780- James **Jones** of Mecklenburg Co., Va to Joseph **Chandler** for 3000 pds. Va. money, 350 acres on **Aaron**'s creek at William **Gill**'s corner, **Applin**'s line, **Harris**'s line, **Jones** and **Harrison**'s lines.
Wts: Wm. **Gill**, Jr., Elizabeth **Harrison**.

80- Aug. 7, 1780- William **Hicks** to Malachiah **Reavis** for 5 shillings 150 acres on **Login**'s and **Reavis**'s lines.
Wts: none.

247

80, 81- May 13, 1780- Charles Rust **Eaton** to William **Locke** for 100 pds. 225 acres on W side of Ruin creek at Jonathan **Kittrell**'s line, in **Benton**'s line-
Wts: John **Major**.

81- Mar. 29, 1780- Reuben **Searcy** to John **Good** for 500 pds. 156 acres on **Bolling** creek at Richard **Searcy**'s corner.

Wts: Asa **Searcy**, Henry **Reardon**.

81, 82- May 19, 1780- George **Tillman** and wife Goodith to William **Tillman** for 60 pds. 200 acres at George **Tillman**'s corner.
Wts: John **Farrar**, Reuben **Morse**.

82- July 2, 1780- Bishop **Hicks** to Jacob **Woodal** for 700 weight of tobacco, 100 acres on William **Reeves**, Thomas **Thomson**'s, Lewis **Parham**'s lines-
Wts: Reuben **Searcy**.

82, 83- May 8, 1780- William **Hickman** to John **Heath** for 500 pds. 178 acres on Grassy creek at his own line and on **Person**'s line.
Wts: David, John **Howard**.

83- July 7, 1780- Abraham **Hester** to Ann **Butler** for 100 pds. 121 acres on branches of Grassy creek in **Glaze**' corner, on **Hunt**'s line.
Wts: David **Smith**, John **Butler**.

83, 84- Feb. 21, 1780- Howell **Lewis**, Sr. to Robert **Mumford** of Mecklenburg Co., Va. for 250,000 weight of tobacco paid in Annual installments, vz of 50,000 weight each year for five years commencing Apr. 25, 1780- 2500 acres on Grassy creek on lines of Phillip **Taylor** and Thomas **Person**'s in Granville Co., N. C, known as *Mountain Tract*, on lines of Robert **Lewis**, James **Downey** and James **Johnston**. .
Wts: John **Kennon**, James **Anderson**, William **Bridgewater**.

84- Aug. 1, 1780- Henry **Pattillo**, clerk, to Richard **Harrison** for 2500 pds. 200 acres or one moiety of land whereon Richard **Harrison** now lives on both sides of **Michael**'s creek, bought by **Pattillo** and **Harrison** of Richard **Wilkins**-

84, 85- Feb. 16, 1780- Phillip **Chavis** (**Chavers**) of Bladen Co., N.C. to Major (Mager) **Evans** of Granville Co., N.C. for 100 pds. 100 acres near the Buffalow Race Paths on his own line to **Hamilton**'s line, **Snelling**'s line.
Wts: John **Nevill**, John **Cook**.

85- Mar. 30, 1780- Henry **Reardon** to John **Hawkins** for 100 pds., 100 acres on **Bolling** creek in **Hawkins'**, **Hudspeth**'s lines.
Wts: Asa and Reuben **Searcy**.

86- Aug. 9, 1780- John **Dickerson** and Elizabeth **Dickerson** to John **Sutton** for 575 pds. 610 acres on Fort Creek on his own line, **Bradford**'s line.
Wts: John **Peace**, Jr.

86- June 12, 1780- John **Hunt** and wife Frances to Joseph **Gooch** for 6666 pds. 13 shillings, 4 pence- 500 acres whereon John **Hunt** now lives on lines of **Cannon**, **Wood**, **Clay**, **Lewis** and **Downey**.
Wts: Gideon **Gooch**, Susaner **Lute**.

87- John **Henderson** produced deed, May 5, 1780, to court, which was made to him by Robert **Lewis** and wife Jane of Goochland Co., Va. for land in Goochland Co., Va. and was proven in Granville Co., N.C.- now asks that Jane **Lewis** be requested to release dower right and John **Hopkins** and William **Holman** of Goochland Co. take deposition of said Jane **Lewis**- She releases her dower right.

87- June 30, 1780- James **Jones** of Mecklenburg Co., Va. to William **Gill**, Sr. of same county and State for 3000 pds. 350 acres on Jonathan's creek, on **Aaron**'s creek on **Gill**'s and **Grant**'s lines in Granville Co., N.C., and on **Aplin**'s line, Jos. **Chandler**'s line, **Harrison**'s line.
Wts: William **Gill**, Jr., Jos. **Chandler**.

88- Mar. 31 1780- Reuben **Searcy** to Henry **Reardon** for 200 pds. 200 acres on Tar river-
Wts: Asa **Searcy**, John **Good**.

88- Mar. 7, 1780- Henry **Reardon** to William Hargrove **Searcy** for 100 pds. 100 acres on **Bolling** creek at **Hudspeth**'s line.

Wts: Asa **Searcy**, John **Tuder**.

248

88, 89 May. 10, 1780- Samuel **Allen** to Henry **Milton** (**Melton**) for 500 pds. 221 acres on **Sneed**'s line and **Milton**'s old line, **Gooch**'s line, **Mitchel**'s line on the main road.

89- Aug. 11, 1780- Richard **Taylor** to his brother Lewis **Taylor** as per contract with him, and for valuable consideration- 474 acres at John **Farris**'s and said Lewis **Taylor**'s corner at Country line in Granville Co.
Wts: Joseph **Taylor**, James **Lewis**.

89, 90- Dec. 4, 1780- Micajah **Bullock** and William **Bullock**. of Amelia Co., Virginia to Samuel **Clay** of Halifax Co., Va. for 800 pds., 1050 acres in Granville Co., N.C. formerly surveyed for George **Morris** at **Mead**'s corner on William **More**'s line, Phil **Walston**'s line-
Wts: Ben **Wade**, Edward **Bullock**.

90, 91- May 7, 1780- Robert **Harris**, Jr. to John **Davis** for 5000 pds. 200 acres which is the land Francis **Falk** bought of Chauncey **Townsend** agent, on Ledge of Rocks creek at corner where George **Byars** lived at George **Miller**'s line. (signed Robert **Harris**, Jr., and Elizabeth **Harris**.).
Wts: Michael **Redwiel**, Jeremiah **Bullock**.

91- July 12, 1780- Edward **Moore** of Montgomery Co., N.C. to Demcey **Moore** of Granville Co., N.C. for 3500 pds. 1203 acres in Granville Co on Fishing creek, at Michael **Wilson**'s, **Benton**'s and **Willis**'s lines, **Hutching**'s line.
Wts: Thomas **Mutter**, Hugh **Galt**.

91, 92- Apr. 18, 1780- George **Wright** to Mary **Phillips** for 100 pds. 212 acres on Nap of Reeds creek at E side of Trading Path on **McCulloh**'s line.-
Wts: Henry **Green**, Joseph **Cash**.

92- July 4, 1780- Wiat **Wilkerson** and wife Mary to Robert **Lewis**, Sr. of Goochland Co., Va. for 832 pds. 10 shls. 325 acres in Granville Co., N.C. on N. side of Tar river on **Wilkerson**'s and **Person**'s lines and **Lewis**'s old line.
Wts: Howel **Lewis**, Sr., Willm **Ridley**, Peyton **Wood**.

92, 93- May 9, 1780- William **Hickman** of Guilford Co., N. C. to William **Cockrell** for 1000 pds. 180 acres in Granville Co., N.C. on Mountain crk in **Hunt** and **Williamson**'s lines.
Wts: David and John **Howard**.

93- Feb. 9, 1780- Ralph **Williams** to William **Green** for 3000 pds. 202 acres on Ledge of Rocks creek on James **Bullock**'s line.
Wts: Micajah **Bullock**, Ben **Wade**.

94- May 4, 1780- John **Powell** of Lunenburg Co., Va. to Thomas **Pool** of Granville Co., N.C. for 13 pds. tobacco, 200 acres in Granville Co. on Grassy creek at Daniel **Grant**'s Spring branch and Robert **Busby**'s line on William **Willingham**'s line.
Wts: Danl **Grant** [Jurat], Joseph **Hart**, Joseph Terry **Davis**.

94, 95- Aug. 7, 1780- John **Tuder**, Sr. to Henry **Tuder** for 50 pds. 8 1/8 acres on N. side of Fishing creek on James **Ellison**'s line.
Wts: Reuben **Searcy**.

95- Aug. 10, 1780- Thomas **Person** to Samuel **Jackson** for 2000 pds. 375 acres on Mill and **Adcock** creek at **Jackson**'s (formerly **Hampton**'s) corner, **Brame**'s and **Wright**' lines, **Clements**' line, **Harris**'s line.
Wts: Francis **Howard**, John **Potter**.

95, 96- May 22, 1780- Daniel **Malone** to John **Hunt** for 5000 pds. 312 acres on Jonathan's creek in **Aplin**'s line, **Royster**'s line, **Gill**'s line.
Wts: Daniel **Malone**, John **Blackwell**.

96- Nov. 1, 1780- Sherwood **Harris** to Benjamin **Beardon** for 1000 pds. 221 acres on Cattail branch where Sherwood **Harris**'s line crosses, formerly Abraham **Cook**'s line.

96, 97- Mar. 9, 1780- John **Adcock** to Robert **Harris**, esq. for 500 pds. 200 acres on Ledge of Rocks creek on S side of Tarboro road on **Holstein**'s and **Hatcher**'s corners.
Wts: Peter **Cash**, Charles **Coleman**.

97, 98- Feb. 18, 1780- John **Whicker** to Reuben **Talley** for 3200 pds. 160 acres on both sides of Harrel's creek on **Hicks**'s, **Bruce'** lines on Mirey branch.-
Wts: Wm. **Currin**, Thomas **Whicker**.

249

98- Nov. 6, 1780- Edward **Willburn** to Francis **Brissie** for 1000 pds. 200 acres on S side of Indian Field creek, at **McCulloh**'s line.
Wts: Will **Kennon**, Barnitt **Pulliam**,
Mary, wife of Edward **Willburn**, relinquishes her dower right.

98, 99- Oct. 7, 1780- Samuel **Hicks** to Thomas **Thomason** for 100 pds. 200 acres on Tabbs creek at **Hicks'**, **Reeves'** lines.
Wts: William **Reeves**, Frederick **Reeves**.

99- Sept. 5, 1780- Samuel **Allen** to Bartlet **Wright** for 500 pds. 189 acres on S side of Old road at **Sneed**'s new line, **Getter**'s line.
Wts: Thos. **Thomason**, Wm. **Wright**, Benj **Hester**.

99, 100- May 27, 1780- Thomas **Bridges** to William **Carrill** of Franklin Co., N.C. for 2000 pds. 240 acres on Beaverdam creek on James **Walker**'s line, being part of tract from Richard **Bradford** to John **Huskey**, Sr. and he to John **Huskey**, Jr. who deedee [sic] to Thomas **Bridges**.
Wts: John **Pope**, John **Whitfield**.

100, 101- May 8, 1780- James **Bennett** and and Sally **Bennett** to James **Manire** of Amelia Co., Va. for 2400 pds. 100 acres in Granville Co., N.C. on Nap of Reeds creek being part of land bought of Alexander **Grey**-
Wts: James **Cozart**, William **Bennett**.

101- Oct. 22, 1780- James **Breckin** (**Breachen**) to Richard **Glasgow** for 400 pds. 337 acres on **Parrish**'s line at Ruin Creek, **Glasgow**'s line.
Wts: Dennis **Driskell**, Charles **Parrish**.

101, 102- Oct. 21 1780- James **Haskins** to Richard Donaldson **Cooke** for 10 pds. 65 acres adjoining the land whereon Richard Donaldson **Cooke** now lives at **Stacey**'s line near **Claxton**'s old path at **Adcock**'s line.
Wts: Francis **Claxton**, Robert **Harris**, Jr.

102- Oct. 30, 1780- William **Chapman** to Richard **Head** for 300 pds. 76 acres on Grassy creek at **Graves**' corner, **Lowe**'s line.
Wts: Henry **Graves**, T. **Satterwhite**.

102, 103- Aug. 7, 1780- Thomas **Brown** to John **Watkins** for 1000 pds. 175 acres at Henry **Fleman**'s corner, John **Hargrove**'s line, country line.
Wts: Thomas and William **Sims**.

103, 104- Sept. 30, 1779- William **Kennon** and wife Elizabeth to Michael **Satterwhite** for 2500 pds. 717 acres on both sides of Hico road being land **Kennon** sold to Col. Robert **Lewis** on **Person**'s line at **Palmer**'s line, on **Bennett**'s line. (signed by Elizabeth and Wm. **Kennon**).
Wts: Thomas **Person**, Rowlan **Thomas**, Jr.

104- Dec. 12, 1780- Elizabeth **Bullock** (Mrs.) deposed before John **Taylor**, and Thos **Satterwhite**, that she freely consents to sale of land sold to Washington **Salter** by her husband William **Bullock**-

104, 105- Feb. 5, 1781- Charles **Williams** to Charles **Farrar** for 50 pds. 230 acres on S side of Ruin Creek at Nathaniel **Williams**' line, and in **Stark**, **Tillman**'s and **Morse**'s lines being the land granted to Charles **Williams** Sept. 4, 1779-
Wts: William **Tillman**, Nathl **Farrar**.

105, 106- Feb. 5, 1781- Daniel **Grant** to John **Owen**, Jr. for 40 pds. 100 acres on S side of Bare branch at Joseph **Gill**'s line.

106- Feb. 6, 1781- Daniel **Grant** to Stephen **Gifford** for love etc, a deed of, gift to his son-in-law Stephen **Gifford** of 425 acres on **Wharton**'s branch of Grassy creek at **Beasley**'s line, **Wilkerson**'s and David **Smith**'s at **Graves**' corner and at **Roberts**' line.

106, 107- Feb. 3, 1781- Daniel **Grant** to Hazelwood **Wilkerson** his son-in-law, a gift of 100 acres on Grassy creek on **Wilkerson**'s own line and adjoining **Busby**'s line on S side of road, at David **Smith**'s line.

107, 108- Jan. 2, 1781- John **Davis** to Michael **Redwine** for 1000 pds. 7 acres which is part of 200 acres **Davis** bought of Robert **Harris**, Jr. on **Davis**'s and **Redwine**'s lines.
Wts: Jeremiah **Bullock**, William **Green**.

108- Dec. 29, 1780- John **Guest** to Leonard **Linsey** for 1000 pds. 287 acres on E side of Tar river to the former line of Luke **Carrell**'s.
Wts: Bennett and Reuben **Searcy**.

250

108, 109- Oct. 6, 1780- **William** James of Franklin Co., N.C. to Andrew **Wade** of county aforesaid, for 5 shillings, 330 acres in Granville Co. on Rocky Branch at **McDaniel**'s and **Person**'s lines, **Dickerson**'s line.
Wts: John **Clayton**, George **James**, James **Wade**.

109- Sept. 4, 1780- Zorababel **Williamson** to William **Bobbitt** for 350 pds. 350 acres in **Edwards**' line, on **Rogers**' and on **Eaton**'s and **Fuller**'s lines.
Wts: Joseph **Mangum**, Samuel **Fuller**.

109, 110- Jan. 6, 1781- William **Douglass** of Orange Co., N.C. to William **Douglass** for 5000 pds. 80 acres in Granville Co., on Fishing creek at **Walker**'s, John **Hudspeth**'s lines.
Wts: Asa and Reuben **Searcy**, Sherwood **Harris**.

110- Nov. 7, 1780- Thomas **Person** to Daniel **Malone** for 10,000 pds. 300 acres on SE side of **Aaron**'s creek on **Harrison**'s line.
Wts: James **Norwell**, William **Thomas**.

111- . . 1780- John **Adcock** to Barnett **Stacey** for 10 pds. 50 acres on John **Adcock**'s Spring branch at James **Claxton** and **Hatcher**'s lines.
Wts: Edmund **Partee**.

111, 112- Jan. 23, 1781- John **Adcock** to Robert **Harris** for 10,000 pds. 300 acres on his own line, **Bullock**'s line on **Williams** Spring branch.
Wts: Henrietta and Robert **Harris**.

112- Jan. 6, 1781- John **Good** to Reuben **Searcy** for 100 pds. 150 acres on **Bolling**'s creek at Richard **Searcy**'s corner.
Wts: John **Searcy**.

112, 113- Dec. 19, 1780- Cutbird **Hudson** of Georgia to Joseph Pumphritt **Davis** of Granville Co., N.C. for 500 pds. 320 acres on Poplar creek at **Parrish**'s and **Hudson**'s lines on **Sneed**'s line, on Lick creek.
Wts: Jonathan **Knight**, William **Byars**.

113, 114- Nov. 30, 1780- James **Currin** to Ambrose **Barker** for 500 pds. 175 acres on Tabb and Nut Bush creeks in

Bullock's, **Sneed**'s lines, **Sears**' and **Currin**'s lines.

114- Feb. 2, 1781- Brereton **Jones** to John **Guinn** for 10,000 pds. 26 acres in Granville. Co.

114- Feb. 2, 1781- Brereton **Jones** to John **Gwinn** for 10,000 pds. 225 acres in Granville Co., N.C. at **Hawkins**' line, on Ledge of Rocks creek on **Williams**' and on **Cooke**'s lines, **Harris**'s line.
Wts: none.

115- Sept, 9, 1780- Traverse **Bowdin** and Pennellopy his wife, to George **Brack** for 20 pds. 60 acres on Thomas **Critcher**'s and on **Brown**'s line.
Wts: Merryman **Barnes**, William **Parrish**, Jr. (**Bowdon**, **Bowden**)

116, 116- Jan. 20, 1781- Samuel **Fuller** to William **Bobbitt** for 10 pds. 100 acres at **Fuller**'s and at **Edwards**' lines.
Wts: Joseph **Mangum**, Elisha **Ward**.

116- Jan. 5, 1781- Thomas **Goss** to Sherman **Goss**, his son, a gift of 100 acres on S side of Tar river being part of tract Thomas **Goss** took up near the road in **Merritt**'s line, Benjamin **Merritt**'s line.
Wts: James **Langston**.

116, 117- Aug. 5, 1780- Jno. **Finch** to John **Huckaby** for 2000 pds. 200 acres on Long creek signed John **Finch**.
Wts: Jenkins **Downey**, Bonner **Bird**.

117, 118- Feb. 5, 1781- Henry **Fuller** to Sarah **Hays** for 10 pds. 46 acres at Joseph **Johnson**'s line, Charles **Eaton**'s corner.
Wts: Samuel **Fuller**, Littleton **Fuller**.

118- Jan. 5, 1781- Robert **Harris**, the elder, to Sherwood **Harris** for 1000 pds. 320 acres on **Adcock**'s creek in **Holstein**'s line.
Wts: William **Ogelvie**, Robert **Harris**, Jr., Harris **Ogelvie**.

118, 119- Oct. 5, 1779- Billey Gosling **Gooch** to Joseph **Hawkins** of Warren Co., N.C. for 2000 pds. 700 acres in Granville Co., N.C. on Deep creek at **Hawkins**' corner.
Wts: Philemon **Hawkins**, Thos. **Williams**.

119- Jan. 23, 1781- William **Tillman** to Osburn **Ball** of Warren Co., N.C. for 20 pds. 186 acres in Granville Co., N.C. on Lick creek at **Parrish**'s and **Loyd**'s corners.
Wts: Joseph **Mangum**, John **Faulkner**.

251

119, 120- Sept. 9, 1780- Mathew **Lowrey** of Wake Co., N.C. to James **Peters** for 200 pds. 200 acres on S side of Buffalow creek being land conveyed by William **Liles** Aug. 5, 1777 to Mathew **Lowrey**.
Wts: Jos. **Hill**, Isaac **Hicks**, William **Liles**, Richard **Rease**.

120- Jan. 22, 1780- Isaiah **Paschal** of Franklin Co., N.C. to William **Paschal** of Granville Co., N.C. for 500 pds. 100 acres in Granville Co., N.C. on a branch.
Wts: Jno. **Lemon**, Wm. **Huckaby**.

121- Sept. 30, 1780- William **Huckaby** of Franklin Co., N. C. to Harberd **Hight** of aforesaid county and State for 5000 pds. 100 acres in Granville Co., N.C. on Buffalow creek.
Wts: John **Hight**, William **Paschal**.

121, 122- Jan. 22, 1780- Isaiah **Paschal** of Franklin Co., N.C. to William **Huckaby** of county and State aforesaid for 500 pds. 100 acres on Buffalow creek in Granville Co., N.C.
Wts: Jno. **Lemon**, Wm. **Paschal**.

122, 123- Jan. 12, 1781- Thomas **Johnson** and wife Patience of Wilks Co., N.C. to Moses **Wood** of Granville Co., N.C. for 400 pds. 300 acres in Granville Co on S. side of Tabbs creek adjoining lands of Saml **Hix**, John **Wright**, **White**'s

land, Avery **Parham**, Isham **Parham**, Joshua **Hays**, John **Parham**, Nathan **Whitlow**'s line.
Wts: Nathan **Moore**, Joseph **Hays**, Wm. **Parrish**, Sr., Joshua **Hays**, Jr, Celia **Hays**.

123- Feb. 5, 1781- Thomas **Norman** to Lemuel **Goodwin** for 2000 pds. 129 acres on both sides of Tabbs creek at **Loyd**'s corner, **Eaton**'s corner being part of 520 acres granted to Thomas **Lowe** by Lord Granville Nov. 28, 1760.
Wts: Demsey **Moore**, Barnett **Pulliam**.

123, 124- Mar. 30, 1780- William **Breachen** of Caswell Co., N.C. to William **James** of Franklin Co., N.C. for 1000 pds. 330 acres on Rocky branch in Granville Co., N.C. at **McDaniel**'s and **Person**'s lines, **Dickerson**'s line.
Wts: John **Clayton**, William **Liles**, Nathan **Jackson**.

124, 125- Oct. 9, 1780- Francis **Howard** to Phillip **Voss** for 195 pds. 306 acres adjoining Thomas and John **Owen**'s lands.
Wts: Richardson **Owen** (Sarah, wife of Francis **Howard**, relinquishes dower.)

125- Feb. 7, 1781- Samuel **Sneed** to Dudley **Sneed** for 2000 pds. 480 acres on both sides of Rackoon branch.

125, 126- Dec. 13, 1780- William **Liles** to Nathan **Jackson** for 5000 pds. 150 acres on W. side of Horse creek on **Liles**' line.

126- July 7, 1780- Elijah **Parrish** to Justus **Parrish** for 1000 pds. 95 acres on Tabbs creek at mouth of the branch.
Wts: Zacharias **Higgs**, Leonard **Higgs**.

127- . . 1779- Lewis **Taylor** and wife Jane to William **Bullock** for 2,066 pds. 13 shillings, 4 pence, land on both sides of Great Island creek, near Cool Spring branch at John **Taylor**'s, Lewis **Taylor**'s lines at line agreed on by Lewis and William **Taylor** which is the land bought of Joseph **Williams** deceased, his heirs or executors, by Lewis **Taylor** except a few acres allotted to William **Taylor** by Lewis **Taylor** adjoining the William **Taylor** Quarter land and now containing 786 acres in all.
Wts: Catherine **Bullock**, John **Taylor**, John **Lewis**.

127, 128- Feb. . .1781- Samuel **Allen** to Reuben **Ragland** for 500 pds. 334 acres on Flatt creek at **Ragland**'s line, **Burton**'s and **Allen**'s lines.
Wts: none.

128- Jan. 2, 1781- Michael **Redwine** to John **Davis** for 1000 pds. 7 acres on Stone creek which was bought of George **Miller**.
Wts: Jeremiah **Bullock**, William **Green**.

129- Oct. 23, 1780- Richard Donaldson **Cooke** to Thomas **Jenkins** for 300 pds. at a line agreed upon between the parties, and at **Jenkins**' line on Reedy creek-
Wts: Rebecca **Cooke**, Wm. **Ogelvie**.

129, 130- Dec. 26, 1780- Philip **Voss** to Thomas **Critcher** for 200 pds. 400 acres on both sides of Grassy creek along **Bridges**' and **Smith**'s lines.
Wts: Ambrose **Barker**, Isaac **Hopkins**.
Elizabeth, wife of Philip **Voss**, relinquishes her dower right.

252

130- July 20, 1780- Richard **Bradford** to Philemon **Bradford**, Jr. for 500 pds. 370 acres at **Fuller**'s corner, **McCullok**'s corner on Beaverdam crk.
Wts: David **Bradford**, John **Bradford**, Benja **Bradford**, Thos **Bradford**.

130, 131- Mar. 27, 1781- Thomas **Bradford** to Philemon **Bradford**, Jr. for 1000 pds. 500 acres at D. **Bradford**'s line, P. **Bradford**'s, J. **Bradford**'s line on Beaver Dam creek with all rights held under law of N.C. since the declaration of Independence.
Wts: Reuben **Searcy**, Asa **Searcy**, Sherwood **Harris**.

131, 132- Dec. 19, 1780- Esther **Critcher**, Samuel **Morse**, Nathaniel **Rochester** and Thomas **Critcher**, executors of the will of Thomas **Critcher** deceased, to Joseph **Taylor** and Phillip **Voss**, tenants in common for 100.000 pds., certain land, as per Will of Thomas **Critcher**, dec'd land on both sides of Fishing creek containing 800 acres at line of lands formerly belonging to **Benton**, Jonathan **White**, **Forgusons**, John **White**'s, **Springfield** which is land conveyed by George **Alston** to Thomas **Critcher**, deceased, July 25, 1774 and also a tract of 100 acres on William **Wright**'s line conveyed by Christopher **Harris** to Thomas **Critcher** deceased, Nov. 4, 1778 and also a tract adjoining the others on Fishing creek at Lewis **Anderson**'s line containing 200 acres being the land conveyed by Thomas **Bradford** executor of Jonathan **White** deceased, to Thomas **Critcher** deceased, Feb. 4, 1778.
Wts: Elijah **Mitchel**.

132, 133- July 12, 1781- Robert **Munford** of Mecklenburg Co., Va. to Phillip **Taylor** of Granville Co., N.C. for 100,000 pds. of Crop Tobacco 1300 acres on Grassy Creek in Granville Co., N.C. on William **Hammock**'s, and **Frazier**'s lines, **Howel**'s, **Taylor**'s corners.
Wts: Otway **Bird** (Byrd), James **Anderson**.

133- May 12, 1781- Robert **Mumford** of Mecklenburg Co., Va. to Otway **Byrd** of Charles City county, Va. a deed of gift of 2000 acres in Granville Co., N.C. on Grassy creek at Robert **Mumford**'s line, Thomas **Person**'s line and known as the *Mountain Tract*, at Robert **Lewis**, James **Downey**, James **Johnston** and at vacant lands.
Wts: John S. **Clack**, Wm. Beverly **Fitzhugh**.
500 acres of the within land adjoining the land of Robert **Mumford** purchased of Phillip **Taylor** is to be reserved to Robert **Mumford**.
Wts: William **Bridgewater**, Thos **Anderson**, John S. **Clack**, Jr., W. B. **Fitzhugh**.

134- Aug. 5, 1780- Richard **Taylor** and wife Lucy to James **Lewis** of Mecklenburg Co., Va. for 100,000 pds. 1986 acres whereon said **Taylor** now lives adjoining **Hawkins'**, **Duncan**'s, **Smith**'s, **Glover**'s, **Terry**'s lands.
Wts: Joseph **Taylor**, Edmd **Taylor**.

134, 135- May 7, 1781- Lucy **Taylor** relinquishes her dower right in land.
Wts: Robert **Burton**, Thomas **Satterwhite** signed- July 28, 1781.

135- Jan. 5, 1781- Ashkenaz **Williams** and wife Sary of Warren Co., N.C. to John **Tanner** for 12, 500 pds. of crop tobacco, 208 acres in Granville Co at Simon **Williams**' and Francis **Williams**' former lines at **Tanner**'s line.
Wts: Thos **Jenkins**, Archles **Williams**, Nimrod **Williams**.

135, 136- Aug. 1, 1781- William **Cooper** to Philip **Purce** (**Peerce**) of Franklin Co., N.C. for 100 pds. 100 acres on **Moxley**'s branch in Granville Co., N.C.
Wts: John **Welch**, J. **Ross**.

136- Nov. 17, 1780- Edward **Harris** to James **Downey** for 10,000 pds. 100 acres on Grassy creek adjoining **Downey**'s, **Person**'s, **Cockril**'s lands.
Wts: David **Knott**, Joseph **Asbell**.

156, 137- Mar. 9, 1781- Benjamin **Bearden** to Richard **Harris** for 75 pds. 300 acres on E side of Cattail creek at **Alston**'s line, crossing Harrisburg road on **Harris**'s line. (Money **Bearden**, wife of Benjamin also signs deed.)
Wts: John **Harris**, Jr., John **Harris**

137- Aug. 1, 1781- William **Gill** and Samuel **Whitehead**, executors of will of William **Gill**, late of Mecklenburg Co., VA., deceased, to Joseph **Gill** of Granville Co., N.C. for 486 pds. 648 acres on both sides of **Jonathan**'s creek at **Baynes**' line.

253

138- Aug. 3, 1781- Peter **Vinson** to Jacob **Vinson** for 10 pds. 150 acres at corner of lands of Alexander **Vinson** and John **Champion** to the corner of **Champion**' and **Henderson**'s lands (John **Henderson**'s) to Nicholas **Holstein**'s line, he now deceased.
Wts: Thos. **Banks**, Ralph **Banks**, John **Champion**, Jr.

138, 139- Aug. 6, 1781- William **Paschal** to Harberd **Hight** of Franklin Co., N.C. for 50,000 pds. land on Buffalow

creek in Granville Co., N.C. on road that runs from **Sims**'s ford to Granville old court house running to Thomas **Smith**'s line to John **Finch**es' line, containing 100 acres.
Wts: John **Hight**, W. **Hight**.

139- Jan. 5, 1781- Robert **Caller**, Sr. of Warren Co., N.C. to Askeenaz (Askhenaz) **Williams** for 25,000 pds. of crop tobacco, 696 acres in Granville Co. at **Bullock**'s and **Smith**'s lines.
Wts: Thos. **Jenkins**, John **Caller**, Wm. **Caller**, John **Tanner**.
signed by Robert **Caller** and Jemima **Caller**.

140- Aug. 4, 1781- Robert **Harris**, Sr. to Robert **Harris**, Jr. for 500 pds. 200 acres on Tarborough road.
Wts: Richard **Harris**, John **Davis**.

140, 141- Aug. 6, 1781- William **Dishazo** to Benjamin **Grisham** for 100 pds. 125 acres on S side of Flat creek at Lick branch where the new road crosses running to Drury **Kimbal**'s and to **Parrish**'s line, Bromfield **Ridley**'s.
Wts: Bromfield **Ridley**'
Nanney, wife of **Dishazo** relinquishes her dower.)

141- June 1, 1781- Abraham **Smith** to Thomas **Hays** for 30 pds., 100 acres on **Linch**es creek at **Merrit**'s corner, **Rogers**' line, to the county line.
Wts: Danl **Hunter**, Saml **Fuller**.

141, 142- Feb. 21, 1781- Abraham **Hester** to John **Landers** (**Landess**) for 33 pds. 6 shillings 8 pence, 120 acres on Grassy creek at Luke **Landers**' corner, along Hazlewood **Wilkerson**'s line.
Wts: David **Smith**, James **Landers**.

142- May 1, 1781- William **Thomas** to William **Williams** for 100 pds. 71 acres on both sides of Tar river at **Barton**'s corner.
Wts: Ralph **Banks**, Cornelius **Cooper**.

143- Aug. 1, 1781- William **Gill** and Samuel **Whitehead** executors of Will of William **Gill**, late of Mecklenburg Co., Va. deceased, to Joseph **Gill** of Granville Co., N.C. for 38 pds. 350 acres on **Jonathan**'s and **Aaron**'s creek in Granville Co., N.C. at Joseph **Gill**'s line, **Grant**'s, dividing line between James **Jones** and Joseph **Chandler** and to **Harrison**'s. and **Gill**'s lines.

143, 144- May 29, 1781- John **Hart** to Joseph **Hart** for 50 pds: the land whereon Joseph **Hart** now lives at **Mutter**'s, **Royster**'s lines, Thomas **Mutter**'s and at **Spaulding**'s lines, **Johnston**'s line, containing 280 acres.
Wts: Lark **Johnston**, Henry Philip **Hart**, John **Johnston**.

144- Aug. 5, 1781- Joseph **Gill** to William **Gill** for 486 pds. 648 acres on both sides of Jonathan's creek.

144, 145- Aug. 1, 1781- William **Gill** and Samuel **Whitehead**, executors of will of William **Gill**, late of Mecklenburg Co., Va. deceased, to Bartley **Greer** of Granville Co., N. C. for 28 pds. 125 acres on **Wade's** corner.

145- Aug. 23, 1779- William **Barton** to John **Mauldin**, for 1000 pds. 275 acres on both sides of Poplar creek on **Standard**'s line.
Wts: Zacharias **Higgs**, Noel **Johnston**, Blake **Mauldin**.

146- Nov. 28, 1780- John **Heflin** to John **Welch** of Halifax Co., N.C. for 4000 pds. 176 acres on Fort creek to **Gilliam**'s line at a ridge between the creek and **Moxley**'s line to John **Peace**, Jr.'s line in Granville Co., N.C.
Wts: John **Peace**, Jr., John **Easter**, Abe **Mayfield**.
Sarah, wife of John **Hefflin**, relinquished dower right.

146, 147- Aug. 4, 1781- Christopher **Harris** to William **Hicks** for 200 pds. 194 acres on Little Ruin creek at courthouse road adjoining Claborn **Harris** and Moses **Kittrell**'s lines.

147- May. 26, 1781- Nathaniel **Hix** gave to his friend Anne **Rainwater**, 3 negroes and all else he owns from this day forward.
Wts: Gillam **Harris**, Susanna **Allen**, Edwd **Harris**.

254

147, 148- July 3, 1781- William **Cox** to Gardner **Tucker** for 40 pds. 150 acres at mouth of branch above William **Cox**'s house on S side of Mountain fork of Jonathan's creek at Joseph **Farmer**'s line.
Wts: William **Gill**, Josiah **Farmer**.

148- Feb. 3, 1779- John **Corder** of Caswell Co., N.C. to Richard **Harris** of Granville Co., N.C. for 5 shls. 11 acres on a branch of Tar river where it crosses the old Trading road and runs to **Boyd**'s line.
Wts: John **Harris**, Joseph **Hart**.

148, 149- July 26, 1781- Isaac **Loyd** to Jonathan **Kittrell**, Jr. for 50 pds. 48 ½ acres adjoining Jonathan **Kittrell**'s old line.
Wts: Zacharias **Higgs**, Ellender **Higgs**.

149- Aug. 7, 1781- Richard **Jones** to Thomas **Person** for 50 pds. 80 acres on S side of Tar river whereon Richard **Jones** now lives adjoining **Person**'s land along **Jones** and **Nevill**'s lines.
Wts: Thos **Rice**, Samuel **Walker**.

150- Mar. 16, 1780- Thomas **Owen** to Thomas **Person** for 6 pds. 10 shls. 162 acres at John **Wilkerson**'s and Thomas **Person**'s lines on **Simmon**'s line.
Wts: William **Palmer**, William **Brisee**.

150, 151- May. 1781- John **Pulliam** to Thomas **Person** for 4000 pds. 250 acres on **Griggs** creek and **Hatcher**'s Run in **Reed**'s line, **Harris**' line, **Person**'s, **Jones**', **Badget**'s, and **Bates**' lines.
Wts: Barnett **Pulliam**, George **Bruce**.

151- Jan, 6, 1780- James **Daniel** to Thomas **Person** for 100 pds. 20 acres between **Shelton**'s and Crooked creek at **Person**'s line, **Allen**'s line.
Wts: Thos. **Critcher**, Phillip **Lewis**.

152- Nov. 6, 1781- Samuel **Hicks** to Moses **Wood** for 20 shillings, 2 acres on my line and his line.
Wts: A. **Barber**.

152, 153- Nov. 5, 1781- Roland **Bryant** to Jonathan **Kittrell**, Jr. for 60 pds. 96 acres on E side of Ruin creek which I bought of Daniel **Hunter** on Jonathan **Kittrell**'s and on George **Woodlief**'s lines, bought in 1763 from **Hunter**-
Wts: James **Jett**.

153- Nov. 5, 1781- Peter **Vinson** to Robert **Jones** of Warren Co., N.C. for- - 43 acres on Cedar creek.
Wts: Jacob **Vinson**, John **Henderson**.

153, 154,- Dec. 12, 1780- Moses **Kittrell** of Gates Co., N.C. to Jonathan **Kittrell** of Granville Co., N.C. for 100 pds. 382 acres in Granville Co., N.C. on head of Rocky branch being all land I own in Granville Co.
Wts: G. **Kittrell**, Samuel **Kittrell**, Joshua **Kittrell**.

154- Oct. 31; 1781- William **Tillman** and Mary (Polly) his wife to John **Craft** for 200 pds. 200 acres on **Tillman**'s, corner.
Wts: Benja **Ragland**, Elizabeth **Farrar**.

154, 155- Oct. 18, 1781- Elisha **Paschal** to Thomas **Key** for 5000 pds. 50 acres on E side of Deep creek at mouth of Maypole branch adjoining lands of Samuel and James **Paschal**.
Wts: William **Berry**, James **Paschal**.

155- May 8, 1780- John **Hunt** of Granville Co. to Richard **Person** of Caswell Co., N.C. for 500 pds. 70 acres on Buffalow creek at **Hunter**'s and **Smith**'s lines in Granville Co., N.C.
Wts: James **Person**, Morris **Floyd**.

156- Sept. 1781- James **Chiles** and wife Catherine of Wake Co., N. C. to James **Johnson** of Granville Co., N.C. for 200 pds. 315 acres on Island creek adjoining **Hester**'s, **Terrill**'s, **Chiles**' and **Gooch**'s lands.

Wts: John **Terrell**, Robert **Hester**, Richard **Chiles** signed James and Caty **Chiles**)

156, 157- Oct. 6, 1781- Edward **Moore** and wife Ann to James **Jett** for 500 pds. 500 acres on both sides of Fishing creek at John **White**'s, George **Harris**'s and **Hamilton**'s lines.
Wts: John **Henderson**, Reuben **Searcy**.

157- May 15: 1781- Isaac **Loyd** to Mark **White** for 75 pds. 106 acres n Ruin creek, William **Spears** on **Higgs**' and **Bryant**'s lines.
Wts: Zacharias **Higgs**, Sherwd **Parrish**.

255

157, 158- Nov. 1781- James **Winningham** to Simon **Hancock** of Franklin Co., N.C. for 100 pds. land at **Bayley**'s and **Fuller**'s lines.
Wts: Philemon **Bowers**, Sherwood **Winningham**.

158- Nov. 1781- James **Winningham** to Sherwood **Winningham** for 500 pds. 436 acres on Newlite creek at **Harris**'s, **Bailey**'s line.
Wts: Simon **Hancock**, Philemon **Bowers**.

158, 159- Nov. 2, 1781- John **Guinn** to Brereton **Jones** for 40 pds. 201 acres on Ledge of Rocks creek at **Hawkins**', **Cooke**'s, **Williams**' lines, **Harris**'s line and also 26 acres formerly property of James Hawkins which Brereton **Jones** purchased and sold to John **Guin**.

159- Oct. 2, 1781- James **Cozart** to Israel **Eastwood** for 500 pds. 270 acres on Windows creek at **Cozart**'s old line, **McCulloh**'s line.
Wts: John **Guinn**.

160- Oct. 2, 1781- James **Cozart** to Israel **Eastwood** for 500 pds. land on Windows creek at **Cozart**'s old line and **Partee**'s line and also a tract adjoining this one containing in the two 371 acres.
Wts: Jno. **Gwin** (**Guinn**).

160- Aug. 15, 1781- Robert **Russell** of Chatham Co., N.C. to William **Wright** of Granville Co., N.C. for 250 pds. 100 acres on N. side of Mill creek to the Mill Race.
Wts: Howel **Ross**, Brereton **Jones**, John **Russel**.

161- Aug. 15, 1781- Robert **Russel** of Chatham Co., N.C. to William **Wright** of Granville Co. for 250 pds. 60 acres on William **Jones**'s line, Isaiah **Phipps**' line, Thomas **Person**'s line.
Wts: Howel **Ross**, Brereton **Jones**, John **Russel**.

161- Aug. 151 1781- Robert **Russel** of Chatham Co., N.C. to William **Wright** of Granville Co., N.C. for 250 pds. 265 acres in Granville Co. on **Jones**' line, **Hampton**'s line.
Wts: Brereton **Jones**, Howel **Ross**, John **Russel**.

162- Nov. 5, 1781- William **White** to Robert **Wilson** for 5000 pds. 250 acres on waters of Ford creek at **Heffernon**'s corner.
Wts: Ralph **Banks**, Wilson **Rogers**, John **Heflin**.

162- Dec. 26, 1780- John **Kittrell** to Jonathan **Kittrell** for 100 pds. 450 acres at **Chavis**'s line.
Wts: Saml **Kittrell**, Isaac **Kittrell**, Joshua **Kittrell**.

163- Sept. 15, 1780- John **Heffernon** to Charles **Heffernon** for 600 pds. 522 acres on E side of Fort creek at John **Bradford**'s line on lines of land of Stephen **Hicks**, John **Sutton**, William **White**, William **Cooper**, **Peace** and **Mayfield**'s lands, Valentine and Abe **Mayfield**'s lines at James **Heffernon**'s line to Fort creek which was granted to John **Heffernon** by the State by Richard **Caswell**, Esq.- Sept. 24, 1779.
Wts: Thos **Banks**, Jas. **Ross**, Wm. **White**.

164- May 1, 1731 Thomas **Howell** to Elias **Peteford** for 25 pds. 107 acres on Tar river at **Lock**'s line, **Moore**'s line,

Parker's and **Taylor**'s lines.
Wts: Benja **Hester**, John **Lock**, Saml **Hunt**.

164, 165- Nov. 1, 1781- Thomas **Bond** to Thomas **Pool** for 60 pds. 169 acres on **Daniel**'s' corner, in Josiah **Daniel**'s' line, Luke **Lander**'s line on **Beck**'s line.
Wts: James **Downey**, Luke **Landers**.

165, 166- Aug. 29, 1781- Miles **King** to Robert **Burton** for 40,000 pds. 205 acres on Little Island creek near **Walker**'s ford on Edmund **Taylor**'s line **Duglasse**'s line to John **Walker**'s land so as to reserve one acre for mill.
Wts: Allen **Robison**, Jonathan **Graves**.

166- Sept. 19, 1781- Richard **Featherston** to Stephen **Sneed** for 10,000 pds. 212 acres at Charles **Williams**' line, J. **Williams** line, **Moss**'s line.
Wts: Saml **Williams**, John **Farrar**, Major **Mitchel**.

167- Sept. 26, 1781- Samuel **Hicks** to Harris **Hicks** for 10 pds. 103 acres on Tabbs creek at **Thomason**'s line, **Moore**'s line.
Wts: Zacharias **Higgs**, David **Hicks**.

256

167, 168- Jan. 7, 1782 Reuben **Searcy** to Moses **Fussel** for 28 pds. 156 acres at Richard **Searcy**'s line.
Wts: Henry **Reardon**.

68- May 23, 1781- David **Harris** to Sherwood **Harris**, son of Christopher **Harris**, for 500 pds. 60 acres on **Adcock**'s creek.
Wts: Richd **Wilkins**, Saml **Harris**.

168, 169- Jan. 9, 1782 John **White** of Chatham Co., N.C. to Thomas **Thompson** of Granville Co., N.C. for 12 pds. 6 ½ acres on John **Tatom**'s corner and west side of Tabbs creek.
Wts: Reuben **Searcy**.

169- Dec. 26, 1781- William **Palmer** to Graves (Groves, Grover?) **Howard** for 100 pds. 400 acres on Little Creek and Reedy creek at John **Kennon**'s line, **Person**'s, **Palmer**'s, **Kennon**'s, **Taylor**'s lines.
Wts: Marke **Howard**, Mary **Palmer**.

170- Jan. 11, 1781- Chas. **Partee** to James **Gallimore** for 50, pds. 400 acres on Little Nap of Reeds creek on **Ross**es line.
Wts: Wm. **Ross**, John [Tenstee], Wm. **Gallimore**.

170- Registered- Feb. court 1782- Thomas **Newby** and Alcey his wife, for 20 pds. 140 acres on Fishing creek at Samuel **Walker**'s line, sold this land to Patrick **Duffy**.
Wts: John **Newby**, Cathsheba **Newby**.

171- Feb. 5, 1782 John **Mitchel** and wife Martha to Thomas **Person** for 300 pds. 385 acres on both sides of Mill creek on George **Gragg**'s former line.
Wts: Reuben **Searcy**.

171, 172- Feb. 4, 1782- (fifth year of our Independence)- William **Puryear** to John **Puryear**. for 200 pds. 213 acres on **Whitehead**'s line, my line and **Chandler**'s line, being part of tract William **Puryear** bought of John **Hightower**. (Wm. **Puryear** to have use of timber for his lifetime.).
Wts: Thornton **Yancey**, Philip **Yancey**, James **Yancey**., Jr.

172- Feb. 4, 1782- William **Puryear** to Robert **Puryear** for 200 pds. gold and silver, 213 acres at William **Puryear**'s, John **Puryear**'s lines south side of **Raymond**'s creek which is land bought by William **Puryear** of John **Hightower**. (Wm. **Puryear** to have use of land for lifetime.).

Wts: Thornton **Yancey**, Sterling **Yancey**, John **Baynes**.

173- Jan. 10, 1782- Robert **Harris** to Zachariah **Wilborn** for 6000 pds. 300 acres which Robert **Harris** bought of John **Adcock** at **Wilborn**'s corner at **Moore**'s corner, **Bullock**'s and **Williams**' line on **Williams** Spring branch.
Wts: Saml **Harris**, Sherwood **Harris**.

173, 174- Feb. 16, 1781- Sherwood **Harris** to Richard **Wilkins** for 500 pds. 309 acres on Tar river at William **Ogelvie**'s line, in old line of Sherwood **Harris**, at School House, Nicholas **Holstein**'s line (**Holston**?).
Wts: Robt **Harris**, Robert **Harris**, Saml **Harris**.

174, 175- Jan. 23, 1782- Nicholas **Jones** to John **Tatom** for 180 pds. my interest in 202 acres granted to Robert **Harris** by **McCulloh** at **Townsend**'s line.
Wts: George **Wright**, Fowler **Jones**.

175- Nov. 18, 1781- Samuel **Glaze** to Robert **Malone** for 500 pds. 150 acres at Mike **Hunt**'s corner on Grassy creek to Jonathan **Knight**'s line at dividing line between Samuel **Glaze** and his father's land, that is Benjamin **Glaze**, his father.
Wts: Lark **Johnston**, John **Hart**.

176- Mar. 19, 1782- Philemon **Bradford**, Sr. to John **Champion**, Jr. for 100 pds. 150 acres on Beaverdam creek at **McCulloh**'s corner.
Wts: Reuben **Searcy**, David **Bradford**.

176- Mar. 19, 1782- Philemon **Bradford** to Bird Booker **Bradford** for 100 pds. 300 acres on Beaverdam branch at **Wright**'s line.
Wts: Reuben **Searcy**, David **Bradford**.

177- Jan. 9, 1781- Thomas **Key** to Thomas **Earl** for 5000 pds. 107 acres on **Sims**'s line.
Wts: William **Guthrie**, William **Berry**, William **Key**.

257

177- Aug. 29, 1781- Dozer **Thornton** of Wake Co., N.C. to George **Taylor** for 10,000 pds. 300 acres on Middle prong of Beaver Dam creek at **Fuller**'s and at **McCulloh**'s line crossing Indian branch which was deeded to Dozer **Thornton** Mar. 1, 1780.
Wts: Reuben **Searcy**, John **Reeves**.

178- May 2, 1782- James **Lunsford** to John **Dickerson** for 50 shillings for every 100 acres, 640 acres on Tar river below **Banks** Mill at mouth of Great Branch in Aquilla **Snelling**'s line on **Dickerson**'s line.
Wts: J. **Peace**, Jr., Robert **Jackson** (**Dickerson** to register grant.

178, 179- Mar. 28, 1782- Thomas **Bonner**, Jr. to Joseph **Oakey**, Jr. for 50 pds. 67 acres on branches of Nap of Reeds creek at **McCulloh**'s line.
Wts: Zephaniah **Walton** (**Welbon**?), Thomas **Jones** [Jurat], John **Gallimore**.

1791- Jan. 8, 1782- John **White** of Chatham Co., N.C. to Joseph **Hays** of Granville Co., N.C. for 300 pds. land on Fishing creek in Granville Co. at **Allison**'s line, **Tuder**'s line, **Hamilton**'s corner.
Wts: John **Allison**, James **Allison**.

180- Feb. 6, 1781- Edmund **Partee** to Edward **Herring** for 25 pds. 140 acres on Ledge of Rocks creek at **McCulloh**'s corner, on **Webb**'s line.
Wts: James **Jett**, George **Lanamore**.

180, 181- May 7, 1782- Isham **Parham** to Stephen **White** for 10,000 pds. 100 acres on Justus **Parrish**'s line.
Wts: Harris **Ogelvie**, Edward **Herring**, Jno. **Minor**.

181- Apr. 24, 1782- Francis **Bressie** to Charles **Partee** for 50 pds. 100 acres at **Hampton**'s corner, to line formerly **McCulloch**, on **Person**'s line.
Wts: Jno. **Minor**, Ephr. **Hampton**.

Wife (unnamed) relinquishes her dower right.

181, 182- May 4, 1782- John **Hunt** to Samuel **Crafton** for 1600 pds. 100 acres on Jonathan creek on **Aplin**'s line, at **Hunt**'s corner.
Wts: Danl **Grant**, Thomas **Grant**.

182- Mar. 21, 1782- Peter **Knowland** to Amos **Tims** of Camblen (Camden) district, South Carolina, for 200 pds. 500 acres on Howel **Rose**'s line at **Gooch**'s line, to Absalom **Ford**'s and William **Wright**'s lines, **Potter**'s and Joseph **Gooch**'s line.
Wts: John **Gwinn**, Jane **Gwinn**.

182, 183- Mar. 5, 1782- Thomas **Merewether** of Halifax Co., VA. to Graves **Howard** of Granville Co., N.C. for 100 pds., 700 acres on Little Creek and on Reedy creek at William **Person**'s corner, on **Dyer**'s line.
Wts: Eliza **Kennon**, Wm. **Kennon**, Robert **Wade**.

183- Dec. 6, 1781- John **Peace**, Jr. to John **Dickerson** for 50 shillings for every 100 acres- 300 acres on Little Creek. at **Fuller**'s corner on John **Dickerson**'s line (and he to register same).
Wts: Zacharias **Higgs**, John **Easter**.

184- Jan. 7, 1782- John **Peace**, Jr. to John **Dickerson** for 50 shls. for each 100 acres, 400 acres on **Pruit**'s corner (he to register same.).
Wts: Zacharias **Higgs**, John **Peace**.

184- Nov. 17, 1781- Kennon **Cooper** to William **Cunyard** of Franklin Co., N.C. for 80 pds. 354 acres on Mountain creek and Sandy creek on lines of land of **Cooper**, **Hawkins'**, **Eaton**'s, **Rogers**, **Christmas**'s lines including plantation whereon Richard **Wooten** settled.
Wts: James **Ross**, Philip **Huckaby**, James **Richards**.

185- Nov. 6, 1781- Reuben **Ransom** to Valentine **White** for 240 pds. 125 acres on Tabbs creek, at Valentine **White**'s, **Dickerson**'s, **Walker**'s lines.
Wts: Thomas **Walker**, Augustine **Woodlief**.

185, 186- Dec. 31, 1781- Goldman **Harris** to Laiborn **Haslip** (**Hazlip**) for 20 pds. 40 acres on Little Creek whereon William **Williams**'s line crosses.
Wts: William **Williams**, Susan **Holston**.

186, 187- Jan. 7, 1781- William **Champion** and wife Sarah to Valentine **Mayfield** for 328 pds. 328 acres on both sides of Fort Creek at Thomas **Banks**' corner, **Mayfield**'s line-
Wts: Thomas **Banks**, Ralph **Banks**, James **Neil**.

258

187- Nov. 2, 1781- John **Sutton** and wife Mary to William **Champion** for 290 pds. 230 acres, on Fort creek at Valentine **Mayfield**'s line, Thomas **Banks** line.
Wts: Thomas **Banks**, Ralph **Banks**, John **Easter**.

187, 188 Anr. 11, 1782- William **Puryear** Sr. to William **Puryear** Jr. for 200 pds. 213 acres at Robert **Puryear**'s corner and on my upper line in John **Puryear**'s line to **Clack**'s creek.
Wts: Thornton **Yancey**, John **Puryear** (William **Puryear** reserves for his lifetime, the use of the land.)

188- Sept. 15, 1781- James **Ross** to George **Laramore** for 50 pds. 50 acres on Ledge of Rocks creek on **Moore**'s and **Green**'s corners, **Ross**'s line.
Wts: Henry **Green**, Mary **Walker**.

188, 189- Jan. 26, 1781- William **Champion** and wife Sarah to Thomas **Banks** for 20 pds. 240 acres on S side of Tar river at, both sides of **Jackson**'s branch on Thomas **Banks**' line, **Mayfield**'s line.
Wts: Ralph **Banks**, Valentine **Mayfield**, James **Neill**.

189, 190- May 6, 1782- Thomas **Pool** to Littleton **Earley** for 60 pds. 169 acres on Grassy creek at **Spaulding**'s line, **Daniel**'s' and **Lander**'s line on **Crenshaw**'s line.
Wts: Daniel **Malone**, John **Blackwell**.

190, 191- Jan. 28, 1781- William **Champion** and wife Sarah to James **Neil** for 60 pds. 100 acres on S side of Tar river at corner between William **Champion** and Abe **Mayfield**.
Wts: Thomas **Banks**, Ralph **Banks**, Valentine **Mayfield**.

191- Mar. 1, 1782- Thomas **Banks** to John **Dickerson** for 15 pds. 437 acres on N side of Tar river adjoining William **Williams**'s and John **Dickerson**'s lines at **Priddy**'s Mill pond.
Wts: John **Allison**, Patrick **Duffey**, James **Bloodworth**.

191, 192- Mar. 20, 1782- William **Ascue** of Franklin Co., N.C. to Philemon **Hawkins** of Warren Co., N.C. for 10,000 pds. 640 acres at **Hawkins**' line-
Wts: Bromfield **Ridley**, Joseph **Seawell**.

192, 193- Dec. 27, 1781- Isabella **Paschal** to Stephen **Turner** for 60 pds. 140 acres on **Roberson**'s corner.
Wts: Dennis and James **Paschal**.

193- July 6, 1782- John **Landish** (**Landers**, **Landess**, **Landis**) and wife Lany (Laney) to John **Potter** for 150 pds. 146 acres on W side of Tar river and on line of land formerly **Roberson**'s.
Wts: Thomas **Wilburn**.

193, 194- July 5, 1782- Jacob **Brazilton** to Isabella **Ray** for 50 pds. 100 acres in Granville Co. (signed by Jacob and Hannah **Brazelton**).
Wts: William **Jones**, Samuel **Adams**.

194- Jan. 15, 1782- Thomas **Smith** to George **Mills** for 10,000 pds. 150 acres on W side of road at Pimple Hill.
Wts: Thomas **Mills**.

194, 195- Mar. 28, 1782- Thomas **Bonner**, Jr. to Charles **Turner** for 100 pds. 209 acres on Nap of Reeds creek at **McCulloh**'s line.
Wts: Zepheniah **Waller**, Thos. **Jones**, John **Gallemore**.

195- Jan. 25, 1782- Jane **Mitchel** to John **Bridges** for 5 pds. 200 acres on Beaverdam and Newlite creeks being part of land granted to David **Mitchel** by Richard **Caswell** Mar. 1, 1780 and Jane **Mitchel** being sole executrix of his will, herein sells the land.
Wts: John **Lunsford**, Gilliam **Harris**.

195, 196- Aug. 4, 1782- William **Byars** attny, for Augustine **Davis**, to George **Gober**-On Sept. 4, 1779 authorized William **Byars** to execute a deed to George **Gober**, since said Augustine **Davis** has removed to the State of South Carolina, for certain land in Granville Co., N.C.- 185 acres on Island creek at **Gober**'s corner and on **Walker**'s line and **Burton**'s line, **Person**'s line.
Wts: William **Webb**, Abraham **Hester**.

196- May 12, 1782- Robert **Beesley** of Lunenburg Co., VA. to John **Wilkerson** of Granville Co., N.C. for 186 pds. 10 shls. -373 acres in

259
on Grassy creek and on Jonathan's creek at George **Malone**'s line, Josiah **Daniel**'s' and John **Blackwell**'s line.
Wts: Daniel and Thomas **Grant**.

196, 197- Nov. 13, 1781- William **Cockrell** to Abraham **Hester** for 80 pds. land on Grassy creek containing 255 acres on **Hunt**'s line, **Pittard**'s and on Gideon **Crenshaw**'s lines, **Brasfield** line, being land whereon **Cockrell** now lives-
Wts: Abram **Crenshaw**, Henry **Spaulding**.

197, 198- Aug. 5, 1782- John **Lock** to Ben **Dass** (**Bass**), for 1000 pds. 581 acres on **Taylor**'s line, **Morris**'s line,

Bagit's old line.
Wts: John **Thomason**, Samuel **Parker**.

198- 1782- Leonard **Sims** from William **Martin**, executor of Will of James **Martin**, deceased, for 17 pds. 16 shls. 1 penny, 166 acres in **Smith**'s branch at **Sims**'s corner.
Wts: Len H. **Bullock**, James **Lewis**, Adam **Rice**.

198, 199- Jan. 15, 1782- George **Mills** to Thomas **Smith** for 10,000 pds. 150 acres on Buffalow creek at **Smith**'s line, Joseph **McDaniel**'s lines and Berry **Lewis**'s corner.
Wts: Thomas **Mills**, Wesley **Paschal**.

199, Mar. 19, 1782- William **Kelly** of Wake Co., N.C. to Jarrett **Sandy** of Franklin Co., N.C. for 65 pds. 250 acres in Granville Co., N.C. at **McCulloh**'s corner at Lick branch.
Wts: Joseph **Taylor**, Henry **Yarbrough**.

200- Nov. 21, 1781- Jacob **Holstein** to William **Ogelvie** for 10,000 pds. 50 acres on S side of **Holstein**'s creek at his corner.
Wts: Elizabeth and Smith **Ogelvie** (Catherine, wife of Jacob **Holstein**, relinquishes her dower right in land.

200- Feb. 1, 1782- Robert **Mumford** of Mecklenburg Co., VA. to William **Randolph** of same county and State **Mumford** conveyed to Otway **Byrd** of Charles City Co., VA. for 250,000 weight of tobacco, certain land on Grassy creek in Granville Co., N.C. which land **Mumford** bought of Howel **Lewis** and **Byrd** has now released all right to land as if no deed had been made, so for 250,000 weight of Neat tobacco, impaled at any ware house on James or Appomatac river above City Point, deeds the land to William **Randolph**.
Wts: James **Anderson**, Mathew **Hawkins**, John **Clark**, Jr., James **Taylor**, and William Beverly **Fitzhugh**.

201- Mar. 11, 1782- John **Williams**, Esq. to Bromfield **Ridley** for 500 pds. 100 acres in **Clanton**'s survey line, on John **Williams**' line.
Wts: T. **Satterwhite**.

201, 202- Aug. 3, 1782- William **Howell** to Jeremiah **Fraizer** for 200 pds. 270 acres on Fishing creek at **Taylor**'s line, Robert **Duke**'s line.
Wts: B. **Pulliam**, Saml **Parker** (signed William and Ann **Howel**.)

202- Aug. 2, 1782- Richard **Henderson** to James **Daniel** for 20 pds. 20 acres on **Anderson**'s fork opposite where Thomas **Burdin** now lives.
Wts: Richd. **Henderson**, A. **Patorn**.

202, 203- Dec. 20, 1781- William **Bailey** and wife Temperance to Arnold **Mann** for 65 pds. 120 acres on both sides of New Light creek being land granted to Gilliam **Harris** by Granville- Dec. 1, 1750 and sold to Jeremiah **Bailey** who deeded to William **Bailey**.
Wts: John **Mann**, Jr.

203, 204- Dec. 20, 1781- William **Bailey** and wife Temperance to Arnold **Mann** for 10 pds. 60 acres on Newlite creek which was granted to Israel **Fuller** and deeded to William **Bailey**.
Wts: Robert **Allen**, Gilliam **Harris**, John **Mann**, Jr.

204- Nov. 20, 1780- Phillip **White** and wife Martha to Thomas **Person** for 1500 pds. the right of dower in land on Fishing creek at **Taylor**'s and **Rochester**'s lines, and John **Walker**'s line being land in which they have dower right, and sell to **Person**.
Wts: John **Pulliam**.

204, 205- Aug. 13, 1782- John **Boyd** to Reuben **Searcy** for sake of doing justice to **Searcy** for land said Reuben **Searcy** bought of my father.

260
Father, Robert **Boyd**, in his lifetime, all my right in the land and its improvements which descended to me at death of my

father Robert **Boyd**, Which land adjoins John **Potter**, Richd **Harris**, Jr., Saml **Johnston**, Ben **Reardon**-
Wts: James **Jett**.

205- July 19, 1782- Allen **Love** of Brunswick Co., Va. trustee for negroes as property of Humphrey **Davis**, also land which was deeded July 25, 1772 for 200 pds. in trust for debt due John **Gordon**. Allen **Love** received the trust deed at end of partnership of **McCall**, **Elliott** and Co. for whom John **Gordon** acted as agent, and now acquits Humphrey **Davis** of all responsibility therefor.
Wts: William **Davis**, Katherine **Low**.

205, 206- July 22, 1782- Humphrey **Davis** to John **Young** for 80 pds. land on Plumbtree branch at **Young**'s corner.
Wts: Grant **Allen**, Thos. **Harton**, John **Smith**.

206- May 9, 1782- Elijah **Parrish** to John **Dunkin**, Jr. for 80 pds. 80 acres on W side of Tabbs creek at Maple Spring branch on Thomas **Parrish**'s line.
Wts: Zacharias **Higgs**, Jesse **Langford**.

206, 207- Oct. 11, 1782- William **Hicks**, Jr. to Benjamin **Harris** for 50 pds. 195 acres on Ruin Creek at Claborn **Harris**'s line, **Kittrell**'s line.
Wts: William and Ann **Hicks**.

207- July 25, 1782- James **Neal** to William **White** for 60 pds. 100 acres on S side of Tar river.
Wts: William **Williams**, Abe **Mayfield**.

208- Aug. 19, 1782- Josiah **Stovall** to Jonathan **Knight** for 50 pds. 52 acres on Grassy creek, being half of tract whereon I live at **Knight**'s corner-
Wts: Lark **Johnston**, Lucy **Johnston**.

208, 209- Nov. 4, 1782- John **Hawkins** and John **Potter** to James **Downey** for 100 pds. 112 acres on Island creek at **Downey**'s corner in John **Kennon**'s line.

209, 210- Oct. 13, 1782- William **Allen** to John **Young** for 200 pds. 260 acres on Grassy creek on John **Young**'s line at John **Morgan**'s corner.
Wts: Thomas **Mutter**, Chas. **Yancey**.

210- May 18, 1782- John Williams **Graves** and wife Mary to Thomas **Bond** for 75 pounds in gold or silver coin, 296 acres on both sides of Grassy creek on Mountain creek.
Wts: Samuel **Pittard**, John **Pittard**, Joseph **Hart**.

210, 211- Aug. 12, 1782- Robert **Mumford**, Otway **Byrd**, William **Randolph** of Mecklenburg Co., VA. to Howel **Lewis** of Granville Co., N.C. Howel **Lewis** of Granville Co., N.C. deeded to Robert **Mumford** certain land in Granville Co., N.C. which **Mumford** by deed of gift conveyed 2000 acres of this land to Otway **Byrd**, his son-in-law. Later Otway **Byrd** released this land to Robert **Mumford** as agreed between them, and **Mumford** sold to William **Randolph**. Now all land is released and conveyed back to said Howel **Lewis** for a quantity of tobacco to be paid by the tenor of first decided deed.
Wts: Henry **Pattillo**, Robert **Crawley**, Howel **Lewis**, Jr.

211, 212- Oct. 12, 1782- Robert **Malone** and wife Mary to James **Smith** for 150 pds. 131 acres on Both sides of Grassy creek on Memucan **Hunt**'s and Jonathan **Knight**'s corners, in lines of land of Robert **Malone** and the Widow **Glaze**.
Wts: Samuel **Smith**, Samuel **Smith**, Jr., Chas. **Breedlove**.

212, 213- Oct. 11, 1782- John **Heath** to John **Oliver** for 100 pds. 342 acres on both sides of Hay Meadow Branch on his old line, on **Person**'s line, **Howard**'s and **Mitchel**'s lines.
Wts: James **Downey**, John **Howard**, John **Downey**.

213- Oct. 22, 1782- Leonard **Lindsey** to William **Longmire** for 175 pds. 287 acres on E side of Tar river on Luke **Carrell**'s line.
Wts: Benjamin **Bearden**, John **Hawkins**, Reuben **Searcy**.

Sarah, wife of Leonard **Lindsey**, relinquishes dower right.

261

213, 214- July 23, 1782- William **Williams** to Laban **Haislip** for 20 pds. 59 acres on Little Nut Bush creek, near the ridge path between Tar river and Little Creek on **William**'s line.
Wts: John **Smith**, William **White**.

214- Nov. 1, 1782- Giles **Hudspeth** of Surry Co, N.C. to Leonard **Lindsey** for 100 pds. 320 acres on Fishing creek on Samuel **Walker**'s line and formerly **Douglas**'s corner.
Wts: Reuben **Searcy**.

215- Feb. 24, 1782- Aaron **Springfield** to Reuben **Talley** of same co. for 50 pds. 70 acres on W side of Fishing creek to the line between Isaac **Arnold** and Sherwood **Harris**.
Wts: James **Currin**, Ben **Grisham**.

215, 216- Oct. 13, 1782- Edward **Herrin** to William **Jones**, Jr. for 50 pd 140 acres on Ledge of Rocks creek at **Moore**'s corner, **McCulloh**'s corner.
Wts: George **Wright**, Zepheniah **Waller**.

216- July 23, 1782- Laban **Haislip** to William **Williams** for 20 pds. 59 acres on Little creek on **Williams**' line.
Wts William **White**, John **Smith**.

216, 217- Aug. 9, 1782- John **Huckaby** to Joseph **Leamon** for 200 pds. 50 acres on **Huckaby**'s line, **Hambleton**'s line.
Wts: William **Watson**, Thomas **Huckaby**.

217, 218- Oct. 20, 1782- Sherwood **Harris** to John **Miner** for 85 pds. 118 acres on 14 side of Cattail creek on **Thomas**'s corner, **Noland**'s line.
Wts: Benj **Reardon** (Ann, wife of **Harris**, relinquishes her dower.)

218- Aug. 6, 1782- John **Huckaby** to James **Watley** of Franklin Co., N.C. for 200 pds. 340 acres on John **Hamelton**'s[sic] line at Buffalow creek.
Wts: William **Watson**, Joseph **Leamon**.

218, 119- Aug. . .1782- John **Leeman** of Franklin Co., N.C. to James **Watley** of same county and State, for 200 pds. 20 acres in Granville Co. on Buffalow creek on **Leamon**'s line.
Wts: William **Watson**. Zach **Dickson**.

219, 220- Feb. 4, 1782- John **Maulden** to Barges **Reeves** for 50 pds. 100 acres, excepting the 2 acres reserved on W. side of Poplar creek.
Wts: Zacharias **Higgs**, Edw. **Grisham**.

220- Aug. 15, 1782- William **Dishazo** to Joshua **Stafford** of Halifax Co., N.C. for 40 pds. 150 acres on Lick creek at **Ricks** corner.
Wts: Zacharias **Higgs**, Garrot **Loyd**.

220, 221- May 12, 1782- John **Dunkin** to William **Yancey** for 25 pds. 218 acres on Grassy creek at **Knight**'s corner, in **Stovell**'s and **Hunt**'s lines.
Wts: Lark **Johnston**, John **Hart**.

221, 222- May 30, 1782- Samuel **Whitehead** and Ursula his Wife; to Thomas **Mutter** for 106 pds. in gold and silver coin, 282 acres on Jonathan's creek in **Mutter**'s and in **Yancey**'s lines, **Thornton** and Phillip **Yancey**'s lines, on John **Puryear**'s line.
Wts: Thomas **Grant**, Phillip **Yancey**.

222- Oct. 4, 1782- William **Ford** and wife Judith, to Thomas **Mutter** for 250 pds. in gold and silver, 354 acres on Grassy Creek and on **Aaron** Creek at Absalom **Pryor**'s line, John **Pryor**'s line, **Smith**'s line, John **Owen**'s and John

Webb's lines, at **Person**'s line.
Wts: Daniel **Grant**, James **Downey**.

23- Nov. 1, 1782- James **Jones** of Wilks Co., Georgia to Jonathan **Kittrell**, Sr. of Granville Co., N.C. for 100 pds. 104 acres on Reedy Branch, in **Spivey**'s line.
Wts: Ransone **Sutherland**.

223, 224- Sept. 10, 1782- James **Gallimore** to William **Tatom** for 50 pds. 300 acres adjoining William **Ross**'s line on Nap of Reeds creek.
Wts: George **Wright**, Stephen **Tatom**.

224 [blank] 1872- Caleb **Brasfield** to Robert **Malone** for 100 pds. 100 acres on Grassy creek at **Butler**'s corner, on **Hunt**'s line, **Smith**'s line.
Wts: John **Heath**, Jarrel **Willingham**.

262

225- Aug. 15, 1782- Samuel **Harris** to John **Potter** for 50 pds. 60 acres on E side of Richard **Wilkins**'s land on main road, on Mirey branch, at **Potter**'s line, and on Tar river.
Wts: Sherwood **Harris**.

225, 226- Dec. 30, 1782- John **Shearman**, Sr. to James **Meadows** for 200 pds. 250 acres on N. side of Stoney creek on Thomas **Person**'s line to the Little Creek.
Wts: Geo. **Roberts**, Michael **Shearman**.

226- Feb. 4, 1783- George **Bristow** to John **Bristow** for 75 pds. 153 acres on W side of Little Ruin Creek in Elias **Guess**'s corner.
Wts: Zacharia **Higgs**, Samuel **Fuller**.

227- Dec. 9, 1782- Zachariah **Higgs** to Jesse **Langford** for 12 pds. 61 acres on Tabbs creek.- -
Wts: John **Bristow**, Sher **Parrish**.

227, 228- Jan. 18, 1783- John **Parham** to Ephraim **Parham** for 10 pds. 107 acres on Tabbs creek whereon Ephraim **Parham** now lives, on **Dunkin**'s and **Bartow**'s lines.
Wts: Zacharias **Higgs,** John **Sute**.

228- Dec. 9, 1782- George **Mills** to Reuben **Insco** for 100 pds. 150 acres on E side of **Dickerson**'s road, on Pimple **Hill**.
Wts: Zacharias **Higgs**, Ben **Smith**.

228, 229- Dec. 27, 1782- Joseph **McDaniel** to Elijah **Parrish** for 100 pds. 150 acres on Tabbs creek at Justus **Parrish**'s land.
Wts: Sherw. **Parrish**. John **Bristow**.

229, 230- Sept. 7, 1782- Zacharias **Higgs** to Thomas **York** of Warren Co., N.C. for 15 pds. 108 acres on Ruin Creek in Granville Co. at **Rogers'**, **Spears'** and **Fuller**'s lines.
Wts: Phillip Hunt **Spears**, William **Spears**.

230- Jan. 23, 1783- James **Owen** to John **Taylor** for 15 pds. 10 shls. 240 acres whereon James **Owen** now lives on Beaver Dam creek at **Taylor**'s corner, and on Jacob **Mitchel**'s line.
Wts: Adam **Smith**, William **Bullock**.

230, 231- Jan 18, 1783- John **Parham** to William **Parham** for 10 pds. 200 acres on Tabbs creek whereon William **Parham** now lives at **Barton**'s line.
Wts: Zacharias **Higgs**, John [**Sute**].

231, 232- Feb. 1, 1783- George **Byars** to Jeremiah **Bullock** for 12 pds. 280 acres on Ledge of Rocks creek in **Veazey**'s corner, at **Beck**'s and **Burford**'s lines, **Jones**'s line- -

signed by George **Byars** and Mary **Bullock**.
Wts: Charles **Bullock**.

232- Jan. 18, 1783- John **Parham** to John **Sute** (**Lute**[3]) for 10 pds. 60 acres on Ruin creek at **Barton** and **Bristow**'s lines.
Wts: Zacharias **Higgs**.

232, 233. . 1780- Joseph **Peace** to John **Dickerson** for 100 pds. 200 acres on Tabbs creek at Christeen **Thomas**'s line.
Wts: Ben **Tuder**, Henry **Smith**, Samson **Hary**. Registered Feb. 1783

233, 234- Jan. 1, 1783- Ephraim **Washington** to John **Washington** for 330 pds. 312 acres, excepting 50 acres which was given to John **Washington**, on both sides of Tar river at **Philpott**'s corner.
Wts: Shearmon **Goss**, Jemima **Hester**.

234- Jan. 1, 1782- Philip **Voss** to John **Webb** for 195 pds. 306 acres on Thomas and John **Owens**'s lines and Thomas **Critcher**'s line.
Wts: none.

234, 235- Jan. 3, 1783- Solomon **Stanton** and Elizabeth his wife, to Ralph **Williams** for 600 pds. 573 acres on Ledge of Rocks creek being land **Stanton** bought of John **Ross** and also a deed from Robert **Wallace** for 200 acres adjoining the tract above near the Trading Path on the road, also a deed from State of N.C. for 173 acres adjoining above tracts on **Grant**'s line to **Wallace**'s former corner- in all 573 acres whereon Solomon **Stanton** now lives.
Wts: William **Green**, Edmond **Cross**.

235, 236- July 13, 1782- Lewis **Taylor** to John **Gomer** Sr. for 25 pds. 50 acres on Island creek at country line, on S side of road.
Wts: John **Jones**, Jerry **Beaver**, Frederick **Caviness**, John **Perry**.

263

236- Dec. 28, 1782- Philip **Chavers** and wife Celia, to John **Penn** for 500 pds., 600 acres on Fork of Tar river and Tabbs creek on William **Dickerson**'s and Edward **Harris**'s lines.
Wts: Rowland **Terry**, James **Byers**, Guilielmus **Byars**.

237- May 6, 1783- Thornton **Yancey**, sheriff of Granville Co., to Christopher **Harris**, the land of George **Alston** and Co. as ordered by court at suit brought, and 300 acres sold to **Harris** as highest bidder Land on **Hatcher**'s Run, Robert **Reid**'s line, near the Meeting house.

238- May 5, 1783- Thornton **Yancey**, sheriff, sold to Solomon **Walker**, as highest bidder, at public sale of property of George **Alston** and Co. which was sold by suit brought for debt.- 150 acres on Fishing creek, **Taylor's** [corner]

239- July 20, 1782- Roger **Thornton** to James **Stark** for 50 pds. 100 acres on James **Stark**'s line, on Philip **Hawkins**' line, Frederick **Weaver**'s corner.
Wts: Isham **Harrison**, William **Cooper** (Catheron and Roger **Thornton** sign.)

239, 240- May 6, 1783- Edmund **Carnes** to William **Jones**, Jr. for 55 pds. 129 acres at Michael **Redwile**'s line on Ledge of Rocks creek at **Wallace**'s line, **Churton**'s line.
Wts: Jeremiah **Bullock**.

240- May 6, 1733 George **Bristow**, Sr. to George **Bristow**, Jr. for 30 pds. 243 acres on Little Ruin Creek at John **Bristow**'s line and at Brissie **Parrish**'s, Philemon and George **Bristow**'s lines.

241- May 6, 1783- George **Bristow** Sr. to Philemon **Bristow** for 30 pds. 243 acres on Little Ruin Creek at William **Floyd**'s corner.

---

[3] Zae wrote this name several times as Lute. I think it is really 'Suit'

241, 242- Apr. 7, 1783- George **Lanemoor** to Joel **Chandler** of Brunswick Co., Va. for 150 pds. 300 acres in Granville Co being State Rights land on **Wilbon**, **Williams**' lines (See George Lane **Moore**).
Wts: John **Manire**, James **Claxton**, Benj **Moore**.

242- May 3, 1783- Josiah **Glass** to Reuben **Fletcher** for 30 pds. 300 acre on Blue ring creek where Caswell Co. intersects the county line.
Wts: Philip **Voss**, Charles **Breedlove**.

243- Feb. 4, 1782- Christopher **Harris** to John **Mauldin** for 50 pds. 100 acres on Ruin Creek at **Kittrell**'s and Benjamin **Harris**'s lines.
Wts: Zacharias **Higgs**, Jonathan **Johnson**.

243, 244- Feb. 16, 1782- David **Harris** to Benjamin **Lunsford** for 16 pds. 100 acres on Newlite creek at William **Lunsford**'s corner and on **Allen**'s line, David **Harris**'s line being part of tract granted to Solomon **Fuller** Mar. 1, 1780.
Wts: William **Lunsford**, James **Lunsford**, John **Lunsford**.

244- Mar. 5, 1783- Rich **Wilkins** to Claborn **Harris** for 140 pds. 125 acres on S side of Mill or Nichlas **Holstan**'s creek, at Samuel **Harris**'s Spring Branch, to the road at the school house, to Wm. **Ogelvie**'s corner.
Wts: J. **Potter**, Sherwood **Harris**.

244, 245- May 6, 1783- Edmund **Taylor** to John **Kennon** for 5½ silver dollars, 230 acres on **Gooch**'s line, at James **Terry**'s line at his own line on Island creek-
Wts: none.

245- May 5, 1783- Edmund **Taylor** to Peter **Wood** for 5½ silver dollars 230 acres on Island creek adjoining his own land.

245, 246- Dec. 1, 1781- Phillip **Voss** to Joseph **Taylor** for 500 pds. one moiety of land known by name of *Harrisburg Tract*, which **Voss** bought of Nathaniel **Rochester** as per deed to Joseph **Taylor** and Philip **Voss** by the executors of **Critcher**. . . Elizabeth, wife of Philip **Voss**, relinquishes her dower right.

246- Aug. 7, 1783- Solomon **Walker** and wife Martha to Joseph **Taylor** for 59 pds. 4 shls. 87 acres at **Taylor**'s corner on Fishing creek, near the road from Harisburg to Oxford.

247- July 31, 1783- Richard **Wilkins** to John **Potter** for 420 pds. 420 acres on Nichilas creek and Tar river.
Wts: Henry **Potter**, Mathew **Hawkins**.

247, 248- Jan. 11, 1783- John **Bridges** to Jones **Fuller** for 50 pds.

264
100 acres on Newlight creek on Ridge Path--.
Wts: James **Winningham**, Elishe **Lunsford**.

248- May 2, 1783- William **Gill** to Bartley **Greer** for 17 pds. 203 acres on **Aaron** creek and Jonathan's creek in **Wade**'s line.
Wts: P. **Yancey**; William **Palmer**.

248, 249- Aug. 2, 1783- George **Head** to William **Graves** for 150 pds. 354 acres on Cedar branch at **Graves**' line, **Smith**'s line.
Wts: Henry **Graves**, Robert **Christmas**.

249- Oct: 14, 1781- Edward **Davis** to William **Kelley** of Warren Co., N.C. for 100,000 lawful money, land on Ledge of Rocks creek at Wake county line-
Wts: Samuel **Davis**, John **Hooker**, John **Durham**.

250- Aug. 2, 1783- Henry **Graves** to William **Graves** for 100 pds. 580 acres on both sides of Spewmarrow creek at his own corner and at Lewis **Yancey**'s line, **Williamson**'s, and **Smith**'s lines.

Wts: Robert **Christmas**, George **Head**.

250- May 4, 1778- William **Graves** to Henry **Graves** for 70 pds. 150 acres on Thomas **Head**'s line, Henry **Graves**'s line, Richard **Head**'s and **Smith**'s line-
Wts; Peter **Bennett**, Ralph **Graves**.

251- June 11, 1783- John **Lunsford** to John **Fuller** for 40 pds. 100 acres on Ridge Path on Newlight creek being part of land deeded from David **Bridges** to John **Lunsford**.
Wts: John **Bridges**, Elisha **Lunsford**.

251, 252- Feb. 24, 1782- Joshua **Stafford** of Halifax Co., N.C. to James **Bishop** for 30 pds. 162 acres on Flatt creek at **Ricks**' line, on Cub creek at **Sneed**'s line, to the road.
Wts: Thos. **Ricks**, Philip **Bishop**.

252- Feb. 5, 1782- Christopher **Harris** to Jonathan **Johnson** for 100 pds. 206 acres on Little Ruin Creek in **Kittrell**'s line, at John **Mauldin**'s, Benjamin **Harris**'s and **Barton**'s lines.
Wts: Zacharias **Higgs**, John **Mauldin**.

252, 253- Dec. 5, 1781- Bartholomew **Kimball** to Roger **Thornton** for 30 pds. 100 acres on N. side of branch at **Weaver**'s corner, James **Godfrey**'s line- signed by Bartholomew and Agnes **Kimball**).
Wts: Frederick **Wever** [Jurat], Solomon **Thornton**.

253- July 25, 1783- John **Blalock** of Surry Co., N.C. to Jeremiah **Blalock** of Granville Co., N.C. for 80 pds. 200 acres on Lowground creek near the path that leads from **Wilkerson**'s to **Bradford**'s at old line.
Wts: Thos. **Bradford**, James **Ellit**, David **Bradford**.

254- Oct. 23, 1782- James **Claxton** to Brereton **Jones** for 50 pds. 100 acres on Ledge of Rocks creek on **Hawkins**' line, **Harris**'s line.
Wts: Micj **Bullock**, Robert **Harris**.

254- Feb. 24, 1783- Daniel **Malone** to Robert **Malone** for 10,000 pds. 300 acres on SE side of **Aaron**'s creek at **Harrison**'s line, Gen. **Harris**'s line-
Wts: Luke **Landers**, Jude **Malone**.

255- Nov. 17, 1782- Hammon **Wilkerson** to Christopher **Kelley**, Jr. for 3 pds. 107 acres on Tarborough road being part of larger survey at Robert **Allison**'s line, John **Champion**'s line, John **Blalock**'s line.
Wts: Joseph **Fuller**, James **Ellitt**.

255, 256- Aug. 2, 1783- Henry **Graves** to William **Graves** for 100 pds. 300 acres on Tar river at mouth of John **Moris** spring branch at Jacob **Head**'s and Robert **Bell**'s lines, Peter **Nolan**'s line.
Wts: Robert **Christmas**, George **Head**.

256- Aug. 2, 1783- Henry **Graves** to William **Graves**. for 10 pds. 40 acres on the road near William **Graves**' lines.
Wts: Robert **Christmas**, George **Head**.

256, 257- Aug. 9, 1783- William **Wright** to Brereton **Jones** for 50 pds. 100 acres on S side of Mill creek at **Hampton**'s line.

257- Dec. 20, 1782- John **Terrell** and wife Ann to James **Johnston** for 100 pds. 412 acres at **Lewis**'s, **Downey**'s, **Chiles**'s lines.
Wts: Samuel **Sugar** (**Lugar**), John **Johnson**, Pemberton **Burch**, Jr.

265

258- Aug. 4, 1783- Millenton **Easley** to Thomas **Glaze** for 60 pds. 169 acres on Grassy creek whereon **Easley** now lives at **Spaulding**'s line and at **Lander**'s line, **Crenshaw**'s line.
Wts: John Williams **Graves**, Arthur **Frazer**.

258, 259- Sept. 21, 1782- James **Gallimore** to William **Trustee** for 12 pds. 100 acres, deeded from Charles **Partee** to **Gallimore** for 400 acres at William **Ross**'s line.
Wts: George **Wright**, William **Tatom**.

259- June 21, 1783- Robert **Hicks**, Sr. gave to his son Robert **Hicks**, Jr. farming tools and live stock, a still and cart etc-
Wts: Thomas **Hicks**, Isaac **Hicks**.

259, 260- June 21, 1783- Robert **Hicks**, Sr. gave to his son. Robert **Hicks**, Jr. charging him 75 pds., all the land he purchased of James **Reeves** Nov. 25, 1765, and also a part of the tract granted to him by Granville Oct. 26, 1752 and also a part of two other tracts as deeds will show, bounded by lands of Robert **Hester**, Thomas **Person**, John **Locks**, Lewis **Anderson**, Isaac **Hicks**, George **Bruce** and B. **Hill** containing 480 acres including the Mill and also 5 negroes. [Dick, Fillie, Bet, Geen, Cato]
Wts: Thos **Hicks**, Isaac **Hicks**.

260- Dec, 13, 1782- Benjamin **Wright** to Benjamin **Morgan** of Franklin Co., N.C. land in Granville Co on Beaverdam creek, at Phil. **Bradford**'s, A. **McCulloh**'s, William **Parnal**'s containing 350 acres including all land bought of Lawrence **Petteford** and Reuben **Bass** and land whereon I now live.
Wts: James **Hornsby**, Reuben **Morgan**.

260, 261- Jan. 13, 1783- Solomon **Fuller** and wife Gilley to John **Moseley** of Franklin Co., N.C. for 120 pds. Va. money, 200 acres on Buck Horn creek at **Docker**'s line, **Bledsoe**'s line.
Wts: Saml **Moseley**, Wm. **New**.

261, 262- Nov. 6, 1783- Richard **Harrison** to Isham **Akin** of Virginia for 400 pds. 200 acres in Granville Co. on both sides of Michael's creek. Anne, wife of Richard **Harrison**, relinquishes dower right.

262- May 21, 1783- Lemuel **Alston** to Robert **Lewis** of Goochland Co., Va. confirms the deed to the land sold by his father Solomon **Alston** of Granville Co., N.C. now deceased, in his lifetime to said **Lewis** for 1215 pds. being on Tar river and the land whereon he then lived containing 2640 acres-
Wts: Zachariah **Hester**, Edmd **Taylor**, Jr. John **Tuggle**.

262, 263- Aug. 15, 17820 Winfield **Wright** to Kemp **Goodloe** for 200 pds. 400 acres on S side of Tar river, at **Champion**'s line where it crosses the Tarborough road and lip road to **Henlie**'s line (**Hendlie**'s?) along James **Kelly**'s and **McGee**'s line- signed by Winfield and Hannah **Wright**.
Wts: Arnold **Mann**, Benjamin **Wright**, Robert **Goodloe**.

263- Aug. 26, 1782- William **Upchurch**, Sr. of Wilks Co., N.C. to William **Upchurch** Jr. of Granville Co., N.C. for 1200 pds. 300 acres on **Walker**'s line in Granville Co., N.C. at **Reardon**'s and **Hawkins**' lines.
Wts: [Alesa?] **Cook**, David **Blalock**.

263, 264- Nov. 3, 1783- James **Butler** to Henry **Williams** for 30 pds. 100 acres on Beaver Dam pond on **Owen**'s line.
Wts: James **Butler**.

264- Oct. 25, 1783- Thomas **Banks**, esq. to William **Hornsby**, schoolmaster, for 30 shillings, 23 acres on Tar river at road and **Banks** and **Hornsby**'s lines-
Wts: R. **Banks**, Thos. **Hicks**, Wm. H. **Searcy**.

264, 265- Oct. 31, 1783- John **Wilkerson** to Josiah **Daniel** for 90 pds. 186½ acres on Grassy creek, S side of **Grant**'s road on Josiah **Daniels'** line.
Wts: Danl **Grant**, Thomas **Grant**.

265- Aug. 4, 1783- Samuel **Sneed** to John **Swan** for 15 pds. 52 acres in Granville Co.
Wts. Z. **Higgs**.

266- Aug. 30, 1783- John **Bragg** of Caswell Co., N.C. to Henry **Graves** of Granville Co. for 150 pds. 400 acres being the land he formerly lived on Spewmarrow creek at Lewis **Yancey**'s, William **Graves**', Thomas **Willson**'s and

Williams **Taylor**'s lines
Wts: Lewis **Yancey**, Ralph **Graves**.

266

266- May 16, 1781- John **Shapard** to Hugh **Snelling** for 80 pds. 50 acres on Tabbs creek at **Chavis**'s old corner on **Ragsdale**'s line, Ben **Sowel**'s line to Ned **Harris**'s line.
Wts: John **Pope**, John **Nevill**, Zorababel **Williamson**.

266, 267- Aug. 20, 1782- Hammon **Wilkerson** to William **Hornsby** for 25 pds. land on S side of Tar river at **Hornsby**'s formerly William **Wilkerson**, Jr.'s line, on **Champion**'s line, **Banks**' line containing 50 acres.
Wts: Robert **Goodloe**, John **High**.

267- Oct. 29, 1783- Thomas **Mutter** to William **Lassiter** for 175 pds. 354 acres on **Aaron**'s and Grassy creeks at John **Pryor**'s line, Abraham **Pryor**'s line, at **Smith**'s, John **Owen**'s, **Webb**'s and **Person**'s lines, Thomas **Critcher**'s line.
Wts: William **Higgs**, Mary **Higgs**.

268- Jan. 23, 1783- Blake **Mauldin** to Lemual **Goodwin** for 10 pds. 86 acres on Ruin creek at Blake **Mauldin**'s line.
Wts: Elisha **Linsey**, Richd **Glasgow**.

268, 269- Jan. 17, 1783- Blake **Mauldin** to Nicholas **Loyd** for 50 pds. 200 acres on Ruin Creek at Moses **Kittrell**'s line, **Loyd**'s corner.
Wts: Charles R. **Eaton**, Henry **Fuller**.

269- Mar. 31, 1783- Nathaniel **Robinson** to Achkinas **Williams** of Warren Co., N.C. for 100 pds. 200 acres on **Jefferson**'s road on **Dick**'s creek on line of land formerly **Miller**'s, **Turner** lines.
Wts: Lewis **Williams**, James **Beckham**, John **Tanner**.

269, 270- Oct. 29, 1783- James **Jett** to Elias **Petteford** for 20 pds. 200 acres on Newlight and Buckhorn creeks at **McCulloh**'s line.
Wts: Philemon **White**, Jemima **White**.

270- Nov [blank], 1783- Sherwood **Harris** to Edmond **Johnston** for 100 pds. land at **Harris**'s line on Tar river at the roadside on **Linsey**'s line.
Wts: none.

270, 271- Nov. 5, 1783- Israel **Eastwood** and wife Mary to Joseph **Waller** for 100 pds. 599 acres at **Dickens**' corner on Nap of Reads creek.
Wts: Thomas **Flint**, Lidey **Eastwood**.

271- Aug. 8, 1783- James **Dunlop** of Bedford Co., VA and David **Ross** of Fluvanna Co., VA. to Simon **Williams** of Granville Co., N.C. for 55,000 pds. 1100 acres on both sides of NutBush creek, two tracts adjoining, and bound by lands of Mary **Robinson**, Askenas **Williams**, Leonard **Sims**, John **Hargrove**, Thomas **Reaves**'.
Wts: William **Williams**, Simon **Williams**, James **Strange**, Hestor **McNeil**.

272- Oct. 22, 1781- William **Palmer** to William **Gill** for 1000 pds. 1000 acres being all land Robert **Mumford** purchased of Chas[4]. . . ., Thomas **Person** and William **Kennon** and sold to me (Mary, wife of William **Palmer**, relinquish her dower right in land.
Wts: M. **Satterwhite**, William **Bressie**.

272, 273- Oct. 22, 1781- William **Gill** to William **Palmer** for 800 pds. 648 acres on both sides of Jonathan's creek.
Wts: M. **Satterwhite**, William **Bressie**.

273- Dec. 12, 1781- Philemon **Hawkins**, Jr. to John **Tanner** of Warren Co., N.C. for 8000 weight of tobacco, 100

---

[4]Part of page cut away.

acres near Virginia line, at Nut Bush creek on **Hawkins**' line, Stephen **Turner**'s corner.
Wts: James **Daniel**, Joseph **Daniel**.
Lucy, wife of Phil. **Hawkins** relinquishes dower right in land.

273, 274- June 16, 1781- Arthor **Jordan** to Philemon **Hawkins**, Jr. for 50 pds. 40 acres on **Anderson**'s swamp at **Hawkins**' line.
Wts: William **Gilliam**, Isham **Harris**.

274- Dec. 11, 1782- William **Gilliam** to Philemon **Hawkins**, Jr. for 40 shillings, one acre on W side of **Anderson**'s swamp.
Wts: John **Mitchell**, Wm. **Steavens**.

275- Jan. 31, 1784 Robert **Callier** of Warren Co., N.C. to William **Hunt** of Granville Co., N.C. for 400 pds. 2 tracts one for 320 acres and granted by H. **McCulloh** to Thomas **George** June 25, 17– and the other to Robert **Callier** for 200 acres- in all 520 acres. in Granville and Orange counties, N.C. on Nap of Reeds creek at trading path.
Wts: Thomas **Person**, Bennett **Wood**.

267

275, 276- Nov. 13, 1783- Thomas **Person** to William **Nailing** for 133 pds. 6 shls. 8 pence 626 acres on Middle creek leading from Neuse to [Harrisburg].
Wts: Thos. **Banks**, Vincent **Voss**, Jr.

276- Nov. 11, 1783- Daniel **Grant** to John **Kennon** for 1000 pds. 1,037 acre on both sides of Grassy creek and Jonathan's creek at Daniel **Grant**'s line, and whereon he now lives.
Wts: Thos. **Owens**, John **Owen**, Elisabeth **Owen**.

277- May 1783- Richard **Stringfellow** to Travis **Bowden** for 20 pds. 3 acres on W side of Nutbush creek in John **Weaver**'s line.
Wts: Ralph **Neal**, Jeremiar **Garner**.

277, 278- Feb. 3, 1784- Thomas **Greenwood** executor of will of George **Bristow**, deceased, to Christopher **Harris** for 150 pds. 240 acres at mouth of **Worley**'s branch, excepting the dower right of Mrs. Elizabeth **Bristow** widow of George **Bristow**, for her lifetime.
Wts: none.

278- Dec. 6, 1783- Samuel **Dyer** of Lincoln Co., N.C. to William **Gill** of Granville Co., N.C. for 150 pds. 375 acres on Reedy creek by **Howard**'s line, and **Gill**'s line-
Wts: Wm. **Kennon**.

279- Feb. 2, 1784- William **Gill** from Graves (Groves[5]) **Howard** for 20 pds. 60 acres on Reedy creek at **Wingate**'s old line, Samuel **Dyer**'s and Wm. **Gill**'s line.
Wts: Groves **Howard**.

279- Feb. 2, 1784- George **Roberts** to John **Sherman** for 100 pds: 307 acres on both sides of Stony creek at road near **Sherman**'s Meeting house on Thos. **Philpott's** line, John **Williams**' and **Eastwood**'s lines.

280- Dec. 14, 1783- Sherwood **Harris** to Robert **Harris**, Sr. for 72 pds. all his interest now or right in at any time, to certain land of 70 acres at Robert **Harris**'s line.
Wts: Reuben **Searcy**; David **Harris**.

280, 281- Feb. 4, 1784, Charles Rust **Eaton**, esq, sheriff of Granville Co. to William **Hunt**, the property of George **Alston** and Co. which was ordered sold to highest bidder by court at suit for debt brought against him. sold 663 acres on Tar river both sides of Cattail branch on main road from Harrisburg to Potter's Mill and to **Benton**'s former line.
Wts: Reuben **Searcy** C. C.-

---

[5] This is the more likely spelling.

281- Feb. 13, 1781- Solomon **Fuller** to William **Heffernon** for 1000 pds. 640 acres on Little Beaverdam creek on **Harris**'s line.
Wts: Gilliam **Harris**, Joseph **Neal**.

281- Jan. 4, 1784- Philemon **Bristow** to Richard **Luit** [**Suite**] of Halifax Co. for 30 pds. 91 acres in Granville Co., N. C.
Wts:, Z. **Higgs**, Jonathan **Kittrell**.

282-.[blank] 1783- Sherwood **Harris** to John **Tuggle** for 24 pds. 60 acres at David **Harris**'s line.
Wts: James **Critcher**, James **Lewis**.

282- Feb. 2, 1784- John **Craft** and Elizabeth, his wife, to John **Chadwick** for 115 pds. 152 acres on Nutbush creek at Frederick and Thomas **Wiggins**' lines-
Wts: William **Bowdon**, James **Bowdon**.

283- July 24, 1783- James **Heffernon** and wife, Ellinor, Charles **Heffernon** and wife Elizabeth to Thomas **Bradford** for 50 pds., a tract of 100 and a tract of 78 acres on Fort creek on **Champion**'s, **Mayfield**'s and **Heffernon**'s lines in Charles **Heffernon**'s and James **Heffernon**'s lines.
Wts: James **Heffernon**, Jr., Wm. **Nailing**.

283- Dec. 13, 178- Benjamin **Harris** to William **Floyd**, for 45 pds. 194 acres on Little Ruin creek at the old field.
Wts: Z. **Higgs**, Elizabeth **Higgs**.

284- Jan. 13, 1784- Vallentine **White** to Thomas **White** for 50 pds. 225 acres on Tabbs creek, **Dickerson**'s and **Walker**'s lines.
Wts: Z. **Higgs**.

284- Dec. 16, 1783- Thomas **Williamson** and William **Williamson**, and James **Williamson** to Samuel **Smith** on behalf of trustees of Ruling Elders of the two United congregations of Presbyterians of Grassy creek and Nut Bush creek, for 300 pds. 300 acres including the house and land whereon the

268
said Thomas **Williamson** now lives, for use and benefit of Church.
Wts: Robert **Christmas**, John **Williamson**, James **Smith** Jr., Robert **Williamson**.

285- May 11, 1783- Wyatt **Hawkins** of Warren Co., N.C. to Thomas **Hilliard** for 2000 pds. 125 acres on W side of Deep creek on Deep branch.
Wts: James **Paschal**.

285- Aug. 4, 1783- Robert **Lewis** of Goochland Co., Va. to his friend Edmund **Taylor**, confirmation of deed to land sold by him, said **Lewis** by John **Henderson** in Granville Co., N.C. and **Henderson** to **Taylor**.
Wts: Edmund **Taylor**, Jr., Howell **Lewis**.

285, 286- Nov. 27, 1782- William **Booth** of Amelia Co., Va. to Gideon **Freeman** of Dunwoody (Dinwiddy) Co., Va. for 500 pds. 500 acres in Granville Co., N.C. on N. side of **Adcock** creek at **Harris**, **Alison** lines on **Hargrove**'s Spring branch.
Wts: John **Howard**, John **Oliver**.

286- Aug. 4, 1783- William **Frazer** to Malichi **Frazer** for 30 pds. 134 acres on both sides of Grassy creek at James **Downey**'s line north of **Cockril**'s Spring Branch.
Wts: David **Knott**, Arthur **Frazer**, Elizabeth **Roberts**.

286, 287- Feb. 1784- Benjamin **Stovall** to Drury **Stovall** for 100 pds. 220 acres on Jonathan's creek to dividing line made by John **Stovall**.
Wts: none-
Anne, wife of Benjamin **Stovall**, relinquishes her dower right.

287- Feb. 3, 1784- William Hargraves **Searcy** to John **Hawkins** for 10 pds. 22½ acres on E side of **Bolling**'s creek.

287- Jan, 30, 1784- Howel **Lewis**, Sr. to Howel **Lewis**, Jr. both of Granville Co., N.C. land on Grassy creek, being 1/3rd of his lands, on **Person**'s line at Lick creek- - deed of gift.
Wts: Robert **Coleman**, Willis **Lewis**.

288- Sept. 26, 1783-Thomas **Banks** to Susanna **Hurt** for 146 pds. 292 acres being part of a tract granted to William **Champion** by the State and deeded to Thomas **Banks** at their lines and Voalentine **Mayfield**'s line at land where James **Jenkins** now lives.
Wts: Wm. **Nailing**, [George] **Priday**, Vollentine **Mayfield**.

289- Nov. 8, 1783- Richard **Davis** to Joseph **Hester** for 100 pds. 229 acres.
Wts: William **Palmer**, David **Smith**, Thos. **Pool**.

289- Jan. 13, 1784- John **Kennon** and wife Elizabeth to Robert **Coleman** 771 acres on both sides of Island creek for 700 pds. being land **Kennon** purchased of Robert **Lewis** and includes all land he owned within the lines of Nicholas **Banks**, James **Terry**, Peyton **Wood**, Joseph **Gooch**, James **Downey**, James **Johnson**, John **Thorp** and Gideon **Gooch**.
Wts: Howell **Lewis**, Jr., Willis **Lewis**, Betsy **Lewis**.

290- Aug. 7, 1781- William **Dishazo** to Bromfield **Ridley** for 118 pds. 100 acres on S side of Flat creek at Drury **Kimball**'s corner on John **Williams**' line-
Wts: Wm. **Byars**.
Nanny, wife of William **Dishazo** relinquishes her dower right.

290, 291- June 16, 1781- Philemon **Hawkins** to Arthur **Jordan** for 50 pds. 40 acres on W side of Indian creek at **Person**'s corner.
Wts: William **Gilliam**, Isham **Harris**.

291, 292- Dec. 28, 1782- John **Mauldin** to Benjamin **Hester** for 109 pds., 175 acres on both sides of Poplar creek at Burges **Reeves**' line to Daniel **Standard**'s line.
Wts: Reuben **Talley**, Daniel **Standard**.
Sarah, wife of John **Mauldin**, relinquishes dower right in land.

292- Apr. 13, 1784- Argil **Hancks** to William **Dodson** for 175 pds. 125 acres on **Dodson**'s branch on NutBush creek at **Hargrove**'s line.
Wts: none. (Fanny, wife of Argil **Hancks**, relinquishes dower right.

292, 293- Apr. 20, 1784- Samuel **Smith**, trustee in behalf of the two United Presbyterian Church congregations of Grassy creek and Nut Bush creek, to Rev. Henry **Pattillo**, 300 acres at line of lands of Samuel **Smith**, James **Hunt**, Thomas **Williamson** by deed from Thomas **Williamson**, William and James **Williamson** made by **Smith** as trustee for Congregation.
Wts: John **Young**, Bartlet **Searcy**.

269

293, 294- May 4, 1782- William **Ogelvie** to John **Potter** for 100 pds. 50 acres at David **Harris**'s line.
Wts: James **Downey**, Jr.

294- May 3, 1784- Wiatt **Wilkerson** and wife Mary to Robert **Lewis** of Va. for 100 pds. 325 acres on N. side of Tar river in **Lewis**'s former line.
Wts: none (Mary, wife of Wiatt **Wilkerson**, relinquishes her dower right.

294, 295- Nov. 1, 1783- Drury **Perkerson** to William **Bradford**, Jr. for 5 pds. 150 acres on E side of Ledge of Rocks creek on **McCulloh**'s line, **Beck**'s and **Bradford**'s lines.
Wts: James **McKlemore**, Nichols **Byars**, William **Jones**.

295, 296- Feb. 6, 1784- Robert **Hicks**, Jr. to George **Jordan** for 100 pds. 180 acres bounded by lands of Isaac **Hicks**, George **Bruce**, W. **Hill**, Robert **Hester**, Robert **Hicks**, Jr., Reuben **Talley**'s, N. side of Huckleberry Pond.

Wts: Thomas **Hicks**, Isaac **Hicks**.

296- Mar. 21, 1782- Elisha **Lunce** to Thomas **Roberts** for 20 pds. 50 acres on a branch of Newlight creek at James **Vinnenam**'s line.
Wts: John **Bridges**, Jones **Fuller**.

296, 297- Oct. 29, 1783- Barnet **Tatom** and wife Mary to Richard **Wilkins** for 100 pds. 100 acres on the old mill on Tabbs creek along **Harris**'s line, Jonathan **White**'s line, along **Medlock**'s line.
Wts: George **Harris**, Jos. Pomfret **Davis**.

298- May 2, 1783- William **Gill** to Samuel **Whitehead** for 200 pds. 207 acres on head of branches of Jonathan's creek at county line on Bartlet **Green**'s line, James **Yancey**'s corner.
Wts: none.

298- Mar. 20, 1784- Joshua **Hays**, Sr. to Zacharias **Higgs** for 12 pds. 60 acres on Tabbs creek.
Wts: John **Bristow**.

299- Mar. 10, 1784- Lewis **Anderson**, Sr. to Lewis **Anderson**, Jr. his son, a gift of 200 acres on Fishing creek (also paid 75 pds. for same.)
Wts: Robert **Hicks**, Jr., Richard **Long**.

299, 300- Feb. 1784- William **Taborn** to Nimrod **Brummett** for 40 pds. 150 acres whereon **Taborn** now lives, excepting one acre sold some years ago to William **Cawthorn** and adjoining his Mill and includes his mill.
Wts: Edmd **Taylor**, Wm. **Cawthorn**.

300- Dec. 1, 1783- Henry **Spaulding** to Samuel **Peace** of New Kent Co., VA. for 5 lawful money, 40 acres at **Royster**'s corner, **Beasley**'s line.
Wts: Larken **Johnston**, Jos. **Hart**, Abraham **Hester**.

300- Dec. 19, 1783- Edward **Page** of Lunenburg Co., Va, to George **Chapman** of Granville Co., N.C. for 100 pds. 350 acres whereon Walter **Campbell** how lives which Edward **Page** purchased of Edmund **Taylor** between the lands of **Roberson**'s orphans, Richard **Hargrove**, Henry **Fleman**, Thomas **Brown** and the county line-
Wts: Richard **Hargrove**, Robert **Hargrove**.

301- Dec. 1, 1783-.Charles **Spaulding** to Samuel **Peace** of New Kent Co., Va, [for 120 pds.], 220 acres on both sides of Grassy creek at **Graves**' line whereon, **Spaulding** now lives.
Wts: Larkin **Johnston**, Jos. **Hart**, Abraham **Hester**.

301, 302- Apr. 7, 1783- Michael **Redwile** to George Lanamoore (Lane **Moore**) for 400 pds. 270 acres on both sides of Ledge of Rocks creek being land sold to **Redwile** by George **Miller** and including 7 acres **Redwile** sold to John **Davis** being part of a larger tract on William **Jones**'s line.
Wts: R. D. **Cooke**, Benja **Moore**.
signed by John **Davis**, Michael **Redwile**, Christiane **Redwile**.

302, 303- Jan. 1, 1784- Thomas **Banks** to William **White** for 37 pds. 94 acres adjoining Thomas **Banks**'s land at Abe **Mayfield**'s line, Susanna **Hart**'s.
Wts: Thos. **Bradford**, Anthony **Cole**, S. **Alston**.

303- May 4, 1784- Burges **Reaves** to Benjamin **Hester** for 30 pds. 100 acres on W side of Poplar creek at **Elwick**'s old line.
Wts: none (Frances, wife of Burges **Reaves**, relinquishes dower.

304- Jan, 31, 1783- John **Davis** to George **Lanemoore** for 100 pds. the land whereon John **Davis** now lives being land bought of Robert **Harris**, Jr.

270
and sold 7 acres to Michael **Redwile**, therefrom, who later released the 7 acres to **Lanemoore** for 7 pds., and the whole

tract is herein sold which lies at corner of land George **Byar**'s lived on and on Geo. **Miller**'s line containing in all 200 acres (signed John and Barbara **Davis**, Michael **Redwile**.
Wts: James **Veazey**, George **Wright**.

304, 305- Feb. 2, 1783- John **Pettycob** to James **Jenkins** for 75 pds. 270 acres at a pine on the mountain near the river thence down the river to **Gilliam**'s corner and along his line to **Lewis**'s branch to **Williams**' line and back to Tar river.
Wts: Wm. **Green**, R. **Seawell**, D. **Hall** (Durham **Hall**).

305- Aug. 5, 1783- Edmund **Taylor** to John **Taylor**, Jr. son of Edmund **Taylor**, for 1000 pds. all that land he bought of his brother Col. William **Taylor** on NutBush creek whereon John **Taylor** now lives.
Wts: none.

305, 306- Mar. 25 1784- Thomas **Banks** to Edmund **Taylor**, Sr. for 100 pds. 323 acres at his own corner on the river to **Hornsby**'s corner, and up river to first beginning.
Wts: John **Tuggle**, Jones **Fuller**, R. **Banks**.

306- Nov. 25, 1783- James **Veazey** to William **Jones** for 50 pds. 50 acres on Nap of Reeds creek.
Wts: Thomas **Flint**, Joseph **Waller**, Charles **Merryman**.

306, 307- May 4, 1784- William **Upchurch** to Edmund **Taylor**, the elder for 20 pds. 130 acres in **Hawkins**' line, **Cawthorn**'s line, **Person**'s line.
Wts: John **Willingham**, Edmund **Taylor**, Jr.

307- Apr. 7, 1783- George **Lanemoore** to Benjamin **Moore** for 100 pds. 200 acres on **Wilborn**'s line, at **Moore**'s corner.
Wts: Charles **Bullock**, Michl **Redwile**.

307, 308- Nov. 20, 1783- Daniel **Standard** and wife Anny to Richard **Wilkins** for 300 pds. 185 acres on south sides of Poplar creek, and a tract of 125 acres which **Standard** bought of Richard **Glasgo** on William **Barton** and also a tract of 50 acres on William **Hicks**' corner on Benja. **Hester**'s line.
Wts: Ransone **Sutherland**, Bernard **Tatom**, George **Harris**.

308, 309- Nov. 11, 1783- Stephen **Gifford** to John **Oliver** for 250 pds. 100 acres on Grassy creek at **Beasley**'s and **Wilkerson**'s lines.
Wts: Joseph **Gill**, John **Roberts**, Larkin **Johnston**.

309, 310- Apr. 1783- Samuel **Hicks** and wife Elizabeth to Solomon **Whitloe** for 40 pds. 135 acres on Tabbs creek on Moss **Wood**'s, Samuel **Hicks**' and **Peyton**'s lines.
Wts: George **Wood**, Jacob **Woodall**, M. **Wood**.

310, 311- Dec, 30, 1782- Askenaz **Williams** and wife Sally to Lewis **Williams** for 4000 weight of inspected tobacco, 133 3/4ths acres of land al Dick's branch being part of tract purchased by sd. **Williams** of Robert **Caller**.
Wts: Phil **Hawkins**, John **Tanner**.

311- Oct, 12, 1775- James **Forster** to Thomas **Person** for 80 pds. 650 acres, on Tar river at **Bennett**'s creek on **Person**'s, **Howard**'s lines.
Wts: Richard **Millner**, Robt. **Russell**.

312- Aug. 3, 1784- Joseph **Taylor** and wife Frances to John **Penn** or 523 pds. 1055 acres on Island creek which **Taylor** obtained by two grants from State adjoining land of John **Taylor**, William **Taylor**, Henry **Graves**, James **Hunt**, Wm. **Pattillo**, Gideon **Gooch**, Lewis **Collins** and John **Penn**.
Wts: none.

312, 313- Feb. 16, 1783- Robert **Malone** to Mary **Oliver** for 100 pds. 100 acres on her line, **Hunt**'s line, and **Smith**'s line.
Wts: John **Oliver**, Sarah **Irby**.

313- Aug, 3, 1782- Robert **Hester** and wife Ann to Zachariah **Bevill** for 2000 pds. 358 acres on Grassy creek in **Smith**'s line.
Wts: none.

271

313, 314- July 28, 1784- Major **Mitchel** and Frances **Mitchel**, widow of James **Mitchel**, deceased, to James **Critcher** for 150 pds. 640 acres on Nut Bush creek, at **Hawkins**' line, **Robertson**'s line, to Widow **Robertson**'s line, as by grant from State to James **Mitchel**.
Wts: John **Mitchel**, Wm. **Hunt**, Jarratt **Loyd**.

314, 315- Jan. 3, 1784- John **Oliver** to Millenton **Easley** for 266 pds. 420 acres on Grassy creek at **Beasley**'s line, **Wilkerson**'s, **Graves**' and **Roberts**' lines.
Wts: Luke **Landers**, Thos. **Pool**.

315- July 30, 1784- Charles **Parrish** and Elishaba **Parrish** his wife, to Dennis **Driskill** for 300 pds. 125 acres on Ruin creek.
Wts: Edward **Grisham**, Drury **Kimball**.

315, 316- July 8, 1784- Joseph **McDaniel** to James **McDaniel** for love and regard for him, a gift of 360 acres on Tabbs creek in **Hunter**'s corner on Thomas **Smith**'s line, **Chavers'** old line, and **Talley**'s line, on Long crk.
Wts: William **Walker**, William **Spears**.

316- July 14, 1784- Bartley **Greer** to Gabrl **Davey** for 250 pds., 328 acres on **Aaron** and Jonathan creek in **Wade**'s corner in county line.
Wts: Robert **Bright**, Robert **Davey**.

316, 317- May 4, 1784- William **Ross** and wife Elizabeth, William **Tatom** and wife Margaret to Rowland **Gooch** for 256 pds. 12 shls. 6 pence, 500 acres at Fowler **Jones**'s line on branches of Nuce river at William **Ross**'s line-
Wts: John **Manire**, Edward **Jones**, Jacob **Brazelton**.

317, 318- May 8, 1781- Jonathan **Parker** to Thomas **Hicks** for 10 pds. 172 acres on Fishing creek at **Bullock**'s, **Hicks'** corners, **Walker**'s line.
Wts: Thomas **Grant**, Pharaba **Parker**.

318- Jan. 5, 1783- Lemuel **Smith** and Bethunia, his wife, of Pittsylvania county, VA. to Samuel **Pointer** of Halifax Co., VA. for 800 pds. 560 acres on W. fork of Grassy creek, in Granville Co., N.C.
Wts: Jno. P. **Smith**, Robert **Flournoy**, Michael **O'Donnell**, Chas. **Hawing**.

319- Sept. 3, 1783- John **Fullilove** to John **Earl** for 200 pds. 200 acres on Tabbs creek at Christopher **Harris**'s line, on **White**'s line, Richard **Harris**'s line.
Wts: Ransone **Sutherland**, George **Harris**.

319- 320- Sept. 18, 1782- George **Heffler** to Abe **Mayfield** for 20 pds. 100 acres at John **Peace**, Jr.'s, Robert **Wilson**'s line.
Wts: John **Peace**, Jr., Valentine **Mayfield**.

320- Apr. 10, 1784- Andrew **Wade** (**Waid**) to William **Wright** for 5 shls. 330 acres on **McDaniel**'s line, at **Person**'s corner, **Harp**'s line, **Dickerson**'s line, **Earl**'s line (Sarah, wife of Andrew **Wade**, relinquishes dower right.
Wts: Benjamin **Hester**, Wm. **Roberts**, Bartlet **Wright**.

320, 321 July. 1, 1784- Thomas **Bond** to Memucan **Hunt** for a negro slave names Sarah, a tract of 263 acres on Grassy creek and on Mountain creek in **Graves**' corner, on **Hunt**'s line where Thomas **Bond** now lives, being part of tract taken up by Samuel **Reed**.
Wts: M. **Hunt**, Anderson **Hunt**, Wm. **Hunt**.

321, 322- Jan. 9, 1784- John **Hooker**, attorney for Thomas **Davis**, to William **Kelley** of Wake Co., N.C. for 100 pds. 200 acres at Edward **Davis**'s corner, in Granville Co., N.C.

Wts: R. **Clark**, Benj **Banks**.

322- Jan. 6, 1784- Elisha **Lunsford** to Jones **Fuller** for 6 pds. 50 acres on E side of Middle fork of New Light creek, being part of tract granted to **Lunsford**.
Wts: John **Moseley**, Jeremiah **Bailey**.

322, 323- Feb. 20, 1781- Hugh **Snelling** and wife Ann to Benjamin **Seawell** of Franklin Co., N.C. for 1000 pds. 800 acres on Tar river at **Claxton**'s line, at county line, on **Evans**', **Williams**'s lines, **Shepard**'s and **Harris**'s and **Chaver**'s old Mill-
Wts: Josah **Cooper**, Henry **Turpin**, Wm. **Nailing**.

272

323- July 30, 784- Richard **Nance** to William **Tanner** for 5 pds. 125 acres on E side of Cowpen fork of Beaverdam creek, at **McCulloh**'s line being part of 530 acres granted by the State to **Nance** in 1780-
Wts: Benja. **Putman**, William **Beck**.

324- July 30, 1784- Benjamin **Whicker** to William **Hester** for 250 pds. 312 acres on Tar river.
Wts: Robert **Hester**, Constant **Hester**.

324- May 3, 1784- Augustine **Woodlief** to Zacharias **Higgs** for 150 pds. 140 acres on **Bryant**'s corner on West side of Ruin creek, at **McDaniel**'s line.
Wts: Mark **White**, Charles R. **Eaton**.

325- Jan. 27, 1783- John **Boyd** and wife Mary to Benjamin **Whicker** for 322 pds. 312 acres on Tar river.
Wts: John and Lucy **Penn**, James **Lyne**.

325, 326- July 26, 1784- Charles **Partee** to Israel **Eastwood** for 50 pd 200 acres whereon he now lives, at **Eastwood**'s line.
Wts: John **Trustee**, Elizabeth **Eastwood**.

326- Jan. 22, 1781- James **Satterwhite** to Solomon **Davis** for 4000 pds. 100 acres on **Michael**'s creek above **Satterwhite**'s plantation, on Rowland **Gooch**'s line and on **Davis**'s line.
Wts: Joseph P. **Davis**, James **Hunt**.

326, 327- Feb. 23, 1784- George **Brister** and Sally **Brister** to Hartwell **Hyde** for 100 pds. 243 acres on Ruin creek at John **Bristow** (also spelled **Brister**) and Bressie **Parrish**'s line, Philemon and George **Bristow**'s lines.
Wts: Avery and John **Parham**.

327- Aug. 2, 1784- Moses **Fussell** and wife Lucretia, to Philemon **White** for 150 pds. 156 acres on **Bolling** creek at Richd **Searcy**'s corner.

327, 328- Dec. 15, 1783- Josiah **Stovall** and wife Mary to William **Easley** for 250 pds. 590 acres on Rattlesnake branch at Jonathan **Knight**'s line.
Wts: John Williams **Graves**, Benjamin **Stovell**, Samuel **Pittard**, Thornton **Yancey**-

328, 329- Dec. 28, 1781- William **Bailey** to Jeremiah **Bailey** for 3 pds. 40 acres which was granted to Israel **Fuller** by the State and from him deeded to **Bailey** (Wm.) on New light creek on **Mann**'s line.
Wts: Arnold **Mann**, Williamson **Rogers**.

329- Nov. 17, 1783- William **Dishazo** to George **King** for 60 pds. 200 acres on the New Road at James **Bishop**'s line, Bromfield **Ridley**'s line.
Wts: Phillip **Bishop**, William **Parrish**.

329, 330- Aug. 4, 1784- Jesse **Newby** to William **Farrer** (**Farer**) for 233 pds. 500 acres on Saml **Walker**'s line and **Hudspeth**'s line, **Ellison**'s line, **Tuder**'s line.
Wts: Wm. **Walker**, Ransone **Sutherland**.

330, 331- Sept. 24, 1784- Thomas **Frohock** of Rowan Co., N.C. to John **Penn** for 856 pds. 642 acres in Granville Co. on S. side of Tar river one tract granted by Granville to Thomas **Parker** Oct. 26, 1752 for 240 acres another tract to John **Frohock** by Granville Dec. 2, 1760 for 402 acres, -adjoining land of William **Davis**, William **Winston**, Thos. **Farrington** and Thomas **Person**.
Wts: Samuel **Spencer**.

331- Sept. 16, 1784- Thomas **Willingham** of Caswell Co., N.C. to John **Stovall** for 50 pds. 96 acres on Jonathan creek at **Pryor**'s and **Royster**'s and **Puryear's** and **Chandler**'s lines.
Wts: Robert and Daniel **Malone**.

331, 332- Aug. 18, 1784- Benjamin **Bass**, Sr. to Benjamin **Bass**, Jr. his son, a deed of gift of 100 acres being part of tract purchased by **Bass** from John **Locke**, bounded by **Taylor**, **Petteford**, and **Moore** lines.
Wts: Joseph and James **Taylor**.

332- Nov. 23, 1782- Randolph **Sandling** to James **Nowlin** for 150 pds. 50 acres formerly granted to William **Mackley** and sold to **Sandling** who sold to Waller **Ownby** who sold to **Going** and from him to **Sandling**.
Wts: John **Pope**, James **Sandling**.

273

333- Apr. 21, 1783- James **Ross** to William **Green** for 100 pds. 100 acres being part of tract I sold to George **Lanemoore** on Ledge of Rocks creek on **Bullock**'s, **Moore**, **Williamson**'s lines in all 150 acres.
Wts: James **Claxton**, Ralph **Williams**.

233, 234- Dec. 17, 1783- James **Williamson** of Montgomery Co., Va. to Thomas **Williamson** of Granville Co., N.C. for 50 shls. 100 acres which was granted to James **Williamson** by The State of N.C. Sept. 4, 1779 on both sides of Spewmarrow creek at **Graves**' corner.
Wts: George **Stovall**, Michael **Williamson**.

334, 335- Apr. 20, 1784- George **Ragland** of Ninety Six District of South Carolina to Stephen **Ragland** of Granville Co., N.C. for 200 pds. 200 acres on S side of Flat creek.
Wts: Samuel **Smith**, John Rochester **Ragland**.

335- Apr. 9, 1784- Jeremiah **Neil** to Benjamin **Morgan** for 20 pds. 100 acres on New Light creek at Joseph **Neal**'s line being land granted to **Fuller** by the State and deeded to David **Harris** who sold to Jeremiah **Neal**.
Wts: Simon **Clement**, Mary **Priddon**, M. **Clement**.

335, 336- Mar. 7, 1783- Roger **Thornton** to William **Fleming** for 100 pds. 100 acres on Merryman **Thorn**'s corner, to John **Besbee**'s line.
Wts: Rhodam **Bole**, James **Godfrey**.

336- [blank] 1784- George **Harris** to William **Floyd** for 2300 pds. 100 acres on Ruin creek at Benjamin **Harris**'s and at **Kittrell**'s lines.
Wts: John **Earl**, William **Wilkins**.

336, 337- Apr. 2, 1784- Bartley **Greer** to William **Hunt** of Mecklenburg Co., Va. for 35 pds. and 1000 weight of inspected tobacco, 125 acres on **Wade**'s corner.
Wts: Presley **Hunt**, Sarah **Greenage** (**Grunage**) Sally **Grunage**.

337, 338- Oct. 30, 1784- Joseph **Rogers** to Joseph **McDaniel** for 10pds. 50 acres on W side of Little Ruin Creek at **McDaniel**'s old line, on **Bristow**'s and on **Campbell**'s lines.
Wts: William **Hornsby**, J. **McDaniel**.

338- Oct. 2, 1784- Sherwood **Harris** to Gideon **Freeman** for 100 pds. 250 acres on **Adcock**'s creek at Col. Robert **Harris**'s corner, to **Holstein**'s line-
Wts: Edward **Freeman**, Robert **Harris**, Jr.
Henrietta wife of Sherwood **Harris**, relinquishes her dower right.

339- Aug. 9, 1784- Howel **Rose** and Amy **Drewry** to George **Elliott** for 240 pds. all land known as ***Rose's** Mill land* on N. side of Tar river including 3 acres on S side of river opposite mill below mouth of **Drewry**'s mill race on **Russel**'s line at **Frazier**'s corner, and on **Shelton**'s creek, containing in all 75 acres.
Wts: Ephraim **Frazer**, Robert **Adcock**.

339, 340- Aug. 5, 1784- Augustine **Woodliff** to Mark **White** for 100 pds. 100 acres on Ruin creek at **Kittrell**'s line, **Higgs**' line.
Wts: Z. **Higgs**, Leonard **Higgs**.

340- Jan. 3, 1784- Philemon **Bristow** to William **Johnson** for 60 pds. 152 acres on Little Ruin Creek at Samuel **Kittrell**'s line to **Floyd**'s line.
Wts: Z. **Higgs**, Thomas **White**.

341- June 3, 1784- Augustine **Woodliff** to Leonard **Higgs** for 4 pds. 3 acres on a creek.
Wts: Mark **White**, Zacharias **Higgs**.

341, 342- Oct. 18, 1784. Edward **Harris** to Elijah **Parrish** for 10,000[sic] pds. 30 acres on **Jones**' Branch at John **Dickerson**'s line on Tabb creek.
Wts: Sherwood and Jeter **Parrish**.

342- Sept. 10, 1784- Bishop **Hicks** to Absalom **Davis** for 50 pds, 550 acreson Poplar creek at **Barton**'s line, **Glasgow**'s line, Pumfret **Davis**'s line at the Glebe corner, **Wilkins**' line.
Wts: Ransone **Sutherland**, Robert **Jeter**.

342- Mar. 24, 1784- Roger **Thornton** and wife Catherine to James **Stark** for 150 pds. 300 acres on **Anderson**'s swamp.
Wts: James **Godfrey**, Frederick **Wiggins**.

274

343- Dec. 9, 1783- Justus **Parrish** to John **Dunkin**, Jr. for 100 pds. 95 acres on Tabbs creek at Joshua **Hays**' field.
Wts: Z. **Higgs**, Susannah **Langford**.

344- July 23, 1784- Nathaniel **Waller** to Thomas **Grant** for $1.00 (dollar), 180 acres on both sides of Ledge of Rocks creek at **Grant**'s and at **Burford**'s corners at **Walker**'s line.
Wts: Zepheniah **Waller**, William **Cole**.

344- Oct, 15, 1784- Harris **Hicks** to David **Hicks** for 25 pds. 103 acres on Tabbs creek at **Thomason**'s line, **Morris**'s line, **Hays**'s line.
Wts: Daniel **Gooch**, James **Terey**.

345- Nov. 2, 1784- John **Bailey** to Jeremiah **Bailey** for 100 pds. 240 acres on Newlight creek at Jones **Fuller**'s line, granted by State 1783-
Wts: Arnold **Mann**, Jones **Fuller**.

345, 346- Nov. 2, 1784- John **White** to Argil **Hanks** for 38 pds. 172 acres on **Taylor**'s Mill creek at county line, at **Collins**' corner and Fields Reeds corner near Meeting House Spring at **Hargrove**'s line.

346- Aug. 15, 1784- Philip **Burford** of Warren Co., N.C. to William **Dodson** of Granville for 133 pds. 6 shls. 8 pence, 140 acres at Bromfield **Ridley**'s corner, Elisha and Sherwood **Sims**'s lines which **Burford** bought of James **Wallace**.
Wts: Wyatt **Hawkins**, Rich **Hargraves**, James **Roberson**.

346, 347- Aug. 30, 1784- John Pryor **Smith** to Anderson **Smith** for 150 pds. 248 acres being land granted by Lord Granville to Charles **Smith** on **Aaron**'s creek.
Wts: Chas. **Allen**, George **Watkins**.

347, 348- Nov. 7, 1782- Abel **Tatom** to Hugh **Snelling** for 200 pds. 300 acres where Abel **Tatom** now lives on

Gibbey **Chavis**'s old line, to Aquilla **Snelling**'s new survey.
Wts: John **Dickerson**, William **Walker**, Joseph **Hill**.

348- Sept. 30, 1783 John **Teatom** (**Tatom**?) to John **Beck** for 100 pds. 202 acres on both sides of Ledge of Rocks creek on **Townsend**'s line.
Wts: George **Wright**, William **Jones**, Jr.

348, 349- Dec. 3, 1782- John **Henderson** and wife Sarah to Edmund **Taylor** for 1520 pds. land whereon we now live containing 2530 acres on both sides of Tar river which we bought of Robert **Lewis** being land east of dividing line agreed on by Robert **Lewis** and myself containing 1386 acres and also a tract I bought of the State containing 580 acres adjoining the old divided land on Fishing creek and Tar river, and also from State a tract of 400 acres on S side of Tar river on **Harp** creek on **Holston**'s line, and a tract from State for 100 acres on W side of Fishing creek on **Cooper**'s line, and a tract from Charles **Ipoc** [?] to me for 75acres on Tar river at Fishing creek at **Henderson**'s line.
Wts:none
(Sarah Relinquishes her dower right).

350- Oct. 18, 1777- William **Wilkerson** to William **Hornsby** for 26 pds. 13 shls. 4 pence, 100 acres on S side of Tar river at William **Hewitt**'s Spring branch crossing road to Thomas **Banks**' line.
Wts: Thomas **Banks**, William **Hewitt**.

350, 351- Nov. 7, 1784- Littleton **Fuller** to Henry **Fuller** for 80 pds. 200 acres on Long Creek.
Wts: Wm. **Hornsby**, Brittain **Fuller**.

351, 352- Feb. 8, 1785- Thomas **Glaze** to Samuel **Peace** for 100 pds. 169 acres which is part of survey deeded by Luke **Landers** on both sides of Grassy creek in **Spaulding**'s, **Landers**', **Daniel**'s line.
Wts: Gid **Crenshaw**, James **Yancey**.

352- Feb. 13, 1782- James **Johnston** and wife Elizabeth to John **Dillion** for 20 pds. 100 acres on Island creek at lower end of tract purchased of John **Chiles** on lines of lands of James **Hunt**, Gideon **Gooch**, James **Johnston**, Robert **Hester**, Drury **Smith**.
Wts: J. **Kennon**, John **Johnston**.

275

352, 353- Feb. 2, 1785- Richard **Banks** of Wake Co., N.C. to William **Laseter** of Granville Co., N.C. for 30 pds. 250 acres on E side of Middle fork of Beaverdam creek at John **Hook**'s corner, **Bradford**'s corner, **McCulloh**'s line.
Wts: John **Brumfield**.

353- Jan. 12, 1785-John **Morris** to Avery **Parham** for 20 pds. 60 acres on a branch of Fishing creek and each side of **Banks** Road at James **Jetts**' and Joseph **Hays'** lines to David **Hicks**'s line.
Wts: Isham **Johnson**, Wm. **Reaves**, Thomas **Thomason**.

Wts: Wm. **Paschal**, John **Finch**.

355, 356- Feb. 8, 1785- Charles Rust **Eaton**, Esq. sheriff of Granville Co. sold at public sale the property of Edmund **Johnston**, at suit brought by Wyatt **Wilkerson** for debt due, and 105 acres adjoining Sherwood **Harris** was sold to John **Hawkins** as highest bidder for same.

356, 357- Dec. 2, 1784- Moses **Wood** and Mary **Wood** to William **Farrer** for 136 pds. 302 acres on S side of Tabbs creek at Solomon **Whitlow**'s line on Avery and Isham **Parham**'s lines and on **Hays**' line, John **Parham**'s.
Wts: Samuel **Walker**, Nimrod **Brummit**, James **Fowler**.

357- Nov. 1, 1784- William **Sauls** of Warren Co., N. C. to Moses **Forkner** of Warren Co., N.C. for 40 pds. 82 acres in Granville Co., N.C. on S side of **Martin**'s creek.
Wts: Joseph **Mangum**, James **Ball**.

358- Dec. 13, 1784- Richard **Person** of Surry Co., N.C. to Thomas **Smith** of Granville Co., N.C. for 30 pds. 15 acres at **Smith**'s old line in Granville Co. on Buffalow creek.
Wts: Wm. **Paschal**, John **Finch**.

358- Dec, 30, 1784- David **Harris**, Sr. to John **Tippet** for 20 pds. 125 acres on Tar river at **Person**'s corner.
Wts: Edmund **Freeman**, Robert **Allison**.

358, 359- Mar. 2, 1784- Edward **Moore** of Montgomery Co., N.C. to Richard **Moore** of same county and State for 200 pds. 200 acres beginning at Nathaniel **Henderson**'s corner and running along his line In Granville Co.
Wts: David **Chandler**, Charles **Carter**.

359- Mar. 8, 1784- Edward **Moore** of Montgomery Co., N.C. Richard **Moore** of same place for 200 pds. 200 acres on Fishing creek in Granville Co. being part of land deeded to William **Jordan** by Augustine **Bates** in 1762, this being the northwest part at **Bass**'s line.
Wts: David **Chandler**, Charles **Carter**.

360- Mar. 7, 1784- Edward **Moore** of Montgomery Co., N. C. to Richard **Moore** of same place for 500 pds. 500 acres in Granville Co., N.C. at Geo. **Harris**', Sarah **Arnold**'s, **Hamilton**'s lines.
Wts: David **Chandler**, Charles **Carter**.

360, 361- Feb. 1, 1784- Edward **Moore** of Montgomery Co., N.C. to Richard **Moore** of same place for 640 pds., 640 acres on N. side of Tar river in Granville Co., N.C.
Wts: David **Chandler**, Charles **Carter**.

276

361- Dec. 1, 1784- Samuel **Smith** to William **Amis** for 120 pds. 225 acres in Granville Co. commonly called *The Glebe Land*, whereon Reverend Henry **Pattillo** lately lived, for the use and benefit of the two congregations of the United Churches of Nut Bush Creek and Grassy creek at [Anderson] **Smith**'s, William **Amis**, Samuel **Smith**'s lands-
Samuel **Smith** is trustee for churches.
Wts: Jon. **Knight**, Samuel **Smith**, Jr., William **White**.

362- Jan. 3, 1785- Joseph **Rogers** to Joseph **McDaniel** for 10 pds. 69 acres in **McDaniel**'s line, W side of Ruin creek, at **Langnford's**, **Hays**' and **Higgs**' lines.
Wts: James **McDaniel**, William **Rogers**.

362- Dec. 13, 1784- Richard **Person** of Surry Co., N.C. to John **Finch** of Granville Co., N.C. for 30 pds. 20 acres on **Stone** creek at **Leaman**'s line.
Wts: James **Sabine**, Wm. **Paschal**, James **Person**.

362, 363- Jan. 25, 1785- John **Brodie** and wife, Mary to John **Keeling** for 226 pds., 12 shls., 6 pence- 181 acres near the Meeting House on **Martin**'s line, **Akin**'s, **Gilasby**'s lines on Meeting House road.
Wts: Sterling **Yancey**, Charles **Mitchel**, John **Williamson**.

363, 364- Sept. 6, 1784- Philip **Burford** of Warren Co., N.C. to Thomas **Clement** of Granville Co., N.C. for 400 pds. 310 acres in Gramville Co. on Cedar creek at Peyton **Clement**'s old corner now Thomas **Clement**'s at the dividing line between Peyton **Clement** and James **Comer (Conner)** to Neuce River.
Wts: Wyatt **Hawkins**, Peter **Twitty**, Phil. **Hawkins**, Jr.

364- Nov. 29, 1783- John **Landers** to James **Downey**, Jr. for 20 pds. 120 acres on Grassy creek at Luke **Landers**' line, **Wilkerson**'s line.
Wts: John **Downey**, Robert **Downey**.

364, 365- Oct. 18, 1784- Robert **Wilson** to William **Williams** for 40 pds. 250 acres on Fort creek at **Heffernon**'s and **Nailing**'s lines.
Wts: Laban **Haislip**, Henry **Beram**.

365- . .1784-. George **Lanemoore** to William **Green** for 16 pds. 50 acres on Ledge of Rocks creek at **Chambless**'s line at **Green**'s corner.
Wts: Zephenah **Walter**, Jeremiah **Bullock**.

365, 366- Mar. 27, 1782- Thomas **Jones** to Chas. **Partee** for 50 pds. 250 acres on Ledge of Rocks creek at **Hall**'s corner, **McCulloh**'s line.
Wts: Edmd **Partee**, Elender **Culverhouse**.

366- Feb. 2, 1785- James **Jett** to Avery **Parham**, Jr. for 15 shls. 3 acres on a branch of Fishing creek.
Wts: Abner **Reeves**, Hardy **Reeves**.

366, 367- Nov. 4, 1784- Isham **Mitchel** to David **Bradford** for 50 pds. 295 acres at Philip **Bradford**'s corner, **Wright**'s line, on Fort creek, mouth of Tarkiln branch.
Wts: Benja. **Morgan**, Thos. **Bradford**.

367- Feb. 7, 1785- Charles R. **Eaton**, sheriff of Granville Co. sold the property of Archibald and John **Hamilton** and Co. ordered sold by court order at suit brought for debt by Larkin **Johnston** for 387 pds.- 160 acres in Granville and Franklin Counties, N.C. sold to Larkin **Johnston** as highest bidder, bounded by lands of **Williamson**, **Finch**. **Leamon**.

368- Jan. 20, 1785- Gabriel **Davey** of Caswell Co., N.C. to Thornton **Yancey** of Granville Co., N.C. for 190 pds. 342½ acres on **Aaron**'s and Jonathan's creek It line of land formerly property of Joshua **Grenage** now belonging to Philip **Meadors**, Charles **Wade** and others bought of Bartley **Greer** by **Davey**-
Wts: Thomas **Mutter**, James **Yancey**, John **Brown**.

368, 369- Jan. 1, 1785- Mary **Briggs** to James **West** for 30 pds. 348 acres on **Taylor**'s corner, **Parker**'s line.
Wts: David **Knott**, Robert **Malone**, John **Knott**.

369- Dec. 22, 1784. Henry **Williams** to Thomas **Lanier** for 5 shls. 150 [acres] on a branch at **Penn**'s line, **Burton**'s line, **David**'s line being part of land granted by Gov. **Martin** of N.C. to Henry **Williams**.
Wts: Elijah **Mitchel**, John **Mitchel**, S. **Sneed**.

369, 370- Jan. 21, 1785- Robert **Harris**, Jr. to Thomas **Wilburn** for 50 pds. 200 acres on S side of Tarborough road on Robert **Harris**'s and **Hatcher**'s lnes to **Holstein**'s corner.
Wts: Henry **Potter**, J. **Potter**.

277

370- Jan. 18, 1769- John **Hamilton** of Halifax Co., N.C. to Littleton **Fuller** of Granville Co., N.C. for 10 pds. 200 acres at head of Long creek on Leonard **Bullock**'s line.
Wts: Stephen **Jett**, Henry **Fuller**.

370, 371- Apr. 5, 1784- Thomas **Key** to Stephen **Turner** for 30 pds. 50 acres on E side of Deep creek at mouth of Maypole Branch.
Wts: Dennis **Paschal**, Thomas **Earls**, Permenis **Williams**.

371- Nov. 5, 1784- John **Tatom** to John **Brodie** for 400 pds. 500 acres at the old mill at John **Harris**'s line along Jonathan **White**'s line, crossing NutBush road to Lewis **Anderson**'s line, **Tatom**'s fence, **Matlock**'s (Nicholas) corner being the land whereon **Tatom** now lives, bought of Jonathan **White**.
Wts: John **Taylor**, Robert **Hester**, T. **Satterwhite**.

372- Feb. 8, 1785- Joseph **Gill** to Lewis **Ackman** for 120 pds. 400 acres on **Aaron**'s and Jonathan's creek at Joseph **Gill**'s line near **Malone**'s path and near **Kennon**'s road at line between Joseph **Chandler** and James **Jones** to **Harrison**'s and Joseph **Gill**'s lines.
Wts: James **Glen** (signed Joseph and Mary **Gill**).

372, 373- May 15, 1784- Claborn **Harris** to Robert **Harris** for 80 pds. 125 acres at mouth of Saml **Harris**'s spring branch to Wm. **Ogelvie**'s line at Nicholas **Holstan**'s creek.
Wts: Temperance **Wilburn**, Saml **Harris**.

373- July 3, 1784- Samuel **Harris** to Robert **Harris**, Sr. for 500 pds. 155 acres on **McCulloh**'s and **Harris**'s lines.
Wts: Claborn **Harris**, Temperance **Wilburn**, Samuel **Harris**.

373-, 374- Dec. 4, 1784- Josiah **Mitchel** to Gilliam **Norwood** for 204 pds. 204 acres on Nut Bush creek.
Wts: John **Lewis**, Robt. **Gillespie**, Joseph **Taylor**.

374- Jan. 25, 1785- Robert **Burton** and wife Agatha to John **Wilson** for 100 pds., 360 acres on both sides of Island creek.
Wts: Sterling **Yancey**, Jas. M. **Burton**, Henry **Wilson**.

374, 375- Oct. 4, 1784- Patrick **Logan** of Surry Co., N.C. to Jonathan **Johnston** of Granville Co., N.C. for 60 pds. 130 acres at Mallakiah **Reeves**' line on Tabbs creek at William **Reeves**' line, Ephraim **Parham**'s line.
Wts: Robert **Lanier**, John **Logan**, Alexa **Douglass**.

375- Mar. 10, 1783- Thomas **Person**, Esq. to John **Penn** for 140 pds. 350 acres near head of a small branch of Island creek along **Collins**' line along **Penn**'s line.

375, 376- Jan. 13, 1785- William **Kennon**, Esq. to William **Gill** for 5pds. 5 acres on Fox creek on **Kennon**'s and **Ring**'s old line.
Wts: Stephen **Merritt**, Francis **Maynard**.

376- Feb. 28, 1785- Edmund **Carnes** to George **Lanemoore** for 40 pds. 111 acres at Michael **Redwile**'s line.
Wts: Micajah **Bullock**, Jeremiah **Bullock**, Ralph **Williams**.

376, 377- Mar. 10, 1785- William **Chavis** to Isaac **Kittrell** for 533 pd, 6 shls. 8 pence, 400 acres on N. side of Tar river both sides of Little creek.
Wts: John **Kittrell**, Joshua **Kittrell**.

377- Mar. 28, 1785- William **Ogelvie** to Harris **Ogelvie** for 100 pds. 180 acres on Claborn **Harris**'s corner in **McCulloh**'s line.
Wts: John **Ogilvie**, Bettey **Ogelvie**.

378- Dec. 9, 1783- Haden **Pryor** of Caswell Co., N.C. to John **Angus** of Prince George Co., VA. for 200 pds. 700 acres at **Person**'s, **Harris**', **Hays**', **Jones**', **Royster**'s lines.
Wts: Thomas **Mutter**.

378- May 1, 1782- Nathan **Jackson** to Robert **Goodloe** for 10 pds. 10 shls.10½ acres on W side of Horse creek at **Goodloe**'s, **Harris**'s, **Jackson**'s corner.
Wts: Kemp **Goodloe**, James **Blackwell**.

288 [sic +10 pages in numbering]
379- July 12, 1784- William **Eaton**, eldest son and heir at law, of William **Eaton**, deceased, to William **Duke**- William **Eaton**, the elder, by his, will dated Feb., 19, 1759 directed that a part of estate be sold by executors to pay his

debts, and whereas his widow Mary **Eaton** and Robert **Jones** were appointed Executors, but both died before paying debts, the said William **Eaton**, Jr. herein sells land containing 180 acres on **Anderson**'s swamp for 150 pds. to William **Duke**.
Wts: Robert **Peebles**, Joseph **Shearen**.

379, 380- Dec. 30, 1784- Richard **Person** of Surry Co., N.C. to George **Finch** for 50 pds. 75 acres on Buffalow creek to **Leamon**'s line, to the county line.
Wts: Wm. **Paschal**, John **Finch**.

380- June 16, 1784- William **Taylor** of Mecklenburg Co., VA. to Nehemiah **Long** for 1000 pds. 1700 acres adjoining lands of John **Taylor**, John **Penn**, Henry **Graves**, William **Bullock**, being part of three surveys, excepting the little exchanged with John **Taylor** before this sale.
Wts: William **Bullock**, John **Taylor**.

380- Dec. 4, 1784- Joel **Chambless** to James **Custerd** for 60 pds. the land whereon I live at Benjamin **Moore**'s line, **Williams**'s line, 150 acres.
Wts: Ann **Williams**, Rebecker **Bailey**, Jacob **Stem**.

381- Apr.- 1785- Ralph **Williams** to Jacob **Ferebow** for 5 pds. 8½ acres at **Williams**' line.
Wts: R. D. **Cooke**, William **Green**.

381- Mar. 30, 1785- John **Hawkins** to William **Longmire** for 80 pds. land on Tar river at Sherwood **Harris**'s line.
Wts: Sherwood **Harris**, Thomas **Minor**, William **Mallory**.

382- Feb. 15, 1785- Peyton **Wood** to Joseph **Gooch** for 5 pds. 55½ acres adjoining his own land on Island creek, at **Clay**'s line.
Wts: Daniel **Gooch**.

382- Apr. 27, 1785- Richard **Head** to Samuel **Smith** for 200 pds. 443 acres whereon Richard **Head** now lives including the land bought of **Chapman** and **Morgan** on E side of Grassy creek where county line crosses on Henry **Hester**'s line, James **Williams**' line, Henry **Montague**'s line, Henry **Graves**' line to land of John **Gordan** and Co, commonly, called Shaeleathers to John **Morgan**'s line.
Wts: Samuel **Smith**, Jr., Rebeckah **Hargrave**, James Webb **Smith**.

382, 383- Apr. 2, 1785- John **Parham**, Sr. to Thomas **Parham** Sr. of Brunswick Co., Va. for 30 pds. 82 acres at Heartwell **Hyde**'s line, **Langford**'s line on branches of Poplar creek.
Wts: James **Jett**, Lewis **Parham**.

383- Dec. 13, 1784- William **Champion** to Alexander **Carter** for 69 pds. land whereon **Champion** now lives containing 230 acres at Col. **Mayfield**'s line on Fort creek.
Wts: Edmund **Taylor**, Sherwood **Harris**.

384- Mar. 29, 1784- James **Winningham**, Sr. to Jones **Fuller** for 40 pds. 190 acres on **Lunsford**'s line, which was conveyed to **Winningham** by N.C.
Wts: John **Pope**, John **Winningham**.

384- Dec. . 1783- William **Spears** to Philip Hunt **Spears**, his son, a gift of 170 acres on Long Creek.
Wts: Wm. **Walker**, William **Spears**.

385- Dec. 29, 1784- William **Graves**, Sr. and Henry **Graves**, Sr. to William **Estes** for 200 pds., 300 acres on Tar river, at John **Mize**'s spring branch along Isaac **Head**'s and Robert **Bell**'s lines on Amos **Penn**'s line, **Ross**'s line.
Wts: Benjamin **Knight**; Lyddal **Estes**.

385, 386- Dec. 24, 1782- Phillip **Pearce** of Franklin Co., N.C. to John **Dickerson** for 20 pds. 100 acres on Fort creek at **Mocksley**'s branch, at John **Pearce**'s line.
Wts: J. **Penn**, Thos **Peace**.

386- Dec. 23, 1784- Stephen **Hix** to Robert **Mills** for, 50 pds. 200 acres in John **Bradford**'s line, to John

Heffernon's line, Robert **Jones**'s line, at **Blackwell**'s line, James **Blackwell**'s line, Isham **Mitchel**'s line.
Wts: Leonard **Higgs**, Robert **Willson**.

289

386- Oct. 26, 1784- William **Beaver** to William **Bullock** for 66 pds. 300 acres whereon **Beaver** now lives, at **Taylor**'s line.
Wts: James **Lyne**, John **Taylor**.

387- Oct. 1, 1784- Joseph **Glover** to Tabitha **Marshal** of Warren Co., N.C. for 238 pds. land on **Chapman**'s branch at the path, on Haw Branch- 238 acres.
Wts: Daniel **Glover** (Phebe, wife of Joseph **Glover**, relinquishes her dower.).

387, 388- May 14, 1784- Henry **Williams** to Augustine **Davis** for 80 pds. 400 acres on Indian fork of Little Island creek at mouth of Rocky branch on **Penn**'s and **Davis**' line with five acres in Indian fork so as to make a straight course at **Burton**'s line.
Wts: William **Byars**, Rowland **Terry**, James **Butler**, Guilelmusie **Byars**.
Priscilla, wife of Henry **Williams**, relinquishes her dower right.

388- Aug. 3, 1785- John **Potter** to Alexa **Boyd** of Mecklenburg Co., VA. for 460 pds. 460 acres in Granville co. at mouth of Nicholas creek at John **Potter**'s field, **Wilburn**'s field along Hillsborough road to Col. Robert **Harris**'s line to William **Ogelvie**'s and Nicholas **Holstein**'s lines, Thomas **Harris**'s line and along river.
Wts: Phil **Hawkins** John F. **Williams**.

388, 389- May 8, 1785- Joseph **Taylor** from Gilliam **Norwood** for 210 pds. 200 acres between the lands of Joseph **Taylor**, John **Taylor** and Benjamin **Norwood** which is the land devised to Gilliam **Norwood** by his father Nathaniel **Norwood**, deceased.
Wts: David **Mason**, Ben **Hancock**.

389- Dec. 1, 1784- John **Hooker** to Darwin **Harris** for 150 pds. 200 acres on Beaverdam creek on **Hampton**'s line and also 86 acres on **Hooker**'s line on R. **Banks** road.
Wts: John **Hooker**, Richard **Nance**.

390- . .1785- Howel **Rose** to Barnett **Pulliam** for 288 pds. 300 acres on Tar river on **Shelton**'s creek at **Hart**'s line, **Graves**' line, **Jones**'s, **Gooch**'s.
Wts: Stephen **Merritt**, Lewis **Wilburn**, Geo. **Bruce**.
signed by Howel and Amey **Rose**.

390, 391- Aug. 3, 1785-Malichi **Reeves** to William **Reeves** for 100 pds. 257 acres on both sides of Tabbs creek.
Wts: Richard **Banks**, Wm. **Ashley**.

391- Jan. 21, 1785- John **Beaver** to Daniel **Scott** for 40 pds. 250 acres at Lewis **Taylor**'s line, William **Bullock**'s line whereon **Beaver** now lives.
Wts: William **Bullock**, John **Terry**.

391, 392- Aug. 3, 1785-Thomas **Johnston** of Rowan Co., N.C. to William **Moore** of Granville Co., N.C. for 120 pds. 100 acres on Tabbs creek at Avery **Parham**'s line.
Wts: **Isham Johnson**, Luke **Landers**.

392- Dec. 31. 1784- John **Tanner** of Warren Co., N.C. to Askenaz **Williams** of same place for 125 pds. land in Granville Co. adjoining the land now belonging to Parmenas **Williams** to Simon **Williams**' line to a corner formerly Francis **Williams**'s and runs to **Turner**'s line containing in the whole 208 acres.
Wts: Lewis **Williams**, Richard **Thomas**, Presley **Thorne**.

392, 393- Dec, 17, 1784- Richard **Suite** of Halifax Co., to William **Johnson** of Granville Co. for 20 pds. 91 acres on River creek at **Floyd**'s line-
Wts: Z. **Higgs**, John **Suite**.

393- Mar. 32, 1782- Bennett **Stacey** to Charles **Partee** for 25 pds. 50 acres on Ledge of Rocks creek at **Hatcher**'s and John **Adcock**'s lines to the Spring branch at Ben **Wade**'s line running to James **Bullock**'s line to James **Claxton**'s line, John **Hatcher**'s line.
Wts: Edm. **Partee**, John **Trustee**.

394- Aug. 1, 1785- Christopher **Harris** to Solomon **Walker** for 200 pds. 240 acres at Samuel **Jeter's** line, and along **Jeter**'s line to White Dirt branch, preserving the 1/3rd part thereof to Elizabeth **Bristow**, relict of George **Bristow** for her lifetime.
Wts: None.

290

[394-395]- Nov. 13, 1784- James **Veazey** to Joshua **Bullock** for 30 pds. 500 acres at **Cash**'s line, on **Cooke**'s line, **Hall**'s line, **Jones**'s line at **Byars**' corner, **Veasey**'s line thence to Thomas **Veazey**'s line, **Claxton**'s.
Wts: Ralph **Williams**, Jeremiah **Bullock**.

395- Apr. 15, 1785-John **Mannin** of Craven Co., South Carolina to Charles **Partee** of Granville Co., N.C. for 100 pds. 133½ acres on Nap of Reeds crk Granville Co., N.C.
Wts: Edmd **Partee**, Wm. **Manning**.

395, 396- Dec. 22, 1784- Henry **Williams** to Robert **Burton** for 5 shls. 95 acres in his own line, on **Davis**'s line, Thomas **Lanier**'s line which was granted by Gov. **Martin** to Henry **Williams**.
Wts: Elijah **Mitchel**, S. **Sneed**, John **Mitchel**.

396- Nov. 13, 1783- John **Potter** to Joseph **Gooch** for 80 pds. 100 acres at **Phipps** corner, on **Bradford**'s and **Nolin**'s lines.
Wts. Joseph **Taylor**, Gideon **Gooch**.

396, 397- Apr. 20, 1785- Lewis **Taylor** to Baxter **Davis** of Mecklenburg Co., VA. for 400 pds. 200 acres on Beaver Pond at the county line on **Davis**'s line.
Wts: Jacob **Mitchel**, John **Smith**.

397- Apr. 9, 1785- Zorababel **Williamson** to Thomas **York** of Warren Co., N.C. for 180 pds. 270 acres on **Collings** creek in Granville Co.
Wts: William **Roberts**, Henry **Fuller**, Wm. **Floyd**, Wm. **Cook**, Richd **Ransom**.

397- Aug. 1, 1785- Owen **Griffin** to John **Young** for 120 pds. land on Drury **Stovall**'s and William **Easley**'s lines to Jonathan **Knight**'s line on N. side of Horsehoe road at **Young**'s line.

398- May 24, 1785- Baxter **Ragsdale** of Franklin Co., N. C. to John **Finch** of Granville Co., N.C. for 200 pds. 185 acres along lines of land of **Clapton**, **Harris**, **Williamson**, **Mores**.
Wts: John **Finch**, Millonton **Finch**.

398, 399- June 24, 1785- John **Penn** to Benjamin **Seawell** of Franklin Co., N.C. for 500 pds. land purchased of Hugh **Snelling** on Tar river and Tabbs creek in Granville Co., N. C. containing 575 acres between lands of Richard **[Clapton]**, William **Smith**, Major **Evans**, Samuel **Jones**, Edward **Harris**, John **Penn**.
Wts: B. **Ridley**, Joseph **Taylor**.

399- Oct. 18, 1784- Thomas **Bridges** to John **Dickerson** deeds 462 acres on Middle creek at **Huskey**'s line, **Weather**'s line, to **Bradford**'s and **Blackwell**'s lines-
Wts: John **Peace** Jr., Wm. W. **Cooper**.

399, 400- Nov. 24, 1783- John **Tatom** to Reuben **Talley** for 200 pds. 300 acres on N. side of Tar river at **Hudspeth**'s line to **Chavis**'s line.
Wts: Joseph Pumfret **Davis**, James **Bristow**, Zachariah **Hester**.

400- May 10, 1784- Wagstaff **Kanady** of Wake Co., N.C. to Mansfield **Jenkins** of Granville Co., N.C. for 50 pds. land on Little Beaver Dam creek at county line at **Kandy**'s corner, **McCulloh**'s corner, contains 220 acres being part of

tract granted by The State to Dozer **Thornton** Mar. 1, 1780- by Richard **Caswell**, Governor.
Wts: James **Heffernon**, Jno. **Humphries**.

400, 401- Mar. 2, 1785- John More **Adams** of Chatham Co., N.C. to Lawrence **Petteford** of Granville Co. for 50 pds. 220 acres on S side of Fishing creek along **Snelling**'s line, **Tatom**'s, **Newby**'s, **Cooper**'s lines.
Wts: Sherwood **Parrish**, Jesse **Parrish**.

401- Aug. , 1785- Brereton **Jones** to Richard Donaldson **Cooke** both of Granville Co., N.C. for 115 pds. 300 acres on **Hawkins** corner along his line to **Cooke**'s line and along line, **Williams**'s line at **Stanton**'s and **Harris**'s lines til intersects **Bullock**'s line at line between **Jones** and **Claxton** and a line between **Jones** and **Hawkins**.
Wts: none.

402- July 30, 1785- George **Brack** and wife Elizabeth to Samuel **Reeves** for 20 pds. 100 acres adjoining land of Thomas **Brame**, James **Brame**, Drury **Kimball**-
Wts: Michael **Jones**, Lewis **Reeves**.

402- May 9, 1785- Robert **Malone** to Josiah **Mitchel** for 150 pds. 233 acres on SE side of **Aaron**'s creek at **Harrison**'s line.
Wts: Thomas **Owen**, James **Mathews**.

291

403- Jan. 7, 1784- Henry **White** to Henry **Smith** for 40 pds. 100 acres on Little Creek at **Williams**' corner.
Wts: John **Welch**, Ruth **Huddleston**.

403- Nov. 24, 1784- William **Burford**, Jr. to Micajah **Bullock** for 50 pds. 200 acres at **Peak**'s line to Widow **Veazey**'s line, **Bailey**'s and **Waller**'s lines.
Wts: Solomon **Burford**, Mitchel **Burford**, Robt. **Baldwin**.

404- July 29, 1785- Henry **Smith** to William **Williams** for 4 pds. 16 shls 15 acres on Little Creek at **Williams**' line.
Wts: Laban **Haislip**, Henry **Williams**.

404- Aug. 23, 1784- William **Duke** of Warren Co., N, C, to Rodham **Atkins** for 400 pds. (**Atkins** of same county) land on S side of **Anderson**'s swamp formerly the property of William **Eaton**, deceased, and by his will ordered to be sold by his excrs.- Nov. 3, 1784- assigned to Phil **Hawkins** by **Atkins**).
Wts: John **White**, Thos. **Atkins**, Isham **Harris** and Wilie **Harris**.

405- Nov. 3, 1784- Rodham **Atkins** of Granville Co. to Philemon **Hawkins** for 105 pds. 180 acres on **Anderson**'s swamp formerly property of William **Eaton**, deceased, and willed to be sold by excrs. and sold to Wm. **Duke**.
Wts: Isham **Harris**, Wilie **Harris**.

405-406- Nov, 8, 1785- William **Hunt**, sheriff of Granville Co., N.C. sold the property of Merriman **Thorn** and wife Winne at public sale at order of court by suit brought by Edward **Wilkins** for debt. Land was bought by Edward **Weaver** as highest bidder for 100 acres.

405- Nov. 16, 1784- Larkin **Johnston** to John **Harp** for 50 pis. 160 acres on Franklin and Granville Co. lines at **Evans**', **Williams**' and **Harp**'s lines-
Wts: Z. **Higgs**, Wm. **Walker**.

407- Nov. 5, 1785- William **Gill** to Charles **Wade** for 100 pds. 140 acres on Aaron's and Jonathan's creeks at Samuel **Whitehead**'s line, Chases **Harris**'s line, **Wade**'s and **Greer**'s lines.

407- Sept. 6, 1785- William **Hart** to Seth **Pettypool** for 74 pds. 10 acres.
Wts: Joseph **Blanks**, Seth **Pettypool**, Young **Pettypool**.

408- Sept. 1784- Wyatt **Wilkerson** to Caleb **Crews** for 100 pds. 140 acres on Tar river adjoining lands of Richard **Searcy**, William **Mallory**, Robert **Lewis**, Archibald **Mitchel** and Reuben **Searcy**.
Wts: Wm. H. **Searcy**, William **Longmire**.

408, 409- July 5, 1785- Gibson **Harris** to John **Penn**-
On Sept, 6, 1756, William **Chavers** (**Chavis**) gave to his. daughter Sarah, wife of Edward **Harris**, and heirs of her body lawfully begotten, 340 acres on Tabbs creek in Granville Co., N.C.- Sarah **Harris** died in January last past, without having conveyed the land to any person, leaving four sons: Gibson, Sherwood, Jesse and Solomon **Harris**-Gibson sells his share for 50 pds. to John **Penn**-
Wts: Reuben **Searcy**.

409- Mar. 20, 1785- Thomas **Banks**, now of the State of Georgia, Wilks county- but lately of Granville Co., N.C. to Lewis **Taylor** of Granville Co. for 450 pds. 1500 acres in Granville Co., N.C. on both sides of Quick Sand creek at **Hornsby**'s line, George **White**'s corner, on Mill ponds at William **White**'s corner, **Hart**'s, **Carter**'s, **Sutton**'s lines, **Bradford**'s corner with a grist mill on the land.
Wts: R. **Banks**, William **Banks**, Joseph **Blackwell**.

410- May 16, 1785- Frederick **Rose** to Zachariah **Eilborn** for 100 pds 100 acres on both sides of Nap of Reeds creek at mouth of Haracane branch at **Knott**'s, **Manire**'s lines, **Veazey**'s corner.
Wts Frederick **Rose**, John **Manire**, Stephen **White**.

410, 411- Dec. 12, 1784- James **Winningham**, Jr. to Robert **Goodloe** for 100 pds. 532 acres on Newlight creek on **Champion**'s line. at Sherwood **Winningham** line, **Bailey**'s line.
Wts: Sherwood **Winningham**.

292

411- Dec. 14, 1784. John **Huckaby** (**Huckabey**) of Wake Co., N.C. to William **Cook** of Granville Co., N. C, for 200 pds. land on E side of Long creek at mouth of Long branch along **Hunt**'s line, **Fuller**'s line, containing 200 acres in Granville Co, N.C.
Wts: John **Dunkin**, John **Parham**.

411, 412- Nov. 24, 1783- James **Veazey** to Joseph **Landess** for 15 pds. 135 acres on Ledge of Rocks creek on **Jones**'s line, **Beck**'s corner, and along **Beck**'s line along Thomas **Veazey**'s line.
Wts: James **Notgrass**, Joseph **Oakey**.

412- Nov. 1, 1785- John **Taylor**, Jr. to Howel **Lewis** for 700 pds., 735 acres on **Bennett**'s creek at [Groves] **Howard**'s, William **Person**'s, Michael **Jones**', Benjamin **Bass**' lines which is land willed to John **Taylor** by his father and upon which he now lives-

413- Oct. 8, 1785-. Elizabeth **Collins** and Edward **Collins** to James **Smith** for 300 pds. 365 acres whereon Elizabeth and Edward **Collins** now live at John **Penn**'s line at **Gooch**'s line, **Cocke**'s (**Cooke**'s) line, on **Read** wagon road, **Person**'s and **Davis**'s lines.
Wts: William **Byars**, Minnies **Mitchel**.

413, 414- Nov. 2, 1785- James **Daniel** to John **Thorp** for 279 pds. 555 acres on N. side of Tar river and Crooked Run adjoining **Person**'s line.
Wts: John **Washington**.

414- Jan. 29, 1785- Zachariah **Wilborn** to Jeremiah **Bullock** for 100 pds. 300 acres on Tar river at [William] **Webb**'s, **Bullock**'s lines, Bridge creek at **Wilborn**'s spring branch, **Moore**'s line.
Wts: R. D. **Cooke**, Edmd **Partee**.

414, 415- Mar. 28, 1785- John **Hunt** and wife Frankey to John **Pomfrett** for 212 pds. 212 acres on Jonathan's creek on **Palmer**'s line, **Aplin**'s line, **Royster**'s line-
Wts: George **Hunt**, Samuel **Crafton**, Peter **Bennett**.

415- Nov. 13, 1784- Judith **Hifiel** (**Highfil**) to Hezekiah **Hifiel** for 20 pds. 130 acres at Samuel **Fuller**'s line.
Wts: William **Floyd**, John **Lawrence**.

416- Aug. 3, 1784- William **Allen** to James **Downey**, Jr. for 50 pds. 65 acres on Grassy creek on side of Courthouse road, along **Malone**'s, **Lander**'s lines.

Wts: Anderson **Hunt**, John **Downey**.

416- Nov. 1, 1785- George **Norman** to Henry **Graves** for 80 pds. 116½ acres on Lick branch at Lattaney **Montague**'s line along Henry **Graves**' line, being the plantation whereon **Graves** now lives.
Wts: Lewis **Yancey**, Ralph **Graves**.

417- Nov. 1, 1785- Lewis **Yancey** to George **Norman** for 200 pds. 227 acres on Lovat **Gates**' line on Lick Branch at Henry **Graves**' line which is the land given me by my father-in-law in Granville Co.
Wts: Ralph **Graves**, Henry **Graves** (signed by Lewis and Mary **Yancey**.

417- Oct. 1, 1785- William **Hart** to Reuben **Jones** for 20 pds. 230 acres in **Pool**'s line, on both sides of the north fork of **Aaron**'s creek with understanding that 10 acres has been deeded to Seth **Pettypool** out of this.
Wts: Thomas **Mutter**, Thornton **Yancey**.

418- Aug. 3, 1784- Nathaniel **Malone** of Caswell Co., N.C. to James **Downey**, Jr. of Granville Co., N.C. for 150 pds. 232 acres on both sides of Mountain creek at **Crenshaw**'s line.
Wts: Anderson **Hunt**, John **Downey**, David **Smith**.

418, 419- Apr. 9, 1785- Henry **Williams** to Thomas **Barnett** for 100 pds. 133 acres on N. side of Indian fork of Island creek at Jesse **Barnett**'s line, at John **Barnett**'s and John **Penn**'s lines.
Wts: Jesse **Barnett**, John **Barnett**.

419- Nov. 5, 1785- Robert **Wilson** to John **Huddleston** for 50 pds. 100 acres on John **Peace**'s line, at James **Jenkins**' line, Harris **Gilliam**'s line
Wts: John **Welch**, Sr., John **Welch**, Jr.

419, 420- Mar. 28, 1785- William **Ogilvie** to Claiborn **Harris** for 100 pds. 120 acres on both sides of Paul's creek, at Samuel **Harris**'s line, **Potter**'s line, David **Harris**'s line, **Freeman**'s corner.
Wts: William **Jacobs**, Patty **Ogilvie**.

293

420- Nov. 71785- David **Mitchel** to Robert **Burton** for 250 pds. 250 S acres on fork of branch below **Burton**'s Tan Yard crossing Hico road about 700 yards above **Mitchel**'s dwelling house, to Buffalow creek on Christmas **Ray**'s line-
Wts: None.

420- Nov. 7, 1785-Samuel **Morse** to Davis **Mitchel** for 50 pds. 50 acres on side of Christmas **Ray**'s spring branch on Buffalow creek at **Mitchel**'s and **Burton**'s lines.
Wts: Thos. **Satterwhite**, Thos **Rice**, R. **Atkins**.

421- Jan. 11, 1786- Samuel **Mors** to Robert **Burton** for 166 pds. 100 acres on NW side of Flat creek to Buffalow branch, along lines of Robert **Burton** and John **Williams**'.
Wts: Thos. **Satterwhite**, Jesse **Rice**.

422- Feb. 3, 1786- John **Hawkins** and wife Sally to Robert **Allison**, Sr. and his son John **Allison** for 170 pds., 609 acres on both sides of **Bowling's** creek at **Hargrove**'s, **Taylor**'s, **Upchurch**, **Walker**'s, **Lindsey** lines.
Wts: J. **Potter**, Henry **Potter**.

422, 423- July 27, 1785- George **Lanemoore** to Bennitt **Phillips** for 80 pds. 212 acres on Nap of Reeds creek on W side of Trading path.
Wts: Jeremiah **Bullock**, William **Green**.

423- Dec. 24, 1785- William **Chavers** gave to his daughter Sarah, wife of Edward **Harris**, 340 acres on Tabbs creek in Granville Co., N. C. and Sarah departed this life in January last past leaving sons, Gibson, Sherwood, Jesse and Solomon **Harris** who inherited the land.
Sherwood **Harris** herein, deeds his share to John **Penn** for 50 pds.
Wts: John **Jordan**, Hamblen **Jordan**, James **Gordan**.[sic]

423, 424- Aug. 17, 1785- Robert **Wilson** to James **Jenkins**, for 100 pds. 169 acres at **Bass**'s old line, to **Banks**' old school path at Abe **Mayfield**'s and John **Peace**'s lines on **Huddleston**'s corner.
Wts: J. **Peace**, Jr., Abe **Mayfield**.

424- Jan. 8, 1785- Joseph **Hester** to William **Palmer** for 130 pds. 229 acres on Jonathan's creek at **Palmer**'s line.
Wts: Luke **Landers**, James Key **Daniel**.

424- May 16, 1785- John **Hight** of Franklin Co., N.C. to John **Hunt** for 20 pds. 20 acres on Buffalow creek on Thomas **Smith**'s line, **Hunt**'s line, **Hunter**'s and Joseph **McDaniel**'s lines.
Wts: Thomas **Smith**, Samuel **Hunt**.

425- Feb, 7, 1786- David **Harris** to John **Tippet** for 50 pds. 125 acres on Tar river on **Allison**'s, **Holstein**'s, **Person**'s lines.
Wts: none.

425- Feb. 7, 1785- Kannon **Cooper** to Joseph **Mangum** of Warren Co., N.C. for 20 pds. part of land granted to **Cooper** on **Martin**'s creek and Sandy creek in 1779 containing 50 acres on the county line at **Cooper**'s line, at **Christmas**'s line, **Mangum**'s line.
Wts: Jonathan **Johnston**, John **Gilliam**.

426- Aug. 17, 1785- Abe **Mayfield** to Robert **Wilson** for 100 pds. 360 acres on Tar river to **Bank**'s old school path at line between John **Peace** and **Mayfield** lands, on **Welch**'s, **Gilliam**'s lines.
Wts: J. **Peace**, Jr., James **Jenkins**.

426- Nov, 26, 1785- Bartholomew **Stovall** to Drury **Stovall** for 5 shls. all my right and title by [omition] in my father's will of all lands believing he meant my brother Drury **Stovall** to have it being the 300 acres willed to my mother for life then to Drury, my brother, whereon. (they live).
Wts: Lewis **Yancey**, Joseph **Hart**.

427- Feb, 6, 1786- Henry **Graves** to Mary **Hester** for 60 pds. 200 acres on lines of Thomas **Williamson**, William **Graves**', **Taylor**'s, **Long**'s, my own line and William **Graves**'s line.
Wts: Ralph **Graves**, Mary **Graves**.

428- May 3, 1785- James **Paschal** to Ashkenas **Williams** for 100 pds. 75 acres at Silas **Paschal**'s line, William **Guthrie**'s to Little Deep creek to James **Paschal**'s spring branch, Ashkenas **Williams**'s line.
Wts: Silas **Paschal**, Archelias **Williams**.

294

428- Feb. 7, 1785- William **Kennon** and wife Elizabeth to Anthony **Lumpkin** (Elizabeth, wife of **Kennon**, is referred to as 'Mary' except in beginning) for 300 pds. 300 acres at **Person**'s corner, near the new road near **Ring**'s old field.
Wts: Joseph **Taylor**.

428, 429- Feb. 7, 1785- William **Kennon** and wife Mary to Reuben **Butler** of King William Co., Va. for 150 pds. 306 acres on **Person**'s line near **Ring**'s old field on **Lumpkin**'s line.
Wts: Joseph **Taylor**.

429, 430- Nov. 23, 1785- Edward **Harris** to Elijah **Ball** of Warren Co., N.C. for 50 pds. 50 acres on Tabbs creek at **Smith**'s branch on John **Penn**'s line.
Wts: Solomon **Thornton**, Osborn **Crabb**, Danl **Ball**.

430- Nov. 10, 1782- Edmund **Partee** from George Thompson **Evans** for 100 pds. 200 acres at **Veazey**'s, **Benet**'s lines, on road that leads from **Newby**'s Folly to Flat river, at **Manin**'s line.
Wts: Benja **Partee**, Mary **Hooker**.

430, 431- Aug. 15, 1785- Edmund **Partee** to Charles **Partee** for 250 pds. 600 acres at **Webb**'s corner to dividing line and bounds of land of Chas. and Edmund **Partee**

Wts: Benja. **Partee**, Jean **Partee**.

431- Dec. 21, 1784- Bartlett **Tyler** to Edmund **Taylor** for 16 pds. 578 acres on Fishing creek which was deeded to **Tyler** Oct. 15, 1783.
Wts: Lewis **Taylor**, John **Gooing**.

431 432- July 23, 1784- John **Moseley** gave to his son Samuel **Mosely** 200 acres whereon I live at [Betty **Ford**]'s line, on Buckhorn creek.
Wts: John Wm. **Cape**, Wm. **Hefflin**.

432- May 6, 1785- John **Harp** to Thomas **Harp** for 32 pds. 10 shillings 150 acres at **Williamson**'s corner, along John **Harp**'s line, along **Finch**'s and **Lemon**'s lines to the county line to the first branch.
Wts: Thomas **Harp**, Jr., Sampson **Harp**.

432- Jan. 18, 1786- Sherwood **Winningham** to Stephen **Turner** for 20 pds. 300 acres on Newlight creek which is part of 640 acres granted by Gov. Alexa **Martin** to **Winningham** Oct. 15, 1783.
Wts: John **Pope**, William **Turner**.

433- Aug. 25, 1784- Edmund **Partee** to Charles **Partee** for 100 pds. 200 acres on Nap of Reeds creek at **Veazey**'s corner, Wm. **Benet**'s line, of his old deeded land on road that leads from **Newby**'s Folly to Flatt river at **Mannin**'s old line.
Wts: John **Trustee**, Benja **Partee**.

433, 434- . . 1786- Elisha **Linsey** to Mary **Guist**, Elizabeth **Linsey**, Ann, Phebe **Linsey** and Sarah **Linsey** his sisters, for 50 pds. 157 acres on both sides of **Bolling**'s creek on the road and at his line, reserving to his mother Sarah **Linsey** for her lifetime then to his five sisters: Mary **Guest**, Elizabeth, Anne, Phebe and Sarah **Linsey**.

434- Jan. 26, 1786- Solomon **Robinson** to Edward **Rowel** of Northampton Co., N.C. for 40 pds. 100 acres which was granted to **Robinson** on Sandy creek, on **Eaton**'s line, to **Hawkins**' line, Thomas **Reeves**' line.
Wts: Joseph **Mangum**, William **Bobbitt**.

434, 435- Jan. 12, 1786- James **McLemore** to Ralph **Williams** for 50 pds. land on Edge of Rocks creek, 193 acres at **Bullock**'s and **Wade**'s (**Waid**'s) lines
Wts: Thomas **Hearne**, John **McLemore**.

435, 436 Mar. 9, 1778- Robert **Hicks** to Robert **Hester** for 50 pds. 57 acres on N. side of **Hicks** Quarter Road, on **Hill**'s corner, **Reeves**' old line.
Wts: Benjamin **Hester**, Robert **Hicks**, Jr.

436- Jan. 2, 1779- Benjamin **Partee** to Charles **Partee** for 500 pds. 300 acres on **Hampton**'s creek.
Wts: Edmd. **Partee**.

436, 437- Mar. 2, 1785-Johnmoore **Adams** of Chatham Co., N.C. to Sherwood **Parrish** of Granville Co, for 25 pds. 70 acres on Fishing creek at **Cooper**'s and **Snelling**'s lines.
Wts: Jesse **Parrish**, Mary **Parrish**.

295

437- Dec. 3, 1785-John Williams **Daniel** to Thomas **Paschal** of Warren Co., N.C. for 60 pds. 178 acres on Deep creek at the county line.
Wts: Jonathan **Graves**, Zadock **Daniel**.

436- Sept. 17, 1785- Dozer **Thornton** of Wilks Co., Georgia to Wagstaff **Kanady** for 40 pds. land in Granville Co., N.C. on Little Beaverdam creek on county line containing 440 acres.
Wts: Thos **Paschal**, Thos **Thornton**, John **White**.

438- Jan. 26, 1786- John **Sutton** to William **Williams** for 40 pds. 200 acres on Fort creek at **Jones**'s line, **Hix**'s line, **Heffernon**'s line.

Wts: James **Jenkins**, John **Rust**.

439- May 2, 1786- William **Hunt**, Esq. sheriff of Granville Co., N.C. by order of court, sold 120 acres belonging to William **Thomas** , for debt at suit brought by Philip **Voss**, and sold to Micajah **Bullock** as highest bidder-land on Tar river at **Noland**'s line.

439, 444- Apr. 24, 1786- William **Hunt**, sheriff, sold at public sale to highest bidder, the land of William **Thomas** at suit brought by Phillip **Voss** for debt, and Reuben **Searcy** was highest bidder for 100 acres at Giles **Hudspeth**'s line formerly now Thomas **Thomason**'s line at **Morris** and **Searcy** lines.

440- 441- Aug. 3, 1784- John **Wadkins** to Thomas **Kelly** for 100 pds. 125 acres on Henry **Freeman**'s line, at the Virginia line, **Fleeman**'s line.
Wts: Dennis **Paschal**, Benjamin **Kelly**, Sherwood **Sims**, Jr.

441- Apr. 1, 1786- William **Stovall** to Joseph **Chandler** for 50 pds. 50 acres on Jonathan's creek at lines of land of Larkin **Johnston** and William **Cleaborn**.
Wts: Peter **Bennett**.

441, 442- Dec. 21, 1785- James **Dyar** to William **Hunt** for 180 pds., 271 acres on Nap of Reeds creek at **Bailey**'s, at William **Hunt**'s line whereon James **Dyer** now lives.
Wts: James **Fleming**, James **Critcher**.

442- Mar. 14, 1786- Thomas **Banks** and wife Susanna of Georgia, to Alexander **Carter** of Granville Co., N.C. for 116 pds. 4 shls. 292 acres granted to Wm. **Champion** by the State and to Thomas **Banks** by the State, being part of two larger tracts, on both sides of Mirey branch and Raccoon branch on S side of Tar river at lines of land of Thomas **Banks**, Alexander **Carter**, Volentine **Mayfield** to Lewis **Taylor**'s at Wm. **White**'s, James **Jenkins**.
Wts: James **Jenkins**, John **Pettycobb**, Wm. **Priddy**.

443- Mar. 8, 1786- Absalom **Pryor** to William **Glass** for 320 pds. 640 acres which was granted to John **Pryor** deceased, by Lord Granville.
Wts: Thomas **Owen**, John **Webb**, Thos. **Owen**, Jr.

443, 444- Apr. 29, 1786- Henry **Green** to Jacob **Ferrebow** for 80 pds. 136 acres on Ralph **Williams** line, to Edward **Jones**'s line, **Moore**'s line.
Wts: Edward **Jones**, Mary **Walker**.

444- May 2, 1786- Richard **Wilkins** to John **Keeling** for 5 shls, 80 acres on Fishing creek in **Walker**'s line, John **Hudspeth**'s line-

444, 445- May 1, 1786- Groves **Howard** to Allen **Howard** for 150 pds. 200 acres on **Taylor**'s line at Hare's branch at **Howard**'s line on **Bennett**'s creek.
Wts: Grant **Allen**, Thos. **Berry**.

445- May 1, 1786- Joseph **Gooch** to Amos **Gooh** for 500 pds. 297 acres on S side of Tar river on **Penn**'s line.
Wts: Amos **Penn**, Daniel **Gooch**.

445, 446- Apr. 29, 1786- James **Custard** to Jacob **Ferrebow** for 20 pds. 20 acres in Ralph **Williams**' line, on Ledge of Rocks creek at Henry **Green**'s line.
Wts: Ralph **Williams**, William **Green**.

446- . . 1786- Amos **Sims** to Joseph **Gooch** for 40 pds., 47.acres.
Wts: Daniel **Gooch**, Amos **Gooch**.

446, 447- May 2, 1786- Richard **Wilkins** to John **Brodie** for 130 pds. 84 acres on Tabbs creek, on **Thompson**'s line.
Wts: None.

447- Nov. 16, 1785- Hazlewood **Wilkerson** to Thomas **Lemay** for 130 pds. 275 acres at **Daniel**'s' corner, **Beasley**'s line, **Downey**'s line.
Wts: Luke **Landers**, Lewis **Lemay**, Saml **Peace**.

447, 448- Mar. 2, 1786- Christopher **Harris** to Robert **Goodloe** for 100 pds. 150 acres at a branch in **Champion**'s corner.
Wts: Nathan **Jackson**, Mark **Lilas**.

448- Feb. 7, 1786- Robert **Wilson** to Surrel **White** for 50 pds. 100 acres on Tar river near **Lunsford**'s Fish traps.
Wts: William **Williams**, James **Jenkins**.

448, 449- Nov. 20, 1785- Harmon **Bayley** and wife Mary to John **Eastridge** for 100 pds. 137 acres on **Davis**'s line, **McCulloh**'s line, **Thornton**'s line.
Wts: William **Bayley**, Thos. **Jenkins**.

449- July 11, 1786- George **Malone** and wife Martha to James **Bedford** of Powhatan Co., VA. for 228 acres on Jonathan's creek on William **Royster**'s line to William **Bailey**'s line to Josiah **Daniel**'s' line, William **Palmer**'s line for 225 pds.-
Wts: John **Pomfrett**, John **Blackwell**, Robert **Coleman**.

450- Aug. 9, 1786- William **Hunt** sheriff of Granville Co. sold at public vendue, the property of Robert **Reid** and Co. which was a tract of land near St George Chappel at Capt. Sherwood **Harris**'s line containing 125 acres- sold to Joseph **Taylor**.

451- Sheriff **Hunt** sold at public sale the land of William **Thomas**, to Edmund **Taylor**, 40 acres in Granville Co.

451, 452- Aug. 9, 1786- Sheriff William **Hunt** sold land of Thomas **Pool** and Abraham **Hester** at public sale, at court order to make money due and owed by them. . . 255 acres on Grassy creek at **Hunt**'s, **Pittard**'s and Gideon **Crenshaw**'s lines, sold to Samuel **Pittard**.

452, 453- Sheriff William **Hunt** sold, by court order, a tract of land belonging to Duncan **Campbell** and Memucan **Hunt** was highest bidder. . Aug. 9, 1786, 100 acres at Bressie **Parrish**'s line.

453- July 22, 1786- Edmund **Taylor**, Sr. to Rowland **Bryant** for 35 pds. 565 acres on Fishing creek for which Bartlet **Tyler** had grant Oct. 15, 1783 excepting 3 acres taken out by **Taylor** for a mill.

453, 454- Aug. 8, 1786- William **Kelly** of Wake Co., N.C. to Richard **Wilkins** for 200 pds., 400 acres in Granville Co. on Wake county line.
Wts: none.

454- May 2, 1786- John **Kennon** to Vinkler **Jones** for 350 pds. 611 acres on **Mitchel**'s and **Lyne**'s lines on the creek.
Wts: Howel **Lewis**, Jr., Lewis **Ackman**.

454, 455- Feb. 22, 1786- Hannah **Wright**, administratix for Susannah **Wright**, William **Wright** of Nash Co., John **Wright** of Halifax Co., Benjamin **Wright** of Franklin Co., N.C. all heirs of Susanna **Wright**, deceased, to John **Pope** for 200 pds. 300 acres on Cedar creek at Peter **Vinson**'s line, on **Bradford**'s line which is part of a larger tract formerly the property of Winfield **Wright** deceased, and by him willed to Susanna **Wright**, now deceased, and we as heirs convey our shares to John **Pope**.
Wts: John **Pope**, Jr., George **Nicholson**, Richd. **Whitaker**, Jr.

455- Aug. 7, 1786- Arthur **Jordan** to Marcellus **Jordan** for 200 pds. 369 acres at Philemon **Hawkins**' line, **Glover**'s line.
Wts Phil **Hawkins**, Jr., David **King**.

455, 456- Aug. 23, 1783- Claiborn **Harris** to Samuel **Kittrell** for 200 pds. 150 acres on Little Ruin Creek.
Wts: Dan **Hunter**, William **Rogers**.

456- Mar. 13, 1786- Richard **Clopton** to Sherwood **Harris** (**Clopton** of Franklin Co., N.C.) for 55 pds. 70 acres on old Ridge Path at Charles **Moore**'s corner, **Harden**'s line to Tabbs creek, Edward **Harris**'s line.
Wts: Thomas **White**, William **Robertson**.

456- Aug 2, 1785- Brereton **Jones** to James **Hawkins** 50 acres for 12 pds. 10 shillings, at line between **Claxton** and **Cooke**'s lands.
Wts: R. D. **Cooke**, Joel **Chambliss**.

457- May 5, 1786- Thornton **Yancey** to Sterling **Yancey** for 200 pds. 342½ acres on county line at Phillip **Mealor**'s and Charles **Wade**'s lines.
Wts: Thornton **Yancey**, Jr., William **Yancey**.

297[no page number on pages 458-461]
458- Mar. 25, 1786- William **Cooper** of Wake Co., N.C. to Harris **Gilliam** of Granville Co., N.C. for 100 pds., 100 acres on Ridges Path at **Welch** and **Peace**'s lines, on John **Peace**'s, **Dickerson**'s line, on **Mockley** branch.
Wts: J. **Peace**, Jr., Sarah **Peace**.

458- May 5, 1786- Stephen **Merritt** to John **Washington** for 247 pds. 267 acres on both sides of Cub creek at John **Washington**'s corner, **Merritt**'s line.
Wts: John **Thorp**, John **Cragg**.

459- Sept. 15, 1781- Isaac **Loyd** to William **Loyd** for 12 pds. 100 acres on Ruin creek, at Roland **Bryant**'s corner.
Wts: Mark **White**, Thomas **White**.

459- Aug. 17, 1785- John **Finch** to Thomas **White** for 100 pds. 185 acres on **Collins**' creek in **York**'s line, Edward **Harris**'s line, to **Jones**' and **Seawell**'s line, **Moore**'s line.
Wts: Z. **Higgs**, Mark **White**
there are pages here numbered the same- -462- - incomplete[6]

[459-460]-- Aug. court 1786- Micajah **Bullock** to John **Minor** for 500 pds. 120 acres on N. side of Tar river on **Harris**'s, **Minor**s's lines.
Wts: Thomas **Owen**, Saml **Harris**.

[460]- Feb. 20, 1786- Richard **Bradford** to John **Moore** for 16 pds. 100 acres on Beaverdam creek.
Wts: [Phil.] **Bradford**, Bird Booker **Bradford**.

[460-461] - June 23, 1786- Chas. **Turner** to Thomas **Bonner** Jr. 209 acres on Nap of Reeds creek at **McCulloh**'s line.
Wts: Joseph **Ellis**, William **Tatum**.

[461] - Jan. 30, 1786- Edward **Rowell** of Northampton Co., N.C., to Samuel **Kittrell** of Granville Co. for 15 pds. 100 acres on Sandy creek, at **Eaton**'s line.
Wts: Wiley **Kittrell**, David **Clopton**.

461-[462] . . 1786- John **Dunkin**, Jr. to Leonard **Clark** for 115 pds. 150 acres on Tabbs creek at **Parham**'s line, **Hays**' line.
Wts: Z. **Higgs**, Charles R. **Eaton**.

462- Dec. 9, 1785- William **Upchurch** to Samuel **Jones** for 30 pds. 200 acres on Buckhorn creek on **Hall**'s, **Bledsoe**'s, **Bailey**'s lines.
Wts: Wm. **Cawthon**, Wm. **Petteford**.

462, 463- Feb. 5, 1786- William **Hornsby**, school master, to William **Floyd**, wheelwright, for 50 pds. 130 acres at Hezekiah **Highfiel**'s line, **Floyd**'s, Henry **Fuller**'s line.

---

[6] Page numbers are missing on the pages. [s] fill in corrections.

Wts: Zacharias **Higgs**, Joshua **Hutchenson**.

463- Feb. 10, 1786- Joseph **Rogers** to Joseph **McDaniel** for 20 pds. 50 acre at Noel **Johnston**'s, and **Hays**' lines on Ruin creek.
Wts: William **Rogers**, Joseph **McDaniel**.

463, 464- Dec. 5, 1785- Thomas **York** to Leonard **Higgs** for 40 pds. 100 acre on Ruin creek at Leonard **Higgs** line, **White**'s, **Spears**', **Fuller**'s, **Floyd**'s and **Rogers**' lines- -
Wts: Z. **Higgs**.

464- Nov. 25, 1785- Edward **Harris** to Solomon **Thornton** for 40 pds. 60 acres on S side of Tabbs creek.
Wts: William **Mills**, William **Dickerson**.

464, 465- Oct. 7, 1785- Frederick **Rose** to Howel **Mangum** for 60 pds. 150 acres on Nap of Reeds creek at mouth of Hurricane creek branch, **McCulloh**'s line, Zachariah **Wilborn**'s line.
Wts: John **Manire**, Zach **Wilborn**, Jemima **Wilborn**.

465- July 8, 1786- Edward **Moore** of Montgomery Co., N.C. to John **Mitchel** of Caswell Co., N.C. for 800 pds. 385 acres in Granville Co. on both sides of Mill creek, a branch of Tar river, at Wm. **Crag**'s line,
Signed Edward **Moore**, by Demcey **Moore**-
Wts: R. **Dickens**.

465, 466- May 28, 1786- Drury **Stovall** to William **Heggie** for 110 pds. 220 acres on S side of Jonathan's creek, which was purchased of Benjamin **Stovall** at John **Stovall**'s corner, on Horseshoe road.
Wts: Lewis **Yancey**, William **Owen**.

298

466- Oct. 14, 1786- Daniel **Scott** to Joseph **Decker** for 40 pds. 150 acres at Lewis **Taylor**'s line, William **Bullock**'s line-
Wts: Robt. **Glover**, Daniel **Glover**.

466, 467- Sept. 13, 1786- Richard **Searcy** to Robert **Burton** for 103 pds. 206 acres on **Bolling**'s creek.
Wts: John **Keeling**, Hezekiah **Glover**.

467- Mar. 15, 1786- William **Burford** of Wilks County, Georgia to Wiat **Wilkerson** of Granville Co., N.C. for 150 pds. 232 acres on N. side of Nuse river below mouth of Nap of Reeds creek.
signed William **Burford** by Solomon **Burford**.
Wts: Thomas **Clement**, Caleb **Brasfield**.

467, 468- Apr. 1, 1786- Robert **Harris** to Thomas **Wilkerson** for 50 pds. 100 acres on Cedar creek.
Wts: Reuben **Searcy**, J. **Potter**.

468- Mar. 25, 1786- John **Smith**, Jr. to John **Duncan**, Jr., merchant, for 20 pds. 79 acres at **Hayes**' field, to **Parham**'s line (**Duncan** spelled **Dunkin**).
Wts: Z. **Higgs**, John **Higgs**.

468- Oct. 11, 1786- Thomas **Grant** of Wilks Co., Georgia to Col. John **Dickerson** of Granville Co., N.C. for 15 pds. 70 acres on waters of Little creek on **Dickerson**'s line.
Wts: Jas. **Baze**, Wm. **Easter**.

469- Oct. 13, 1786- Samuel **Pittard** to John **Hart** for 75 acres, 255 acres on Grassy creek whereon Abraham **Hester** now lives on **Hunt**'s, **Pittard**'s, and Gideon **Crenshaw**'s line.
Wts: Larkin **Johnston**, Abraham **Hester**, Theodorick **Johnston**.

469- Dec. 17, 1785- John **Harp** to Thomas **York** of Warren Co., N.C, for 30 pds. 100 acres on my own line and along **Harp**'s line, **Right**'s and **Finches**' lines.
Wts: Samson **Harp**, Philemon **York**.

470- Jan. 4, 1786- John **Bristow** to Jonathan **Kittrell**, Jr. for 75 pds. 153 acres on Little Ruin Creek at Elias **Guess**'s line-.
Wts: John **Higgs**, William **Johnston**.

470- Jan. 5, 1785- Frederick **Beck** to Michael **Beck** for 5 pds. 50 acres on E side of Ledge of Rocks creek, part of land whereon Frederick **Beck** now lives on **Farmer**'s Spring-
Wts: Ephraim **Emry**, Ben **Clark**.

471- Nov. 25, 1784- James **Veazey** to William **Jones**., Sr. for 50 pds. 50 acres on Nap of Reeds creek at William **Jones**'s line, George **Alston**'s line.
Wts: George **Wright**, Howard **Cash**, Thos **Veazey**.

471- Nov. 4, 1786- John **Knott** to Jacob **Brazelton** for 150 pds. 225 acres on Nap of Reeds creek at Frederick **Ross**'s line, Robert **Dickens'** line.
Wts: John **Knott**.

472- Nov. 8, 1786- William **Fleming** to William **Weaver** for 25 pds. 50 acres at Merryman **Thorn**'s line-
Wts: Frederick **Wiggins**, Edmund **Weaver**.

472- Jan. 16, 1784- Hugh **Snelling** to Samuel **Jones** for 50 pds., 50 acres on John **Finch**'s line, **Harris**'s line.
Wts: Solomon **Thornton**, Bartlet **Tyler**.

472, 473- Oct. 14, 1786- Thomas **Grant** of Wilks county, Georgia to Col. John **Dickerson** of Granville Co., N.C. for 15 pds. 70 acres on Tabbs creek at **Walker**'s and **Fuller**'s lines.
Wts: Jas. **Baer** (**Barr**), William **Easter**.

473- Nov. 7, 1786- John **Wilkerson** to Robert **Jordan** of Halifax Co., Va. for 150 pds. 698 acres on Grassy creek at **Pryor**'s line, **Simmon**'s line, **Owen**'s and **Edwards'** lines, Davis **Wilkerson**'s corner, John **Wilkerson**'s line in Granville Co.
Wts: Samuel **Pointer**, Thomas **Owen**.

473, 474- Aug. 16, 1786- Stephen **Ragland** of Wilks Co., Georgia to Thomas **Wiggins** of Granville Co, N.C. for [blank], 405 acres in Granville Co. at **Harrison**'s line on Indian creek, at James **Stark**'s, Bartholomew **Kimball**'s, Thomas **Rowland**'s, Edward **Weaver**'s, Charnick **Cox**'s lines.
Wts: James **Currin**, Jesse **Newby**.

474- Feb. 2, 1786- Robert **Malone** to William **Elixon** for 100 pds. 100 acres.

299
at lines of land of James **Mitchel**, **Gill**'s, at line between me and Patrick **Stewart** and lying on NE side of **Aaron**'s creek.
Wts: Thos **Pool**, Josiah **Mitchell**.

475- Aug. 1786- Joseph **Manghum** to Charles **Partee** for 10 pds. 100 acres at George Thomson **Evans** corner, **Mannin**'s line, **Manghum**'s line.
Wts: John **Maniers**, Robert **Reid**.

475- Nov. 23, 1785- Joseph **Langston** to Thomas **Goss** for 40 pds. 160 acres on Tar river, on Mountain and **Merritt**'s creek on **Merritt**'s line.
Wts: Stephen **Merritt**, Mary **Merritt**.

476- Sept. 24, 1785- Jarett **Landey** to Abraham **Lawrence** 250 acres on Lick Branch at **McCulloh**'s line. signed Jarrett **Sandey**.
Wts: William **Lawrence**, James **Patron**.

476- Jan. 5, 1785- Frederick **Beck** to Michael **Beck** for 10 pds. 200 acres on Ledge of Rocks creek at **Beck**'s line.
Wts: Ephraim **Emry**, Ben **Clark**.

477- Aug. 26, 1786- Mary **Harrison** to Joseph **Chandler** for 100 pds. 180 acres on **Aaron**'s creek on **Chandler**'s line, to the road.
Wts: James **Chandler**, Robert **Bevill**.

477- May 20, 1785- Thomas **Harp** to Thomas **York** of Warren Co., N.C. for 53 pds. 13 shls. 4 pence, 150 acres on **Williamson**'s corner, along John **Harp**'s line, to **Finch**'s line to the county line at dividing line between John and Thomas **Harp**.
Wts: Joseph **Mangum**, Kennon **Cooper**.

478- Oct. 29, 1785- Edmund **Taylor**, Sr. and Edmund **Taylor**, Jr. from Bartle **Tyler** for 60 pds. 325 acres whereon **Tyler** now lives lying between the lines of Col. **Dickerson**, Hugh **Snelling**, Sherwood **Parrish**, Fishing creek and Tar river.
Wts: William **Dickerson**, Solomon **Whitlar**.

478- Oct. 20, 1786- Ralph **Williams** to Jacob **Ferebow** for 5 pds. 9 acres on Ledge of Rocks creek, at Ralph **Williams**'s line.
Wts: Micajah **Bullock**, Edmund **Carns**.

478, 479- Oct. 3, 1786- Ambrose **Barker** to Thomas **Rice** for 220 pds. 225 acres on Tabb, Fishing and Nutbush creeks at **Currin**'s corner near his sho[p] thence to **Person**'s line and to **Bullock**'s line-
Wts: Sterling **Yancey**, Vincent **Rice**.

479- Nov. 4, 1786- John **Gomer** to Daniel **Scott** for 40 pds. 166 acres on Island creek at the county line.
Wts: Joseph **Duke**, Robt. **Smith**.

480- Feb. 7, 1786- Henry **Langford** to John **Dunkin** for 50 pds., 173 acres on Ruin creek at John **Parham**'s line, to **Bristow**'s line.
Wts: Z. **Higgs**, Ioshun **Hutchinson** (Joshua **Hutchinson**).

480- Nov. 7, 1786- Thomas **Hammock** and Maryann **Hammock** of Pittsylvania Co., Va. to Howel **Lewis**, Jr. for 50 pds. 200 acres at George **King**'s line along **Parker**'s and **Hill**'s lines in Granville Co., N. C.
Wts: None-

481- Jan. 31, 1786- Phillip **Lewis** to Jacob **Slaughter** for 200 pds. 320 acres on both sides of **Shelton**'s creek adjoining land of Thomas **Person** on Jacob **Slaughter**'s corner.
Wts: Wm. **Gill**, Jacob **Slaughter**.

481, 482- Nov. 11, 1785- William **Burford**, Jr. to John **Tatom** for 200 pds. 200 acres on both sides of Ledge of Rocks creek, at Frederick **Beck**'s line and a second tract adjoining his own and John **Beck**'s line containing 285 acres, and a third tract at **Waller**'s corner on **McCulloh**'s line on Little Ledge of Rocks creek at **Beck**'s and **Burford**'s lines containing 150 acres, and the 4th tract at **Byars**', **Burford**'s corners containing 37 acres- in the whole 672 acres-
Wts: George **Wright**, Benja **Wheler**, William **Tatom**.

482- Nov. 10, 1784- James **Veazey**, Jr. to Micajah **Bullock** for 200 pds. 640 acres on Nap of Reeds creek, in **McCulloh**'s line, **Dyar**'s line, **Callier**'s line and to the county line.
Wts: Ralph **Williams**, R. D. **Cooke**.

300

482, 483- Nov. 18, 1784- James **Veazey**, Jr. to Micajah **Bullock** for 150 pds. 457 acres on Cedar creek at **Waller**'s corner, **Brazelton**'s corner, on **McCulloh**'s line, **Peak**'s and William **Burford**'s lines.
Wts: Ralph **Williams**, R. D. **Cooke**.

483- Nov. 18, 1784- James **Veazey**, Jr. to Micajah **Bullock** for 200 pds. 500 acres on Nap of Reeds creek at James **Veazey**'s line to county line.
Wts: Ralph **Williams**, R. D. **Cooke**.

484- Oct. 12, 1786- William **Glass** to [Ambrose] **Barker** for 600 pds. 640 acres on **Aaron**'s creek.

Wts: Nicholas **Talley**, James **Crews**.

483- Nov. 3, 1786- John **Owen**, Sr. to John **Owen**, Jr. his son, land on Grassy creek at a stump on **Owen**'s line containing 8½ acres.
Wts: Thomas **Grant**, Elisabeth **Owen**.

485- Grant from Henry **McCulloh** to George **Milnor** for 320 acres on the 100,000 granted to him, **McCulloh**, by the King of England-
signed by agents Alexa **McCulloh** and John **Campbell**.
George **Milnor** agrees to pay to Lord Granville the quit rents on this land bought of **McCulloh**.

486- Oct. 18, 1786- Caleb **Brasfield** to Anderson **Smith** for 100 pds. 350 acres on W side of Grassy creek being all land Caleb patented adjoining the land whereon his mother lives except 100 acres he sold to Mrs. **Oliver** whereon she now lives.

486, 487- Oct. 10, 1786- Elizabeth **Brasfield** to Anderson **Smith**-
Elizabeth, Caleb and George **Brasfield** sell to Anderson **Smith** for 200 pds. 262 acres on W side of Grassy creek at **Smith**'s line, being all land George **Brasfield**, deceased, bought of Mathew **Tanner**.
Wts: Samuel **Smith**, Sr. and, Jr.

477, 478- Aug. 17, 1785- Thomas **White** to John **Finch** for 50 pds. 225 acres on Tabbs creek, at **Thomason**'s line, **Walker**'s line, **Dickerson**'s line.
Wts: Z. **Higgs**, Mark **White**.

488- Jan. 19, 1787- Thomas **Thomason** and wife Anna to Hardy **Reeves** for 80 pds. 200 acres on Tabbs creek, at **Hicks**' corner, in **Reeves**' line, and James **Jett**'s corner.
Wts: John **Gilliam**, John **Parham**.

488- Feb. 15, 1787- James **Jett** to Joseph **Taylor** for 600 pds. 500 acres on both sides of Fishing creek at John **White**'s line, George **Harris**' line, Sarah **Arnold**'s corner and **Hamilton**'s line.
Wts: none.

489- Feb. 6, 1786- Hugh **Currin** to John **Brodie** for 100 pds. 136 acres on **Thompson**'s line.
Wts: Wm. **Hunt**.

489- Feb. 5, 1787- Thomas **Hicks** to Francis **Hester** for 10 pds. 100 acres on Fishing creek at corner of the *Folly Land*, in **Walker**'s line.
Wts: Robert **Hicks**, Jr., Zachariah **Hester**.

489, 490- Dec. 23, 1780- Isham **Mitchel** to James **Weathers** for 42 pds. 200 acres on side of Great Path on W fork of Fort creek, at mouth of Tarkiln branch.
Wts: John **Pope**, George **Nicholson**.

490- Aug. 13, 1784- Edmund **Taylor** the elder, gave to his son Edmund **Taylor** the younger, the land whereon Edmund, Jr. now lives which is the tract he bought of Thomas **Banks** and that Edmund **Taylor**, Sr. bought of John **Henderson** on S. side of Tar river and adjoining land he lives on with 3 small islands in the river being more convenient to him than the lands whereon I live- in all 1500 acres.
Wts: Robert **Johnson**, John **Taylor**.

490- Aug. 17, 1785- Mark **White** to John **Finch** for 50 pds. 100 acres on E side of Tabbs creek, in **Loyd**'s line along **White**'s line.
Wts: Z. **Higgs**, Thomas **White**.

491- July 27, 1785- Bennet **Phillips** to William **Jones**, Jr. for 100 pds. 100 acres on Nap of Reeds creeks-
Wts: William **Green**, Jeremiah **Bullock**.
signed Bennett **Phillips**, Mary **Moore**.

301

491- Feb. 3, 1787- Joel **Pope** of Caswell Co., N.C. to Thomas **Daniel** of Granville Co., N. C. for 100 pds. 200 acres on both sides of N. fork of **Aaron**'s creek at **Pryor**'s corner.
Wts: Gabriel **Davey**, Thos **Pool**.

492- Feb. 6, 1787- George **Elliott** of Northampton Co., N.C. to Ephraim **Frazier** for 100 pds. 75 acres known as **Ross**'s Mill Land, on N. side of Tar river, including 3 acres opposite the mill to mouth of **Drury**'s Mill run on **Frazier**'s Spring branch and N branch **of Shelton**'s creek.
Wts: M. **Satterwhite**.

492, 493- Mar. 7, 1785- John **Wilkerson** to Wm. **Bailey** for 50 pds. 186½ acres on Grassy creek being a half the land bought of Robert **Beasley** adjoining William **Royster**, Joseph **Hart**, George **Malone**, Josiah **Daniel**.
Wts: M. **Satterwhite**, David **Wilkerson**, Brereton **Jones**.

493- Dec. 1, 1786- Stephen **White** of Sulivan Co., to Joshua **Hays** of Granville Co., N.C. for 500 pds. 100 on **Parrish**'s and **Hays**' lines.
Wts: M. **Searcy**, Francis **Searcy**.

493- Jan. 9, 1787- Robert **Bevill** to Robert **Sandford** for 60 pds. 154½ acres on **Aaron**'s creek on **Chandler**'s and **Pool**'s lines.
Wts: Robert **Malone**, R. **Wade**- -
signed by Robert and Elizabeth **Bevill**.

404- Dec. 26;1786- William **Bowden** to John **Moss** for 60 pds., 120 acres on both sides of Crooked Run on Reuben **Moss**'s line, Thomas **Wiggins**' line to Rocky Branch along Samuel **Moss**'s line.
Signed William and Mary **Bowden**.
Wts: Reuben **Moss**, Edmund **Smith**, John **Mears**.

494, 495- Jan, 6, 1787- John **Tuggle** to Robert **Allison** for 24 pds. 60 acres on Tar river at David **Harris**'s line.

495- Sept. 26, 1786- James **Owen** to John **Taylor** for 53 pds. 6 shls. 8pc. 200 acres whereon Mrs. **Owen** now lives on Beaverdam, adjoining lands of Thos **Taylor**, Jacob **Mitchel**, Wm. **Owen** and Guy **Smith**.
Wts: Francis **Taylor**, Ann **Bullock**, William **Bullock**, John **Lewis**.

495- Dec. 12, 1784- Milleton **Earley** to John **Oliver** for 250 pds. 420 acres on Grassy creek along **Beasley**'s line, on S side of road on **Wilkerson**'s line to David **Smith**'s line at **Graves**' line, **Roberts**' line.
Wts: Luke **Landers**, Joseph **Hart**, Tyree or Jesse **Landers**, Wm. **Easley**.

496- Feb. 3, 1786- John **Dunkin**, Jr. to Henry **Langford** for 50 pds. 80 acres on W side of Tabbs creek to mouth of Spring branch and along **Smith**'s line, **Clark**'s line.
Wts: Z. **Higgs**, Joshua **Hutchinson**.

496- Dec. 23, 1786- William **Nailing** to William **Minor** for 40 pds. 100 acres on Middle creek on **Shepperd**'s line.
Wts: John **Massey**, Wm. **Cook**.

497- Dec. 26, 1786- Daniel **Hunter** to Joshua **Kittrell** for 300 pds. 661 acres on both sides of Long creek, a branch of Tabbs creek on **Hunter**'s corner, **McDaniel**'s corner at mouth of Mountain Branch which land was granted to Daniel **Hunter** by John **Searcy** and wife and by Wm. **Chavers**.
Wts: William **Hunt**, Isham **Kittrell**.

497- July 3, 1784- Robert **Harris**, Sr. to Kimbrough Tinsley **Ogelvie** for 500 pds. 200 acres at Sherwood **Harris**'s, **Alixon**'s, William **Hunt**'s, lines on Cedar branch.
Wts: Saml **Harris**, Smith **Ogelvie**.

498- Dec. 10, 1786- James **Harrison** of Ninety Six District, South Caroline to Isham **Harrison** of Granville Co., N.C. for 200 pds, 300 acres on both sides of Nutbush creek called Indian creek being the plantation that James **Harrison** bought of Phillip **Hawkins**, Sr. and bounded by Phillip **Hawkins**, Jr., James **Stark**. as per original grant of this land
Wts: Reuben **Daniel**, Anne **Harrison**.

498, 499- May, 9, 1787- John **Williams**, Bromfield **Ridley**, John **Summerville**, Howel **Lewis**, Sr., Thornton **Yancey**, Phil **Hawkins**, Jr., Robert **Coleman**, Samuel **Smith**, Commissioners of the town of Williamsborough, Granville Co., N.C. sold to Reuben **Searcy** for 6 pds. town *lot No. 56.*
Wts: Stephen **Sneed**.

302

409- Feb. 2 1787- John **Gomer** to Samuel **Smith** for 30 pds. 100 acres at dividing line between Daniel **Knott** and myself to the road-
Wts: Robert **Malone**, John **Gomer**, Sr.

499- . . 1787- Philemon **White** to William **Parham** for 50 pds. 106 acres on branches of **Bolling**'s creek, at line formerly **Alston**'s and Co. to Philemon **White**'s spring branch.
Wts: Reuben **Searcy**.

500- May 8, 1787- James **Smith** to Lewis **Amis** for 131 pounds, 131 acres on Grassy creek at **Hunt**'s corner on **Knight's** line on **Glaze**'s line.

500- Feb. 27, 1787- John **Barnett** to Thomas **Goldsmith** for 50 pds. 128 acres on **Harper**'s line.
Wts: William **Byars**, Elizabeth **Byars**.

501- Oct. 26, 1782- John **Pope**, Sr. to John **Pope**, Jr. for 5 shillings 153½ acres on W side of Cedar creek on **Bridges**' line.
Wts: Osborn **Pope**, Samuel **Pope**.

501- Jan. 31, 1787- Benja **Morgan** to John **Woodburn** of Franklin Co., N.C. for 500 pds. 350 acres on Beaverdam creek in Granville Co., N.C. on Philemon **Bradford**'s line, **McCulloh**'s old line, to Wm. **Parnal**'s corner.
Wts: Simon **Clement**, George **White**.

502- May 5, 1787- Thomas Wilmon **Culverhouse** to Jeremiah Culverhouse **Gilmore** for 5 pds. 150 acres at branch, dividing line between James **McLemores**' and Thomas Wilmon **Culverhouse**'s plantations and on Picture Branch-Year: 1940; Census Place: San Antonio, Bexar, Texas; Roll: m-t0627-04202; Page: 12A; Enumeration District: 259-58
Wts: James **McLemore**, Thomas **Bonner**, George **Wright**.

502- Feb. 4, 1786- Henry **Smith** to John **Dickerson** esq. for 10 pds. 50 acres on N. side of Little creek at **Haislip**'s corner, on **Barton**'s old line til it strikes Great Branch.
Wts: Joseph **Peace**, Jr., James **Barr**.

503- May 8- [registered 1787] John **Badgett** to his son William **Badgett**, a deed of gift of 150 acres on N. side of Tar river.
Wts: James **Forsyth**, Joseph **Hester**.

503- May 8, 1787- John **Badgett** gave to his son Peter **Badgett**, 150 acres on N. side of Tar river whereon Peter **Badgett** now dwells.
Wts: James **Forsythe**, Joseph **Hester**.

504- Nov. 10, 1785- James **Smith** to John **Williams** for 93 pds., 6 shls, 8 pence, 70 acres on W side of Fishing creek at line which formerly divided lands of Sherwood **Harris** and Isaac **Arnold** and along **Harris**'s line-
Wts: Solo. **Walker**, Augustine **Davis**.

504- Jan. 2, 1787- Sherwood **Harris** to John **Penn** for 50 pds. 70 acres on Tabbs creek which is land Sherwood **Harris** bought of Richard **Clapton**.
Wts: William **Byars**, Eliza **Taylor**.

505- Jan. 6, 1787- Thomas **White** to John **Penn** for 100 pds. 185 acres on both sides of Long Creek bounded by lands of Charles **Moore**, Thomas **York**, Baxter **Ragsdale** and **Penn**.
Wts: John **Higgs**, Thos **Hendrick**.

505- Feb. 21, 1787- Robert **Lewis**, Sr. of Goochland Co., VA, to Robert **Coleman** of Granville Co., N.C. for 300 pds., a half of a tract of land on S side of Tar river which said **Lewis** bought of Solomon **Alston** quantity not yet known, this tract adjoins Edmund **Taylor**, on Tar river.

Wts: William **Longmire**, Wiatt **Wilkerson**, Robert **Lewis**, Thos **Payne**, Elizabeth **Woodson**-

506- May 8, 1787- William **Hunt** to James **Bradey** for 30 pds. land at Robert **Reid**'s line on the old road.
Wts: Thos **Ligon**.

506- Apr. 23, 1787- William **Ellixon** to Patrick **Obrient** for 100 pds. 100 acres on N. side of **Aaron**'s creek at line between myself and Josiah **Mitchel** on **Gill**'s, **Owen**'s and the line between myself and Patrick **Obrient** along to **Duty**'s line.
Wts: Thomas **Pool**, Josiah **Mitchel**, John **Akin**.

507- Jan. 21, 1787- John **Tatom** to Benjamin **Whealer** for 100 pds. 340 acres on **Clark**'s and **McCulloh**'s lines, in **Tatom**'s corner.
Wts: William **Beck**, John C. **Beck**, John **Tatom**.

303

507, 508- Dec. 17, 17-2- Solomon **Walker** to Robert **Burton** for 210 pds. 310 acres on Lick Branch bounded by the lands of Vinkler **Jones**, William **Glover** and others, being land bought of Joseph **Davenport** and wife Aug. 19, 1769 and another tract deeded to **Walker** by William **Gober** Aug. 10, 1782. (Amey, wife of Solomon **Walker** releases right in land).
Wts: A. **Robison**, John **Keeling**, Jas **Burton**.

508- Mar. 5, 17– Robert **Burton** to Ambrose **Barker** for 158 pds. 560 acres on **Bolling**'s creek at boundaries of John **Turer**'s land, now belonging to Thomas **Williams**.
Wts: John **Brodie**.

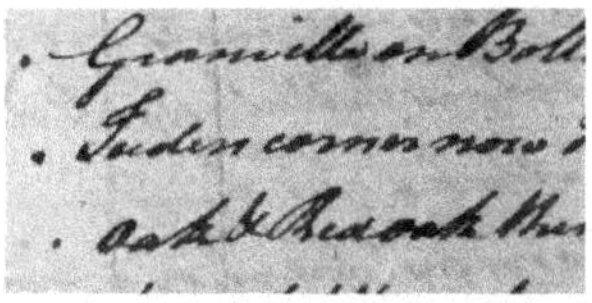

509- Mar. 15, 1787- Jonathan **Kittrell** to Samuel **Walker** for 70 pds. 153 acres on E side of Little River creek to Elias **Guest**'s corner.
Wts: Wm. **Walker**, Rowland **Bryant**.

509- May 5, 1787- Charles **Wade** to Robert **Wade** for 300 pds. 300 acres on E side of the creek along **Harris**'s, **Jones**'s lines and crossing **Aaron**'s creek.-
Wts: Samuel **Harris**, Dennis **Reardon**.

510- Nov. 15, 1787- William **Wright** of Wilks County, Georgia, to William **Stovall** of Granville Co N.C. for 20 pds. 39 acres in Granville Co., N.C. on, Jonathan's creek at **Hunt**'s line, **Stovall**'s line.
Wts: Drury **Stovall**, Richd **Griffin**, George **Pool**.

510- Dec. 4, 1786- Hammon **Wilkerson** of Granville to James **Paschal** of Warren Co., N.C. for 50 pds. 433 acres on Beaverdam creek along **Bradford**'s, **Hall**'s line to Tarborough road to the creek.
Wts: James **Hefferlin**, William **Wilkerson**.

511- Feb. 20, 1787- Robert **Coleman** to Edmund **Duke** of Goochland Co., VA. 550 pds. 577 acres in Granville Co., N.C. being part of land bought of John **Kennon** and bounded by Gideon **Gooch**, Nicholas **Burch**, Sr., James **Terry** Sr., Peyton **Wood**, Joseph **Gooch**, Christian **Scum**, James **Downey** and James **Johnston**.
Wts: [Wm. **Manor**[7]], Anderson **Thomason**, Andrew **Ware**, Wiatt **Wilkerson**, William **Longmire**-

511, 512- Aug. 8, 1786- John **Pope** Sr. to John **Pope**, Jr. for 200 pds. 300 acres on both sides of Cedar creek at Peter

7 Also looks like 'Marrow'.

Vinson's line, on **Hawley**'s branch (**Henley**'s branch?) to **Bradford**'s line which land is part of tract sold by Winfield **Wright**, Susannah **Wright**, now deceased, and deeded from Hannah **Wright**, administrix, John **Wright**, Benjamin **Wright**, joint heirs of Susannah **Wright**, deceased, in equal parts of the 300 acres.
Wts: Saml **Fuller**.

512- Feb. 15, 1787- John **Tatom** to George **Wright** for 100 pds. 140 acres on E side of Ledge of Rocks creek at John **Beck**'s line to Frederick **Beck**'s corner and along Benjamin **Wheeler**'s line.
Wts: Samuel **Adams**, Bennet **Phillips**.

512, 51-3 Dec, 4, 1786- Gilliam **Harris** to John **Welch** for 30 pds. 139 acres on Beaverdam creek at David **Harris**'s corner to **Mitchel**'s line, **Bridges**', **Harris**', Robert **Allin**'s line.
Wts: Shem **Cooke**, Susannah **Allin**.

513, 514- Mar. 13, 1787- Joseph **Gill** of Franklin Co., N.C. to John **Baird** and John **Angus** of Prince George Co., VA. for 300 pds., 827 acres on both sides of Andrew Branch in Granville Co., at William **Ellixson**'s and **Harrison**'s, **Lewis**'s lines.
Wts: John **Morton**, David **Irving**, Alexander **Will**.

514- Apr, 28, 1784- Reuben **Talley** to James **Smith** for 70 pds. 70 acres on W side of Fishing creek to the dividing line between Isaac **Arnold** and Sherwood **Harris** and along **Harris**'s line.
Wts: Barnett **Pulliam**, Mathew **Snipes**.

514, 515- Oct. 3, 1786- John **Hart** to Larkin **Johnston** for 60 pds. 200 acres on Grassy creek at dividing line between John **Hart** and Joseph **Hart** on John **Williams**, **Graves**'s line, to **Mutter**'s line and along his line.
Wts: Samuel **Pittard**, Abraham **Hester**.

304

515- May 2, 1787- Samuel **Harris** to Smith [**Ogilvie**] for 10 pds. 30 acres On Tar river near head of Paul's creek on **Jenkins**' and [**Ogilvie**]'s lines.
Wts: Kimbrough [**Ogilvie**], Wm. **Ogilvie**.

515, 516- Nov. 15, 1786- John **Terry** and wife Mary to Daniel **Marrow** of Mecklenburg Co., VA. for 150 pds. 260 acres in Granville Co., being part of tract granted to William **Terry**, deceased, by Lord Granville on both sides of Great Island creek in James **Lewis**'s line.
Wts: Henry **Williams**, John **Gomer**, G. **Sims**.

516- Jan. 20, 1783- Augustine **Davis** to John **Mitchel** for 200 pds. 420 acres at mouth of Little Watery branch in **Lanier**'s line, **Gober**'s and **Terry**'s lines.
(Mary, wife of Augustine **Davis**, relinquishes dower).
Wts: Samuel **Williams**, James **Byars**, Richd **Davis**.

517- May 1787- Phillis **Mitchel**, sole heir and executrix of John **Mitchel**, deceased, to Stephen **Sneed** for 200 pds. 420 acres at mouth of Little Watry branch along **Lanier**'s line, **Burton**'s, **Person**'s, **Terry**'s lines.
Wts: none.

517, 518- Mar. 16, 1787- Howel **Lewis**, Sr., John **Young**, Leonard Henley **Bullock**, Robert **Burton**, Bromfield **Ridley**, John **Somerville**, Philemon **Hawkins** and Thornton **Yancey** of Granville Co., N.C. commissioners of the Town of Williamsborough, N.C. to Samuel **Smith** for 6 pds. *lot No. 24* in Williamsborough, N.C.
Wts: Sterling **Yancey**, Stephen **Sneed**.

518- Mar. 15, 1787- Howel **Lewis**, Sr., John **Young**, Sr., Len Henley **Bullock**, Robert **Burton**, Bromfield **Ridley**, John **Somerville**, Philemon **Hawkins**, Thornton **Yancey**, commissioners of the town of Williamsborough, N.C. sold to Samuel **Smith**, *lot No. 5* in the town.
Wts: Stephen **Sneed**, Sterling **Yancey**, Stephen **Sneed**.

518-519- Mar. 7, 1785- John **Somerville** and wife Mary to John **Hunt** for 200 pds. 150 acres in the first tract, on **Mead**'s line at Joseph **Bass**'s corner, at Robert **Hicks**'s line, and a tract of 100 acres on Fishing creek, and another of 200

acres on Fishing creek at **Mead**'s line to Henry **Day**'s corner.
Wts: Ro. **Burton**, Thos **Satterwhite**.

519, 520- Feb. 5, 1786- William **Hunt**, sheriff of Granville, to John **Brodie**, the land of John **Mosely** as per order of court at suit brought by Solomon **Fuller** for debt due him. 200 acres on both sides of Buckhorn creek on **Dockery**'s line.
Wts: Lewis **Potter**.

520- Aug. 7, 1787- Charles **Parrish** to Drury **Kimball** for 300 pds. 191 acres at George **Brack**'s line, on **Kimball**'s own line, Dennis **Driskill** line.
Wts: Frederick **Wiggins**, Joseph **Hays**.

520, 521- Aug. 6, 1787- Reuben **Searcy** to John **Morris** for 100 pds. 99 acres on both sides of **Hatcher**'s Run in **Moore**'s line and **Mooris**'s line.
Wts: Micajah **Bullock**.

521- Aug. 7, 1787- James **Woodall** and Jacob **Woodall** to Lewis **Parham** for 40 pds. 50 acres on Tabbs creek in Granville Co., NC. on lines of Lewis **Parham** and Samuel **Hicks**.
Agness **Woodall** relinquishes her dower right in land (wife of which?)

521- 522- Mar. 27, 1787- . Benjamin **Smith** and wife Sarah to his brother John **Smith** for 31 pds. 41 acres on **Kittrell**'s and **Talley**'s lines and also an acre adjoining John **Smith** including the Spring thereon.
Wts: Charles **Blackley** and James **Blackley**.

522- Jan. 17, 1787- John **Tatom** to William **Knight** for 20 pds. 149 acres on Ledge of Rocks creek, **Grant**'s and **Whealer**'s lines, **Swiney**'s line on John **Beck**'s corner.
Wts: B. **Clark**, Elisha [**Dyar**].

522, 523- Aug. 7, 1787- Thomas **Newby** to William **Farrar** for 233 pds. 500 acres on **Walker**'s line, **Allison**'s and **Tuder**'s, **Hudspeth**'s line, **Couch**es' line.
Wts: none.

523- Dec. 8, 1785- Joseph **Langston** to William **Oakley** for 5 shls. 50 acres on Cub creek in the county line.
Wts: Stephen **Merritt**, Hezekiah **Hobgood**, John **Williams**.

305

523, 524- Feb. 21, 1787- Joseph **Langston** of Greenville County, South Carolina to Arthur **Moore** of Caswell Co., N.C. for 200 pds. 1395 acres in Granville Co., N.C. at **Merritt**'s corner, on **Goss**'s line, **Sherman**'s road, on **Mangum**'s line, on **Langston**'s line, to the county line, **Wills**' and **Philpot**'s lines-
Wts: John **Manire**, Stephen **Merritt**, Winfret **Merrill**.

524, 525- July 16, 1787- Phillip **Yancey** to Thornton **Yancey** for 22 pds. 17 shls. 6 pence, 15 1/4 acres on Grassy creek where the Virginia line crosses Quarter branch in **Yancey**'s own line whereon Philip **Yancey** lives.
Wts: Sterling and Thomas **Yancey**.

525- Mar. 15, 1786- James **Meadows** to Joseph **Hester** for 100 pds. 50 acres on Tar river at mouth of Horse branch on **Person**'s line and Stoney creek.
Wts: William **Gilliam**, Allen **Howard**.

525, 526- Jan. 8, 1787- Woodson **Daniel** of Wake County to Nicholas **Derning** for 40 pds. (**Derning** of Orange Co.) 200 acres on Cedar creek at **Clements**' corner on **McCulloh**'s line.
Wts: Elijah **Veazey**, Hubard **Sykes** (**Lykes**).

526- Aug. 8, 1787- Thomas **Philpott** to John **Washington** for 30 pds. 50 acres on Tar river at **Person**'s corner, on **Washington**'s old line.
Wts: Joseph **Hester**.

526, 527- Dec. 11, 1785- Charles **Jones** to Joseph **Langston** for 5 shls. 245 acres whereon **Jones** now lives at

Meadow branch of Cub Creek and on Nap of Reeds creek on S side of the road on **Mangum**'s line.
Wts; Stephen **Merritt**, Howel **Rose**, Thos. **Hobgood**.

527- July 24, 1787- Gideon **Gooch** to John **Johnston** for 120 pds. 200 acres being part of tract formerly property of John **Thorp**, purchased from him on James **Johnston**'s line to Robert **Coleman**'s line, formerly, now Edmund **Duke**'s.
Wts: Robert **Coleman**, Joseph **Gooch**, Peyton **Wood**.

527, 528- July 23, 1787- John **Thorp** to Gideon **Gooch** for 200 pds. 302 acres on W side of Island creek in **Lewis**' line and **Minter**'s line.
Wts: Peyton **Wood**, John **Johnson** James **Terry**.

528- Jan. 4, 1787- William **Hicks** to Micajah **Debruler**, a gift of130 acres on S side of the road from Harrisburg to the old courthouse on **Reeves**' line to **Barton**'s line.
Wts: William **Mathews**, William **Hicks**.

528, 529- May 9, 1787- Commissioner of the town of Williamsborough, N.C. sold to Stephen **Sneed** for 6 pds. *lot no 62* in the town.
Wts: Wm. **Byars**.

529- Oct. 28, 1787- James **Brodie** to Jacob **Anderson** for 30 pds. 100 acres at **Bearden**'s and Robert **Reed**'s lines.

529, 530- Feb. 17, 1787- Thomas **Craft** and wife Elizabeth to William **Shemwell** for 80 pds. 320 acres at George **Brack**'s and **Critcher**'s lines on **Hawkins**' corner, **Norman**'s line, **Parish**'s corner.
Wts: Thos **Norman**, Joshua **Hutchenson**.

530- Oct. 29, 1787- Benjamin **Grisham** to Drury **Kimball** for 200 pds. 125 acres on Flat creek on the new road at Drury **Kimball**'s corner in **Parish** line and Bromfield **Ridley**'s line.
Wts: Harris **Hicks**, Sion **Kimball**.

531- July 1, 1784- John **Champion** to Champion **Allen** for 50 pds. 350 acres on Horse and Cedar creeks, at **Winningham**'s line, which is part of Grant to John **Champion** for 350 acres.
Wts: John **Pope**.

531, 532- Oct. 29, 1787- John **Keeling** to John **Somerville** for 200 pds. 180- acres on **Martin**'s line, at road near Meeting house, at **Akin**'s line.
Wts: Thos **Satterwhite**, Stephen **Sneed**.

532- Nov. 5, 1787- Christopher **Harris** to Nathaniel [**Snipe**] for 200 pds. 360 acres on both sides of **Hatcher**'s Run at Robert **Reid**'s corner.
Wts: Reuben **Searcy**, Sherwood **Harris**.

532, 533- Oct. 27 1787- Joseph **Hart** to Samuel **Harrison** for 20 pds. 150 acres on both sides of Gallion branch near **Grant**'s road, **Johnston**'s line, to line agreed on by **Hart** and **Harrison**.
Wts: John **Downey**, Thomas **Mutter**, Jr., Thomas **Mutter**, A. **Hunt**.

306

533- Nov. 8, 1787- Edward **Nowling** (**Nowland**) to John **Minor** for 20 pds. 213 acres on N. side of Tar river on **Minor**'s line, old road.
Wts: Jeph. **Parker**, Benja **Rearden**.

533, 534- May 26, 1787- James **Kelley** of Mecklenburg Co, Va to Major **Evans** for 50 pds. 100 acres on both sides of Middle creek at John **Rogers**' line being part of 588 acres, granted to John **Pope** who sold to James **McGehee** and he sold to James **O'Kelley**.
Wts: John **Pope**, George **Nicholson**.

534- Nov. 3, 1787- Joseph **Chandler** to John **Chandler** for 30 pds. 50 acres on S side of Jonathan Creek.
Wts: Thornton **Yancey**, William **Chandler**.

534, 535- Nov. 6, 1787- Claburn **Harris** and wife Judith to Harris **Ogelvie** for 100 pds. 120 acres on both sides of Paul's creek at Samuel **Harris**'s corner and along his line to **Freeman**'s line.
Wts: John **Tipet**.

535- Dec. 5, 1786- Samuel **Jones** to Baxter **Ragsdale** of Franklin Co., N.C. for 50 pds. 50 acres in Granville Co. at Thomas **White**'s corner on John **Penn**'s line, **Harris**'s line.
Wts: Thomas **White**, Edw **Ragsdale**, Thomas **Devaugh**.

535, 536- Oct. 17, 1787- Arthur **Moore** to Stephen **Merritt** for 200 pds, 1395 acres on Tar river, **Goss**'s line, **Jones**' line, **Shermon** road, **Mangum** line, **Langston**'s line to the county line, **Willis** and **Philpott's** lines.
Wts: Chas. **Partee**, R. D. **Cooke**.

536- Oct. 29, 1787- Jacob **Holstein** (**Holston**) to Claborn **Harris** for 100 pds. 230 acres on N. side of **Holstein**'s creek on **Hampton**'s line This is signed by Jacob **Holstein**, Elizabeth **Jacob** and Katty **Holstein** Elizabeth **Jacob** relinquished her right of dower-
Wts: Harris **Ogelvie**, Sherd **Harris**, Wm. **Jacob**.

537- Oct. 9 1787- Lawrence **Petteford** to Nathan **Bass** for 50 pds. 170 acres on Fishing creek adjoining land of Hugh **Snelling**, Thomas **Newby** and Col. **Taylor** and Elijah **Parrish**'s land.
Wts: Peyton **Wood**, Thomas **Crews**.

537- Aug. 18, 1787- Luke **Landers** to Josiah **Daniel** for 150 pds. 300 acres on Grassy creek on **Daniel**'s' line, Samuel **Peace**'s line, Gideon **Crenshaw**'s line.
Wts: Wm. **Bailey**, Mary **Bailey**.

538- Nov. 6, 1787- John **Sherman** to Samuel **Walker** for 55 pds. 307 acres, on Tar river at road near **Sherman**'s Meeting house at Thos **Philpot**'s and John **Williams**'s lines, **Eastwood**'s line.
Wts: Ephr **Frazier**, Abner [**Russel**].

538- May-- 1787- John Conrad **Farmer** to Charles **Partee** for 50 pds. 116 acres on Ledge of Rocks creek at **Amis**'s line, John **Beck**'s line.
Wts: Absalom **Baker**, Mary **Tatom**.

539- Aug. 16, 1782- William **Gober** to Solomon **Walker** for 5 shls.110 acres on Island Creek at **Burton**'s corner in **Walker**'s line.

539- May 9, 1787- Town Commissioner of Williamsborough, N.C. to William **Shemwell** for 6 pds. *lot No. 15* in the town.
Wts: Stephen **Sneed**.

540- Feb. 2, 1787- Drury **Stovall**, Dorcas **Stovall**, Anne **Stovall** wife of Drury **Stovall**, to John **Young** for 350 pds. 300 acres (excepting 1/16th of an acres whereon are graves) where I now live at the corner of land belonging to John **Young**, William **Stovall** and William **Yancey** and Drury **Stovall**, at Jonathan creek on William **Higgs** line on Mill road.
Wts: John **Young**, John Smith **Young**, William **Young**.

541- Dec. 22, 1787- Reuben **Searcy** to Charles **Harris** for 22 pds. 10 shls, 45 acres on Cattail creek on **Beardon**'s line at **Harris**'s own corner.

541- Dec. 8, 1787- John **Hall** to David **Blalock** for 100 pds. 100 acres on Beaverdam creek at Richd **Bradford**'s corner, Ephraim **Bradford**'s line and on Tarborough road.
Wts: Phil **Bradford**, Jere **Blalock**.

307

541, 542- Oct. 4, 1787- Jesse **Searcy** to Henry **Graves** for 100 pds. 100 acres on both sides of Lick creek on lines of Henry **Graves**, John **Smith**, at Lovet **Gates**' house.
Wts: William **Haggis**, Ralph **Graves**.

542- Jan. 19, 1788- Henry **Fuller** to Daniel **Edwards** of Franklin Co., N. C, for 150 pds. 200 acres on both sides of Long Creek on Charles Rust **Eaton**'s line-
Wts: Britain **Fuller**, Jonathan **Fuller**.

542, 543- Dec. 1, 1781- John **Winningham** to Jones **Fuller** for 74 pds. 100 acres on **Bailey**'s line.
Wts: Valentine **Austin**, Bartholomew **Fuller**.

543- Nov. 9, 1787- John **Weaver** to Susanna **Weaver** for 20 pds. 60 acres at **Mitchel**'s corner in **Hawkins**' line, Widow **Robertson**'s line, Thomas **Rowland**'s line-
Wts: Merryman **Barnes**, Thomas **Rowland**.

543, 544- Feb. 3, 1785- William **Huitt** to John **Hefflen** for 45 pds. 125 acres on N. side of Middle prong of Beaverdam creek at Hammon **Wilkerson**'s line and the Tarborough road.
Wts: Ellick **Sandervenson**, John **Holt**.

544- July 3, 1786- Mary **Bradford** and Thomas **Bradford** to Charles **Heffernon** for 50 pds. 178 acres at **Champion**'s line on Fort creek and this containing 100 acres and the other 78 acres at **Mayfield** and at **Heffernon**'s lines-
Wts: David **Bradford**, John **Massey**, Valen **Alston**.

545- Jan. 22, 1788- William **Allen** to John **Badget** for 97 pds. 233 acres being part of larger tract taken up by William **Meadows** at Jacob **Slaughter**'s line at **Mathews**' line.
Wts: Wm. and Seth **Badget**, James **Pool**.

545, 546- June 4, 1787- Ezekiel **Fuller** of Franklin Co., N.C. to James **Carden** of Granville for 40 pds. 50 acres on Tabbs creek at Edward **Harris**'s line and John **Dickerson**'s line.
Wts: Nathaniel **Jarret**.

546- Feb. 2, 1788- Valentine **Austin** to Jones **Fuller** for 40 pds. 97½ acres on **Bailey**'s line, **Winningham**'s line.
Wts: Bryant **Cavnees**, Jeremiah **Bailey**.

546, 547- Jan. 4, 1787- Simon **Hancock** to John **Winningham** for 50 pds. 100 acres on **Bailey**'s line, at **Fuller**'s line.
Wts: John **Harris**, Valentine **Austin**.

547- Nov. 7, 1787- Joab **Glover**, Daniel **Glover**, Robert **Glover** and David **Glover** to James **Lewis** for 103 pds. certain land which their father, Joseph **Glover**, willed to his son, Robert, Daniel and David and whereas Robert, Daniel and David, this land which they inherited from their father to James **Lewis** for 103 pds. and Joab brother of the within named Daniel, Robert and David **Glover** also sold his inheritance which was land whereon his father lived and whereon he then lived, to James **Lewis** for 200 pds.
Wts: Jordan **Norwood**.

548- Dec 10, 1785- Joseph **Roberts** to Brereton **Jones** for 125 pds. 596 acres in **Daniels'** line adjoining Robert **Hester** and Henry **Graves**, **Oliver**'s, **Edwards**' lands.
Wts: Larkin **Johnston**, Peter **Bennett**

548- Nov. 30, 1782- Hammon **Wilkerson** to John **Hall** for 100 pds. 100 acres on Beaverdam creek at Richd **Bradford**'s corner, Thos. **Bradford**'s line and Tarborough road.
Wts: Phil and Richd **Bradford**.

548, 549- Jan. 911788- Elias **Peteford** to Harnett **Pulliam** for 40 pds. 107 acres on Tar river at **Taylor**'s line, **Ross**'s and **Moore**'s line at **Parker**'s corner.-
Wts: Ephraim **Frazier**, Lewis **Peteford**.

549- Nov, 1, 1787- Benjamin **Smith** to John **Smith** for 110. pds. 117 acres on both sides of Little creek at **Inscoe**'s spring branch, John **Smith**'s line.
Wts: John **Kittrell**.

308

550- Oct. 5, 1787- Jesse **Carrell** to John **Dickerson** for 180 pds. 240 acres on Beaverdam creek at James **Walker**'s line, being the land deeded from Jess **Carrell** to **Dickerson**.
Wts: James **Barr**, Joseph **Peace**.

550- Feb. 5, 1788- Richard **Glasgow** to John **Mayfield** of Warren Co., N.C. for 100 pds. 170 acres on Ruin Creek at Charles **Parrish**'s line, **Davis**'s corner.-

551- July 24, 1787- Alexander **Vincent** to Peter **Vincent** for 20 pds. 63 acres adjoining lands of John **Champion**, Peter **Vincent**.
Wts: Jacob **Vincent**, John **Holt**.

551, 552- Jan. 15, 1787- John **Sutton** to Presly **Wilson** for 50 pds. 100 acres (**Wilson** of Warren Co., N.C.) being part of tract granted to John **Dickerson** Jan, 15, 1773 on Fort creek at **Bradford**'s and **Jeffers**'s lines- granted by the State.
Wts: Elias and James **Jenkins**, Nelson **Nailing**.

552- Jan. 27, 1788- William **Kelley** to William **Wilkins** for 50 pds. 100 acres on Ledge of Rocks creek at Edward **Davis**'s old corner in **Emry**'s line on Ephraim **Emry**'s corner.
Wts: James **Patterson**, A. **Lawrence**.

552; 553 - - 1787- Richard D. **Cooke**, Jacob **Stem** for 80 pds. 100 acres on Ledge of Rocks creek at George **Lanemoore**'s line and on **Bullock**'s and **Claxton**'s corners, James **Harkin**'s line.
Wts: Jeremiah and Charles **Bullock**, Samuel **Harris**.

553- Feb. 5 1788- Richd **Wilkins** to William **Wilkins** for 15 pds. 200 acres on Ledge of Rocks creek at Edward **Davis**'s old corner and **Swiloban**'s corner, Abraham **Lawrence**'s line, **Kelly**'s line.
Wts: none.

554- Jan. 25, 1788- Benjamin **Lunsford** to Thomas **Stephens** for 50 pds. 100 acres adjoining lands of Robert **Allen**, **Witcher**, Jane **Mitchel** and Joseph **Neal**.
Wts: Wilson and John **Bailey**.

554- Aug. 3, 1787- William **Hunt**, sheriff of Granville Co., to Lewis **Potter**, the land of John **Potter** at order of court at suit brought by administrators of Charles E. **Taylor** and Elijah E. **Graves**: 546 acres on both sides of Tar river whereon John **Potter** then lived, and which he bought of John **Gwin**, also a tract he bought of John **Landish** adjoining.
Wts: James **Hurst**.

555- Jan. 18, 1788- William **Hunt** to Gideon **Freeman** for 500 pds. 588 acres on Cedar creek at **Smith**'s line on Tarborough road, **Allison**'s line, at Horse creek-
Wts: Robert **Allison**, David **Parish**.

555- June, 26, 1787- William [**Huet**] to James **Heflin** for 100 pds. 280 acres on Beaverdam at **Holt**'s line, at John **Heflin**'s corner.
Wts: Phil. **Bradford**, John **Heflin**.

555, 556- Jan. 25, 1788- Thomas **Gowing** (**Gooing**) to John **Simmons** for 120 pds. 150 acres on both sides of **Taylor**'s creek, being lower part of tract granted to John **McKisock** and sold to Thomas **Goving** (**Gowing**).
Wts: John **Carrel**, John **Simmonds**, Thos. **Symmonds**.

556- Dec. 9, 1787- William **Cook** of Rowan Co., N. C. to John **Tippet** of Granville Co., N. C. for 40 pds. 96 acres on **Adcock**'s creek at mouth of **Hargrove**'s Spring branch on **Booth**'s line at **Holstein**'s line.
Wts: John **Minor**, Charles **Coleman**.

556, 557- Dec. 15, 1787- Major **Evans** to James **Blackley** for 71 pds. land whereon **Evans** now lives which he purchased of John **Gowen** containing 100 acres on line of Kemp **Goodloe**'s land deceased, William **Nailing**, Thomas and Robert [**Predders**] ?
Wts: William **Dickerson**, John **Peace**, Saml **Hopkins**.

557- Dec. 15, 1787- John **Dillon** to James **Downey** Jr. for 9pds. 10 shls. 100 acres on Island creek, lower end of tract James **Johnston** bought of John **Chiles** on James **Hunt**'s, Gideon **Gooch**'s, James **Johnston**'s, Robert **Hester**'s and Drury **Smith**'s lines-
Wts: James **Downey**, Edward **Burrage**.

309

557, 558- Mar. 3 1787- Benjamin **Moore** to Charles **Bullock** for 100 pds. 200 acres at **Jones**'s line, **Chandler**'s corner.
Wts: Jeremiah **Bullock**, Rchd D. **Cooke**.

558- Feb. 7, 1788- Thomas **Wilburn** to Robert **Burton** Esq. for 90 pds. 300 acres adjoining lands of Micajah **Bullock**, Kimbrough **Oglevie**, Gideon **Freeman** and John **Hefflin** as by two deeds from Robert **Harris** to Thomas **Wilburn**.

558, 559- Mar. 8, 1788- Duncan **Rose** of Dinwiddie Co., VA. attorney to John **Banister** of Battersea, in same County and State, with John **Banister**, Jr. also as attorney- appointed Edward **Clarke** of the aforesaid County my substitute that he may in my name to take possession of a tract of land in Edgecombe Co., now Granville Co. being the land patented by Ephroditus **Moore**, also a tract in same County of 500 acres patented to William **Moore** and also a tract in same County for 200 acres patented to Benjamin **Hill**, and, 640 acres granted to said Benjamin **Hill** which lands have been purchased of David **Meade** of Maycocke by the said John **Banester**, Sr. of Battersea.
Wts: John **Brander**, John **Smitton**, Wm. **Hunter**
Duncan **Rose** attests and deposes before William **Davis**, notary public for Petersburg District, VA. and acknowledges power of attorney May 1787
May 20, 1787- William **Davis**, notary public, takes deposition of David **Meade** of Maycocke, Prince George Co., VA. who states that is his act and delivers certain implements as above stated in presence of Joseph and Elizabeth **Westmore**, Salley **Warrington** and Mary **Davis**.

559, 560- May 20, 1787- David **Meade** of Maycocke, Prince George Co., VA. to John **Banester** of Battersea, Dinwiddie Co, VA. four tracts of land in Granville Co., N.C. which is delivered by his attorney, Charles R. **Eaton** in Granville Co.
Wts: Elizabeth and Joseph **Westmore**, Sally **Warrington**, Mary **Davis**, William **Davis**-

560, 561- May. 20, 1787- David **Meade** of Maycocke, Prince George Co., VA. to John **Banester** of Battersea, Dinwiddie Co., VA. for 200,000 pds. of crop tobacco, 300 acres in Granville Co, formerly Edgecombe Co., which was granted to Ephroditus **Moore** July 25, 1743 and 400 acres granted to William **Moore** July 27, 1743, also 200 acres granted to Benjamin **Hill** Apr. 11, 1745 and 640 acres granted to **Hill** on same date, all in Granville Co. and were bought severally by David **Meade** of Nansemond Co. father of said David **Meade**, now deceased. John Rust **Eaton** of Granville as attorney delivered land with good deeds to same.
Wts: Jos. **Westmore**, Elisabeth **Westmore**, Sally **Warrenton**, Mary and Wm. **Davis**.

561, 562- Mar. 15, 1787- Stephen **Merritt** to Robert **Dickens** of Caswell Co for 600 pds. 633 acres being part of 3 tracts on both sides of Tar river at **Goss**'s line, **Washington**'s line.
Wts: Thomas **Person**, Reuben **Butler**.

562- Mar. 29, 1788- Timothy **Driskill** to John **Taylor** for 110 pds. 175 acres in **Johnson**'s line, **Taylor**'s line, **Norwood**'s line, **Harper**'s line.
Wts: Jordan **Norwood**, William **Byars**.

562, 563- Sept. 23, 1787- Micajah **Bullock** to William **Beck** for 50 pds. 80 acres at **Landess**'s and **Beck**'s corners.
Wts: [Matthew] **Pryor**, Peter [**Cash**].

563, 564- Jan. 11, 1787- Thomas **Clements** to George **Brasfield** for 160 pds. 200 acres on Cedar creek (signed by Thomas and Ann **Clement**).
Wts: Ellis **White**, Wm. **Prichard**, Caleb **Brasfield**, John **Tuggle**.

564- Jan. 11, 1787- Thomas **Clements** to George **Brasfield** for 160 pds. 640 acres excepting the 50 acres whereon John **Tuggle** now lives, on Cedar creek at **McCulloh**'s corner in his own line, John **Tuggle**' line
Wts: Wm. **Prichard**, Caleb **Brasfield**, John **Tuggle**.

565- Nov. 19, 1787- Lewis **Amis** from Reuben **Glaze** for 75 pds. 112 acres on Jonathan **Knight**'s line to the Widow **Butler**'s line, William **Knight**'s line being 1/3rd, whereon Benjamin **Glaze**, deceased, resided.
Wts: John **Oliver**, Anderson **Hunt**.

310

565, 566- Jan. 18, 1780- William **Floyd** to Samuel **Kittrell** for 280 pds. 60 acres on N. side of Tabbs Creek in **Kittrell**'s line, Joseph **Parrish**'s line-
Wts: Jonathan **Kittrell**, Wm. **Hornsby**.

566- Nov. 12, 1787- Benjamin **Dispain** to William **Bettes** of Franklin Co., N. C. for 60 pds. 180 acres on Nuce river on Horse creek.
Wts: Wyatt **Betts**, Thos **Bradford**.

566, 567- Aug. 8, 1786- William **Hewit** to William **Lawrence** of Wake Co., N.C. a tract of 180 acres in Granville Co., N.C. on S aide of Tarboro road at **Robertson** creek, at corner between William **Wilkerson** and John **Hefflin** on **Holt**'s and Sandy **Vincent**'s line, at **Champion**'s corner.
Wts; John **Guin**, John **Champion**. Wm. **Jones**.

567- Sept. 12, 1787- Elizabeth **Tuder** and Valentine **Tuder** to John **Morris** for 100 pds. 160 acres on W side of Fishing creek at line formerly **Hudspeth**'s and now **Alison's**, and at **White**'s line, now **Allison's**.
Wts: Reuben **Searcy**, Z. **Higgs**.

567, 568- Feb. 4, 1787- Thomas **Clements**. to John **Tuggle** for 50 pds. 150 acres on Cedar creek at **Bagby**'s line.
Wts: George and Caleb **Brasfield**.

568- Feb. 1, 1788- Nicholas **Loyd** to Jonathan **Kittrell** for 40 pds. 100 acres on **Eaton**'s line and his own line.
Wts: Stephen **Jett**, Z. **Higgs**.

568, 569- Mar. 17, 1787- William **Floyd** to Thomas **White** for 85 pds. 294 acres on Ruin creek on **Johnston**'s and **Kittrell**'s lines, **Locke**'s line-
Wts: Z. and John **Higgs**.

569- May 1, 1788- Anderson **Smith** to Lewis **Amis** for 220 pds. 208 acres on N. side of Grassy creek at **Smith** line.
Wts: William and M. **Hunt**.

570- Jan. 10, 1788- John **Duncan**, Jr. to Thomas **Peyton** for 100 pds. 173 acres on Ruin creek at John **Parham**'s and **Bristow**'s, **Johnston**'s lines-
Wts: Samuel **Kittrell**, Wiley **Kittrell**.

570, 571- Aug. 6, 1718- John **Young**, sheriff, to Lewis and Henry **Potter** the land of John **Potter** by order of court at suit of George **Bristow** vrs. John **Potter** containing 663 acres on Tar river near Breverdam and on **Harris**'s line, Nicholas creek and also a tract on David **Harris**'s corner containing 53 acres and a tract of 25 acres-
Wts: Reuben **Searcy**, Joshua **Bell**.

571- Feb. 12, 1788- Robert **Bell** of Franklin Co., N. C. to John **Brodie** of Granville for 200 pds. 277 acres in Granville which was deeded by Robert **Hicks**, Sr. to Robert **Bell** in 1769, on Tabbs creek at **Thompson**'s and **Reeves**' lines.
Wts: Elizabeth **Minskis**.

571, 572- Aug. 18, 1787- James **Critcher** and Major **Mitchel** (**Critcher** of Orange Co., N.C.) to Samuel **Reeves** for 233 pds. 6 shls, 8 pence, 640 acres in one tract and 50 acres in another tract on E side of Nutbush creek at Major **Mitchel**'s corner at **Hawkins**' and **Robertson**'s lines in Granville Co., and at Widow **Robertson**'s line, Thomas **Critcher**'s line.

Wts: Samuel **Sneed**, Barnett **Jeter**.

572- Jan. 28, 1788- Thomas **Kelley** to George **Chapman** for 6 pds. 5 acres in the County line in **Chapman**'s line at a large path that leads from **Chapman**'s to Kingsford road.
Wts: Robert **Hargrove**, James **Mathis**, James **Hargrove**.

572, 573- Aug. 24, 1787- Cornelius **Cooper** to Edmund **Taylor** Sr, for 63 pds. 180 acres being land **Cooper** holds on both sides of Fishing creek at **Taylor**'s corner.
Wts: Henry **Duncan**, Joseph **Renns**.

573, 574- May 24, 1788- James **Lyne** from Gillam **Norwood** and his wife Catherine for a Negro man named Simon, a black horse, 20 pds., & 2 barrels of corn- a tract of land containing 204 acres on Nutbush crk on **Mathews** branch.
Wts: William **Byars**, David **Mason**.

311

574- Aug. 4, 1788- Samuel **Harris** to Richard **Harris** for 200 pds. 260 acres being land thereon Ro. **Harris** deceased, did live on S side of Nicholas creek adjoining land of Samuel **Harris**, William **Ogelvie**, Thomas **Jenkins** and Alexander **Boyd**.
Wts: Thomas **Wilburn**. L. **Potter**.

574- Oct. 23, 1786- William **Jones**, Sr. to Moses **Jones** for 100 pds. 100 acres on Nap of Reed creek.
Wts: John **Manire**, Joseph **Walker**, John **Rusell**.

575- Aug. 1, 1788- William **Cauthon** (**Cawthorn**) to Edmund **Taylor** for 57 pds. 10 shls. 57½ acres at **Taylor**'s corner near his mill path.
Wts: Jno. **Marshall**, John **Upchurch**.

575- Oct. 13, 1786- Thomas **Grant** of Wilks Co., Georgia to William **Chavis** of Granville Co., N. C. for 4 pds. 10 shls, 20 acres. on Tar river at **Chavis**'s line and **Snelling**'s line.
Wts: Molten **Grey**, Barnet **Snelling**.

575, 576- May 19, 1788- John **Moore** to John **Brown** for 100 pds. 100 acreson Beaverdam creek at Phil **Bradford**'s line, **Pascal**'s line, **Hall**'s corner.
Wts: James **Paschal**, Lenrd. **Moye** (**Mays**).

576- Aug. 4, 1788- Jonathan **Johnston** to Gideon **Johnston** for 100 pds. 206 acres on Little Ruin creek on road in **Kittrell**'s line, John **Sute**'s line, Thomas **White**'s line, **Barton**'s line.
Wts: John and Z. **Higgs**.

576, 577- Oct. 12, 1785- Thomas **Pool** and wife Obedience to John **Blackwell** for 120 pds. 200 acres on Grassy creek in John **Kennon**'s spring branch, Robert **Burley**'s line, William **Willingham**'s line.
Wts: Thomas **Boyd**, Isaac **Butler**, John **Pomfrett**.

577, 578- Sept, 13, 1787- William **Lasiter** to Cornelius **Cooper** for 100 pds. 150 acres at John **Hooper**'s corner on W side of middle fork of Beaverdam creek at **McCulloh**'s line, and **Bradford**'s corner.
Wts: Peter **Bennett**, R. **Searcy**.

578, - July 25, 1788- Robert **Jordan** of Halifax Co., VA. to David **Wilkerson** of Granville Co. N.C. for 5 pds. 6 acres on Bear Skin creek at David **Wilkerson**'s line.
Wts: Samuel **Pointer**, Wm. **Wilkerson**.

578- July 25, 1788- David **Wilkerson** to Robert **Jordan** of Halifax Co., VC for 5 pds. 12 acres in Granville Co., N. C. on Bearskin creek.
Wts: Saml **Pointer**, Wm. **Wilkerson**.

578, 579- Feb. 23, 1788- Elijah **Parrish** to Joel **Moore** for 25 pds. 30 acres on W side of Tabbs creek at William **Minor**'s line.

Wts: John **Higgs**, John **Langford**, Parish **Langford**.

579, 580- Oct. 30, 1787- William **Knight** of Surry Co., N.C. to James **Walker** for 40 pds. 149 acres on W side of Ledge of Rocks creek at **Whealer**'s corner, **Grant**'s line, on **Beck**'s line.
Wts: James **Ringgold**, Benj **Bonner**, John **Knight**.

580- Sept, 3, 1787- Slomon **Roberson** to Samuel **Reeves** (**Roberson** of Linkhorn Co, N.C.) for 40 pds. 120 acres being part of tract granted to **Roberson** at Kingston Sept. 4, 1779 and is on Robert **Roberson**'s corner in Granville Co., N. C. running to Edward **Rowls**' and at **Mitchel** and **Hawkins**' lines, including the plantation whereon S. **Roberson** lives.
Wts: Niccols and Robert **Roberson**, Sugar **Fortner**.

580, 581- July 31, 1788- Henry **Reardon** to William **Hester** for 200 pds. 200 acres on Tar river.
Wts: Allen **Howard**.

581- 1788- William **Wright** to Thomas **York** for 150 pds. 150 acres on Long Creek on **Dickerson** and **Ragadale**'s lines, **Finch**es line to **Harp**'s line.
Wts: Z. **Higgs**, Elijah **Ball**.

581, 582- Jan. 5, 1788- Joseph **Chandler** to James **Chandler** for 200 pds. 178 acres on S side of **Aaron**'s creek where road crosses at said **Chandler**'s line.
Wts: Joseph **Chandler**, Jr., Susanna **Chandler**.

312

582- Aug. 6, 1787- Robert **Beasley** and Betty his wife, of Lunenburg Co., VA. to Stephen **Beasley** of Granville Co., N.C. for 100 pds. 427 acres on lands of Charles **Edwards**, Thomas **Searcy**, Josiah **Daniel** and John **Blackwell**.
Wts John **Blackwell**, Anne **Pomfrett**, John **Pomfrett**.

582, 583- Aug. 30, 1787- Samuel **Smith** to Daniel **Marrow** of Mecklenburg Co., VA. for 32 pds. 84 acres at Lewis **Taylor**'s line, Daniel **Knot**'s former line, **Ellexon**'s line, James **Lewis**'s line and on main road.
Wts: William **Byars**, Wm. **Ellexon**.

583- Aug. 28, 1787- Daniel **Scot** to Daniel **Marrow** of Mecklenburg Co., VA for 24 pds. 83 acres which was bought by **Scot** from John **Gower**, Sr. whereon Daniel **Scott** now lives adjoining Lewis **Taylor**, John **Gower**, William **Ellixon** and Anderson **Smith**.
Wts: Wm. **Byars**, Wm. **Ellixon**.

583, 584- Aug. 5 1788- Simon **Clement** Sr. to Peter **Bennet** for 125 pds. 250 acres adjoining land of Samuel and Obadiah **Clement** and Israel **Eastwood**.

584- Nov. 4, 1758 Lewis **Potter** to Lewis **Bennett** for 400 pds. 446 acres, which formerly belonged to John **Gwinn** on S side of Tar river, and a tract that belonged to John **Landis** adjoining this one.

584, 585- Nov. 4, 1788- Lewis **Bennett** to John **Lemay** of Mecklenburg Co VA. fort 240 pds. 275 acres on Grassy creek on **Satterwhite**'s line, **Daniel**'s line.

585- Feb. 10, 1788- William **Chavis** to Elijah **Ball** for 20 pds. 20 acres on **Snelling**'s line.
Wts: Thomas **Newby**, Joshua **Hutchinson**.

585, 586 Apr, 6, 1784- Richard **Banks** of Wake Co., N.C. to Harmon **Bagley** of Warren Co., N. C. for 20 pds. 137 acres in Granville Co. on W side of Beaverdam creek on **Thornton**'s and **Davis**'s line and at County line.
Wts: George **Brogdon**, Benjamin **Clark**.

586- Apr. 15, 1788- John **Tatom** to Richard **Omery** for 80 pds. 330 acres on **Waller**'s line at **Bonner**'s corner, **McCulloh**'s.
Wts: Thomas **Bonner**, James **Walker**.

586, 587- Nov. 1, 1788- John **Collins** and wife Mary to Catherine **Mackay** for land containing 100 acres on **Collin**'s

line at the county line.
Wts: Thomas **Collins**, Henry **Fleman**.

587- Sept. 27, 1788- Nathaniel **Waller** to James **Cannon** of Mecklenburg Co., VA. for 200 pds. 200 acres at **Bullock**'s corner, **Waller**'s corner.
Wts: [?] **Hardaway**, David William **Pigg**.

587- Dec. 18, 1787- Major **Evans** to Elijah **Ball** for 50 pds. 100 acres on **Harp**'s line, **York**'s line, **Penn**'s line.
Wts: Daniel **Ball**, Solomon **Thornton**.

588- Feb. 12, 1788- William **Hefflin** to Absalom **Mangum** for 100 pds. 100 acres on Little Beaver Dam at **Hefflin**'s line.
Wts: James **Mangum**, James Williams **Capes**.

588- Aug. 20, 1788- Reuben **Searcy** to Arthur **Johnston** of Amelia Co., VA. for 400 pds. 820 acres on both sides of Hatcher's Run at John **Morris**'s corner Thomas **Thomson**'s corner on **Taylor**'s line, **Mitchel**'s line.
Wts: Micajah **Bullock**, Edmund **Freeman**.

589- Nov. 1788- Richard **Nance** to John Williams **Capes** for 50 pds. 107 acres on Beaverdam creek at John **Moore**'s corner, Banjamin **McCulloh** and Samuel **Smith**'s lines.
Wts: P. **Bradford**, J. **Peace**, Jr.

589. 590- Nov. 5, 1788- Charles **Partee** to Susanna **Notgrass**, widow, for 60 pds. 116 acres on Ledge of Rocks creek at **Beck**'s corner on John and Frederick **Beck**'s lines.
Wts: Joseph **Landess**, William **Philpott**.

590- Nov. 6, 1788- Thomas **Kelley** to John **Johnson**, Jr., of Mecklenburg Co., VA. for 60 pds. 170 acres at John **Hargrove**'s line on the country line, Henry **Fluman**'s line.
Wts: Daniel **Johnson**, William **Hendricks**.

313

590, 591- Sept. 26, 1788- William **Tanner** to William **Buchanon** for 60 pds. 70½ acres on **Nance**'s branch in **Glasgow**'s corner, on **McCulloh**'s line.
Wts: James **Paschal**, Silas **Paschal**.

591- Oct. 31, 1788- Richard **Nance** to John **Moore** for 120 pds. 201 acres on Beaverdam creek, on **Taylor**'s line, **Hooker**'s **line. Banks** road, to **Hooker**'s and **Glasgow**'s lines, **Buchanon**'s line.
Wts: Micajah **Bullock**, Frederick **Nance**.

591, 592- Nov. 1, 1787- Malachiah **Reaves** to Reuben **Talley** for 400 pds. 477 acres on W side of Tabbs creek at **Johnson**'s line, **Barton**'s line.
Wts: William **Hicks**, Jr., Frederick **Reaves** (signed Malachiah and Elizabeth).

592- Jan. 29, 1787- Jonathan **Parker** and wife Ann to Michael **Jones** of Amelia Co., VA. for 35 pds., 400 acres on **Parker**'s line, **Hill**'s, **Howard**'s, **Taylor**'s lines on a creek.
Wts: Elijah **Parker**, George **Parker**.

592- Oct. 24, 1788- Bartholomew **Kimball** and wife Agnes to Thomas **Rowland** for 125 pds. 400 acres on **Stark**'s, **Rowland**'s lines.
Wts: Isham **Harrison**, Saml **Kittrell**.

593- Dec. 13, 1788- Jacob **Woodall** to John **Duncan** for 50 pds. 100 acres on Tabbs creek at William **Reeves** line, Hardey **Reeves** line to Lewis **Parham**'s line to the creek.
Wts: Am. **Woodall**, James **Woodall**, Leamon **Duncan**.

593- Feb. 4, 1788- John **Holt** to Alexander **Vincent** for 40 pds. 100 acres at John **Holt**'s, William **Huitt**'s and Alexander **Vincent**'s on **Roberson** fork of Beaverdam creek to mouth of Flag pond branch.

Wts: Rolley **Holt**, Jacob **Vincent**.

594- Feb. 3, 1789- Samuel **Pointer** of Halifax Co., VA to John P. **Smith** of Granville Co., N.C. for 800 pds. 560 acres on West fork of Grassy creek.

594- Feb. 5, 1788- Nathan **Bass** to Gideon **Crews** for 50 pds. 100 acres on **Harrell**'s creek at **Crews**' line, Reuben **Talley**'s line, Thomas **Crews** line.
Wts: Saml **Clay**, Peyton **Wood**.

594, 595- Mar. 29, 1788- Darwin **Harris** to Richard **Glasgow** for 150 pds. 200 acres on Beaverdam creek at Andrew **Hampton**'s corner and a tract of 86 acres on **Nance**'s branch at **Hooker**'s line, **Nance** and **Banks**' lines.
Wts: Richard **Wilkins**, William **Glasgow**.

595, 596- Sept. 3, 1788- Zachariah **Wilburn** to James **Carrington** for 100 pds. 100 acres at mouth of Hurricane branch at Frederick **Rose**'s line, by **Nott**'s line, **Manier**'s line at **Veazey**'s and **Harrison**'s lines.
Wts: John Wm. **Manire**, P. **Bennett**.

596- Jan. 24, 1789- Stephen **Merritt** to William **Philpott** for 10 pds. 100 acres on S fork of Cub creek at **Philpott's** corner.
Wts: John **Washington**, John **Thorp**.

596, 597- May 21, 1788- Nathan **Megehe** Sr. to Nathan **Megehe**, Jr. for 25 pds. 119 acres on S side of Tar river which is part of grant from Granville to Robert **Mills**, deceased, Dec. 1760.
Wts: Willm **Dickerson**, John **Dickerson**.

597- Nov. 21, 1788- Samuel **Whitehead** sold to Henry **Bohannon** for 200 pds. 270 acres on a branch of Jonathan's creek in the county line at Sterling **Yancey**'s corner, running to James **Yancey**'s line.
Wts: William **Inge**, Thornton **Yancey**.

597, 598- Feb. 2, 1789- Drury **Mitchel** to John **Puit** for 25 pds. 100 acres being part of land granted to David **Mitchel** Mar. 1, 1780 on Beaverdam crk.
Wts: Phil **Bradford**, Joseph **Puit**.

598- May 21, 1787- Nicholas **Loyd** to Lemuel **Goodwin** for 20 pds. 50 acres on W side of Ruin creek along **Goodwin**'s line.
Wts: Wm. **Hunt**, Robert **Reid**.

598, 599- May 3, 1788- Joseph **Decker** of Mecklenburg Co., VA. to William **Bullock** of Granville Co., N.C. for 40 pds. 150 acres at **Busby**'s corner on a branch on **Bullock**'s own line.
Wts: William **Bullock**, Jr., James **Bullock**.

599,- Aug. 30, 1788- Hugh **Snelling** and Lettice **Snelling** to John **Taylor** for 490 pds. 1,040 acres, one tract of 640 acres at Little creek on

314
Snelling's line, and another tract of 300 acres whereon **Snelling** now lives which he purchased of Abel **Tatom**, and a tract of 100 acres whereon Lettice **Snelling** now lives adjoining the others.
Wts: Edmd **Taylor**, Josiah **Rucks**.

599, 600- Aug. 27, 1788- John **Williams** to Isham **Johnston** for 55 pds. 70 acres on W side of Fishing creek to the former dividing line between Isaac **Arnold** and Sherwood **Harris** and along **Harris**'s line.
Wts: Barnett **Pulliam**, William **Ester**.

600- Jan. 30, 1789- John **Chandler** to John **Boswell** for 54 pds. 50 acres on S side of Jonathan's creek between Larkin **Johnston** and William **Clayton**.
Wts: Thornton **Yancey**, William **Chandler**.

600, 601 May- -1788- John **Young**, sheriff, to **Jonathan Kittrell**, the land of Ozborn **Ball** as per order of court at suit brought against **Ball** for unpaid debt, in Warren Co., N.C. -186 acres in **Gilliam**'s line, on Lick creek at **Parrish**'s corner, **Glasgow**'s and **Loyd**'s lines. **Kittrell** was highest bidder.

601- Sheriff John **Young**, sold at public sale, the property of Edward **Moore** as ordered by court at case brought against him for debt. On May 5th 1789, 200 acres at **Bass**'s line was sold to Mary **Badget** as highest bidder for same.

602- Nov. 3, 1787- Thomas **White** to John **Sute** for 50 pds. 100 acres on Little Ruin creek on **Kittrell**'s line, **Johnson**'s line, **White**'s line.
Wts: John **Higgs**, Z. **Higgs**.

602, 603- Apr. 7, 1789- Ephraim **Hampton** of Rowan Co., N.C. to Joseph **Gooch** of Granville Co., N.C. for 300 pds. 400 acres on S side of Tar river in **Harris**'s line, **Jackson**'s line, **Sneed**'s line on Mill creek to **Bennett**'s line.
Wts: John **Minor**, John **Hampton**.

603- Oct. 2, 1788- Arthur **Moore** to Robert **Cate** for 30 pds. and a negro man, [Cato] two tracts of land in Granville Co. on Nap of Reeds creek at William **Bennett**'s corner containing 238 acres and the other tract on Arthur **Moore**'s line, **Bowling**'s, **Manning**'s, **Bennett**'s lines containing 56 acres.
Wts: John **Cate**, James **Carrington**.

604- Mar- 1789- Richard **Bradford** to John **Mann** for 60 pds. 154½ acres on a fork of Beaverdam creek at **Brown**'s and **Paschal**'s lines.
Wts: P. **Bradford**, Ephraim **Bradford**.

605- Mar. 21, 1789- Robert **Mills** to John **Bradford** for 50 pds. 200 acres at John **Bradford**'s line, on Charles **Heffernon**'s line, Robert **Jones**'s line James **Blackwell**'s line, Isom **Mitchel**'s line.
Wts: John **Mann**, Ephraim **Bradford**, P. **Bradford**.

605- May 4, 1789- Howel **Lewis**, Jr. to John **Brodie** for 6 pds. *lot No. 40* in Williamsborough, N.C.
Wts: S. **Potter**, John **Pulliam**.

605- May 4, 1789- Howel **Lewis** to John **Brodie** for 6 pds. *lot No. 39* in Williamsborough, N.C.
Jno. **Potter**, John **Pulliam**.

605, 606- May 2, 1789- Daniel **Scott** to Benjamin **Robinson** of Mecklenburg Co., VA. for 20 pds. 100 acres on the country line at James **Lewis**'s line.
Wts: Leonard **Smith**, William **Byars**.

606- Sept. 3, 1788- Grant **Allen** and Francis **Allen** to Thomas **Mutter**, Jr. for 182 pds. the land whereon William **Allen** deceased, lived and died and willed to Grant **Allen.** On S side of Grassy creek at John **Young**'s line in Thomas **Allen**'s line on **Love**'s corner at Elizabeth **Morgan**'s line to the creek, containing 281 acres.
Wts: Graves **Howard**, Peter **Badget**.

607- Oct. 21, 1788- Thomas **Allin** of Mercer Co., Ky to Thomas **Mutter** of Granville Co., N.C. for 178 pds. 178 acres on Spewmarrow creek at John **Young**'s line, in Granville Co., N.C. at corner of land sold by Grant **Allen** to Thomas **Mutter**.
Wts: John **Brown**, William **Heggie**.

315

607- May 2, 1789- Rowland **Grant** to Edward **Burrage** for 150 pds. 394 acres on a creek at **Melton**'s line, **Davis**'s line.
Wts: John **Higgs**, Z. **Higgs**.

608- Mar. 10, 1789- John **Williams**, esq. to Nathaniel **Williams** for 10 shls. 30 acres at Cotton Patch branch of Ruin creek at line dividing John **Williams** and Charles **Williams** lands.
Wts: Charles **Williams**, James **Anderson**.

608- May- 1787- Bartlet **Tyler** to Edmund **Taylor** Sr. and Edmund **Taylor**, Jr. for 42 pds. 2 shls. 8 pence, 325 acres I live which was granted Oct. 28, 1785 and, suppose to be 338 acres which is in dispute with **Taylor**, and this deed is for all that remains of the tract which is bounded by Col. **Dickerson**'s land and on the river etcetc.
Wts: Jno. **Cocke**, B. **Ridley**.

609- Nov. 8, 1788- Reuben **Butler** to Howel **Lewis** Jr. for 200 pds. 306 acres being ½ of land **Butler** purchased of William **Kennon** joining Anthony **Lumpkin**, William **Gill** and Thomas **Person** lands.
Wts: Willis **Lewis**, Nicholas **Burch**.

609- Dec, 19, 1788- Samuel **Crafton** to John **Pomphrett** for 91 pds. 5 shls 100 acres on Jonathan's creek on **Appling**'s line, **Royster**'s line, **Pomprett**'s.
Wts: Thomas **Appling**, Pomprett **Blackwell**.

610- May 6, 1789- Howel **Lewis** to Charles **Lewis** of Mecklenburg Co., Va for 900 pds. 720 acres at Howel **Lewis**, Sr.'s line at fork of Mountain branch at **Munford**'s corner.

610- May 1789- John **Young**, sheriff, to John **Dickerson** 100 acres lately property of Henry **Smith**, on Little creek at **Wilkerson**'s corner.
Wts: Peter **Bennett**.

610, 611- May 9, 1787- John **Williams**, Bromfield **Ridley**, John **Somerville**, Howel **Lewis**, Sr., Thornton **Yancey**, Phil **Hawkins**, Jr., Robert **Coleman**, John **Young**, commissioner of town of Williamsborough, N.C. to Howel **Lewis**, Jr. for 6 pds. *Lot No. 40* in the town.
Wts: Robert **Coleman**, Stephen **Sneed**.

611- May 9, 1787- Commissioners of Williamsborough, N.C. to Howel **Lewis**, Jr. for 6 pds. *Lot No. 39* in Williamsborough, N.C.

611, 612- Commissioners of Williamsborough, N.C. to John **Brodie** for 6 pds. *lot No. 41* in Williamsborough, N.C. May 9,1787.

612- May 9, 1787- Commissioner to John **Brodie** for 6 pds. *lot No. 63* in Williamsborough, N.C.

612- July 29, 1789- Philemon **White** and William **Parham** to William **Hester** for 500 pds. 206 acres on **Bolling** and Cattail creeks at Ambrose **Barker**'s, Charles **Harris**'s lines.
Wts: William **Currin**.

613- Feb. 2, 1789- James **Cannon** to Nathaniel **Waller** (**Cannon** of Warren Co.) for 96 pds. 260 acres on Nap of Reeds creek at lines of Izabella **Ray**, Micajah **Bullock** and Nathaniel **Waller** being whole of land I bought of Nathaniel **Waller**-
Wts: Joseph **Taylor**, Wm. **Hunt**.

613- Feb. 2, 1789- Edmund **Carnes** to George **Lanemoore** for 120 pds. 224 acres on both sides of Ledge of Rocks creek on the sd. **Moore**'s corner at corner of **Chambless**'s land, Benjamin **More**'s, Jeremiah **Bullock**'s lines.
Wts: Micajah **Bullock**, Phillip **Bullock**.

614- Dec. 7, 1788- Richard **Nance** to John **Hooker** Sr, for 40 pds. 55 acres on E side of **Banks** road at **Nance**'s, **Taylor**'s, **McCulloh**'s line, **Glasgow**'s.
Wts: Micajah **Bullock**, Abraham **Lawrence**.

614, 615- Feb,14, 1789- James **Hefflin** to James **Paschal** for 57 pds. 280 acres on Beaverdam creek being where William **Wilkerson** lives on **Paschal**'s and **Hefflin**'s lines, John **Holt**'s line, **Smith**'s line.
Wts: Richard **Glasgow**, William **Wilkerson**.

615- Oct. 30, 1787- Berry **Lewis** of Franklin Co. N.C. to Thomas **Harp** of Granville Co. for 50 pds. 100 acres at **Smith**'s line.
Wts: Seth **Mabry**, Thomas **Turpin**.

316

615, 616- Feb. 10, 1789- Thomas **Lanier** to Elizabeth **Taylor**, William **Bullock**, Joseph **Taylor**, William **Penn** executors of John **Taylor** deceased for 84 pds. 10 shls. 169 acres on Beaverdam creek at **Taylor's** corner, Baxter **Davis's** line.
Wts: James **Lewis**, William **Bullock**, Jr.

616- June 26, 1789- Obadiah **Smith** of Chesterfield Co., Va. to Anderson **Smith** of Granville Co., N.C. for 300 pds. 469 acres in Granville Co. on both sides of middle fork of **Aaron**'s creek in **Smith**'s line- Luke **Smith**, Sr. of Halifax Co., Va. willed to his son Drury **Smith** the land whereon he did then live (Luke lived on land) and Drury **Smith** was to make a good deed to his brother Zachariah **Smith** for land in Carolina whereon John **Powel** then lived. Zachariah **Smith** died soon after and Drury **Smith** omitted making deed to land and Obediah **Smith** then claimed land and he willed to Obediah **Smith** who deeds it to Anderson **Smith**.
Wts: Robert **Burton**, Esq.

616, 617- Apr. 8, 1789- Rd **Banks** to John **Peuit** for 100 pds. 100 acres on Beaverdam creek at **Banks** and **Peuit**'s corner which was granted by State to R. **Banks**.
Wts: John **Pope**, B. **Bradford**.

617- Jan. 20, 1789- James **Carrington** of Orange Co., N.C. to Willm **Mangum** for 110 pds. 100 acres on Nap of Reeds creek at mouth of Hurricane branch at Frederick **Rose's** line, **Veazey**'s line.
Wts: John **Carrington**, Abraham **Davis**.

618- Mar. 13, 1789- Baxter **Ragsdale** to William **Penn** for 100 pds. 60 acres being land **Ragsdale** bought of Saml **Jones** and bound on every line by lands of John **Penn**.
Wts: Seth **Mabry**, John **Pope**, David **Ragsdale**.

618- June 25, 1785- Thomas **Key** to Norris **Pardue** for 50 pds. 100 acres on **Duke**'s branch on Ben **Guy**'s line, **Martin**'s line.
Wts: Salley **Reddin**, James **Harrison**.

618, 619- Dec. 19, 178?- Robert **Glover** and David **Glover** to Daniel **Glover** for 500 pds., all their share of land willed them by Joseph **Glover**, deceased, on both sides of Little Island creek containing 780 acres at Jesse **Harper**'s corner, **Buzbee**'s, Edward **Smith**'s, James **Lewis**'s corners to William **Marshall**'s line, **Hawkins**', along line formerly **McHarg**'s, to **Taylor**'s line, Ben **Norwood**'s line.
Wts: William **Byars**, Gulielmus **Byars**, James **Byars**.

619, 620- Mar. 21, 1789- Jonathan **Kittrell** to George **Alston** for 264 pds. 8 shls. 148 acres on River creek at my old corner on line of land I lately bought of Nicholas **Loyd**.
Wts: Dan. **Hunter**, William **Hunt**, Isham **Kittrell**.

620- May- 1789- Charles **Kennon** of Halifax Co., Va, to Dennis **Obryan** for 240 pds. 415 acres on both sides of Reedy creek at **Howard**'s corner, **Person**'s line.
Wts: John **Kennon**, Chas **Lewis**.

620- Apr. 3, 1768- Edmund **Taylor** of Mecklenburg Co., Va. gave to Timothy **Smith** and his wife Ann **Smith** the land whereon they now live containing 200 acres which I bought of Benj **Mitchel** and Timothy **Smith** agrees to will all his estate to Lewis **Taylor** son of Edmund **Taylor**, at his decease and at decease of wife Ann **Smith** and if Lewis **Taylor** die without heir then to Richard, son of Edmund **Taylor**.
Wts: James **Anderson**, Hen **Pendleton**, Ann **Brown**.

621- Mar. 11, 1789- John **Williams** esq. to William Johnston **Pattillo** son of the deceased, Henry **Pattillo**, for 6 pds. *lot No. 34* in the town of Williamsborough, N. C.
Wts: Leonard **Sims**, R. **Henderson**, Henry **Potter**.

621, 622- Aug. 1, 1789- William **Royster** Sr of Mecklenburg Co., Va. to Francis **Royster** of Granville Co., N. C. for 100 pds. 625 acres in Granville Co. at William **Royster**, Jr.'s line at lines of land of John **Stovall**, Thomas **Mutter**, and on Jonathan's creek, Grassy creek, Robert **Burley**'s line.
Wts: Thomas **Appling**, William **Royster**, Jr.

317

622- June 5, 1789- John **Woodburn** to John **Chappelear** for 75 pds. 300 acres at Philemon **Bradford**'s corner at James **Walker**'s line.
Wts: Z. **Higgs**, Joshua **Hutchinson**.

623- Feb. 12, 1789- John **Holt** to John **Quals** for 110 pds. 312 acres on both sides of **Robertson**'s fork of Beaverdam creek at Alexander **Vincent**'s line on Flag Spring branch at **Freeman**'s, **Bullock**'s, **Smith**'s lines to John **Thomas**'s corner
Wts: Micajah **Bullock**, Evan **Freeman**.

623, 624- Jan. 16, 1789- Isham **Harrison** and wife Amey to Samuel **Reaves** for 270 pds. 300 acres on Cedar creek in **Robinson** line to Arthur **Jordan**'s corner and **Eaton**'s line along Drury **Kimball**'s line on Indian creek.
Wts: Wm. **Gilliam**, Lewis **Reaves**, Thos. **Reaves**.

624- Nov, 3, 1789- Samuel **Sneed** to Bishop **Hicks** for 25 pds. 40 acres near the head of Flat creek on **Hicks**' line.
Wts: none.

624, 625- Mar. 2, 1789- Leonard **Clark** to Zachariah **Higgs** for 113 pds. 150 acres on W side of Tabbs creek at Joshua **Hays**' line on **Parham**'s line and on **Floyd**'s line.
Wts: James **Clark**, Charles C. **Clark**.

625- Sept. 10, 1787- Zachariah **Bevell** (**Bevil**) to David **Malone** for 100 pds. 258 acres on Grassy creek in **Smith**'s line to the road.
Wts: John **Oliver**, Robert **Malone**.

625, 626- Nov. 1, 1788- Henry **Langford** to George **Floyd** for 100 pds. 80 acres at mouth of Maple Spring branch at John **Smith**'s line to Leonard **Clark**'s line.
Wts: Z. **Higgs**, Sollomon **Higgs**.

626- June 19, 1789- David **Mitchel** administrator of John **Robison**, dec'd to Samuel **Revis** for 280 pds. 300 acres on **Lowe**'s line.
Wts: Sterling **Yancey**, Reuben **Morse**.

626, 627- Oct 2, 1788- Micajah **Bullock** to Mathew **Pryor** for 100 pds. 212 acres on W side of Ledge of Rocks creek at **Bullock**'s line, James **Claxton**'s line on **Byars** line.
Wts: Phillip **Bullock**, Philip **Pryor**.

627- Aug. 1, 1789- William **Royster** Sr. of Mecklenburg Co., Va. to John **Royster** of Granville Co., N.C. for 100 pds. 548 acres N.C. in Granville Co. N.C. on Grassy creek called Jonathan's creek at corner of William **Royster**'s land in John **Pomprett**'s line to William **Shatard**'s line at John **Stoval**'s on [Joel] **Chandler**'s line, Bartholomew **Stovall**'s line.
Wts. William **Royster** Jr., Thomas **Appling**.

628- Aug. 1, 1789- William **Royster**, Sr. of Mecklenburg Co., Va. to William **Royster**, Jr. for 100 pds. 500 acres at John **Stovall**'s line in James **Jones** on **Boling** road on John **Pomfret**'s line at William **Palmer**'s line and James **Bradford**'s line (**Bedford**) on Jonathan creek.
Wts: Thomas **Appling**, John **Royster**.

628, 629- Sept. 29 1788- Thomas **Satterwhite** and wife Ann to John **Somerville** for 54,200 weight of tobacco inspected at Peterburg, Va. 542 acres on N. and S sides of Little Nutbush Creek which **Satterwhite** purchased of James **Hunt** and adjoins **Somerville**'s land and on Thomas **Lanier**'s line, at David **Mitchel**'s line, on N. side of road.
Wts: Ro. **Burton**, Henry **Potter**.

629, 630- Nov. 5, 1789- John **Thomason** to Thomas **Satterwhite** for 62 pds. 157 acres on Fishing creek at **Hicks**'s corner, **Satterwhite**'s corner (formerly Isaac **Hicks**'s) on **Person**'s line, to **Tatome** (formerly **Brodie**'s) line.
Wts: None.

630- Oct. 8, 1789- Samuel **Peck** of Wake Co., N.C. and John Comer (Conner) **Peck** of Granville Co., N.C. for himself and as attorney for Henry **Peck** and Charles **Peck** to Caleb **Brasfield** of Granville Co, N. C. for 320 pds. a tract of land formerly the property of Leonard **Peck**, deceased, containing 153 acres and a half, which was willed to Lucy **Peck** his wife, for her life time or widow hood and who has since the death of Leonard **Peck**, married Caleb **Brasfield**. and we sell to them the land left her for life which

318
is on Neuse river at Richard **Benneham**'s line, John C. **Peck**'s line on Nap of Reeds creek.
Wts: Wm. **Hunt**, Jr., Jesse **Rice**, J. C. **Parker**.

630, 631- Oct. 15, 1789- Caleb **Brasfield** and Lucy his wife, to Richard **Benneham** of Orange Co., N. C. for 213 pds. 153 acres on Neuse river at **Benneham**'s corner on Nap of Reeds creek at John Comer **Peck**'s line.
Wts: none.

631- Aug. 15, 1789- Memucan **Hunt** and wife Mary to Anderson **Hunt** for love and affection, a deed of gift of 143 acres on N. side of Tar river being land whereon Elizabeth **Williams**, deceased, formerly lived which was bequeathed by William **Williams**, deceased, to his son Stephen **Williams** who transferred it to Thomas **Critcher** by deed of trust who sold it to Memucan **Hunt**.
Wts: E. **Hunt**, Willm **Healy**, Polly **Hunt**, Thomas **Hunt**.

632- Dec. 23, 1789- Lewis **Taylor** to Frederick **Owen** for 7, 200 pds. weight of neat mercantile tobacco 100 acres on S side of Island creek at Daniel **Marrow**'s line, Nathl **Parrot**'s line, David **Christopher**'s line.
Wts: Micj **Bullock**, Edmd **Taylor**, Jr., John **White**.

632, 633- June 13, 1787- Nathan **Harris** to Robert **Allin** for 50 pds. land on **Beckham**'s creek at Isaac **Fuller**'s line on **Harris**'s line which was granted June 1783 by Alexa **Martin**, esq., governor of N.C. to **Harris**.
Wts: Jeremiah **Bailey**, Samuel **Bailey**.

633- Feb. 2, 1789- William **Mangum**, Jr. of Orange Co., N.C. to Arthur **Frazer** of Granville Co., N.C. for 110 pds. 100 acres on both sides of Nap of Reeds creek at **Nott**'s line at mouth of Hurricane branch, **Harrison** branch.
Wts: James and John **Knott**.

634- Sept. 2, 1788- Reuben **Searcy** to Robert **Burton** for 100 pds. *lot No. 56* in Williamsborough, N. C.
Wts: Henry **Potter**.

634- Nov. 17, 1787- Edward **Noland** to Reuben **Searcy** for 5 shillings 149 acres on branches of Tar river at Benjamin **Beardennn**'s line **Johnson**'s line and line formerly Richard **Harris**'s, **Potter**'s and **Noland**'s corner.
Wts: Benjamin **Bearden**.

635- Nov, 28, 1789- John **Finch** to Thomas **Jenkins** of Warren Co., N.C. for 180 pds. 275 acres on Tabbs creek at **Thomas**'s and **Finch**'s corner to Joshua **Kittrell**'s line, **Loyd**'s line, **Walker**'s, **Mason**'s, **Dickerson**'s lines.
Wts: John **Walker**, William **Hunt**.

635, 636- July 3, 1789- John **Young**, sheriff of Granville Co. to Sarah Crosha **Barnett** for 200 pds. land lately property of Thomas **Barnett**, deceased, sold at public auction.
Wts: P. **Bennett**.

636- Jan. 16, 1790- Thomas **Thompson** to Charles **Lewis** for 200 pds. land on Tabbs creek whereon I now live, on Glebe road at George **Harris**'s line which was bought of Nicholas **Matlock**, William **Hicks**, John **White**.
Wts: Joseph **Taylor**, James **Butler**.

636, 637- Feb. 2, 1790- Samuel Farrer **Williams** to Reuben **Morse** for 300 pds. 200 acres on both sides of Great Nutbush creek at **Morse**'s corner at old Trading Path at **Wiggins**' corner, **Person**'s corner, **Williams**' line.
Wts: Howel **Morse**, Frederick **Wiggins**.

637- 638- Jan. 9, 1789- Richard **Wilkins** to Absalom **Davis** for 266. pds., 355 acres, one tract of 185 acres on both sides of Poplar creek the 2nd tract 120 acres at William **Barton**'s line to **Standard**'s old corner, the 3rd tract of 50 acres on William **Hicks** line, Benjamin **Hester**'s and on Poplar creek.

Wts: Jas. P. **Davis**, Darwin **Harris**, Allen **Wilkins**.

638- Dec. 24, 1787- Nathan **Jackson** of Virginia to George **Cavener** of Granville Co. for 120 pds. 140 acres on Horn creek at **Goodloe**'s corner being part of land bought of William **Liles** by **Jackson**.
Wts: William **Lile**, Chas. **Champion**, Jackson **Lile**.

319

638, 639- Nov. 2, 1789- Zacharias **Higgs** to Micael **Wood** for 75 pds. 150 acres on W side of Tabbs creek on Joshua **Hays'** line.
Wts: Joshua **Hutchinson**, Sothoron **Higgs**.

639- Dec. 3, 1789- John **Gilliam** to Joseph Pomfret **Davis** for 102 pds. 6 shillings, 341 acres on both sides of Lick branch at **Loyd**'s corner .
Wts: Absalom **Davis** , Isham **Akin**, E **Mitchel**, J. **Critcher**.

640- Jan. 28, 1790-John **Craft** to Stephen **Sneed** for 300 pds. 200 acres at **Craft**'s corner, **Brown**'s line.
Wts: Henry **Potter**, E. **Mitchel**

640, 641- Sept. 2, 1788- Reuben **Searcy** to Robert **Burton** for 100 pds. 149 acres on Tar river on Samuel **Johnston**'s line, **Bearden**'s corner, **Burton**'s line formerly **Potter**'s, on line formerly Richard **Harris**'s line Henry **Potter**, Francis **Bussier** witnesses.

641- Jan. 1, 1790- John **Lemay** and Samuel **Lemay** to Lewis **Lemay** for 50 pds. 475 [acres] at **Daniel**'s, **Beesley**'s, **Smith**'s, **Downey**'s lines.
Wts: Joseph **Hart**, Wm. **Gill**.

641, 642- Feb. 1, 1789- John **Owens** to William **Owens**, Sr. for 100 pds. 400 acres whereon William **Owens**, Sr. now lives on Beaverdam creek at Henry **Montague**'s line, **Davis**'s line, **Mitchel**'s line.
Wts: Henry **Graves**, Frederick **Owens**.

642- Dec. 23, 1789- Lewis **Taylor** to David **Christopher** of Mecklenburg Co., Va. for 65 pds. 111 acres on S side of Island creek on **Parrot**'s line.
Wts: Edmd **Taylor**, John **White**.

642, 643- Dec. 23, 1789- Lewis **Taylor** to John **White** of Mecklenburg Co., Va. for 73 pds. 111½ acres on S side of Island creek at William **Bullock**'s line in Granville Co., N.C.
Wts: Edmd **Taylor**, Jr., David **Christopher**.

643- Jan. 30, 1790-Samuel **Harris**, son of Robert **Harris**, to Samuel **Harris**, son of Richard **Harris**, for 50 pds. 18 acres.
Wts. none.

644- Dec. 26, 1789- William **Millner** to Richard **Millner** for 150 pds. 150 acres on S side of Mountain creek on Jonathan's creek at Thos. **Mutter**'s line, Joseph **Farmer**'s line.
Wts: Charles **Crenshaw**, John **Gess**.

644, 645- Nov. 15, 1787- Rowland **Bryant** to Joseph **Peace** for 50 pds. 565 acres at mouth of Fishing creek along **Taylor**'s line, in **Cooper**'s line along **Snelling**'s line on bank of the river.
Wts: Henry **Hays**, John **Peace**, Jr.

645- Feb. 1, 1790- William **Owens** to John **Owens** for 100 pds. 400 acres whereon John **Owen** now lives on Beaverdam creek at B. **Davis**'s, Henry **Montague**'s, Anderson **Smith**'s lines.
Wts: Henry **Graves**, Frederick **Owen**.

645, 646- Aug. 7, 1789- John **Holt** to John **Chadwick** for 60 pds. 200 acres on **Roberson**'s creek on **Vincent**'s line along **Lawrnese**'s line.
Wts: P. **Bradford**, James **Paschal**.

646- Apr. 4, 1789- Isaac **Hicks** of Wake Co., N.C. to Thomas **Satterwhite** of Granville Co., N.C. for 30,000 weight of tobacco 500 acres in Granville Co., N.C. on Reuben **Talley**'s line, formerly John **Wilkes**' line, at Edward **Bass**'s line on Reuben **Talley**'s and James **Crews**' lines, Robert **Hicks**, Jr.'s line being the tract of land Robert **Hicks**, Sr. conveyed to his son Isaac **Hicks**- Dec. 29, 1779.
Wts: Jno. **Brodie**, Solo. **Walker**, Fra **Eastwood**.

647- Feb. 2, 1790- William **Hunt** to Benjamin **Beardin** for 40 pds. 200 acres on Cattail creek on the old road at line formerly **Alston**'s land.
Wts: none.

647- Aug. 29, 1789- John **Chadwick** to Frederick **Wiggins** for 65 pds. 152 acres on both sides of Nutbush creek down Great Branch at Frederick **Wiggins**' line, Reuben **Moss**'s line, Thomas **Wiggins**' line.
Wts: Reuben **Morse**, Charnick **Cox**.

320

648- July 2, 1789- John **Young**, sheriff of Granville Co., N.C. to Garrott **Goodloe**, administrator of Kemp **Goodloe**, deceased, for 175 pds. land that was property of Kemp **Goodloe**, deceased, at lines of land of **Champion**'s at Tarborough road near James **Kelley**'s line on the creek.
Wts. P. **Bennett**.

648, 649- Apr. 25, 1790- Charles **Partee** to John **Williams** for 300 pds. 100 acres on N. side of **Webb**'s Mill creek to Isham **Johnston**'s line on **Parker**'s line at Jefferson road along Edmund **Partee's** line at **Bowling**'s Mountain to the corner of Widow **Cozart**'s land on **Eastwood**'s line at **Partee**'s and **Williams**' lines to Benja **Partee**'s corner at Samuel **Jackson**'s line and on William **Webb**'s line, **Clements'** line.
Wts: Benja **Fowler**, Abner **Partee**, Isham **Johnston**.

649, 650- Feb. 3, 1787- Ralph **Williams** to Benjamin **Moore** for 85 pds. 193 acres on Ledge of Rocks creek on **Bullock**'s line, **Wade**'s line.
Wts: Rd. D. **Cooke**, Jeremiah **Bullock**.

650- Dec. 2 8, 1789- Manus **Weaver** to Thomas **Rowland** for 50 pds. 75 acres on E side of Nutbush creek on **Rowland**'s line at John **Weaver**'s Spring Branch.
Wts: Thomas **Reavis**, Lewis **Reavis**.

650, 651- May 3, 1790-John **Williams** to Solomon **Williams** for 5 shld. 133 acres on north side of Tar river at **Hunt**'s line.
Wts: William **Walker**, William **Philpott**.
End of Book - - -O

Book N 1790-1793

321

1- Mar. 11, 1788- William **Nailing** to William **Jeffreys** for 65 pds. 100 acres on E side of Middle creek on **Shepperd**'s line.
Wts: Nelson **Nailing**, Phil **Bowers**, J. **Peace**, Jr.

1, 2- July 17, 1789- Gideon **Gooch** to James **Smith** for 50 pds. 100 acres on Island creek at **Gooch**'s, **Penn**'s lines, **Person**'s line and on New road.
Wts: John **Hall**, John **Gooch**.

2- Aug. 3, 1787- Edmund **Carnes** to [Joel] **Chambless** for 50 pds. 153 acre on William **Swinney**'s corner, on W side of Ledge of Rocks creek, at Richard D. **Cooke**'s corner, George L. **Moore**'s line, **Cash**'s.
Wts: Micajah **Bullock**, Ralph **Williams**.

2, 3- Oct. 10, 1789- William **Smith** to Daniel **Edwards** of Franklin Co., N.C. for 30 pds. 45 acres on **Eaton**'s line on main road at **Smith**'s line and at Samuel **Fuller**'s line.
Wts: Wm. **Cook**, Britain **Fuller**, Danl **Hunter**.

3- Aug. 1, 1789- William **Jones**, Sr. to William **Jones**, Jr. for 100 pds. 100 acres on Nap of Reeds creek on George **Alston**'s line.
Wts: Jeremiah **Bullock**, Joseph **Cash**.

4-.. 2, 1784- John **Mize** to William **Rose** for 133 pds. 6 shls. 8 pence 177 acres on S side of Tar river.
Wts: John **Manire**, Howel **Rose**.

4- Dec. 29, 1789- Richard **Harris** to Samuel **Harris** for 200 pds. 260 acres at Samuel **Harris**'s spring branch on the road, at Smith **Ogelvie**'s line, Nicholas **Holstein**'s creek.
Wts: Absalom **Ford**, Priscilla **Harris**, Lewis **Bennet**.

5- July 22, 1788- Edward **Noland** to William **Jones** for 100 pds. 80 acres on Tar river on Mill Path, at Reuben **Searcy**'s line to the old road running to John **Minor**'s line and **Bearden**'s line.
Wts: Benjamin **Bearden**, Abraham **Lawrence**.

5, 6- Apr. 24, 1790-Fowler **Jones** to William **Jones**, Jr. for 100 pds. 200 acres known as *Tract no. 12* at Michael **Wilson**'s corner.
Wts: David **Parker**, Benjamin **Fowler**.

6- Nov. 7, 1789- Joseph **Taylor** to **Stewart** and **Muir**, merchants, of Halifax, N.C. On Feb. 5, 1787 James **Jett** sold to Joseph **Taylor** 118 acres on west side of Tabbs creek but conveyed 500 acres to **Taylor** instead of the 118 as deeded. This indenture deeds to **Stewart** and **Muir**, merchants, of Halifax, N.C. at request of father of James **Jett**, namely Stephen **Jett**, he now deeds 381 acres on East side of the creek.
Wts: Joseph **Taylor**, Jr., Archd **Jett**.

6, 7- Nov. 3, 1789- Daniel **Malone** to William **Irby** for 50 pds. 250 acres on Grassy creek in **Smith**'s line to the road.
Wts: James **Downey**, Jr., J. **Kennon**.

7- Feb. 19, 1787- William **Rose** and Stephen **Merritt** to Brereton **Jones** for 200 pds. 177 acres on S side of Tar river.
Wts: Mary **Merritt**, Phil **Noland**, Wm. **Jones**.

8- May 15, 1789- Ezekiel **Fuller** to Cornelius **Cooper** for 49 pds. 82 acres on Tar river at **Fuller**'s and **Dickerson**'s line, **Williams** line, at **Thomas**'s corner.
Wts: Jonathan **McKassick**, Henry **Williams**.

8, 9- Feb. 1, 1790- Bartholomew **Stovall** to John **Stovall** for 5 pds. 7½ acres at line 25 ft. from Jonathan creek.
Wts: George **Stovall**, David **Stovall**, Thos **Voss**.

9 Apr, 23, 1790-Sherwood **Harris**, the elder, to Josiah **Rucks** for 78 pds. 156 acres whereon Josiah **Rucks** now lives on Tar river at **Longmire**'s corner.
Wts: Edmd **Taylor**, Nath. **Moore**.

322

9, 10- Apr. 20, 1790- Demcey **Moore** to Charles **Mitchel** for 1100 pds. 1203 acres on Fishing creek to Michael **Wilson**'s former corner and at **Benton's** former line, **Willis**'s former line, **Smith**'s former line, **Hutching**'s former line.
Wts: Joseph **Taylor**, Fr. **Busiere**.

10, 11- Aug. 3, 1790- Samuel **Smith**, Esq., sheriff, to Joseph **Taylor** the land of Reuben **Butler**, ordered sold by court at suit for debt. William **Kennon** sued Reuben **Butler** 200 acres sold to Joseph **Taylor** as highest bidder for same on **Person**'s old field.

11,12- Aug. 3, 1790- Samuel **Smith**, William **Bullock**, a tract of land as property of Nehemiah **Long** at suit brought by Alexander **Black** and Nathaniel **Allen** for debt in Northampton Co.1700 acres sold to William **Bullock** as highest bidder, adjoining land of John **Taylor** deceased, William **Penn**, Mary **Hester**, Ralph **Graves** and George **Norman**, and William **Bullock**, being land Nehemiah **Long** bought of Wm. **Taylor**- June 16, 1774.

12- Aug. 5, 1790- Memucan **Hunt** to Edward **Hunt** for 5 pds. and love he bears for his son Edward, 263 acres on both sides of Grassy creek being land he bought of Thomas **Bond** July 31, 1784 on Mountain Creek at **Graves**' corner.

13- Dec. 26, 1789- Sherwood **Parrish** to William **Minor** for 25 pds. 35 acres on E side of Fishing creek at **Taylor**'s line.
Wts: Elijah **Parrish**, Reuben **Inscoe**.

13- Jan. 13, 1790- Richard **Glasgow** to Bressie **Parrish** for 400 pds. 361 acres on S side of **Nance**'s branch and on N. side of middle fork of Beaverdam creek, on John **Moore**'s corner, William **Lawrence**'s corner.
Wts: John **Hooker**, William [**Hooker**].

13, 14- July 31, 1790- Lewis **Taylor** to Edmund **Taylor**, Jr. for 700 pds. land on N. side of Island creek at Lewis **Taylor**'s line containing 1000 acres adjoining land of William **Bullock**, Jacob **Mitchel**, Anderson **Smith**, the country line, Daniel **Marrow**, James **Lewis**.
Wts: Edmund **Taylor**, Sr., Nathl **Moore**.

14. .1790- William **Gill** to William **Shepard** for 40 pds. 228 acres on **Puryear**'s and James **Yancey**'s corners to **Bohannon**'s corner, **Wade**'s corner and on Charles **Harris**'s line.

14, 15- Jan. 19, 1789- John **McKissack** of Caswell Co., N.C. to John **Simmons** of Granville Co. for 6 pds. 100 acres granted to John **McKissock** for 600 acres May 2, 1752 of which this is part.
Wts: William **McKissock**, John **Simmons**.

15, 16- Nov. 7, 1785- Sherwood **Winningham** to John **Whitfield** for 40 pds. 340 acres which is part of tract granted to **Winningham** Oct. 15, 1783 for 1650 acres on Cedar and Beaverdam creeks in **Pope**'s line, **Huskey**'s and **Whitfield**'s lines.
Wts: Ozborn **Pope**, John **Husketh**s, and John **Husketh**, Jr.

16- Dec. 12, 1789- Edward **Loyd** to George **Alston** for 24 pds. 12 shls. 41 acres on Ruin creek on **Alston**'s, formerly **Kittrell**'s, corner near Church Spring branch.
Wts: John **Nuttall**, Elisha **Linsey**, Sherd **Cawthorn**.

16, 17- Feb. 16, 1790- Joel **Chambless** to George **Lanemoore** for 80 pds. 153 acres on **Lanemoore**'s line on Ledge of Rocks creek at William **Searcy**'s and Richard D. **Cooke**'s corners, **Parker**'s line. Wm. **Jones**' line.
Wts: Wm. **Webb**, Jeremiah **Bullock**.

17, 18- Sept. 10, 1789- Baxter **Davis** and wife Amelia, of Mecklenburg Co., Va. to Anderson **Smith** for 200 pds. 200 acres at the county line, on **Smith**'s line, Lewis **Taylor**'s line.
Wts: Thomas **Mutter**, John **Stamper**.

18- Sept. 10, 1789- Baxter **Davis**, and wife Amelia of Mecklenburg Co., Va. to Anderson **Smith** for 200 pds. 250 acres on Beaver Pond creek at **Davis**'s corner on country line.
Wts: Thomas **Mutter**, John **Stamper**.

323

18, 19- Sept. 10, 1789- Baxter **Davis** to Anderson **Smith** for 500 pds. 400 acres on both sides of Beaver Pond creek at the country line.
Wts: Thomas **Mutter**, John **Stamper**.

19, 20- Sept. 18, 1789- Baxter **Davis** of Mecklenburg Co., Va. to Anderson **Smith** for 100 pds. 250 acres adjoining lands of Jacob **Mitchel** and Baxter **Davis** at Virginia line on **Maynard**'s Ferry road.
Wts: Thomas **Mutter**, John **Stamper**.

20- Aug. 3, 1790- James **Downey**, Sr. to James **Downey**, Jr. for 250 pds. 350 acres on both sides of Grassy creek at James **Johnston**'s line, **Davis**'s line, **Smith**'s line, Baxter **Davis**'s line.
Wts: Allen **Howard**, J. **Kennon**.

20, 21- July 31, 1790- Edmund **Taylor** to Lewis **Taylor** for 700 pds. 1540 acres on S side of Tar river at **Lewis**'s line, **Holsteins**'s. line adjoining **Champion**, **Hornsby** and **White**'s lines.
Wts: Nathl **Moore**, Edmd. **Taylor**, Sr.

21- Feb. 14, 1788- Joseph **Johnston** to Charles Rust **Eaton** for 49 pds. 49 acres on Reedy branch on **Eaton**'s line.
Wts: Reuben **Searcy**.

21, 22- Nov. 29, 1787- Augustine **Wright** of Wake Co., N.C. to John **Pope**, Jr. of Granville Co. for 40 pds. 300 acres on S side of Cedar creek on Peter **Vinson**'s corner, and at **Hindley**'s branch being part of tract whereon Winfield **Wright** formerly lived and by him conveyed to Susanna **Wright** by will (Augustine **Wright**, heir of Thomas **Wright**).
Wts: Benjamin **Morgan**, Ozborn and John **Pope**.

22- Feb. 20, 1787- Brereton **Jones** to Robert **Hester** for 120 pds. 596 acre in **Daniel**'s line on **Hester**'s own line, **Graves'** and **Oliver**'s lines, and at **Edwards**' and **Wilkerson**'s lines, **Bennett**'s line.
Wts: Luke **Landers**, Stephen **Hester**.

23- May 21, 1787- Nicholas **Loyd** to Charles Rust **Eaton** for 20 pds. 49 acres in **Eaton**'s line on the old road at **Locke**'s line.
Wts:, Wm. **Hunt**.

23, 24- May 5, 1790- Stephen **Merritt** to William **Oakley** for 46 pds. 100 acres on N. side of Cub creek.
Wts: Thos. and John **Oakley**.

24- July 29, 1790- John **Dickerson** to Laban **Haislip** for 30 pds. 100 acres on Fort creek at John **Peace**, Jr. line.
Wts: John **Dickerson**, H. **Williams**.

24, 25 - Mar. 12, 1790- James Minge **Burton** to Bromfield **Ridley** for 5 shl 100 acres which is the land devised to Frances **Keeling**, now wife of Bromfield **Ridley**, by will of John **Sims**, deceased, on N. side of Reedy branch, in Warren County, N.C.
Wts: James **Ridley**, Reuben **Ragland**.

25, 26- May 11, 1790- Bromfield **Ridley** and wife Frances to James Minge **Burton** for 5 shls. 100 acres on N. side of Reedy branch being the land devised to Frances **Keeling** by John **Sims**, deceased, in Warren county, N. C. now wife of Bromfield **Ridley**.
Wts: Reuben **Ragland**, James **Ridley**.

26- July 25, 1761- Grant from Lord Granville to John **Rowe** (**Roe**) of Granville Co. for 433 acres on both sides of Island Creek at **Davonport**'s corner, **Lyne**'s line, **Glover**'s line.
Wts: J. **Montford**, Jos **Edwards**.

27- Apr. 11, 1788- James **Hogg** deposes before William **McCauley** and William **Lytle**, J. P. of Orange Co., Va. that John Minge **Burton** bought from James **Hogg** Oct. 11, 1779 certain lands in Virginia which is part of grant to [Richard **Henderson** and Co] at mouth of the river.

27, 28- Oct. 11, 1779- Williamsburg, Va. Capital of Virginia In 1778 Richard [**Henderson**], Esq and Co. for quieting the minds of the Indians, was granted land on the river Ohio at the mouth of Green River and SE side of Ohio River and by several courses thereof 12½ miles turning right 12½ miles each way from Green river

324
James **Hogg**, copartner, of Orange Co., Virginia for 2000 pds. conveys his share of the lands granted to Richard [**Henderson** and Co], to Robert **Burton** which is 1/8th of the whole grant, excepting ¼ of the 1/8th which I sold to William **Day** and 12,500 acres heretofore sold to Robert **Burton** which he sold to Dorsey **Penticost**, being part of grant made to Richard **Henderson** and Co.
Wts: [Nathl **Rochester**],Thos. **Burke**, John **Penn**.

28-[29]- Oct. 28, 1790- Barnett **Pulliam** to John **Pulliam** for 110 pds. 147 acres in Granville Co. on **Harrol**'s creek at **Crew**'s line and on Mirey branch to Anderson **Ford**'s line.
Wts: Jo. P. [**Davis**].

29, 30- Aug. 28, 1790- Jonathan **Knight** to Thomas **Mutter** for 56 pds. 10 shls. 6 pence, 21½ acres on Grassy creek at **Young**'s line which is at corner of land purchased by **Mutter** of Allen **Love**.
Wts: Samuel **Smith**, M. **Hunt**.

30- Aug. 16, 1790- Solomon **Walker** to Bishop **Hicks** for 128 pds. 171 acres whereon **Hicks** now lives at Samuel **Jeter**'s corner at mouth of **Worley**'s branch.
Wts: Joseph **Taylor**, John **Brodie**.

30, 31- Dec. 26, 1785- Henry **Williams** and wife Priscilla to Henry **Townes** of Mecklenburg Co., Va. for 45 pds. 100 acres being land taken up by James **Butler** and registered in Book N. folio 107 on Beaverdam branch at John **Taylor** and Jacob **Mitchel** lines.
Wts: John **Smith**, John **Reaves**, J. **Downey**, Jr.

31- Nov. 2, 1790- Thomas **Lanier** to William **Lanier** for love and good will toward his son, a deed of gift of 900 acres and 11 negroes reserving use for myself for my lifetime.. . land on Nutbush creek and reserving to wife Judith for her lifetime, the land and hands which is at John **Somerville**'s line, to the chimney at south end of my dwelling house thence by the middle wall of house to chimney in north end of house, and west to a branch at Mr. **Somerville**'s other line. This part of land to my wife Judith for her lifetime, and my son to support my daughter Mary for her lifetime, then all to be his in fee simple.
Wts: Thomas **Satterwhite**, [James] **Vaughn**, John **Brodie**.

32- Mar. 21, 1778- John **Williams** to Robert **Burton** a deed of gift John **Williams**, Thomas **Hart**, Nathaniel **Hart**, William **Johnston**, James **Hogg**, John **Lutsell**, David **Hart**, Len Henley **Bullock** in reference to the grant of Richard **Henderson** and co. who bought of the Cherokee Indians on Mar. 17, 1775, land on the Ohio River.
John **Williams** gave to Robert **Burton**, ¼ th. part of his, **Williams**'s, 1/8 part of the land purchased of the Cherokees.
Wts: Bromfield **Ridley**, Adam **Rice**.

32, 33- Dec. 6, 1788- William **Wright** to Wm. **Thomason** for 50 pds. 100 acres on Fishing creek near the road in Granville Co.
Wts: Wm. **Reaves**, Robert **Smith**.

33- Aug. 25 1788- Reuben **Searcy** to Reuben **Parker** for 25 pds. 50 acres on Cattail and **Bolling** creek at **Beardon**'s line.
Wts: Lewis **Page**, Sarah **Mitchel**.

33, 34- Oct. 4, 1790- Robert **Crawley** and wife Mary of Mecklenburg Co., Va. to James **Lewis** of Granville Co. for 170 pds. 176 acres in Granville Ce. on both sides of **Gillam**'s branch at **Crawley**'s and **Lewis**'s lines, in the county line.
Wts: Field **Rudd**, James [**Wortham**].

34, 35 1790- Barnett **Pulliam** to Samuel **Clay** for 40 pds. 54 Acres on **Harrell**'s creek in Granville Co. at **Meades**', **Clay**'s and **Boyd**'s lines.
Wts: Jo. P. **Davis**.

35- Sept, 3, 1790- Ezekiel **Fuller** to his son Benjamin **Fuller** a gift of the land whereon he now lives containing 268 acres on Cornelius **Cooper**'s and Capt Samuel **Walker**'s lines.
Wits: Ja. **Johnston**, Isaiah **Smith**.

325

35, 36. Jan, 13, 1790- Brissie **Parrish** to Richard **Glasgow** for 150 acres on E side of Little Ruin Creek.
Wts: John **Hooker**, William **Hooker**.

36- Nov. 1, 1790- William **Penn** to Richard **Taylor** of Mecklenburg Co., Va for 1200 pds. 1900 acres in Granville Co., N.C. being whole of tract purchased by John **Penn** in his lifetime of William **Chavis**, Benjamin **Seawell**, Thomas **Frohock**, Gibson and Sherwood **Harris**, Baxter **Ragsdale**- 164 acres in forks of Tar river not included in this grant-

37- Nov. 27, 1790- Robert **Crawley** and wife Mary of Mecklenburg Co. to Lucy **Crawley** for 5 shls. and love of her, our daughter, 239 acres in Granville Co., N.C. on country line at James **Lewis**'s corner.
Wts: Hannah **Crawley**, Gilliam **Norwood**, James **Aiken**, Samuel **Smith**.

37, 38- May 4, 1789- Molten **Gray** to William **Cawthorn** for 100 pds. 300 acres on Ridge path to the new road at Champion **Allen**'s line and on **Roberts**' line, **Huskey**'s line.
Wts: Richard **Hudspeth**, Jesse **Cawthorn**.

38- Feb. 21, 1788- John **Whitfield** to Morton **Gray** for 40 pds. 300 acres on Ridge Path to the new road at Champion **Allen**'s line, **Roberts**' and **Huskey**'s lines.
Wts: Edmund and James **Taylor**.

38, 39- Feb. 3, 1791- Bird Booker **Bradford** to Harris **Bradford** for 100 pds. 150 acres on Reedy branch of Beaverdam creek. at **Pewet**'s line and **Clement**'s line.
Wts: Joseph **Peuit**, James **Mann**.

39- Feb. 7, 1790- Reuben **Morse** to Stephen **Sneed** for 20 pds. 15 acres on **Sneed**'s line.
Wts: Charles **Williams**, John **Moss**.

40- Feb. 8, 1791- James **Lewis** to William **Shanks** for 20 pds. 40 acres at **Taylor**'s Ferry road on **Marrow**'s line, **Shanks**' corner, the country line at Island creek bridge on **Taylor**'s ferry road.
Wts: none.

40, 41- Jan. 27, 1791- Vinkler **Jones**, Sr. to John **Williams**, esq, for 5 shls. 20 3/4ths acres on S side of Flat creek on **Williams**'s line.
Wts: Elijah **Mitchel**, Micajah **Bullock**.

41- William **Wright** (**Right**) to Richard **Thomason** for 100 pds. 176 acres on **McDaniel**'s line, **Smith**'s corner, **Harrison**'s corner, **Dickerson**'s line.
Wts: Thomas **Thomason**, Francis **Thomason**, Sr.

41, 42- May 14, 1790- Woodson **Daniel** of Wake Co., N.C. to Nicholas **Derning** of Orange Co., N.C. for 40 pds. 225 acres on Cedar creek at lines of Henry **McCulloh**'s *tract No 1.*
Wts: Elijah **Veazey**, B. **Clark**.

42- Oct. 29, 1790- Benjamin **Robinson** of Mecklenburg Co to William **Shanks** for 20 pds. 100 acres in Granville Co. on the country line at Island creek on James **Lewis**'s line.
Wts: Daniel **Marrow**.

43- Aug. 17, 1790- Lewis and Henry **Potter** to Solomon **Walker** for 600 pds. 700 acres being whole tract purchased of sheriff of Granville Co on S side of Tar river including the mill and adjoining lands of Alexander **Boyd** and Samuel

Harris.
Wts: A. **Henderson**, Joseph **Taylor**, Chas. **Mitchel**.

43, 44- Feb. 9, 1791- Robert **Burton** to Bartholomew **Strum** for 26 pds. land at **Taylor**'s line (John **Taylor**), on the road, which divided lands of **Strum** and **Sheppard**.

44- Nov. 24, 1790- Frederick **Rose** to James **Meadows** for 204 pds. 300 acres on Nap of Reeds creek crossing **Kemp** creek.
Wts: John **Washington**, John **Williams**.

44, 45- Mar. 26, 1789- Thomas **Williams** to Archibald **Mitchel** for 100 pds. 103 acres on **Bolling** creek at Richard **Searcy**'s line, **Linsey**'s line.
Wts: James and John **Sample**.

326

45, 46- May 9, 1787- Commissioners of Williamsborough, N.C. to Howel **Moss** for 6 pds. *Lot No 17* in the town.
Wts: Stephen **Sneed**.

46- Feb. 7, 1791- Peter **Bennett** to Chesley **Daniel** for 111 pds. 275 acres whereon **Bennett** now lives on Grassy creek in **Hester**'s line, formerly **Roberts**'line, **Wilkerson**'s line.
Wts: Mary and Jane **Daniel**.

46, 47- May 28, 1790- Brereton **Jones** to Simon **Clement** for 53 pds. 10 shls. 177 acres on S side of Tar river on William **Graves**' and Stephen **Clement**'s lines.
Wts: Obed **Clement**, Saml **Clement**.

47, 48- Oct. 24, 1790- Jonathan **Knight** to William **Amis**, Jr. for 25 pds. 190 acres on Grassy creek at **Amis**'s corner, Jonathan **Knight**'s line.
Wts: Lewis **Amis**, Thomas **Mutter**, Jr.

48- Aug. 4, 1788- George **King** to John **Williams** for 50 pds. 200 acres on Lick branch on the new road at James **Bishop**'s line, Bromfield **Ridley**'s line.
Wts: Chas. **Williams**, John **Nucholds**.

48, 49- Aug. 23, 1790- Edmund **Taylor** of Mecklenburg Co., Va. to Daniel **Marrow** of Granville Co., N.C. for 90 pds. 450 acres on N. side of Island creek at a branch above the house where **Marrow** now lives and on road to **Taylor**'s ferry on Capt. James **Lewis**'s line.
Wts: David **Christopher**, Thos. **Field**, Thos. **Hord**.

49, 50- Feb. 3, 1791- John **Pewit** to Harris **Bradford** for 100 pds. 70 acres on Reedy branch of Beaverdam creek in his own line at **Bradford**'s and **Clement**'s line.
Wts: Joseph **Puit**, John **Pewit**, Jr.

50- Nov. 1790- John **Holt** to John **Chadwick** for 80 pds. 125 acres on Beaverdam creek at **Quall**'s corner, **Smith**'s corner.
Wts: James **Paschal**, James **Hefflin**.

50, 51- Jan. 7, 1791- David **Glaze** of Wilks Co., Georgia to Lewis **Amis** of Granville Co., N.C. for 75 pds. 112 acres on Grassy creek at Jonathan **Knight**'s corner in Elizabeth **Butler**'s line on Memucan **Hunt**'s line.
Wts: A. **Hunt**, John **Reaves**, Thomas **Mutter**.

51- May 1790- George Lane **Moore** to Benjamin **Moore** for 10 pds. 18 acres on Ledge of Rocks creek at **King**'s corner, in my own line and Benjamin **Moore**'s to **Bullock**'s line.
Wts: none.

52- Feb. 9, 1791- Robert **Burton** to Stephen **Sneed** for 45 pds. 10 acres on the old road on the church lot at the middle of Ferry road.

52, 53- Dec. 13, 1783- William **Trusty** to Fowler **Jones** for 50 pds. 100 acres on Nap of Reeds creek at **Ross**'s line.
Wts: William **Jones**, John **Boling**.

53- Feb. 16, 1791- Seth **Pettypool** to Ambrose **Jones** for 50 pds. 60 acres on S side of **Aaron**'s creek at John [**Pettypool**]'s line, in Ambrose **Jones**'s line.
Wts: James **Jones**, Stephen **Jones**, Robert P. **Pool**.

54- Mar. 18, 1791- John, Wm., Orston and Valentine **Parrish** to Thomas **Ricks** for 25 pds. 100 acres on Tabbs creek on **Kimbal**'s line, on Charles **Parrish**'s line (Mary **Parrish**, widow, relinquishes her dower right).
Wts: Z. **Higgs**, S. **Higgs**- signed John **Parrish**, William **Parrish**, Orston **Parrish**, Valentine **Parrish**.

54, 55 -[day of] -1791- James **Downey**, Jr. to Thomas **Voss** for 120 pds. 120 acres on Grassy creek at Abraham **Crenshaw**'s liner on Mountain creek at **Smith**'s corner, formerly Daniel **Malone**'s line, and another tract on Courthouse road on Gideon **Crenshaw**'s line, **Malone**'s and **Daniel**'s lines for 65 acres and 120 acres adjoining at **Landers** (Luke) **Daniel**'s line In all 417 acres.
Wts: Gid **Crenshaw**, John **Downey**.

327

55- Mar. 26, 1790- Joseph **Hester** to James **Meadows** for 100 pds. 50 acres on Tar river at mouth of Horse creek to Stony creek.
Wts: John **Nuttall**, Geo. **Alston**.

56- Feb. 15, 1791- Nicolas **Loyd** to Elisha **Lindsey** for 100 pds. 221 acres on Ruin Creek at **Alston**'s line (wife relinquishes her dower right).
Wts: Sion **Kimball**, Craddock **Gober**.

56, 57- Mar. 4, 1791- William **Knight** and Pattatiel, his wife to Samuel **Smith** for 250 pds. 300 acres on lines of Samuel **Smith**, Thomas **Mutter**, William **Amis**, and Lewis **Amis** on Grassy creek.
Wts: Wm. **Smith**, J. **Smith**, Thomas **Voss** (wife relinquished her dower right.)

57- Apr. 28, 1791- Jobe [**Henson**] to Thomas **York** for 40 pds. 150 acres on **Dickerson**'s line, **Ragsdale**'s, **Finch**'s lines, **York**'s line.
Wts: Robert **Thomason**, Richd. Pollard **Thomason**.

57, 58- May 15, 1784- John **Pope** to Osborn **Pope** for 50 pds. 152½ acres on S side of Cedar creek at Arthur **Fuller**'s line, George **Nicholson**'s line, **Bradford**, John **Pope**'s, Richard **Bridges**' lines.
Wts: James **Weathers**, John **Pope**, Jr.

58- Feb. 28, 1791- Robert **Burton** to James **Vaughn** for 95 pds. 2 lots in Williamsborough, N.C. *Nos. 6 and 7.*
Wts: Saml **Griffin**, David **Mitchel**.

59- Mar, 28, 1791- Thomas **Peyton** of Cumberland Co., N.C. to James **Hunt** of Granville Co., N.C. for 200 pds. 173 acres on Little River creek at John **Parham**'s line, **Bristow**'s and **Johnston's** lines.
Wts: Rowland **Bryant**, Joseph **Rogers**.

59, 60- Oct. 28, 1790- James **Meadows** to Lemuel **Goodwin** for 600 pds. 430 acres on both sides of Stony creek a fork of Tar river on **Person**'s line, along the old road.
Wts: John **Washington**, Wm. **Walker**.

60- Aug. 3, 1789- John **Williams**, esq. to Harris **Hicks** for 100 pds. 150 acres whereon **Hicks** now lives on the new road to James **Bishop**'s line on Bromfield **Ridley**'s line.
Wts: Henry **Pattillo**, John **Nichols**, James M. **Burton**.

60, 61- July 23, 1789- John **Somerville** to Robert **Burton** for 200 pds. land which John **Somerville** bought of Jno. **Keeling** agreeable to the deed thereto.
Wts: Thos. **Satterwhite**, John **Brodie**, Jas. **Vaughn**.

61, 62- May 1, 1791- William **Penn** of Mecklenburg Co., Va. to John **Askew** of Granville Co., N.C. for 55 pds. 60 acres on Tabs creek in Granville Co. at Sterling **Hardin**'s line, Charles **Moss**'s line, Edward **Harris**'s line to the old Ridge path.
Wts: acknowledged by **Penn**.

62- Oct. 8, 1790- Isham **Johnston** to William **Fraizer** for 50 pds. 70 acres at the dividing line between Isaac **Arnold** and Sherwood **Harris**, formerly, W. side of Fishing creek along **Harris**'s line.
Wts: Chas. **Partee**, John **Williams**, B. **Pulliam**, Abd. **Clement**.

62, 63- Feb. 17, 1791- John **Pettypool** and Jesse **Pettypool** of Union County South Carolina to Seth **Pettypool** of Granville Co., N.C. for 30 pds. all that land bequeathed to them by their father in Granville Co., N. C., on N. side of a creek at John **Pettypool** Sr.'s old line containing 200 acres.
Wts: Young **Pettypool**, Mary **Pettypool**.

63- May 3, 1791- Howell **Moss** to Archibald **Henderson** for 6 pds. *Lot No. 17* in Williamsborough, N.C.
Wts: Henry **Potter**, A. **Potter**.

63, 64- May 3, 1791- Edmund **Taylor**, Sr. sold to James **Terry** and Nicholas **Burch**, a tract of land on Great Island creek which they have divided to and between themselves and at that time told them that when he had: patented land adjoining this they were entitled to 1/3rd thereof and now for 5½[8] dollars **Taylor** deeds to them 230 acres adjoining their lands to be equally divided between them.

328

64- Sept. 10, 1790- Ezekiel **Fuller** of Franklin Co., N.C. to William **Smith** of county and State aforesaid for 100 pds. 600 acres in Granville Co., N.C. on Tar river and Tabbs creek at **Hawley**'s Mountain to John **Dickerson**'s line at **Fuller**'s corner, **Cooper**'s and Capt. **Walker**'s lines.
Wts: Robert **Hight**, Samuel **Fuller**.

65- May 4, 1791- John **Young**, former sheriff of county, to Robert **Burton** at suit brought against Miles **King** and John **Potter** and the land sold to **Burton** belonging to Miles **King** near Williamsborough is part of the land held by his wife of said **Potter** and which he died siezed of. ..the wife now married to Miles **King**-now released to **Burton**.
Wts: James **Downey**.

65, 66- May 14, 1790- William **Parham** to Charles **Clark** for 35 pds. 90 acres on Poplar creek on **Burton**'s line.
Wts: Z. **Higgs**, Southorn **Higgs**.

66- Apr. 30, 1791- Philemon **Bradford**, Sr. to Bird Booker **Bradford** for 100 pds. 150 acres on middle fork of Beaverdam creek at Philemon **Bradford**'s corner.
Wts: P. **Bradford**, J. **Mann**.

66, 67- Aug. 28, 1790- Benjamin **Bradford** to William **Moore** for 43 pds. 180 acres at **Bradford**'s line, Jeremiah **Blalock**'s line on **Banks'** road up Tarborough road to Highland pond on David **Blalock**'s line.
Wts: Nathl **Moore**, Edmund **Taylor**, Sr.

67- July 31, 1790- Lewis **Taylor** to Nathaniel **Moore** for 226 pds. 420 acres on upper side of Quicksand creek at **Hornsby**'s line, **Bradford**'s corner.
Wts: Edmd. **Taylor** Sr. and Jr.

67 68- July 19, 1790- Bromfield **Ridley** to Drury **Kimball** for 150 pds. on S side of Flat creek containing 100 acres on Drury **Kimball**'s and John **Williams**' line (Frances **Ridley**, wife, relinquishes her dower right).
Wts: R. **Henderson**, James M. **Burton**.[9]

---

[8] Corrected from $5½,00.

[9] This line was typed over with the data from the following deed.

68-13 Jan 1791- Stephen **Merritt** of Caswell Co., N.C. to Bennett **Williams** of the same place, for 8 pds. 175 acres at corner of **Philpott** and **Merritt**'s lands to the county line at William **Oakley**'s line.
Wts: Thos. **Mallard**, Nathl. **Clark**.

69- May 23, 1791- Stephen **Merritt** of Granville Co., N.C. to Abraham **Meadows** for 59 pds. 324 acres on Knap of Reeds creek at **Hobgood**'s line on **Person**'s corner to Joseph **Mangum**'s line.
Wts: Robert **Dickens**, Bennett **Williams**.

69- Oct. 15, 1790- Stephen **Merritt** to Hezekiah **Hobgood** for 6 pds. 20 acres on S side of Cub creek at mouth of **Hobgood**'s Spring branch.
Wts: David **Roberts**, Fowler **Hobgood**.

70- Aug. 4, 1791- Hezekiah **Hobgood** to Thomas **Hobgood** for 5 pds. 180 acres being land Hezekiah **Hobgood** now lives on at Joseph **Langston**'s line on N. side of Cub creek at **Hobgood**'s spring branch.
Wts: Fowler **Hobgood**.

70, 71- Oct. 12, 1790- John **Hudspeth** of Surry Co., N.C. to Thomas M. **Thomason** for 260 pds., 520 acres on S side of Fishing creek, at mouth of Spring branch at **Keeling's**, **Linsey**'s lines.
Wts: George **Thomason**, Richd **Hudspeth**, James **Thomason**.

71, 72- Oct. 16, 1790- Nathaniel **Waller** to Lee **Griggs** of Westmoreland Co., Virginia for 400 spanish milled dollars, land on Knap of Reeds creek in Granville Co., N.C.
Wts: Wm. **Hunt**, Robert **Griggs**.

72- Aug. 1, 1791- Willis **Roberts** to Obediah **Vosvel** for 12 pds. land on **Knott**'s and **Fraizer**'s line, **Person**'s line containing 80 acres.
Wts: none.

72, 73- Jan. 8, 1791- John **Huddleston** to William **Byrum**, Jr. for 80 pds. 100 acres on James **Jenkins**' line, John **Peace**'s, John **Welch**'s line.
Wts: W. **Welch**, A. **Byrum**.

73- May 2, 1791-Jonathan **Knight** of Mecklenburg Co., Va. to William **Knight**, Jr. his son, of Granville Co., N.C. a gift of 300 acres on N. side of Grassy creek in Granville Co., N.C. now in his possession on **Hunt**'s, **Easley**'s, Jonathan **Knight**'s, Lewis **Amis**'s lines.
Wts: Thomas **Mutter**, William **Heggie**, John **Brown**.

329

73, 74- Dec. 23, 1790- Samuel **Walker** to Joseph **McDaniel** for 20 pds. 152 acres of land on River creek at **Glasgow**'s line.
Wts: John **Walker**, Hezekiah **Walker**.

74, 75- Aug. 26, 1760 Grant from Lord Granville to Joseph **Gray** for 239 acres in Granville Go., N.C. on Flat creek.

75- Mar. 13, 1760 Grant from Lord Granville to Young **McLemore** for 640 acres on both sides of Flat creek in Granville Co.

76- Feb. 28, 1789- Christopher **Harris** to Bromfield **Ridley** for 678 pds. 500½ acres on N. side of Flat creek whereon **Harris** now lives at **Jones**' and **Gober**'s corner, Jonathan **Tyne**'s line, Judge **Williams**'s line, **Ridley**'s.
Wts: Elizabeth **Ridley**, E. **Henderson**.

76, 77- May 10, 1791- Jacob **Slaughter** to Ambrose Harrison **Duncan** for 100 pds. 80 acres on **Shelton**'s creek.
Wts: Wm. **Gill**, Abraham **Slaughter**.

77- May 10, 1791- Jacob **Slaughter**, Sr. to George **Dunkin** for 100 pds. 80 acres on **Shelton** Creek at Harrison **Dunkin**'s corner.
Wts: Wm. **Gill**, Abraham **Slaughter**.

78- Aug. 2, 1791- Elisha **Lindsey** to George **Thomason** for 50 pds. 157 acres on Fishing creek at **Duglass**'s corner, **Thomason** and **Walker**'s lines.
Wts: Richd **Bearden**.

78, 79- May 5, 1789- Thomas **Person** to William **Frazier** for 5 pds. 75 acres on Grassy creek adjoining lands of **Johnson** and others at **Frazier**'s and **Person**'s corner, **Johnson's** and **Lewis**'s lines.
Wts: William **Lasiter**, Cornelius C. **Cooper**.

79- July 28, 1791- Edmond **Taylor** of Mecklenburg Co, Va. to William **Taylor**, Sr of same place for 150 pds. 400 acres on W side of Island Creek, at Daniel **Marrow**'s line on **Taylor**'s Ferry road, Jacob **Mitchel**'s line.
Wts: Robert **Coleman**, John **Grisham**.

79, 80 July 30, 1791- Charles **Wade** to John **Downey** for 400 pds. 590 acres at **Harris**'s line on both sides of **Aaron**'s creek, at **Bohannon**'s and **Yancey**'s lines at road near plantation whereon I now live, on the Virginia line with **Winfree**'s line, Robert **Wade**'s lines.
Wts: M. **Hunt**, James **Downey**, Nancy **Smith**.

80, 81- Aug. 1, 1791- Micajah Greenfield **Debruler** to John **Earl** for 75 pds. 130 acres on S side of road from Harrisburg to the old court house, at **Reeves'** and **Barton**'s lines.
Wts: Wm. **Hicks**, Jr., Elizabeth Ann **Hicks**.

81- July 10, 1791- Thomas **Oakley** to Hezekiah **Hobgood** for 5 pds. 160 acres whereon I now live at Joseph **Langston**'s line to Cub Creek.
Wts: Thos **Hobgood**, Fowler **Hobgood**.

81, 82- Nov. 10, 1790- Jonathan **Parrish** to George **Floyd** for 30 pds. 30 acres on W side of Tabbs creek on Samuel **Kittrell**'s line, **McDaniel**'s and **Rogers**' lines.
Wts: Z. **Higgs**, John° **Higgs**.

82- July 31, 1790- John **Champion**, Jr. to Simon **Clement**, Sr. for 80 pds. 150 acres on Beaverdam creek.
Wts: Samuel **Clement**, Henry **Morris**.

83- Aug. 1, 1791- Reuben **Talley** to John **Taylor** for 200 pds. 300 acres on N. side of Tar river at John **Taylor**'s line, Isaac **Kittrell**'s line.
Wts: Wm. **Hicks**, Jr.

83, 84- Nov. 8, 1791- **Stewart** and **Muir** and Co., of Halifax, N.C. to John **Nuttall** for 142 pds. 10 shls. 427½ acres on Fishing creek on **Allison**'s line, **Taylor**'s, **Hopkins**', **Hicks**' and **Page**'s lines, **Morris**'s.
Wts: Archd **Jett**, Wm. **Perkins**.

84- Nov. 5, 1791- Robert H. **Harris** to Samuel **Lemay** for 30 pds. 50 acres on **Holston**'s Creek

84, 85- Nov. 12, 1791- Robert H. **Harris** to Samuel **Lemay** for 150 pds. 150 acres at Saml **Jackson**'s line.

85- Oct. 28, 1791- Samuel **Packer** of Wake Co., N.C. to Jonathan **Badget** of

330
Granville Co., N.C. for 104 pds. 250 acres on Cedar creek near **Clements'** and **West**'s corner.
Wts: Saml **Harris**, Thos. **Tomlinson**.

85, 86- Nov. 3, 1791- Elisha **Shemwell**, brother and Heir of William **Shemwell**, deceased, of Wake Co., N.C. to Elijah **Mitchel** of Granville Co., for 6 pds. lot No. 15 in Williamsborough, N, C.
Wts: William **Chandler**, John **Brodie**.

86- Oct. 7, 1791- Robert **Lewis** of Goochland Co., N.C. to William **Malory** for 55 acres which is part of the tract of land **Lewis** sold to John **Marshall**, and was to deliver deed to him when he had paid for same, and since that time **Marshall** sold 25 acres to **Mallory**. this deeds releases that land to William **Malory**.

Wts: Chas. **Mallory**, Howel **Lewis**, Henry **Tuggle**.

86, 87- Jan. 20, 1789- John **Hooker**, Sr. to John **Hooker**, Jr. for 100 pds. 100 acres on Beaverdam creek at **McCulloh**'s and **Cooper**'s lines.
Wts: William **Hooker**.

87, 88- Jan. 30, 1789- Hardy **Reeves** to Lewis **Page** for 130 pounds, 200 acres on Tabbs creek at **Hicks**' corner, **Reeves**' line, James **Jett**'s line.
Wts:, Wm. **Thomason**, William **Reeves**.

88- Aug. 30, 1791- Samuel **Harrison** of Halifax Co., Va. to George **Petty** of Granville Co., N.C. for 15 pds. 140 acres on **Grant**'s road, **Peace** and **Johnston**'s corner along **Johnston**'s line to **Royster**'s line.
Wts: Gideon **Williams**, Thornton **Yancey**.

88, 89- Nov. 8, 1791- Lewis **Page** to Micajah G. **Debruler** for 50 pds. 200 acres on Tabbs creek in John **Duncan**'s, John **Nuttal**'s former line of land he sold to Thomas **Hester**, on **Reeves'** line.
Wts: Wm. **Hicks**, Jr., Benja. **Mathews**.

89- Nov. 9, 1791- Edward **Buridge** to Samuel **Creath** for 150 pds. 394 acres on **Howlet**'s creek at **Melton**'s line.
Wts: William **Smith**.

89, 90- Oct. 23, 1790- John **Harp** to Westwood A. **Jones** of Franklin Co., N.C. for 75 pds. 60 acres in Granville Co., on Thomas **Harp**'s branch.
Wts: John **Bobbitt**, Sarah **Harpe**.

90- Oct. 12, 1789- William **Jones** to David **Harris** for 100 pds. 80 acres on Tar river at Reuben **Searc**y's line, John **Minor**'s line, **Bearden**'s line.
Wts: John **Minor**, Sherwood **Harris**.

90, 91- Aug. 13, 1788- John **Hooker**, Sr. to Cornelius **Cooper** for 50 pds. 83¼ acres on S side of the creek at [black Jack on] **Hooker**'s line[10].
Wts: John **Williamson**, William **Hooker**.

91- Aug. 12, 1790- Ezekiel **Fuller** of Franklin Co., N.C. and Thomas **Person** of Granville Co., to Cornelius **Cooper** of Granville Co., for 50 pds. 45 acres on Tar river at lands of Cornelius **Cooper**, **Williams**' line.
Wts: B. **Bennitt**, Francis **Taylor**.

92- Feb. 25, 1791- Solomon **Thornton** to James **Cardin** for 40 pds. 60 acres on S side of Tabbs creek.
Wts: William **Wilkerson**, John **Ball**.

92, 93- Jan. 10, 1791- Tabitha **Marshall** of Warren Co., N.C. to William **Marshall** for 250 pds., 238 acres in **Chapman** branch on Granville Co.
Wts: Dixon **Marshall**, Mathew **Marshall**.

93- Sept. 12, 1791- Elijah **Veazey**, executor of will of Edward **Veazey** deceased, to David **Bundrige** for 275 pds. 320 acres on Nap of Reed creek on lines of James **Veazey** and George **Laco?**'s[11]
Wts: Wm. **Hunt**, Fentrull **Hall**.

93, 94- Sept. 13, 1791- Zebulon.**Veazey** to Thornton **Mallard** for 60 pds. 148 acres on Nap of Reed creek at James **Bennett**'s line, on W side of Don's creek in **Ross**'s line.
Wts: Blackmun **Pardue**, James **Veazey**.

---

[10] Gwynn has this as Jackson **Hooker**'s line

[11] Smeared in court record.

94- Jan. 1, 1790- Leonard **Adcock** to David **Cozart** for 12 pds. 20 acres whereon David **Cozart** now lives at Jeremiah **Bullock**'s line, Francis **Bressie**'s line, Leonard **Adcock**'s line.
Wts: Wm. **Webb**, Mary **Cozart**.

331

95- July 28, 1789- Wm. **Jeffreys** to Philemon **Bowers** for 200 pds. 278 acres on Fort creek along **Carter**'s line, **Taylor**'s line, **Wilson**'s line.
Wts: S. **Cook**, Claborn **Cook**.

95, 96- Feb. 3, 1791- John **Puet** to Joseph **Puit** for 100 pds. 186 acres on Reedy branch of Beaverdam creek at David **Bradford**'s line.
Wts: Harris **Bradford**, John **Pewit**, Jr.

96- Jan. 1, 1792- David **Cozart** to Jeremiah **Bullock** for 10 pds. 42½ acres (also David **Cozart**'s wife, Josebell, deeds with her husband, the land) in the old road at Jeremiah **Bullock**'s line, **Bressie**'s and **Ogelvie**'s lines.
Wts: Wm. **Webb**, Philip **Bullock**, Jas. **Webb**.

96, 97- Sept. 13, 1791- David **Bundrige** to Elijah **Veazey**, for 183 pds. 214 acres on Knap of Reeds creek at Edward **Veazey**'s corner on **Bullock**'s line.
Wts: Wm. **Hunt**, Feliterell **Hall**.

97, 98- Nov. 9, 1791- John **Dickerson**, Jr. to James **Hunter** for 93 pds. 10 shillings, 170 acres on N. side of Tar river at mouth of Deep branch.
Wts: Dan **Hunter**, William **Hunt**, John **Walker**.

98- July 13, 1787- Micajah **Bullock** to John **Jarrott** for 56 pds. 200 acres in the county line, Peyton **Matterson**'s line.
Wts: Peyton **Madison**, Benjamin **Wade**.

98, 99- Apr. 13, 1791- John **Moss** to Vinkler **Jones** for 155 pds. 120 acres on both sides of Crooked creek on Reuben **Moss**'s line, Thos. **Wiggins**' line.
Wts: Vinkler **Jones**, Jr., Merryman **Barnes**.

99, 100- Nov. 12, 1791- Robert **Coleman** of Mecklenburg Co., Va. to Willis **Lewis** and Charles **Lewis**, his brother, of Granville Co., N.C. for 300 pds. 200 acres which is one moiety of land sold by Robert Lewis **Byrd** to John **Williams** who sold it to Robert **Coleman** on S side of Tar river.
Wts: Joseph **Taylor**, Thomas **Taylor**.

100- Feb. 4, 1792- Roderick **Wright** and Joseph **Wright** of Halifax Co., N.C. to James **Blackwell** of Granville Co., N.C. for 102 pds., 100 acres on N. side of Cedar creek at **Champion**'s corner on Hillsborough road on **Goodloe**'s line to **Hendley**'s line to the Great Branch at **Pope**'s corner which is land whereon Winfield **Wright**, Sr. formerly lived.
Wts: James **Judge**, Jon **Murden**, William **Smith**.

100, 101- Feb. 5, 1792- Daniel **Williams** to Leonard **Smith**, Jr. for 120 pds. 220 acres adjoining lands of Field **Rudd**, Wm. **Collins**, William **Dunkin**, Leonard **Smith**, Sr., John **Hargrove**.
Wts: none.

101, 102- Feb. 4, 1792- Samuel **Pittard** to Edward **Hunt** for 50 pds. 200 acres on both sides of Mountain creek which was bought of James **Williams** on Feb. 2, 1779 on **Crenshaw**'s lines.
Wts: John **Downey**, John **Hart**, M **Hunt**.

102- Apr. 2, 1791- Reuben **Morse** to Vinkler **Jones** for 40 shillings 50 acres on W side of Crooked Run on **Morse**'s line on Ruin creek and bounded by lands of Samuel **Morse** at which Reuben **Morse** in the lifetime of said Samuel **Morse** failed to make good deed for.
Wts; Elijah **Mitchel**, B. **Ridley**.

103, 104- May 10, 1792- Micajah **Bullock** to James **Vaughn** and Bromfield **Ridley** land of Benjamin **Ragland** sold at public sale at suit brought by William **Byars** for debt due and unpaid. Land was 200 acres adjoining **Ridley**'s, John **Wilson'**s, Reuben **Ragland**'s and known as ***Raglands*** *Neck*. This deed is made by Micajah **Bullock**, sheriff of Granville Co.

105- Apr. 23, 1792- David **Witherspoon** admstr. de bonis non of Abner **Nash**, deceased to John **Webb** and John P. **Smith** for 300 pds. 750 acres on

332
Grassy creek at **Pryor**'s, **Laseter**'s, **Crutcher**'s lines, **Pointer**'s line, **Person** line and at W.O **Pope**'s corner of land bought several years ago of Thomas **Person** which is same land bought by Abner **Nash** of Thomas **Person** Dec. 30 1785-
.
Wts: Ro. **Burton**, Wm. **Shapard**, Jr.

106- Mar. 15, 1792- Champion **Allen** to John **Carrol** for 50 pds. 170 acres on S side of Cedar creek which is part of tract of 700 acres granted to John **Champion**, Sr.
Wts: John **Pope**, Jr., James **Weathers**.

106, 107- Aug. 12, - - Zachariah **Bevill** to John **Burg** for 100 pds. 100 acres on Island creek at William **Erby**'s line and to **Johnson**'s line.
Wts: John **Johnson**, William **Gooch**, Absalom **Johnson**.

107- Dec. 13, 1785- Thomas **Person** to Abner **Nash** for 3000 pds. 750 acres on Grassy creek in Granville Co., N.C. at W. O. **Pryor**'s line, to **Lasiter**'s and **Crutcher**'s lines in **Pointer**'s line, **Person**'s line.
Wts: Thos. **Haslin** (Registered in Book Q, **Page** 432, Craven Co., N.C.)

107, 108- Jan. 3, 1791- Samuel **Mosely** of Orange Co., N.C. to Roger **Jones** of Franklin Co., N.C. for 100 pds. 209 acres on Newlight branch at **Mann**'s and **Mitchel**'s lines to the county line, in **Mosley**'s corner.
Wts: William **Hefflin**, John **Mosely**.

108- May 7, 1792- Mary **Badget** to Lewis **Anderson** for 150 pds. 200 acres in **Bass**'s line.
Wts: Joseph **Taylor**, Wm. **Shapard**.

108, 109- Nov. 8, 1790- Edmund **Carnes** of Montgomery Co., N.C. to Mathew **Pryor** of Granville Co., N.C. for 10 pds. 8 acres on Picture branch at **Parker**'s corner on **Jones**'s line.
Wts: Micajah **Bullock**, Philip **Pryor**.

109, 110- Dec. 14, 1791- John **Owen** to William **Lassiter** for 25 pds. 203 acres on **Aaron**'s creek at **Gill**'s corner, **Briant**'s line, **Person**'s and **Owen**'s lines.
Wts: Thos. **Pool**, J. P. **Smith**.

110- Aug. 14, 1782- David **Harris** to Joseph **Neall** for 60 pds. 200 acres on Beaverdam creek on **Lansford**'s line, **Mitchel**'s corner being land granted- Mar. 1, 1780 by Richard **Caswell**, Governor.
Wts: William **Heffernon**, Fielding **Heffernon**.

110, 111- Feb. 19, 1789- William **Bobbitt** of Franklin Co., N.C. to William **Smith** of Granville Co., N.C. for 150 pds. 350 acres on **Linches** creek on County line at **Eaton**'s corner including the plantation whereon **Smith** now lives.
Wts: Joseph **Mangum**, Benjamin **Johnston**.

111- Feb. 20, 1792- Robert **Coleman** of Mecklenburg Co., Va. to Christian **Strom** of Prince Edward Co., Va. for 200 pds. 250 acres on Island crk at John **Gooch**'s line.
Wts: Bartholomew **Strom**, Ro. **Lewis**, James **Roberts**.

112- Nov. 12, 1791- Peter **Vincent** to Michael **Cockleree** of Orange Co., N.C. for 45 pds. 150 acres on **Allerson**'s line, on both sides of Horse crk.
Wts: Jacob **Holston**, Henry **Strator**.

112, 113- Apr. 26, 1792- James **Akin**, Sr. to Samuel **Smith** for 75 pds. 100 acres on Island creek on E side of Lick branch.
Wts: James [**Lyne**], Henry **Lyne**.

113- Mar. 27, 1792- Wm. **Ogelvie**, Sr. to Smith **Ogelvie** for 50 pds. 218 acres on S side of road from Hillsborough along **Bullock**'s line along **Cooke**'s line (Mary, wife of Wm. **Ogelvie** relinquishes dower).
Wts: Saml **Harris**, Christph. **Harris**.

113, 114- Dec. 28, 1791- Henry **Graves**, Jr. of Caswell Co., N.C. to Thomas **Edwards** of Granville Co., N.C. for 70 pds. 125 acres on Mountain creek at David **Smith**'s line to Thomas **Voss**'s line on Thomas **Person**'s, John **Oliver**'s lines.
Wts: L. **Johnston**, Josiah **Daniel**.

114- Apr. 30, 1792- William **Palmer** to Henry **Melton** for 150 pds. 200 acres on Jonathan's creek adjoining lands of John **Pumfret**, William **Royster**, James **Bedford** to Church path.
Wts: Thomas **Voss**, William **Royster**.

115- Feb. 1, 1791- David **Wilkerson**, Sr. to William **Wilkerson** for 80 pds.

333
tract of 80 acres on Bearskin creek at Rob. **Hester**'s line to Lick branch at mouth of **Wharton**'s branch.
Wts: Wm. **Gill**, P. **Bennett**.

115, 116- May 20, 179[smeared]- Samuel **Parker** of Wake Co., N.C. to James **Kanedy** of Person Co., N.C. for 75 pds. 360 acres on head of **Norris**'s creek at **Hill**'s line adjoining John **Knott** and James **West**.
Wts: None. Registered- May 1792.

116- Jan. 20, 1792- Zacharias **Higgs** to Elijah **Parrish** for 10 shls. one acre on Tabbs creek at the Mill.
Wts: John **Higgs**, K. **Higgs**.

116, 117- May 8, 1792- Thomas **Grant** of Wilks Co., Georgia by power of attorney to Thomas **Owen**, to David **Parker** of Granville Co., NC, for 40 pds. 70 acres on Tar river at **Cooke**'s line, **Jones**'s corner.
Wts: Lewis **Bennett**, Joshua **Bell**.

117- Dec. 28, 1786- William **Huet** to Kimbrough **Ogilvie** for 500 pds. 52 acres on Cedar crk. on Tarborough road at **Ogilvie**'s line.
Wts: Chas. **Hill**, Danl **Harris**, Cal^n **Harris**.

117, 118- Aug. 13, 1791- Solomon **Davis** to Benjamin **Searcy** for 30 pds. 100 acres in **Satterwhite**'s line, **Person**'s line in **Gober**'s line near the creek.
Wts: James **Satterwhite**, William **Akin**.

118- Apr. 21, 1790- Claburn **Harris** to William **Ogilvie** for 30 pds. 16½ acres on Claborn **Harris** and **Ogilvie**'s line on Spring branch.
Wts: Benjamin **Bearden**, Sherwood **Harris**.

118, 119- Feb. 1, 1791- David **Wilkerson**, Sr. to David **Wilkerson**, Jr. for 50 pds. 50 acres on Bearskin creek, at **Wilkerson**'s and **Person**'s lines to John **Wilkerson**'s line.
Wts: Wm. **Gill**, P. **Bennett**.

119- Mar. 30, 1790- William **Floyd** to George **Floyd** for 100 pds. 164 acres on Ruin creek at Samuel **Kittrell**'s line.
Wts: Z. **Higgs**.

120- Mar. 27, 1792- James **Vaughn** to Stephen **Sneed** for 327 pds. *Lots No. 6 And 7* in Williamsborough, N.C.
Wts: Wm. **Norwood**, Sam. **Searcy**.

120- Nov. 9, 1791- Peter **Vinson** to Henry **Strater** for of Orange Co., N.C. for 100 pds. land on Horse creek at **Holston**'s line on **Champion**'s line.

Wts: Robert **Allison**, Jacob **Holston**.

121- Oct. 27, 1791- Kanon **Cooper** to Philemon **Hawkins** for 25 pds. 147 acres on S side of Sandy creek in Granville County and Warren, on **Hawkins**' and **Conyard**'s lines, at Jos. **Mangum**'s line.
Wts: Joseph **Mangum**, Arthur **Cooper**, Wm. **Howel**.

121, 122- Jan. 19, 1789- Thomas **Person** to William **Little** for 10 pds. land on So Et sides of Great Nutbush creek and both sides of Indian creek bounded by **Henderson**'s corner on the bank of Nutbush crk. to **Bearden**'s line, **Bullock**'s, **Daniel**'s, **Gilliam**'s, **Jordan**'s, **Wiggins**, **Williams**'s lines containing 1200 acres and also a tract on both sides of **Michael**'s creek at **Akins**' and **Penn**'s lines containing 800 acres- in all 2000 acres.
Wts: James **Robinson**, William **Penn**, John **Smith**, Samuel **Smith**.

122, 123- Mar 10, 1789- Charles **Williams** to Nathaniel **Williams** for 5 shls 6 acres being part of tract whereon Charles **Williams** now lives on a line between Jno. and Charles **Williams** on River creek.
Wts: none.-

123, 124- May 13, 1791- Phil **Hawkins**, Jr. of Warren Co., N.C. to Richard **Inge** of Mecklenburg Co., Va. for 580 pds. 700 acres in Granville Co., N.C. on W side of Lick swamp at line formerly **Trevillion**'s line which was granted by Lord Granville to **Hawkins**- Feb. 6, 1762 and he deeded to Phil **Hawkins** called Col. Philemon **Hawkins**, Jr.
Wts: Saml **Hopkins**, Jr., Chas. **Davis**.

124- May 12, 1791- Phil **Hawkins**, Jr. of Warren Co., N.C. to Phil **Hawkins**, Sr. father of Phil **Hawkins**, Jr. (Granville Co) gives in exchange for other land given him by his father, 400 acres on Sandy creek at Nicholas

334

Roberson's line of land whereon Kennon **Cooper** formerly lived and Col. Charles **Eaton**'s lines being part of lane taken up by Humphrey **Ballard** Mar. 9, 1761 and conveyed to Phil **Hawkins** who deeded it to Phil **Hawkins**, Jr.
Wts: William **Allen**, James **Mitchel**.

125- Jan. 31, 1792., James **Peit** to John **Bridges** for 25 pds. 100 acres on Beaverdam creek at **McCullow**'s line being part of tract granted to David **Mitchel**- Mar. 1, 1780.
Wts: Jacob [**Britwell**], Moley **Bridges**.

125, 126- Feb. 25, 1792- Daniel **Williams** to, John **Somervell** for 600 pds. 700 acres bounded by lands of Henry **Lyne**, Leonard **Sims**, William **Bullock**, Robert **Burton**, Mathew **Clay**, John **Somerville**, William **Martin** estate.
Wts: James **Vaughn**, James **Lyne**.

126- Feb. 21, 1792- Champion **Allin** to Charles **Taylor** for 20 pds. 100 acres on John **Whitfield**'s line at John **Carrel**'s line, Thomas **Roberts**' line.
Wts: Arnold **Mann**, J. **Mann**.

126, 127- Mar. 13, 1792- Claborn **Harris** to Jeremiah **Bullock** for 90 pds. 160 acres on **Holstein**'s creek at mouth of a branch along **Ogelvie**'s line, at **Bressie**'s line, **Adcock**'s, **Jackson**'s line, **Lemay**'s corner.
Wts: [Saml] **Lemay**, James **Bradley**.

127, 128- Nov. 7, 1791- Ephraim **Bradford** to Philemon **Bradford**, Jr. for 100 pds. 420 acres on Beaverdam creek on **Bradford**'s, **Blalock**'s, **Brown**'s line on Tarborough, road from B. **Bradford** to D. **Bradford**'s lines.
Wts: John **Hardaway**, John **Mann**.

128- July 10, 1792- Richard Donaldson **Cooke** to William **Webb** for 30 pds. land on both sides of **Jefferson**'s tract containing 200 acres at **Wilbourne**'s line to Lane **Moore**'s line.
Wts: Jeremiah **Bullock**, J. **Webb**.

128, 129- May 21, 1790- Samuel **Sneed** of Caswell Co., N.C. to Phillip **Sneed** for 300 pds. 431 acres on Buffalo Creek at Joshua **Ball**'s corner to **Sneed**'s line, **Wood**'s, **Parrish**'s Lines.
Wts: Steph **Sneed**.

129, 130- Apr. 14, 1788- Joseph **Hays** to Thomas **Johnson** for 42 pds. 140 acres on Fishing creek at James **Jett**'s line near **Banks**' road to **Hicks**' line.
Wts: Noel **Johnston**, John **Hays**.

130- Aug. 17, 1792- Solomon **Whitlow** to Jeremiah **Frazier** for 100 pds. 135 acres on **Hays**' line, on **Farrar**'s line, Samuel **Hicks**'s line, David **Hicks**'s line.
Wts: William **Bolling**, [Epm] **Frazier**.

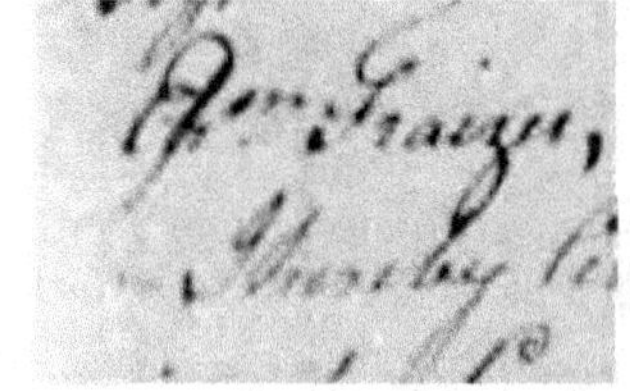

130, 131- July 28, 1790- Samuel **Kittrell** to Jonathan **Kittrell** for 5 pds. 26 acres on W side of Tabbs creek.
Wts: Charles R. **Eaton**, John **Potter**, Danl **Hunter**.

131- Apr. 8, 1792- Samuel **Harris**, Sr. and wife Margaret to Alexander **Brodie** for 100 pds. 23½ acres on Tar river at corner of Samuel **Harris**, Sr.'s line, and in Harris **Ogilvie**'s line.
Wts: Danl **Gooch**, Reuben **Searcy**, John **Norman**.

131, 132- Jan. 3, 1792- George **Dunkin** to Harrison **Dunkin** for 52 pds. 80 acres on **Shelton**'s creek, **Person**'s line, near **Gill**'s road to Harrison **Dunkin**'s corner.
Wts: Jacob **Slaughter**, William **Owen**.

132- Dec. 22, 1790- Anthony **Person** of Southampton Co., VA to Littleton **Howard** for 70 pds. land on N. fork of Tar river called **Bennett**'s creek at **Hill**'s corner near the courthouse road on **Person**'s line near **Knott**'s and Randal **Bearden**'s lines
Wts: M. **Satterwhite**, Graves **Howard**.

132, 133- July 5, 1792- Israel **Eastwood** to John **Eastwood** for 50 pds. 150 acres on **Cozart**'s branch, **Hampton**'s Mill creek at John **Eastwood**'s spring branch, **Bennett**'s line.
Wts: Obediah **Clement**, Abra **Eastwood**, Eliza **Eastwood**.

335

133- Nov. 6, 1791- Joseph **Taylor** to Thomas **Taylor** for 5 shls. a gift of 306 acres on Fox creek which **Taylor** purchased at sheriffs sale as property of Reuben **Butler**.

134- Jan. 30, 1792- John **Williams** to Charles **Partee** for 500 pds. 1000 acres on both sides of the creek whereon Chas. **Partee** now lives at lines of Israel **Eastwood**, **Clements** and Samuel **Jackson** which is land **Williams** purchased of **Partee**.
Wts: Jos. **Robards**, Brereton **Jones**.

134, 135- Nov. 9, 1792- Ralph **Williams** to Joel **Chambless** for 76 pds. 280 acres at **Williams**' old line to Jacob **Ferebow**'s line on Ralph **Williams**' line, on **Moore**'s road to the big road.
Wts: William **Green**, Obed **Clement**.

135, 136- May 14, 1792- John **Angus** of Prince George Co., Va to William **Shepard** of Granville Co., N.C. for 20,000 pds. of inspected crop tobacco, 700 acres at **Person**'s formerly now **Kimball**'s corner, on **Harris**'s line., on **Royster**'s line.
Wts: James **Lyne**, William **Cowles**.

136- Sept. 12, 1792- Dorothy **Scribnor** to John **Finch** for 10 pds. 20 acres on Buffalo creek at Thomas **Smith**'s line, Richard **Thomason**'s line.
Wts: John **Harp**, Chas. **Moore**.

136, 137- Sept. 1, 1792- Samuel **Fuller**, Sr. to William **Walker** for 270.00 silver dollars. 270 acres on Tabbs creek at Littleton **Spivey**'s branch on Henry **Fuller**'s branch, Henry **Jones**' line.

Wts: Wm. **Fuller**, Lydda **Huckabey**.

137, 138 - - May 1792- William **Haynes** from Thomas **York** for 7 pds. 10 shls 25 acres on W side of Franklin county line.
Wts: William **Paschal**, William **Leeman**.

138, 139- Sept. 20, 1792- Micajah **Bullock**, sheriff, to James **Vaughn** as highest bidder, the property of Leonard **Smith** who was sued by Archibald **Henderson** and Henry **Potter** for unpaid debt, and court ordered. property sold- For 58 pds. 222 acres on Island creek at James **Lewis**'s Joseph **Akin**'s, Jno **Hargrove**'s, Wm. **Duncan**'s, and Sion **Smith**'s lines.
Wts: John **Brodie**, John **McAden**.

139, 140- Nov. 6, 1792- Joshua **Hays** to Henry **Hays** for 50 pds. 50 acres on W side of Tabbs creek being part of my own tract on John **Parham**'s line.
Wts: Noel **Johnston**, William Moore **Johnson**.

140, 141- July 13, 1792- Joseph **Cash** to Brian **Cash** for 25 pds. 260 acres on W side of Picture branch at corner of **Culverhouse**'s land, to **Bonner**'s corner.
Wts: John and Thomas **Culverhouse**.

141- Aug. 7, 1792- Francis **Hester** to John **Huddleston** of Halifax Co., N.C. for 15 pds. 100 acres on Fishing creek on **Walker**'s line.
Wts: John **Bristow**, Ezekiel **Huddleston**.

141, 142- Nov. 7, 1792- John **Webb** to John P. **Smith** for 200 pds. 540 acres which **Webb** and **Smith** purchased of David **Witherspoon** administrator of Abner **Nash** deceased, on **Smith**'s line and **Daniel**'s' line.
Wts: William **Webb**, Lewis **Hening**.

142- Nov. 7, 1792- John **Webb** from John P. **Smith** for 200 pds. 348 acres being part of tract **Smith** and **Webb** purchased of David **Witherspoon**, as administrator of Abner **Nash**, deceased, on **Daniel**'s' line at **Crutcher**'s corner.
Wts: William **Webb**, Lewis **Henning**.

143- Mar. 21, 1792- Samuel **Fuller**, Sr. to Roger **Jones** of Franklin Co., N.C. for 71 pds. 39 acres in Granville Co., with the *mill tract* thereon on Long creek on old mill pond on **Weaver**'s line.
Wts: John **Jones**, John **Bobbitt**.

143, 144- Nov. 6, 1792- Robert **Reed** to Edward **Harris** for 90 pds. 302 acres on Newlight creek in **Harris**'s line.
Wts: Elijah **Mitchel**.

336

144- Mar. 20, 1792- James **Winfree** to David **Winfree** of Halifax Co., Va. for 20 pds. 100 acres on Wolf Pit Branch at State line on **Wade**'s corner on road to **Pulliam**'s mill, to **Wade**'s road.
Wts: John **Wade**, Wrn. **Taylor**, Robert **Wade**.

145- Oct. 6, 1792- John **Finch** to William **Haynes** of Franklin Co., N.C. for 50 pds. 133½ acres Buffalo creek on **Thomason**'s line.
Wts: James **McDaniel**, John **Haynes**.

145, 146- May 17, 1792- Joseph **Leman** of Franklin Co., N.C. to William **Leman** of Granville Co. for 100 pds. 125 acres on S side of Buffalo creek in counties of Granville and Franklin, N.C. at Western **Jones**'s corner, John **Finch**'s line, **Haynes**' and **York**'s lines.
Wts: John **Finch**, Reuben **Ransom**.

146- Nov. 9, 1792- William P. **Thomason** to Reuben **Talley** for 55 pds. 10 shls. 100 acres on Fishing creek near the road.
Wts: Phillip **Bullock**, Thomas **Satterwhite**.

146, 147- May 15, 1789- Richard **Banks** of Wake Co., N.C. to Thomas **Tucker** of same place, for 30 pds. 300 acres in Granville Co., N.C. on Ledge of Rocks creek at Wake Co. line, on **McCulloh**'s line, **Person**'s line, **Burford**'s line. Wts: Ephraim **Emery**, Elijah **Green**.

147, 148- Apr. 28, 1788- Joel **Chambless** and James **Custard** to Ralph **Williams** for 100 pds. 280 acres on **Wilburne**'s line, **Williams**' line.
Wts: William **Webb**, William **Green**.

148, 149- May 15, 1789- Richard **Banks** of Wake Co., N.C. to Ephraim **Emery** for 16 pds. 4 shls. 108 acres on Ledge of Rocks creek.
Wts: Elijah **Green**, John **Brumfield**, Thomas **Tucker**.

149- Nov. 2, 1792- William **Easley** to John **Young** for 295 pds. 590 acres on both sides of Rattle Snake creek on **Knight**'s line.
Wts: John **Brown**, Thomas **Mutter**.

149, 150- Nov. 3, 1792- Daniel **Marrow** to James **Lewis** for 36 pds. 9 shls. 27 acres being part of tract **Marrow** purchased of John **Terry** on W side of Great Island creek on Horseshoe creek where **Lewis**'s and **Marrow**'s lines cross.
Wts: Wm. **Neal**.

150, 151- Feb. 8, 1786- Robert **Crawley** (acting executor of the Will of the late Ellis **Drury**, deceased, of Mecklenburg Co., Va.) to Thomas **Person**, land of Ellis **Drury** deceased, sold in order to pay debts of the deceased, and Thomas **Person** became highest bidder for 200 acres in Granville Co., N.C.
Wts: Ransone **Sutherland**, Chesley **Daniel**.

151, 152- Jan. 1, 1793- Thomas **Person** to Rev. George **McKeljohn** for 17 pds. 5 shLs. 70 acres including the house wherein he now lives.
Wts: John **Wynne**, Richd **Thomas**, Jr., Thomas **Owen**, Sr.

152-153- Jan. 17, 1789- By order of Granville Co., Court, the land of Sarah **Harris**, deceased, was divided among her heirs. One part to William **Penn**, executor of John **Penn**, deceased, and he awarded east part of land by paying other claimants 10 pds. which was 1/2 of 413 acres on both sides of Tabbs creek on **Penn**'s line at **Harris**'s corner.
Wts: John **Rust**, John **Kendrick**.

153- Jan. 26, 1793- William **Smith** of Franklin Co., N.C. to George **Alston** of Granville Co. for 155 pds. 10 shls. 622 acres on W side of Tabbs creek to John **Cardine**'s line, E side of Holly Mountain branch at **Walker**'s and at Ben **Fuller**'s lines.
Wts: Saml **Rust**, Nathl **Hight**, Nicholas **Loyd**.

154- Feb. 1, 1793- Ezekiel **Fuller** to George **Alston** for 155 pds. 10 shls. in full for William **Smith**'s order drawn in my favor being purchase money for land conveyed by **Smith** to **Alston**- Jan. 6, 1793.
Wts: Reuben **Talley**, Benjamin **Hester**, Gideon **Johnson**.
Fuller relinquishes all right in land to **Alston**.

337

154, 155- Dec. 10, 1792- Alexander **Boyd** of Mecklenburg Co., Va. to Edward **Cheatham** of Granville Co., N. C. for 42,000 pds. of Petersburg Inspected tobacco the land John **Potter** sold to Alexander **Boyd** Aug. 3, 1785- excepting the acres James **Harris** may recover due to his entry thereon now pending.
Wts: Leonard **Sims**, John **Creath**, Ro. **Burton**.

155, 156- 5th [day of] 1793- Isaac **Butler** and wife Mary of Granville Co., to Joseph **Hillyard** (**Hilliard**) of King William Co., Va. for 100 pds. 56 acres adjoining Benjamin **Hillyard**, John **Boyd** and Thomas **Butler**, **Frazier**'s lines.
Wts: Henry **Potter**.

156- Jan. 5, 1793- John **Thorp**, Sr. gave to his son John **Thorp**, Jr. 435 acres on waters of Tar river at Crooked Run on **Person**'s, **Badget**'s line, and a negro [boy named Major]
Wts: Thomas **Owen**, Sr., James **Terry**.

157- Aug. 20, 1792- Benjamin **Bradford** to Philemon **Bradford**, Jr. for 300 pds. 300 acres on Quick Sand creek on Tarborough road at **Bradford**'s corner, **Warthorn**'s line, **Taylor**'s corner.
Wts: James **Paschal**, Charles **Taylor**.

157, 158- Feb. 4, 1793- R. D. **Cooke** to John Donaldson **Cooke** and Richard **Cooke** for 5 shillings, 619 acres on Camp creek to be equally divided in quantity and quality between them on **Knott**'s line, **Eastwood**'s line, **Ross**'s line on the county line crossing Camp creek with **Mangum**'s line, **Roberts**' line to **Veazey**'s line and back to **Eastwood**'s line.
Wts: James **Claxton**, Joshua **Bullock**.

158- Feb. 3, 1793- Peter **Badgett** to William **Badgett** for 10 pds. 150 acres on N. side of Tar river.
Wts: none.

158, 159- Feb. 5, 1793- John **Wilson** to Henry **Wilson** for 20 pds. 177 acres on headof Little Island creek on **Gober**'s line.
Wts: M. **Bullock**, J. **Potter**.

159- Nov. 8, 1792- Samuel **Hicks** to Robert **Frazer** for 60 pds. 200 acres on Tabbs creek at Micajah **Debruler**'s line to David **Hicks**'s line, Jeremiah **Fraze**r's line, Nathan **Whitlow**'s, Lewis **Parham**'s line.
Wts: Zachariah **Hester**.

160- Jan. 28, 1793- Robt. **Lewis** of Goochland Co., Va. to Charles **Lewis** and Willis **Lewis** of Granville Co., N.C. for 300 pds. 150 acres on S side of Tar river in Granville Co., N.C. being the upper part of the *Great Low Grounds* and all Robert **Lewis** owns on S side of river bounded by lines of Charles and William **Lewis** sons of Howel **Lewis**, the elder, **Person**'s lines.
Wts: John **Boyd**.

160, 161- Dec. 11, 1792- Richard **Fenner** of Frankland Co., N.C. to Charles R. **Eaton** of Granville Co., N.C. for 367 pds. 2560 acres being a donation from the State granted on Camp creek for personal services during the late war at SW corner of the heirs of Benjamin **Porter**'s to Elmore **Duglass**'s corner-
Wts: Robert **Bell** (**Ball**), John **Geddy**.

161- Feb. 5, 1793- Harris **Hicks** to Phillip **Bishop** for a negro woman and children delivered to him, 150 acres being the land whereon James **Hill** now lives on Flat creek on New rode (Road) on James **Bishop**'s line, Bromfield **Ridley**'s line (Tempey, wife of Harris **Hicks** relinquished dower right).
Wts: James **Satterwhite**.

162- Dec. 15, 1792- John **Thorp**, Sr. to James **Terry**, Jr. for 60 pds. 120 acres on Crooked Run to the mouth of Big Branch in **Person**'s line.
Wts: John **Thorp**, Jr.

162, 163- Jan. 30, 1793- Shearman **Goss** to John **Badgett** for 10 pds. 300 acres on **Badgett**'s own line, **Moore**'s whereon **Badgett** now lives.
Wts: Benton **Badgett**, James **Badgett**, Andrew **Badgett**.

163- Feb. 2, 1793- Robert **Lewis** of Goochland Co., Va. to John **Marshall** of Granville Co., N.C. for 500 pds. 450 acres on N. side of Tar river being the part of The *Great Low Grounds* tract Robert **Lewis** owns below the mouth of Bowling creek being all land he owns below the creek bounded by the river and the lines of Edmund **Taylor**, Thomas **Person**.
Wts: James **Robards**, Henry **Mullins**

338

163, 164- Feb 5, 1793- Joseph **Johnston** to Charles R. **Eaton** for 25 pds. 50½ acres on both sides of Reedy creek at **Eaton**'s line.
Wts: William **Hunt**, Isham **Kittrell**

164- Dec., 17, 1792- Isaac **Kittrell** to George **Kittrell** for 100 pds. [80] acres on W side of Tabbs creek at mouth of Maple Spring on John **Smith**'s and Michael **Wood**'s lines.

Wts: Rowland **Bryant**, Joshua **Kittrell**, Jonathan **Kittrell**.

165- Nov. 16, 1792- William **Loyd** to Benjamin **Hester** for 50 pds. 265 acres on Ruin creek on William **Barton**'s line, **Glasgoe**'s line, in **Gilliam**'s line, **Loyd**'s line.
Wts: John **Nuttall**, Geo. **Alston**, Jarrot **Loyd**.

165, 166- Nov. 9, 1792- Thomas **Steel** to Edward **Bass** for 75 pds. 206 acres on **Boling**'s creek, at John **Tuder**'s corner, Richard **Searcy**'s line.
Wts: John **Brodie**, Thos. **Satterwhite**.

166- Aug. 15, 1792- Samuel **Fuller** to Joseph **Smith** of Franklin Co., N.C. for 50 pds. 195 acres on *Old Mill tract* to head of Little Branch, Henry **Fuller**'s line.
Wts: John **Woodlief**, Henry **Thompson**.

167- Mar. 10, 1789- Nathaniel **Williams** to Charles **Williams** for 5 shls. 6 acres on S side of Ruin Creek a[t] clift of Rocks at edge of Mill pond.
Wts: none.

167, 168- The property of John **Marshall**, deceased, divided in the following manner - - For Dixon **Marshall**- No. 1129, 228 acres, no. 1130. 640 acres, No. 1132, 640 acres- To Wm. **Marshall** No. 1111, 640 acres 1128, 640 acres, 1134, 228 acres, For Mathew **Marshall** No. 1113, 640 acres, 1131, 640 acres, 1127, 640 acres; For Chas **Marshall**, No. 1133, 640 acres, 1135, 640 acres, 1068, 640 acres, This is an accounted acres and no. of grants to each above named and there is 412 acres to be divided to Mathew and 400 acres to Charles, also a like amount divided to Dixon and William **Marshall**- Aug. 29, 1791- signed by Dixon **Marshall**, Wm. **Marshall**, Mathew **Marshall**, Charles **Marshall** witnessed by George **Allin**, Nathan **Turner**, Jamey **Turner**/May 10, 1792.

168, 169- Sept. 8, 1792- Charles **Parrish** to Drury **Kimball** for 150 pds. 157 acres on Ruin Creek at Dennis **Driskall**'s line.
Wts: Drury **Kimball**, Jr., **Harris Hicks**.

169, 170- Nov. 7,1792- John **Dickerson** to John **Cardin** for 154 pds. 127½ acres on Tar river along James **Hunter**'s line on Samson **Harp**'s and E. **Fuller**'s lines, Cornelius **Cooper**'s line.
Wts; Joel **Moore**, Jeremiah **Rust**, Robt. **Cardin**.

170- Feb. 4, 1793- James **Claxton** to Joshua **Bullock** for 50 pds. 206 acres in Granville Co., N. C.
Wts: Rchd **Cooke**, Rd D **Cooke**.

171- Feb. 28, 1793- Gideon **Gooch** to Amos **Gooch** for 300 pds. 560 acres on Reedy creek on **Mize**'s and **Partee**'s lines.
Wts: Joseph and Daniel **Gooch**.

171, 172- Apr. 24, 1793- Gideon **Crenshaw** to Thomas **Voss** for 5 pds. 10 acres on Mountain creek on the old road.
Wts: none.

172- Feb. 25, 1793- John William **Manire** to Absalom **Weaver** for 100 pds. 50 acres at mouth of **Dun**'s creek on W side of Nappareeds creek.
Wts: Arthur **Frazer**, Richard **Ogelvie**.

173- Mar. 29, 1792- James **Forsythe** to Joseph **Hester** for 100 pds. 88½ acres on Picture branch at **Bullock**'s corner, **Forsythe**'s corner being part of land deeded to **Forsythe** by James **Cash** and title made good by Act of General Assembly in 1790.
Wts: Jonathan **Badgett**.

173- May 1, 1792- John **Dunking** (**Dunkin**) to [Semor] **Dunkin** for 50 pds. 100 acres on Tabbs creek joining William **Reeves**, Hardy **Reeves**, Lewis **Parham**'s lines.
Wts: John **Hall**, William **Reeves**.

339

174- Feb. 16, 1793- Charles **Parrish** to Thomas **Ricks** for 20 pds. 150 acres on Ruin Creek at William **Parrish**'s line.
Wts: Phillip **Bishop**, John **Ricks**.

174, 175- May 8, 1793- Richard D. **Cooke** to Richard **Cooke** for 36 pds. 141 acres on Ledge of Rocks creek at **Cash**'s corner, **McLemore**'s line.
Wts: George **Bullock**, Benjamin **Bullock**.

175- The land of Sarah **Harris**, deceased, ordered divided by Charles R. **Eaton**, Samuel **Walker**, Jno. Russ, Jonathan **Kittrell**, Jr., Roland **Bryant**, that is to divide the half that was devised to Jesse and Solomon **Harris** the other was divided to Wm. **Penn**. . Feb. court 1789- The land divided adjoined William **Penn**'s land and Solomon and Jesse **Harris** recieved equal shares- Mar. 13, 1789 Both the **Harris** had 192 acres at **Penn**'s, **Dickerson**'s lines on Tabb creek, each recieving 96 acres.

175, 176- Aug. 24, 1791- William **Bettes** to Robert **Goodloe** for 50 pds. 145 acres on Horse creek at **Champion**'s line.
Wts: James **Harvey**, J. **Peace**, George **Cavernor**.

176,[12] - (there is no page 177)- Apr. 26, 1793- David **Bundrage** to Bryan **Stonum** for 40 pds. 106 acres on Knap of Reeds creek at Elijah **Veazey**'s line in **Bullock**'s, **Benneham**'s line (the deed is unfinished).
[Wts: Wm **Hunt**.]

[177- May 1793- William **Hicks** for love and good will towards my daughter, Anne **Matthews** and her husband William **Matthews**, grant 130 acres on waters of Poplar Creek on **Barton**'s line at the road leading to Hillsborough to Halifax, **Hester**'s and **Davis**'s line.
Wts: Micajah **Debruler**, Mary **Debruler**, William **Hicks**, Jr.]

[177, 178- 8 May 1783-][13] (this is the latter part of a deed)
William **Minor** to Rite **Bass** for 30 pds. 35 acres on Fishing creek, at **Lawhorn**'s line, at Nathan **Bass**'s line, **Tabor**'s, John **Easter**'s lines.
Wts: R. **Cardin**, Wm. **Nailing** - May court 1793- .

178- Jan. 17,1793- Joseph **Peace** to John **Easter** for 50 pds. 258 acres on E side of Fishing creek at John **Smith**'s line at **Lawhorn**'s and **Bass**'s lines at **Taylor**'s Mill land.
Wts: Joseph **Peace**, Jr., Meredith **Peace**.

179- Feb. 3, 1792- Joseph Cash **Hall** of Montgomery Co, N.C., Roadey **Griggs** of Granville Co., N.C. for 80 pds. two tracts of land of 288 acres in Granville Co. at **McLemore**'s, **Culberhouse**'s lines, **McCulloh**'s and **Partee**'s lines, **Bullock**'s line.
Wts: Robert **Allison**, Micajah **Bullock**, Gabrel **Hall**, Robert **Grigs**.

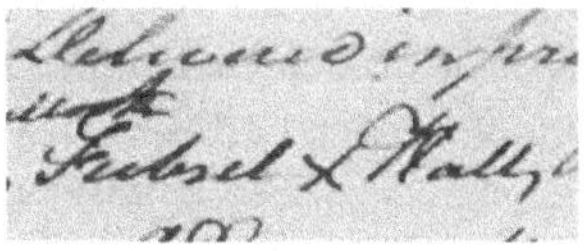

179, 180- 1792- James **Lewis** of Wake Co., and Robert **Lewis** of Granville Co., N.C., William **Lewis** of Orange Co., N.C. to Howel **Lewis** of Granville Co., N.C. for 400 pds, 318 acres on both sides of Island creek in Granville Co., N.C. at **Hawkins**' line.
Wts: George **Taylor**, James **Taylor**, Thos. **Hines**.

180- May 7, 1793- Grove **Howard** to Barnet **Howard**, his son, for love etc, a deed of gift of 150 acres on a branch in **Morris**'s line at **Howard**'s line.
Wts: Thomas **Owen**, William **Glass**.

---

[12] Familysearch film 7513647 skips page 177 in book N.

[13] Last of the info from page 177 before the manuscript picks up with Gwynn's transcription.

181- Jan. 21, 1793- Larkin **Johnston** of Person Co., N.C. to Ezekiel **Henderson** (**Hendrickson**) of Granville Co., N.C. for 20 pds. 100 acres in Granville Co., N.C. on N. side of Grassy creek, **Graves**' line, **Grant**'s road, **Peace**'s line. Wts: George **Petty**, Joseph **Petty**.

181, 182- Aug. 25, 1792- Israel **Eastwood** to Joseph **Ellis** for 33 pds. 6 shls., 8 pence, 175 acres on **Waller**'s and on **Veazey**'s lines, **Oakey**'s line.
Wts: Edwd **Jones**, Bennett **Phillips**, Wm. **Jones**.

182- Jan. 10, 1793- Gillam **Harris** to Robert **Allin** for 30 pds. 100 acres on Newlite creek.
Wts: Jeremiah **Bailey**, Samuel **Bailey**.

182, 183- Feb. 2, 1793- Joseph **Peace**, Sr., to John **Smith** for 50 pds. 100 acres in Granville Co., N.C.
Wts: John **Easter**, Joseph **Peace**.

183- Nov. 24, 1792- John **Dickerson**, Jr. to Uel **Crowder** for 50 pds. 50 acres on Tar river at Ezekiel **Fuller**'s lines, Henry **Fuller**'s line, to the mountain and to John **Cardin**'s line.
Wts: John **Dickerson**, W. **Williams**.

184- July 30, 1792- Benjamin **Fuller** to John **Dickerson** for 34 pds. 69 acres at **Dickerson**'s line.
Wts: Sothoron **Higgs**, Wm. **Martin**, Thos. **Jenkins**.

184, 185- Feb. 11, 1793- Philemon **Hawkins** of Warren Co., N.C. to Phil **Hawkins**, Jr. of same place for a tract of land in Granville Co. already deeded, a certain tract on Lick swamp containing 700 acres at a line formerly **Trevillion's** which land was granted to P. **Hawkins** by Granville Feb. 7, 1762.
Wts: John **Hazard**, Robert **Nicholson**.

185- July 19, 1792- Nicholas **Durning** of Orange Co., N. C, to George **Horner** for 125 pds. 225 acres in Granville Co., N.C. on Cedar creek at a line of Henry E. **McCulloh**'s land.
Wts: Elijah **Veazey**, Thomas **Horner**.

186- Apr. 13, 1793- Thomas **Rowland** and wife Sary (Sarah) to James **Stark** for 78 pds. 200 acres at **Wiggins**' corner, Thomas **Rowland**'s line.
Wts: Merryman **Barns**, Samuel **Barns**.

186- Feb. 29, 1792- Mical **Beck** and Anne **Beck** to William **Smith** for $200.00 silver, 200 acres at Susanah **Notgrass**'s spring branch to Ephraim **Emry**'s line.
Wts: Robert **Smith**, Wm. **Beck**.

187- Aug. 7, 1793- John **Somerville**, John **Young** and Robert **Hyde**, surviving executors of the Will of Jesse **Harper**, late of Granville Co., N.C. to Robert **Burton** for 566 pounds, all the lands that belonged to Jesse **Harper**, in Granville Co., at the time of his death on both sides of Little Island creek containing 1350 acres bounded by lands of Jordan **Norwood**, Benjamin **Norwood**, John **Taylor**, William **Sheppard**, Thomas **Barnett**, Thomas **Golden**, William **Penn**, John **Taylor**, Sr.'s estate, Miles **Busby** and Daniel **Glover**.
Wts: none.

187, 188- Aug. 7, 1793- Robert **Burton** to Robert **Hyde** for 566 pds. 1350 acres on, both sides of Little Island creek which formerly was property of Jesse **Harper**, deceased., in Granville Co., N.C.

188- Aug. 1, 1793- Thomas **Mutter** to Abraham **Crenshaw** for 190 pds. 282 acres on N. side of Jonathan's creek in **Mutter**'s corner, James **Yancey**'s line to Thornton **Yancey**'s line, Phillip **Yancey**'s line, John **Puryear**'s line along **Chandler**'s line to **Mutter**'s corner.
Wts: James **Downey**, Thomas **Brown**.

189- Aug. 4, 1793- John **Bridges** to Drury **Bridges** for 10 pds. 210 acres on Beaverdam creek.
Wts: Daniel, Molley and Joseph **Bridges**.

189, 190- Feb. 18, 1793- Richard **Champion** of York County, South Carolina to Lewis **Lemay** of Granville Co., N.C. for 138 pds. 231 acres in Granville Co., N.C-

Wts: J. **Peace**, Jr., J. **Peace**, Abraham **Champion**.

190- Aug. 6, 1793- John **Dickerson** to James **Barr** for 100 pds. 200 acres on W side of Tabbs creek on head of Great branch at Christian **Thomas**'s line, **Snelling**'s line.

191- Nov. 20, 1791- Samuel **Moseley** of Orange Co., N.C. to Reuben **Hoof** of Warren Co., N.C. for 20 pds. 100 acres being part of land granted to **Moseley** and which other part was deeded to Saml **Jones** on Buck Horn creek in Granville Co., N.C.
Wts: Doctor **Collier**, Saml **Hancock**.

191, 192- Dec. 29, 1792- Shearmon **Goss** to Thomas **Goss** for 37 pds. 100 acres on Tar river at spring branch near a high hill on main road at Benjamin **Merritt**'s line.
Wts: Mary W. **Badett**, John **Goss**.

192- July 9, 1793- Henry **Green** to Levin **Fletcher** for 100 pds. 300 acres on Nap of Reeds creek in Granville Co. Edward **Jones**, Nicholas **Green**.

192, 193- Mar. 6, 1793- Howel **Rose** to Simon **Clement**, Sr. for 55 pds. 80 acres on S side of Tar river adjoining lands of William **Graves**, and Joseph **Gooch** and others.
Wts: Stephen **Clement**, Samuel **Clement**.

341

193- Mar. 1, 1793- John **Taylor** to Simon **Clement**, Sr. for 60 pds. 150 acres on S. side of Tar river.
Wts: James **Cozart**, Saml **Clement**, Stephen **Clement**.

193, 194- Aug. 6, 1793- Joseph **Gooch** to Daniel **Gooch** for 300 pds. 250 1 acres on Tar river at John **Landers**'s line on N. side of river.
Wts: none.

194-195- Feb. 13, 1793- Bartholomew **Stovall** to John **Stovall** for 175 pds. 202½ acres on E side of Jonathan's creek at mouth of spring creek and including ½ the spring (excepting the 1/16 of an acre where my wife and children are buried).
Wts: William **Chandler**, Robert **Puryear**, Mary **Bryan**.

195- May 21, 1793- John **Cardin** to John **Keeton** for 20 pds. 40 acres on Tar river at Mathew **Crowder**'s line at John **Cardin**'s line, to James **Hunter**.
Wts: Joel **Moore**, Robert **Cardin**.

195, 196- May 9, 1787- John **Williams**, Bromfield **Ridley**, John **Somerville**, Howel **Lewis**, Sr., Thornton **Yancey**, Phil **Hawkins**, Jr., Robert **Coleman** and Samuel **Smith**, commissioners of the town of Williamsborough, N.C- to Francis **Bussier** for 6 pds. *Lot No. 3* in Williamsborough.
Wts: S. **Sneed**.

196- Aug. 3, 1784- Jesse **Cozart** to Ralph **Williams** for 10 pds. land on Ledge of Rocks creek in **Harris**'s line, **Staton**'s line.
Wts: Charles **Bullock**, Saml **Searcy**.

196, 197- May 25, 1793- Francis **Bussiere** to Stephen **Sneed** for 6 pds. *Lot No. 3* in Williamsborough, N.C., Granville Co.
Wts: Thomas **Critcher**.

197, 198- Dec. 1, 1792- Thomas **Jenkins** to Thomas **Blacknall** for 130 pds. 275 acres on Tabbs and Long creeks at **Thomas**'s and **Finch**'s lines, on Jochun **Kittrell**'s corner, **Loyd**'s, **Hunt**'s, **Dickerson**'s lines.
Wts: John **Hays**, John **Blacknell**.

198- Feb. 5, 1793- Lewis **Ackman** to David **Stovall** for 120 pds. 400 acres on Jonathan's and **Aaron**'s creeks at John **Baird**'s line formerly Joseph **Gill**'s line near the road on **Malone**'s line, **Chapman**'s line, **Apling**'s line at line made

by James **Jones** and Joseph **Chandler** south to **Beard**'s and James **Chandler**'s lines.
Wts: John **Stovall**, Thos. **Pool**, John **Pomfrett**.

This book is followed by an index to Land grants and 342 pages of grants from State of North Carolina 1779-1792

About the abstractor- Bonnie Zae Hargett Gwynn

Bonnie Zae Hargett Gwynn was a prolific genealogist and author who made significant contributions to documenting the history and records of several counties in North Carolina.

She was born 30 June 1906 in Prague, Lincoln, Oklahoma and died 31 December 1968 in Tucson, Pima, Arizona. [1] She was born in Oklahoma because her parents moved from Tennessee there in 1901 and returned to Halls, Lauderdale, Tennessee in 1909. [2]

She was the 5th of 9 children, 8 girls and 1 boy. The oldest was born in 1896 and my mother was the last in 1918.[3]

She graduated from Halls high school in 1924 and attended West Tennessee State Teachers College, Memphis, Shelby, Tennessee .

She married Henry Norburne Gwynn in 1928, and they lived in Memphis, Tennessee, where her husband was a founder of an advertising firm. He was 1/2 of Simon and Gwynn Advertising Agency in Memphis. It was very successful so Aunt Zae had all the resources needed to pursue her genealogy passion. Therefore she was able to live in North Carolina for weeks and months while researching in the Court Houses. And she could afford to hire researchers to help when needed.[4]

Notable Works[5]

Gwynn authored numerous books and publications, including:

- Abstracts of the wills and estate records of Granville County, North Carolina
- Guardian accounts of Granville County, North Carolina, 1810-1856
- Court minutes of Granville County, North Carolina, 1746-1820
- Kinfolks of Granville County North Carolina, 1756-1826
- Abstracts of the early deeds of Granville County, North Carolina, Vol 1 & 2

She also self-published several works, such as:

- Abstracts of the records of Jones County, North Carolina 1779-1868
- The 1850 Census of Craven County, North Carolina
- Records of Onslow County, North Carolina, 1734-1850, Vol 1 & 2

Memberships and Legacy

Gwynn was an active member of the Zachariah Davies Chapter of the Daughters of the American Revolution (D.A.R.) in Brunswick, Tennessee, and the Southern Arizona Genealogical Society in Tucson, Arizona. Her contributions to preserving genealogical records and family histories in North Carolina were significant, and her works continue to be valuable resources for researchers and genealogists.

Due to respiratory issues, Gwynn and her husband eventually moved to Arizona for her health. She passed away in 1968 due to pulmonary emphysema and asthmatic bronchitis, leaving behind a rich legacy of genealogical works.

---

[1] Arizona Department of Health Services; Phoenix, AZ; Arizona Genealogy Birth and Death Certificates. [Her dob is 1907 on her tombstone-tdl]

[2] Email 11 Apr, 2024 from nephew Joe Brown, Jackson, TN. <jactn@icloud.com>

[3] Ibid.

[4] Ibid

[5] Find a Grave, database and images (https://www.findagrave.com/memorial/10327154/bonnie_zae-gwynn: accessed May 28, 2024), memorial page for Bonnie Zae Hargett Gwynn (30 Jun 1907–31 Dec 1968), Find a Grave Memorial ID 10327154, citing Halls Cemetery, Halls, Lauderdale County, Tennessee, USA; Maintained by Allen Reedy Curtis (contributor 47745134).

www.ingramcontent.com/pod-product-compliance
Lightning Source LLC
LaVergne TN
LVHW061239100826
845148LV00008B/990

* 9 7 8 0 7 8 8 4 2 8 6 5 4 *